LONGMAN CLASSICS *in* POLITICAL SCIENCE

Party
Politics
in America

Twelfth Edition

MARJORIE RANDON HERSHEY
Indiana University

Foreword by
JOHN H. ALDRICH
Duke University

PEARSON
Longman

New York San Francisco Boston
London Toronto Sydney Tokyo Singapore Madrid
Mexico City Munich Paris Cape Town Hong Kong Montreal

Executive Editor: Eric Stano
Senior Marketing Manager: Elizabeth Fogarty
Production Manager: Eric Jorgensen
Project Coordination, Text Design, and Electronic Page Makeup:
  Pre-Press Company, Inc.
Cover Design Manager: John Callahan
Cover Image: Dave Cutler/Images.com
Manufacturing Buyer: Roy L. Pickering, Jr.
Printer and Binder: RR Donnelley & Sons Co.
Cover Printer: Phoenix Color Corp.

Library of Congress Cataloging-in-Publication Data
Hershey, Marjorie Randon.
    Party politics in America / Marjorie Randon Hershey; foreword by
John H. Aldrich.—12th ed.
        p. cm.—(Longman classics in political science.)
    Includes bibliographical references and index.
    ISBN 0-321-41491-8 (alk. paper)
    1. Political parties—United States. I. Title. II. Series.
JK2265.H477 2006
324.273—dc22
                                    2006002846

Please visit us at www.ablongman.com

ISBN 0–321–41491–8

2 3 4 5 6 7 8 9 10—DOC—09 08 07 06

Brief Contents

Detailed Contents

Figures and Tables

Foreword

Why should you be interested in studying political parties? The short answer is that virtually everything important in American politics is rooted in *party* politics. Political parties are at the core of American democracy and make it what it is today—just as they have virtually from the Founding.

Why should you use this book to guide you in the search for understanding democratic politics in America? The short answer is that this book is the best guide you can have, and it has been the best guide in this search for quite a long time. Now, let's turn to the longer answers.

I first encountered this text at the same stage in my life you are in now: as an undergraduate; although in my case that was back in the 1960s. I read it in a form called mimeograph—think of it as a very smelly, smudgy Xerox copy—while the second edition was being prepared. At that point, the book was authored by a young, up-and-coming scholar named Frank Sorauf. Following on the heels of his important study of the impact of political parties on the Pennsylvania legislature,[1] *Party Politics in America* established him as arguably the leading scholar of political parties of his generation. In those days—less so today—it was common for a "textbook" (that is, a book designed to be used in class) to do more than just tell you what others had written about its subject. Rather, books written for undergraduates were also designed to make a coherent argument about its subject matter—to engage you, the reader, intellectually. So it was then, and with this book, so it remains today.

In the sixth edition, published in 1988, Frank brought in Paul Allen Beck as coauthor. Paul took over the authorial duties beginning with that edition, and Marjorie Randon Hershey did so beginning with the ninth edition in 2001, leading to the book that you are about to read today. Each did so with considerable respect for the substance and the perspective that characterized the previous editions. This has brought a high degree of intellectual continuity to *Party Politics in America*. There are three important continuities (the first two of which are things you might want to keep in mind for the exams!). First, Sorauf, Beck, and Hershey very effectively use a three-part division in the discussion of political parties. More specifically, they divide the political party into its electoral, governing, and organizational roles. These three aspects of a party create a coherent system that (sometimes loosely, sometimes more tightly) provides a degree of integration to the diverse workings of any one political party. In those cases, the electoral, governing, and organizational aspects of the political party all pull together. However, as you will learn, there are often strains within and among these three divisions. What, for example, would you do if you were an adviser to the Republican Party faced with the following choice? There is a policy stance that will help your presidential nominee win votes

[1]Frank J. Sorauf, *Party and Representation, Legislative Politics in Pennsylvania* (New York: Atherton Press, 1963).

xvii

from undecided (typically moderate) voters and thus perhaps help your party win the presidency. That same stance, however, will hurt your party's candidates for the U.S. House of Representatives in their fund-raising campaigns and thus put at risk the narrow majority they currently hold in the House. Is it more important to hold a majority in the House or to hold the presidency? Should you risk losing potential support from moderate voters to maintain close ties with more extreme groups key to your organizational strength in fund-raising?

The second continuity is that Sorauf, Beck, and Hershey see the two major political parties in the United States as a system. The two-party system has long played a central role in the historical evolution of American politics (see especially Chapter 7). Although this two-party system has important implications for the dynamics of American politics, they also see the two-party system as a part of the intermediary groups in society. By this, the authors mean that the parties serve as points of contact between the public and its government (see their Figure 1.1, a figure that I believe has graced this book for twelve editions now).

The third continuity is that each is a terrific scholar of political parties, and although these continuities have allowed this book to keep its unique intellectual stamp, the transition among authors has also allowed each to bring to the work his or her particular strengths. In the end, this has made the twelfth edition of the book richer and stronger than ever before. As I noted earlier, Frank Sorauf used his expertise to explain the role of the political party in government. Since then, he became one of the nation's leading experts on the role of money in politics and in later editions reflected that increasingly important but perennially controversial subject.[2] Paul Beck brings a distinguished career of scholarship, examining the role of political parties in the electorate and adding nicely to Frank's expertise about the governing role.[3] Paul is, like Frank and Marjorie Hershey, an expert on American politics. However, Paul is also, more than most of us who study American politics, genuinely knowledgeable about comparative politics. Indeed, he has not only been at the center of the study of "dealignment" from parties in the American electorate (that is, an apparent increase in the people withdrawing from partisan politics) but is also a leading scholar of dealignment in many other nations as well.[4] Marjorie, through her expertise, has made important contributions to one of the most difficult questions to study: how candidates and their campaigns shape and are shaped by electoral forces.[5] This interaction links the two most important components of the party, elections and governance, into a more coherent whole. It has allowed her to bring clarity to what

[2]See, for example, Frank J. Sorauf, *Money in American Elections* (Glenview, IL: Scott Foresman/Little, Brown College Division, 1988) or *Inside Campaign Finance: Myths and Realities* (New York: Yale University Press, 1992).

[3]He has written a great deal on this subject. One illustration that has long been one of my favorites is his "A Socialization Theory of Partisan Realignment," which was originally published in *The Politics of Future Citizens*, edited by Richard Niemi (San Francisco, CA: Jossey-Bass, 1974, pp. 199–219), and reprinted in *Classics in Voting Behavior,* edited by Richard Niemi and Herbert Weisberg (Washington, DC: CQ Press, 1992).

[4]Among his many writings, see his edited book with Russell J. Dalton and Scott Flanagan, *Electoral Change in Advanced Industrial Democracies: Realignment or Dealignment?* (Princeton, NJ: Princeton University Press, 1984).

[5]See especially her books, *Running for Office: The Political Education of Campaigners* (Chatham, NJ: Chatham House, 1984) and *The Making of Campaign Strategy* (Lexington, MA: D.C. Heath-Lexington, 1974).

has become an increasingly confused portion of the field. Marjorie also has closely studied the role of gender in politics, a dimension of party politics that has not only been of long-standing importance from at least the granting of women's suffrage but has also become especially critical with the emergence and growth of the "gender gap."[6] Finally, she has made a long series of contributions to help us understand how to bring meaning to complex events.[7] One special feature of this book is the increased use of narratives from well-known and little-known party figures alike, narratives that serve to bring the subject matter to life.

One issue critical to all who study American politics is the understanding that politics matters in your life, that this is your government, and that the political parties are ways in which you can help shape what your government and elected officials do. This is one of the most important meanings of American political parties. They, and the government that they create, are the consequences of you and your political actions. So saying allows me to move more directly to the longer answer about the study of political parties themselves.

At the outset, I mentioned that you should want to study political parties because they are so important to virtually everything that happens in American politics and because political parties are so central to the workings of any democracy. Great, but you are probably asking, "So what questions should I keep in mind as I read this book? What questions will help me understand the material better?" Let me propose as guidelines three questions that are neither too specific nor too general. We are looking, that is, for questions somewhere in between "Are parties good?" on the one hand and "Why did the House Majority Leader, Tom DeLay (Republican, Texas), speak so strongly against campaign finance reform when he was House Minority Leader on February 13, 2002?" on the other hand.

You are well aware that today politicians can appear magnanimous and statesmanlike if they say that they will be nonpartisan and if they call for Congress to "rise above" partisan politics to be bipartisan. Yet essentially every elected official is a partisan, and essentially every elected official chooses to act in a partisan way much of the time. Why do politicians today, you might ask, speak as if they are of two minds about political parties? Perhaps they actually are. Even if you dismiss this rhetoric as just words, it is the case that the public is of two minds about parties, too. This book, like virtually all written about American political parties, includes quotes from the Founding Fathers warning about the dangers of party and faction, often quoting such luminaries as John Adams, Thomas Jefferson, and James Madison. Yet these very same men not only worried about the dangers of party but they were the founders and first leaders of our first political parties. So the first question is why are people—leaders and followers, founders and contemporary figures alike—both attracted to and repulsed by political parties?

---

[6]An especially interesting account of the ways the political parties reacted to female suffrage can be found in Anna L. Harvey, *Votes without Leverage: Women in American Electoral Politics, 1920–1970* (Cambridge: Cambridge University Press, 1998).

[7]See, for example, "Constructing Explanations for U.S. State Governors' Races: The Abortion Issue and the 1990 Gubernatorial Elections," *Political Communication* 17 (July–September, 2000): 239–262; "The Meaning of a Mandate: Interpretations of 'Mandate' in 1984 Presidential Election Coverage," *Polity* (Winter, 1995): 225–254; and "Support for Political Women: Sex Roles," in John C. Pierce and John L. Sullivan, eds., *The Electorate Reconsidered* (Beverly Hills, CA: Sage, 1980), 179–198.

Let me suggest two books that might give you additional ways to think about this question. One is Richard Hofstadter's *The Idea of a Party System: The Rise of Legitimate Opposition in the United States, 1780–1840* (Berkeley: University of California Press, 1969). This book is a series of public lectures that Hofstadter gave in which he roots political parties deeply in the American democratic tradition, arguing that they represent the outward manifestation of a change in philosophic understanding of the relationship between citizens and leaders in this, the world's first practicing democracy. Austin Ranney, in *Curing the Mischiefs of Faction: Party Reform in America* (Berkeley: University of California Press, 1975), connects Hofstadter's view of the role of philosophic ideas and American democratic practice from our first 60 years to the contemporary era. Ranney was a leading scholar of political parties, but in this case he was also writing this book in reflection upon his time spent as a member of the so-called McGovern-Fraser Reform Commission, which revised the rules for the Democratic Party and advocated the reforms that led to the current presidential primary system. Thus, there is both a theoretical and practical dimension to this work.

This question of the purpose of parties in our democracy, both theoretical and practical, leads easily to a second major question that should be in your mind as you work through this book and your course: How does the individual connect to the political party? There are two aspects to this question. One is fairly direct—what do parties mean to the individual and how, if at all, has this changed over time? The great work that laid out this relationship in the modern era is *The American Voter* by Angus Campbell, Philip E. Converse, Warren E. Miller, and Donald E. Stokes (New York: John Wiley & Sons, 1960). Many argue that this connection has changed fundamentally. At one extreme, Martin P. Wattenberg has written about the declining relevance of political parties to the voter, such as in his *The Decline of American Political Parties, 1952–1996* (Cambridge, MA: Harvard University Press, 1998), using such striking evidence as a dramatic decline in the willingness or ability of citizens to say what they like or dislike about either of our two major political parties. Others disagree with Wattenberg. Larry Bartels, for example, has shown that partisanship remains as influential in shaping the vote as ever.[8] A second dimension of the question is whether any apparent decline, irrelevance, or dealignment of parties reflects growing distancing from the government itself. It is certainly the case that today we hear people say, "The government, they . . . ," and not "The government, we . . . ." I suspect that few of us think that way. It is certainly common to hear politicians call for a tax cut by claiming that doing so will give the people back their money. Such a statement would not make sense if we thought of the government as being composed of us, ourselves, and thus thought of our taxes as sending our money to work in our government, doing our bidding by enacting our preferences into legislation selected by our representatives whom we chose. The question can, however, be cast even more broadly, asking whether the people feel removed from social, cultural, economic, and political institutions, generally, with political parties and the government therefore only one more symptom of a larger ill. This is certainly a part of the concerns that motivate Robert D. Putnam in his *Bowling Alone: The Collapse and Revival of American Community* (New York: Simon & Schuster, 2000).

---

[8]Larry M. Bartels, "Partisanship and Voting Behavior, 1952–1996," *American Journal of Political Science* 44 (2000): 35–50.

The change from a trusting, supportive, identified public to one apparently dramatically less so is one of the great changes that took place in American politics over the past half century. A second great change is what is often called "polarization," a growing distance between the elected officials of the two parties. That is, compared with 50 years ago, today the Democrats are more liberal and consistently more so than Republicans, who in turn are much more conservative than in the Eisenhower administration. Although this is not to say that there is anything close to an identical set of beliefs by the members of either party, there is a greater coherence of opinion and belief in, say, the congressional delegations of each party than in earlier times. Even more undeniable is a much clearer divergence between the policy interests and choices of the two parties than, say, 50 years ago. You might refer to *Polarized Politics: Congress and the President in a Partisan Era* (Washington, DC: CQ Press, 2000), edited by Jon R. Bond and Richard Fleisher, for a variety of indications of this fact. The question then is not whether there is greater polarization today; the question is whether this relative clarity of polarization matters. As usual, there are at least two ways to understand the question. One is simply to ask whether a more polarized Congress yields policies very different from a less polarized one. The readings in Bond and Fleisher generally support that position. Others, for example, Keith Krehbiel in *Pivotal Politics: A Theory of U.S. Lawmaking* (Chicago, IL: University of Chicago Press, 1998) and David W. Brady and Craig Volden in *Revolving Gridlock: Politics and Policy from Carter to Clinton* (Boulder, CO: Westview Press, 1998) argue that the Founders' creation of checks and balances makes polarization relatively ineffectual in shaping legislation due to vetoes, compromises necessary between the two chambers, and so on. Even more generally, however, David R. Mayhew has argued in *Divided We Govern: Party Control, Lawmaking, and Investigations, 1946–1990* (New Haven, CT: Yale University Press, 1991) that our system generates important legislation regardless of which party is in control or whether they share power under divided partisan control of government. This carefully considered argument raises the question of whether the party really matters. As you might expect, there has been considerable interest in the challenge that Mayhew, Krehbiel, and Brady and Volden have raised. One set of responses can be seen in the Bond and Fleisher volume. Another can be found in the book *The Macro Polity* by Robert S. Erikson, Michael B. MacKuen, and James A. Stimson (Cambridge, UK: Cambridge University Press, 2002).

As you can see, we have now reached the point of very recently published work. We are, that is, asking questions that are motivating the work of scholars today. So, let's get on with it and turn to the book and the study of political parties themselves.

JOHN H. ALDRICH
Duke University

Preface

In the year when the first edition of *Party Politics in America* was published, a Republican president won a narrow victory in his second try for the office. A number of commentators declared that the Republicans were fast becoming the nation's majority party. American troops were fighting a war far from home. As the death toll mounted, more and more groups and individuals questioned the reasons for American involvement and called for the quick withdrawal of the troops. At home, campaign finance scandals prompted new calls for reform.

The year was 1968; the president was Richard Nixon, and the war was in Vietnam. Should we conclude that the more things change, the more they stay the same? Only in part. If readers of the first edition had been asked to imagine the world of party politics in the early 2000s, would they have predicted the impact of instant worldwide communication on the Internet, billion-dollar presidential campaigns, and the September 11 attacks? The political environment has clearly changed, yet political parties continue to play a vital role as they adapt to that environment.

As the third author of *Party Politics*, I have had the great advantage of building on the foundation provided by Frank J. Sorauf and Paul Allen Beck, two of the foremost scholars of political parties. Frank Sorauf inaugurated this text and continued to revise and perfect it for almost two decades. Paul Beck brought the book into the late 1980s and 1990s with the intellectual vision and the meticulous care that has marked his research on parties and voting.

The book that they nurtured has long been known as the "gold standard" of political parties texts. Instructors and students have valued previous editions because they have provided, quite simply, the most thorough and definitive coverage of the field. These editions of *Party Politics in America* have been both an essential reference and an invitation to more than a generation of students. My aim has been to build on the book's great strengths—its comprehensive coverage, conceptual clarity, and the comparative perspective that is woven into every chapter—while making it even more readable and engaging.

This edition contains updated versions of the features that have been so well received in the last two editions. The boxes titled "A Day in the Life" tell the personal stories of individuals whose experiences help to illustrate recent changes in the parties. Many of my students see political parties as remote, abstract, and a bit underhanded—something that might interest elderly people but not teens and twentysomethings. I hope these stories will change their minds. As in the case of a young military veteran who joins the College Republicans, in part to act on his religious beliefs, and the challenges faced by the first person to win and hold a U.S. House seat as an "out" lesbian, these are compelling stories that can show readers why studying party politics is worth their time.

In other chapters, the features titled "Which Would You Choose?" present students with major debates about party politics—for instance, whether encouraging greater voter turnout would help or harm American democracy (see Chapter 8) and whether legislators ought to be listening mainly to their legislative party leaders or to their constituents (in Chapter 13). These summaries, using the point-counterpoint format with which undergraduates are familiar, could serve as the basis for classroom debate on these and many other fundamental concerns.

There's much that is new in the twelfth edition. Chapter 2 presents a new discussion of the safety of congressional seats and its consequences for political polarization. Examples of the involvement of the Christian Right in state and local politics have been added to Chapter 3. Chapter 6 incorporates a broader range of approaches to understanding party identification. Chapter 7 reassesses the concept of realignment—perhaps the most significant change in the new edition. This chapter moves away from the more disputed aspects of the concept and focuses on the central question of changes over time in the relationships between social groups and partisanship. The chapter includes new material about the sixth party system, how it has changed from the New Deal system, and how best to characterize the nature of the change. Throughout the book and especially in Chapter 11, there is extensive information about the 2004 and 2006 elections, including the national parties' use of database targeting. A much-expanded treatment of the impact of the Bipartisan Campaign Reform Act (BCRA) on national and state parties and campaigns can be found in Chapter 12, as well as a fuller discussion of 527 and 501(c) groups. Partisanship in the judicial nomination process, from the "nuclear option" to the "Gang of 14," receives more attention in Chapter 14, and there is expanded discussion of party polarization in Congress and the electorate in Chapters 13 and 15.

As in previous editions, I've tried to make the reader's job easier by putting important terms in boldface and making sure that they are clearly defined, emphasizing the central points even more, and making some of the long tables into figures or into shorter, clearer tables. And for instructors, I have worked to make sure that each chapter can stand alone so that teachers can assign chapters in any order they choose without leaving their students puzzled because relevant concepts were explained elsewhere.

Like political parties and elected officials, textbooks have constituents. However, as many elected officials find, accountability to the constituency takes a lot of effort. Textbook writers have a hard time getting detailed information as to what readers like and don't like about a book, what could be clearer, and what could be more interesting. I have been very lucky to get reactions from users of *Party Politics in America*, but I would like to receive many more. As you read the book, then, whether you are a teacher, a grad or undergraduate student, or a political practitioner, I would appreciate your suggestions and reactions. You can reach me at hershey@indiana.edu.

I owe thanks as well to the many people who have been so gracious with their help: to my graduate and undergraduate students; to present and former colleagues at Indiana University, particularly Bob Huckfeldt, Ted Carmines, John Williams, Leroy Rieselbach, Jerry Wright, and Mike Ensley; and to departmental staff members Margaret Anderson, Fern Bennett, Scott Feickert, Steve Flinn, Marsha Franklin, Loretta Heyen, Sharon LaRoche, and James Russell.

Austin Ranney, Leon Epstein, Jack Dennis, and Murray Edelman were most responsible for my interest in party politics and for my training in political science. Murray Edelman deserves special mention in that group, not only as a mentor and model for so many of us but also as a much-beloved friend. John Aldrich, one of the most insightful and systematic analysts of political parties, was kind enough to write a foreword. Other political scientists have also been among my best and favorite teachers: Bruce Oppenheimer, Gerry Pomper, Tony Broh, Jennifer Hochschild, Burdett Loomis, Richard Fenno, Anthony King, John Kingdon, Mike Kirn, Brian Silver, Jim Stimson, and Brian Vargus. For this edition, I have appreciated the comments and contributions of Paul C. Clark II and Ian Stirton of the Federal Election Commission, Alan Abramowitz, Tony Corrado, Mary Ellen Diekhoff, Shane Kennedy, Mary Grisez Kweit, Michael Malbin, Quin Monson, Keith Poole, Brad Warren, and the excellent research assistance of Jennifer Hayes Clark.

Reviewers of the eleventh edition—Jay A. DeSart, Utah Valley State College; Jae-Jae Spoon, University of Michigan; Reed Welch, West Texas A & M University; Christina Wolbrecht, University of Notre Dame—were generous with their time and constructive comments, which helped me continue adapting the book to meet students' and instructors' needs. And it remains a pleasure to work with the people at Longman: Editor Eric Stano, Donna Garnier, and Kara Wylie; and Beth Kluckhohn and the other members of the Pre-Press Company, Inc. production team.

Most of all, I am very grateful to my family: my husband, Howard, and our daughters, Katie, Lissa, Lani, and Hannah. Everything I do has been made possible by their love and support.

MARJORIE RANDON HERSHEY

PART ONE

Parties and Party Systems

Who decides how old you must be to drink beer legally? Who determines whether the kitchen of your favorite pizza place is sanitary, and what "sanitary" means? Who made the decision that you need a license to get married but you don't need a license to have a baby?

All three questions have the same answer. It's government that makes these decisions and thousands more that affect your life every day. In fact, you would have to look very hard to find an aspect of your life that is *not* affected by government action. The federal government decides whether the meat in your hamburgers needs to be tested for salmonella contamination and whether schools are allowed to serve irradiated beef. State governments have decided which sex acts can be prosecuted. It is the political system that plays the most important role in deciding, as a famous political scientist put it, "who gets what, when, how."[1]

Because government decisions affect almost everything we do, large numbers of groups have mobilized to try to influence these decisions as well as the selection of the men and women who will make them. In a democracy, the political party is one of the oldest and most important of these groups. Parties have a lot of competition, however, Organized interests such as the Gun Owners of America and the National Gay and Lesbian Task Force also work to get the government policies they want, as do pro-life and abortion rights groups, the Christian Coalition, and People for the Ethical Treatment of Animals. Even organizations whose main purpose is nonpolitical, such as universities, beer makers, and MTV, understandably try to influence the government decisions that affect them.

All these groups serve as *intermediaries*—links or connections between citizens and the people in government who make the decisions that affect our lives (Figure I.1). By bringing together people with shared interests, they amplify these people's voices in speaking to government. They raise issues that they want government to solve. They tell people what government is doing. They keep an eye on one another's behavior as well as on the actions of public officials.

Different intermediaries specialize in different political activities. Parties focus on nominating candidates, helping to elect them, and organizing those who win. Most organized interests represent narrower groups; they are unlikely to win popular majorities so they try instead to influence the views of elected and appointed officials. Still others work mainly to affect public opinion and media coverage. Groups like these in other

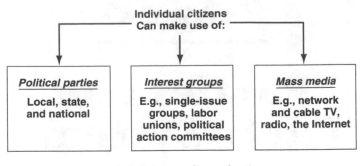

to influence or learn about

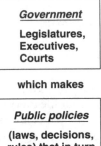

which makes

Public policies

(laws, decisions, rules) that in turn affect citizens

FIGURE I.1   Parties and Other Intermediaries Between Citizens and Government.

democracies may play different roles. The American parties, for example, tend to concentrate on election activities, whereas parties in Europe have been more committed to spreading ideologies and keeping their elected officials faithful to the party's program.

The competition among these intermediary groups is fierce. Parties, of course, compete with one another. They vie with interest groups for money, expertise, and volunteer help and then, with those resources in hand, for the support of individual citizens and elected officials. Getting people's attention and support is difficult in an age when TV and web-surfing soak up the free time of so many prospective activists and voters. Parties must even fight for a major role in political campaigns; the American parties are not nearly as dominant in the business of campaigning as they were a century ago.

Adding to their burden, parties fight for power in a culture that both loves and hates them. On the one hand, many writers have celebrated the American parties as the tools with which we build and repair our democracy and as the "distinguishing marks" of a modern government.[2] In a reflection of that belief, when many nations in Eastern Europe threw off Communist rule almost two decades ago, one of the first things democratic activists did was to form political parties.[3]

On the other hand, political parties have been the targets of suspicion and ridicule since the United States began. James Madison and the other founders were very wary of organized factions in their new republic. About a century later, the Progressive movement—

reformers intent on rooting out political corruption and returning power to middle-class people like themselves—targeted the parties' "boss rule" as the enemy to overcome. Disgust with party power in the 1960s and 1970s led to another series of party reforms that has helped to reshape current politics. Many Americans remain skeptical and even hostile to the ideal of political parties.[4]

Public hostility has led, in turn, to a host of restrictions on how parties can organize and what they can do. Parties have tried to adapt to these rules over time by changing their organizations and the nature of their activities. The political parties of the early 2000s would hardly be recognizable to politicians of a century ago, and the parties that we know today may change dramatically in the coming decades.

The aim of this book is to explore the American parties: how they have developed, how they affect us, and what they are capable of contributing to a democratic politics. Given the rise of the Internet, the growth of single-issue groups, and the many other ways in which we can learn about and affect government, are political parties really as essential to the survival of a democracy as many have assumed? Are they a boon to both candidates and voters, or do they deserve the distrust with which so many Americans—and probably you yourself—view them?

Chapter 1

What Are Political Parties?

If we had listened to George Washington, there would be no political parties in the United States today. Washington declared in his Farewell Address: "Let me warn you in the most solemn manner against the baneful effects of the spirit of party," which he considered the "worst enemy" of popular government. Two centuries later, many Americans agree; in survey after survey, many respondents say that they think of political parties with suspicion—like the cat at the bird feeder—if they think of them at all.

We may be a little late, but suppose we take Washington's advice. Imagine that as President Bush nears the end of his second term, the parties simply vanish. There are no party organizations to hold primary elections, no party leaders to advise or support the candidates, and no party labels to guide the voters. Would we do a better job of choosing the next president?

Of course, we will have to find another way to trim down the thousands of presidential wanna-bes to the very few who will run in the general election. Without party primaries and caucuses, who would make that decision? Members of Congress? Not in a system designed to separate legislative from executive powers. Nomination by the nation's mayors and other elected officials, as happens in France? A special edition of the television series *Survivor*? The answer is not obvious, though it is obviously vital to our future.

Assuming that problem is solved, many other challenges remain. Strong party organizations help bring voters to the polls. Without any political parties, will voter turnout, already lower in the United States than in most other industrialized democracies, decrease even further? Most people are not very interested in politics, so how will voters decide on a candidate without the guidance that party labels provide? Will they spend hours researching each candidate's stands on the issues, or will they choose the candidate with the most attractive personality, at least as seen on TV? When the new president takes office, how will he or she gain majority support for new programs from a Congress elected as individuals, with no party loyalties to unite them?

What is this political organization that is so necessary and yet so distrusted? Does the concept of party include only the politicians who share a party label when seeking

5

and holding public offices? Does it also include the activists who work on the campaigns and the ordinary citizens who support a party's candidates? Or is a party any grouping that chooses to call itself a party, whether Democratic or Boston Tea?

A THREE-PART DEFINITION OF PARTIES

Most scholars would agree that *a party is a group organized to nominate candidates, to try to win political power through elections, and to promote ideas about public policies.* Who is included in the definition of party? To the analysts quoted in "What Is a Political Party?" on page 7, the central figures are the candidates and elected officials who share a party's label (see, for example, Edmund Burke's and Anthony Downs's definitions). Many parties in democratic nations, including the United States, began as groups of political leaders who organized to advance certain programs.

Most observers, however, see the American parties as including more than just candidates and officeholders. As John Aldrich's definition (see "What Is a Political Party?") reminds us, parties are organizations; they are institutions that have a life, and a set of rules, of their own. Interested individuals can become active in them and help set their goals and strategies, just as one would do in a sorority or a church youth group. These activists and organizations are central parts of the party, too.

It is tempting to close our definition at this point and to view the American parties solely as teams of political specialists—elected officials, candidates, party leaders, activists, and organizations—who compete for power and then exercise it. That leaves the rest of the population on the outside of the parties, a position that many citizens may well prefer. Yet this would ignore an important reality: Parties are rooted in the lives and feelings of citizens as well as candidates and activists. Even though the American parties do not have formal, dues-paying "members," many voters develop such strong and enduring attachments to a particular party that they are willing to tell a pollster, "I'm a Democrat" or "I'm a Republican." Further, when writers refer to a "Republican realignment" or a "Democratic area," they see parties that include voters as well as officeholders, office seekers, and activists.

The Progressive movement of the late 1800s and early 1900s, which promoted party registration and the practice of nominating candidates in primary elections, strengthened the case for including a citizen base in a definition of American parties. Voters in primary elections make the single most important decision for their party: who its candidates will be. In most other democracies, only the party leaders and activists have the power to make this choice.

Because American voters have the right to nominate the parties' candidates, the line that separates party leaders from followers in most other nations becomes blurred in the United States. American voters are not only consumers who choose among the parties' "products" (candidates) in the political marketplace but also managers who decide just what products will be introduced in the first place. Making consumers into managers has transformed political parties, just as it would revolutionize the market economy. Taking this into account in our definition of parties, as do the Chambers and Key definitions in the box on page 7, makes for a messier concept of political party, but a more realistic one in the American setting.[1]

WHAT IS A POLITICAL PARTY?

A party aims to promote certain policies:

[A] party is a body of men united, for promoting by their joint endeavors the national interest, upon some particular principle in which they are all agreed.

Edmund Burke (1770)

It works to gain power in government:

In the broadest sense, a political party is a coalition of men seeking to control the governing apparatus by legal means . . . [through] duly constituted elections or legitimate influence.

Anthony Downs (1957)

It is an organization with rules and durability:

Political parties can be seen as coalitions of elites to capture and use political office. . . . (But) a political party is . . . more than a coalition. A major political party is an institutionalized coalition, one that has adopted rules, norms, and procedures.

John H. Aldrich (1995)

It inspires loyalty among voters:

[A] political party in the modern sense may be thought of as a relatively durable social formation which seeks offices or power in government, exhibits a structure or organization which links leaders at the centers of government to a significant popular following in the political arena and its local enclaves, and generates in-group perspectives or at least symbols of identification or loyalty.

William Nisbet Chambers (1967)

A political party is all of the above:

Within the body of voters as a whole, groups are formed of persons who regard themselves as party members. . . . In another sense the term party may refer to the group of more or less professional political workers. . . . At times party denotes groups within the government. . . . Often it refers to an entity which rolls into one the party-in-the-electorate, the professional political group, the party-in-the-legislature, and the party-in-the-government. . . . In truth, this all-encompassing usage has its legitimate applications for all the types of groups called party interact more or less closely and at times may be as one.

V. O. Key, Jr. (1958)

In short, we can most accurately see the major American political parties as having three interacting parts. These three are the ***party organization,*** which includes party leaders and the many activists who work for party causes and candidates; the ***party in government,*** composed of the men and women who run for public office on the party's label and who hold public office; and the ***party in the electorate,*** or those citizens who express

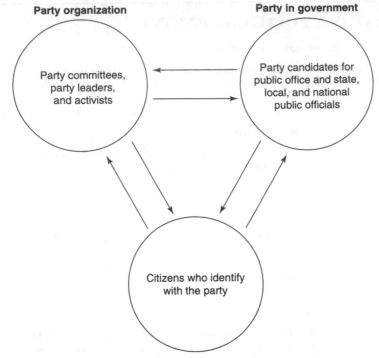

FIGURE 1.1   **The Three Parts of American Political Parties.**

an attachment to the party (see Figure 1.1).[2] We explore each of these parts separately, keeping in mind that the character of the American parties is defined by the ways in which they interact.[3]

The Party Organization

The party organizations are made up of people who hold jobs with titles—the national and state party chairs and officers; the county, city, ward and precinct leaders and committee people—and those who don't, but who are devoted enough to volunteer their time, money, and skills to the party. These are groups of people who work to promote *all* of the party's candidates and its perspectives on major issues, not just an individual candidate or two. Some party leaders or activists may be waiting for the right time to run for public office (and thus cross over into the party in government); others have been pressed into service as candidates for Congress or city clerk when nobody else wants the job. Many party activists prefer the tasks of answering phones in the party headquarters and plotting strategy, however, rather than the frenzied days and anxious nights that are the life of a political candidate.

The Party in Government

The party in government consists of the candidates for public office and those who hold office, whether elected or appointed, who share a party label. The major figures here are presidents, governors, judges, mayors, Congress members, state legislators, bureaucrats, and local officials who hold the same party affiliation.

Interactions between the party in government and the party organization can be like those of siblings: part loyalty and part rivalry. They regularly work together to meet shared goals, but they may have different priorities in reaching those goals. A senator, for example, may be trying to raise as much campaign money as possible in order to win a big victory that will boost her chances of later running for president. At the same time, the party organization's leaders may be hoping to convince the same campaign contributors to support more vulnerable party candidates instead, in the hope of gaining a party majority in Congress.

These two parts of the parties also jockey for leadership of the party as a whole. When reporters want to get a "Republican view" on an issue, they will often interview a source in the White House, if the president is Republican, or a Republican leader in Congress; these members of the party in government are often assumed to speak for the party. Leaders of the party's organization, such as the chair of the New York Republican State Committee, might prefer to put a different spin on the issue. But presidents and congressional party leaders do not have to clear their pronouncements with the party organization, nor can they be controlled by it. These tensions, which can lead the party organization and the party in government to compete for scarce resources, show why it is helpful to treat them as separate parts of the party.

The Party in the Electorate

The party in the electorate is the least well defined of the three parts. It consists of the men and women who *see themselves* as Democrats or Republicans: citizens who feel some degree of loyalty to the party, even if they have never set foot in the party's headquarters or met its candidates. We call them *partisans* or *party identifiers.* Many of these partisans have declared themselves to be a Democrat or Republican when they registered to vote; more than half of the states require citizens to register by party. Others regard themselves as partisans even if they do not register to vote under a party label or even if they do not vote at all.

These members of the electoral party are inclined to support their party's candidates and issue stands, but they are not under the party organization's control. In general elections, they may vote for one party candidate and reject another; in primaries, they may decide to saddle the party with a candidate that the organization can't stand. However, they are vitally important as the core of the party's electoral support; without this base, the party would have to work much harder to win and keep power.

This relationship between the party organization and party in government, on the one hand, and the electoral party, on the other, is one of the most striking characteristics of the major American parties. Other political organizations—interest groups such as teachers' unions and environmental groups—try to attract supporters in addition to their members, but these supporters remain outside the group's organization. That is not true of American parties. The party in the electorate is more than an external group to be mobilized. In addition to its power to choose the parties' candidates by voting in primaries, in many states the electoral party helps select local party officials, such as precinct committee leaders. So the major American party is an open, inclusive, semipublic organization. The extent to which citizens can affect the choice of its leaders, and thus influence its character, sets it apart from other political organizations and from parties in most other democracies.

WHAT PARTIES DO

Political parties in every democracy engage in three sets of activities to at least some degree. They select candidates and contest elections; they try to educate citizens about issues important to the party, and they work to influence government to provide certain policies and other benefits.[4] Parties and party systems differ in the degree to which they emphasize these individual activities, but no party can completely ignore any of them.

Electing Candidates

Parties often seem to be completely absorbed by their efforts to elect candidates. Electoral activity so dominates the life of the American party that its metabolism follows almost exactly the cycles of the election calendar. Party activity reaches a peak at election time; between elections, many parties go into hibernation. Parties are goal-oriented, and in American politics, achieving one's goals ultimately depends on winning elections.

The need to elect candidates serves as the primary force connecting the three parts of the parties. Party leaders and activists committed to a particular elected official often join with other members of the party in government and with party voters to return that official to office. When the election is won or lost, they will frequently drift apart again. These groups of individuals from different parts of a party, drawn together to elect a particular candidate, are like the nuclei of the party.[5]

Educating (or Propagandizing) Citizens

Parties also try to teach or propagandize citizens. The Democrats and Republicans do not promote all-inclusive ideologies like those of a fundamentalist Islamic party. They do, however, represent the interests and issue preferences of the groups that identify with and support them. In this sense, the Republicans and Democrats can be seen as the parties of business or labor and of the wealthy or the disadvantaged. (You'll find more on this later in the chapter.) Party positions on issues have become clearer and more polarized since the 1960s.

Governing

Almost all American national and state elected officials ran for office as either Democrats or Republicans, and their partisan perspectives affect every aspect of the way government works. The legislatures of 49 states[6] and the United States Congress are organized along party lines. On some issues, party cohesion may break down. Yet, in general, there is a surprising degree of party discipline in voting on legislation. In executive branches, presidents and governors usually choose cabinet officers and agency heads of their own party. Even the courts show evidence of the organizing and directing touch of the parties, though in more subtle ways.

The American parties, however, do not have a monopoly on any of these three activities. They compete regularly with interest groups, other political organizations, and even the media in all these areas. Even though the parties organize state legislatures and Congress, they must contend with interest group pressures and legislators' own beliefs to influence legislators' votes. In nominating candidates, especially at the local level, other organizations such as groups backing or opposed to a new sports stadium or a display of the Ten Commandments on public property try to influence primaries or urge candidates to run. In promoting issues, the major parties are often overshadowed by the efforts of single-issue groups, minor (third) parties, individual public figures, and the media.

Because the American parties' activities center on electing candidates, the party in government dominates the party to a degree unusual among western democracies. In parties more strongly committed to educating citizens about the party's ideology—European Marxist parties, for instance—party organizations are more likely to be able to dictate to the legislative parties, telling them what to emphasize and holding them accountable for their votes.

THE EFFECTS OF PARTY ACTIVITY

How do these party activities affect American politics? First, parties help people make sense of the complexities of politics. Most of us don't pay much attention to government. Parties simplify issues and elections for us; thus, people can make sensible choices in politics, by using their party attachment as a guide for evaluating candidates and issues, even when they don't have a lot of political information. By making it easier for citizens to form political judgments, parties ease the way for people to become politically active. In fact, parties preach the value of political commitment. They take part in Americans' political education by transmitting political information and values to large numbers of current and future voters.

Second, the American parties help aggregate and organize political power. They put together individuals and groups into blocs that are powerful enough to govern. So in the political world as well as within the individual, parties help to focus political loyalties on a small number of alternatives and then to build support for them. Parties also provide an organized opposition. That is not a popular role to play; the behavior of a constant adversary may seem like that of a sore loser. But an organized opposition is vital to a democracy because it has a natural incentive—its own ambition—to serve as a watchdog on a powerful government. Few of us would be willing to devote the time and effort to play this important role on our own.

Third, because they are so focused on contesting elections, the parties dominate the recruitment of political leaders. Large numbers of legislators, political executives, and even judges entered public service through a political party or partisan candidacy for office. Because the parties work at all levels of government from local to national, they can encourage the movement of leaders from one level to another. Further, because they are constants in the election process, parties help to make changes in government leadership more routine and orderly. In nations where parties are not stable from one election to the next, leadership changes can be much more disruptive.

Finally, the parties help unify a divided American political system. The U.S. government was designed to fragment political power, to make sure that no single group could gain enough of it to become a tyrant. The division between the national government and the states, multiplied by the separation of powers at each level, does an impressive job of fragmenting power. The challenge is to enable these fragmented units to work together to solve problems. The two major national parties are a unifying force in

American politics. Their ability to bridge the separation of powers has limits, but the major parties can provide a basis for cooperation in a government marked by decentralization and division.

HOW DO PARTIES DIFFER FROM OTHER POLITICAL GROUPS?

We have seen that parties have a lot of competition as intermediaries in politics. *All* political organizations, not just parties, try to educate at least some citizens and mobilize their supporters either to win public office or to influence those who do win. How, then, do parties differ from these other political organizations?

Parties Are Paramount in Elections

Above all, a party can be distinguished from other political organizations by its role in structuring elections. In most elections, candidates are listed on the ballot as "Democrat" or "Republican"; they are not listed as "National Rifle Association" or "AIDS activist." It is the major parties that normally enlist the election clerks and the poll watchers, not the Chamber of Commerce. The parties are paramount among political groups in contesting elections.

They Have a Full-time Commitment to Political Activity

The major American parties are fully committed to political activity; it is the sole purpose of their existence. Interest groups and most other political organizations, in contrast, move freely and frequently from political to nonpolitical activities and back again. The Steelworkers' Union, for example, is fundamentally concerned with collective bargaining for better pay and working conditions. It may turn to political action to support sympathetic candidates or to lobby Congress for favorable legislation, but its interests are rooted in the workplace. Parties live entirely in the political world.

They Mobilize Large Numbers

An interest group, such as a political action committee representing the corporations that make diet pills, does not need millions of supporters to try to convince Congress to go easy on regulating the ingredients in diet pills; it may be able to succeed with only a few strategists and a small, well-mobilized clientele. Because winning elections is so vital to parties' goals, however, parties must recruit and mobilize an enormous range of supporters to win large numbers of races. The result is that in a system such as that of the United States, party appeals must be broad and inclusive; a major party cannot afford to represent only a narrow range of concerns.

They Endure

Political parties, at least in the United States, are also unusually stable and long-lived. Single-issue groups and most business and environmental groups are fleeting by comparison. The size and abstractness of the parties and their ability to transcend individual candidates give them a much longer life. Both major American parties can trace their histories for more than 150 years, and the major parties of other western democracies also have impressive life spans. This remarkable endurance adds to their value for voters. The parties are there as points of reference, year after year, election after election, and candidate after candidate, giving continuity to the choices Americans face and the issues they debate.

They Serve as Political Symbols

Finally, political parties differ from other political organizations in the extent to which they operate as symbols, or emotion-laden objects of loyalty. For tens of millions of Americans, the party label is a social identity, like that of an ethnic or religious group. It is the chief cue for their decisions about candidates or issues; it relates their values to the real options of American politics.

Remember, however, that the differences between parties and other political organizations are differences of degree. Interest groups do become involved in elections, even extensively involved, and the larger organized interests serve as political symbols, too. They can recruit candidates, give political cues to their members and friends, and get their supporters to the polls on Election Day. Other nonparty groups may do the same. Interest groups also promote issue positions, try to influence officeholders, and give money to campaigns. They do not, however, and in most localities cannot, offer their names and symbols for candidates to use on the ballot.

In some respects, the major parties have more in common with some of the larger interest groups, such as the Chamber of Commerce and the American Association of Retired Persons (AARP), than they do with minor or third parties. Most minor parties are electoral organizations in name only. Their candidates are in no danger of needing a victory speech on election night. They may have few or no local organizations. Their membership base, often dependent on a single issue, may be just as narrow as that of most interest groups (see, for example, the box on page 14: "Is This a Party?"). However, minor parties may qualify to be listed on the ballot, and their candidates can receive public funding where it is available and where they can meet the criteria for it. In these ways (and sometimes *only* in these ways), they can be more like the major parties than the large interest groups.

HOW THE AMERICAN PARTIES DEVELOPED

The world's first political parties developed in the United States. For more than 200 years, their history has been entwined with the expansion of popular democracy. A key part of this story is the shift in the relative positions of the three parts of the party as first the party in government, then the party organizations, and then both the parties in government and in the electorate enjoyed their period of dominance.[7]

The Founding of American Parties

Although the founders of the American government were hostile to the idea of political parties, the seeds of parties were sown shortly after the new government was created. Groups within the Congress disagreed about how much power the new national government should have, relative to the states. The dominant group came to be called *Federalists;* led by the ambitious young treasury secretary, Alexander Hamilton, they championed

IS THIS A PARTY?

In early September 2000, the Natural Law Party formed a coalition with the Reform Party. As one reporter pointed out, with understatement, "They'll have to iron out a few differences in philosophy." The Reform Party was founded by Ross Perot, a billionaire who argued for reducing the national debt and limiting congressional terms. When Perot declined to run again as the party's presidential candidate in 2000, one faction of his party decided to nominate Pat Buchanan, a controversial conservative writer and speaker. Some Reform activists opposed that idea and looked for another candidate.

The candidate they chose was John Hagelin, who was also the leader of the Natural Law Party (now known as U.S. Peace Government). Begun by followers of the Maharishi Mahesh Yogi, a Hindu guru, Hagelin's party calls for conflict-free politics based on Transcendental Meditation (TM). Meditation, they believe, will reduce crime, violence, sickness, and accidents in the United States. An important accompaniment to TM is "yogic flying," in which meditation is said to lift the individual's body off the ground, inch by inch, beginning with "hopping" and, eventually, sailing away.

Some of the more earthbound Reform Party activists struggled mightily to mesh with their new Natural Law allies. "I don't know anything about yogic flying, but I had a sled, an American Flyer, when I was a kid," said Perot's former aide, Russ Verney, at the Natural Law convention. Another worried Reform worker asked Hagelin if he could fly and was reassured that the answer was no. Whether he was further reassured by the candidate's acceptance speech, in which Hagelin declared that, "the unified field percolates infant universes at the rate of 10 to the 143rd per cubic centimeter per second," was not noted.

Source for the quotations: Dana Milbank, "The Reform Party, Feelin' Guru-vy," *Washington Post,* September 2, 2000, page C1.

centralized (federal government) control over the economy, a central banking system, and high tariffs to protect fledgling American industries (see the box on page 15).

The opposition rallied around Thomas Jefferson and James Madison, who wanted to protect the states' rights from national government interference. Each group gathered in meetings, called "caucuses," to plan strategy. During the 1790s, these alignments began to take more enduring form. Their differences, as is the case now, were both principled and personal; as historian David McCullough reports, the animosity between Hamilton and Jefferson "had reached the point where they could hardly bear to be in the same room. Each was certain the other was a dangerous man intent on dominating the government."[8]

These early "parties," then, were formed "from the top" by their party in government, rather than by activists at the grassroots. They focused initially on issues that animated the national leaders who formed them rather than on local issues, as would be expected at a time when most Americans played only a marginal or indirect role in politics. In the first years of the Republic, the vote was limited in almost every state to those free men who could meet property-owning or taxpaying requirements. Even these relatively small numbers of voters had limited power, as the writers of the Constitution intended. The president was chosen not directly by the voters, but indirectly by the Elec-

THE AMERICAN MAJOR PARTIES

In more than 200 years of U.S. history, only five political parties have reached major party status, and only the Democrats and Republicans have retained it to this day.

1. **The Federalist Party, 1788–1816.** The champion of the new Constitution and strong national government, it was the first American political institution to resemble a political party, although it was not a full-fledged party. Its strength was rooted in the Northeast and the Atlantic Seaboard, where it attracted the support of shopkeepers, manufacturers, financiers, landowners, and other established families of wealth and status. Limited by its narrow electoral base, it soon fell before the success of the Democratic-Republicans.

2. **The Democratic-Republican Party, 1800–1832.** Many of its leaders had been strong proponents of the Constitution but opposed the extreme nationalism of the Federalists. This was a party of the small farmers, workers, and less-privileged citizens, plus southern planters, who preferred the authority of the state governments and opposed centralizing power in the national government. Like its leader, Thomas Jefferson, it shared many of the ideals of the French Revolution, especially the extension of the right to vote and the notion of direct popular self-government.

3. **The Democratic Party, 1832–Present.** Growing out of the Jacksonian wing of the Democratic-Republicans, it was the first really broad-based, popular party in the United States. On behalf of a coalition of less-privileged voters, it opposed such business-friendly policies as national banking and high tariffs. It also welcomed the new immigrants (and sought their votes) and opposed nativist (anti-immigrant) sentiment.

4. **The Whig Party, 1834–1856.** This party, too, had roots in the old Democratic-Republican Party, but in the Clay-Adams faction and in opposition to the Jacksonians. Its greatest leaders, Henry Clay and Daniel Webster, stood for legislative supremacy and protested the strong presidency of Andrew Jackson. For its short life, the Whig Party was an unstable coalition of many interests, among them nativism, property, and business and commerce.

5. **The Republican Party, 1854–Present.** Born as the Civil War approached, this was the party of northern opposition to slavery and its spread to the new territories. Therefore it was also the party of the Union, the North, Lincoln, the freeing of slaves, victory in the Civil War, and the imposition of Reconstruction on the South. From the Whigs it also inherited a concern for business and industrial expansion.

toral College. Although election to the House of Representatives was entrusted to a direct popular vote, election to the Senate was not; senators were chosen by the respective state legislatures. This cautious start for democratic self-government produced very rudimentary political parties.

The party groupings in Congress made some limited efforts to reach out to the voters at home. Party organization at the grassroots level began as "committees of correspondence" between national and local leaders. Each side established a newspaper to propagandize on behalf of its cause. And public sentiment found its way to the Capitol. Organized popular protest against some unpopular administration measures was directed at the party in Congress, and fights broke out occasionally between rival party mobs.

One of these two incipient parties, the **Democratic-Republicans** (led by Jefferson), began organizing in the states and local communities in time for the 1800 elections. The more elitist Federalists, who had earlier dominated the Congress, failed to keep up; splits arose within their caucus, and the Federalists began to disappear in most states soon after the defeat of their last president, John Adams, in 1800. In short, the pressures for democratization were already powerful enough by the early 1800s to scuttle an infant party whose leaders in the government could not adapt to the need to organize a mass electorate, especially in the new states of the frontier. Yet the Federalists gave a historic gift to American democracy. They accepted Adams's defeat in 1800 and handed control of the presidency to their Democratic-Republican rivals.[9]

The Democratic-Republicans, who were the party of agrarian interests and the frontier, quickly established their electoral superiority and held a one-party monopoly for 20 years. They dominated American politics so thoroughly by the time of James Monroe's election in 1816 that the absence of party and political conflict was called the "Era of Good Feelings." Despite the decline of one party and the rise of another, however, the nature of party politics did not change much during this period. It was a time when government and politics were the business of an elite group of well-known, well-established men, and the parties reflected the politics of the time. Without party competition, leaders felt no need to establish larger grassroots organizations, so the parties' further development was stalled.

American politics began to change sharply in the 1820s. By then, most states had eliminated the requirement that only landowners could vote, so the suffrage was extended to all white males, at least in state and federal elections. The growing pressure for democratization also led governments to make more and more public officials popularly elected rather than appointed.[10]

The most obvious change in the 1820s was the emergence of the presidential election process that has lasted to this day, and that accompanied a shift of power within the parties. The framers of the Constitution had crafted an unusual arrangement for selecting the president, known as the Electoral College. Each state, in a manner selected by its legislature, would choose a number of presidential voters (electors) equal to the size of its congressional delegation. These electors would meet in the state to cast their votes for president; the candidate who received a majority of the states' electoral votes was the national winner. If no candidate received a majority, the president was to be selected by the House of Representatives, with each state casting one vote.

This Electoral College was an ingenious invention. By leaving the choice of electors to the state legislatures, the framers avoided having to set uniform election methods and voting requirements, issues on which they strongly disagreed (and which involved, of course, the explosive question of slavery). This also eliminated the need for federal intervention in a question on which the states had previously made their own decisions and which might have produced state opposition. Requiring electors to meet simultaneously in their respective states helped prevent a conspiracy among electors from different states to put forward their own choice for president.

At first, states used a variety of methods for selecting presidential electors, but by the 1820s, popular election was the most common method.[11] This growing enthusiasm for democratic practices also eroded the power of the party's congressional caucus to nominate a presidential candidate. Caucus nominations came to be criticized as the action of a narrow and self-perpetuating elite. The congressional party caucus, then, was losing its role as the predominant force within the parties.

The caucus system also began to fall apart from within. The Democratic-Republicans' attempt to nominate a presidential candidate in 1824 ended in chaos. No candidate won a majority in the Electoral College, so the House of Representatives had to choose among John Quincy Adams, William H. Crawford, and Andrew Jackson. Although Jackson was the front-runner in both the popular and electoral votes, the House chose Adams. Jackson, in turn, defeated Adams in 1828; by then, the nation was entering a new phase of party politics.

THE EMERGENCE OF A NATIONAL TWO-PARTY SYSTEM

The nonparty politics of the Era of Good Feelings gave way to a two-party system that has prevailed ever since. The Democratic-Republicans had developed wings or factions that chose divorce rather than reconciliation. Andrew Jackson led the frontier and agrarian wing of the Democratic-Republicans, the inheritors of the Jeffersonian tradition, into what is now called the ***Democratic Party.*** The National Republicans, another faction of the old Democratic-Republicans who had earlier promoted Adams for president, merged with the ***Whigs*** (an old English term referring to those who opposed the dominance of the king, by whom they meant Jackson). That created two-partyism in the United States.

Just as important, the parties as political institutions developed even more of a nationwide grassroots base. The Jacksonian Democrats held the first national nominating convention in 1832 that, appropriately, nominated Jackson himself for a second term. (The smaller Anti-Masonic Party had held a more limited convention a year before.) Larger numbers of citizens were now eligible to vote, so the presidential campaign became more concerned with reaching out to the public; new campaign organizations and tactics brought the contest to many more people. Jackson was then sent back to the White House for a second term as the leader of a national political party.

Party organization in the states also expanded. Candidates for state and local office were increasingly nominated by conventions of state and local leaders, rather than by the narrower legislative caucuses. By 1840, the Whigs and the Democrats were established in the first truly national party system and were competitive in all the states.

During the 1840s and 1850s, the bitter issue of slavery increasingly fractured both parties. The Whigs, who were particularly divided, collapsed. Antislavery sentiment moved into a new group calling itself the ***Republican Party.*** The Republicans had formed mainly to demand the abolition of slavery but then adopted the Whigs' commitment to protect American businesses with high tariffs and to levy high taxes in order to subsidize industrial development—roads, railroads, and settlement of the frontier. The Republicans organized throughout the nation, with the exception of the South and the Border States, which were Democratic strongholds, and won the presidency in 1860. The party system and the nation split into North and South.

In short, modern political parties similar to those we know today—with their characteristic organizational structures, bases of loyal voters, and lasting alliances among governmental leaders—had developed by the middle of the 1800s.[12] The American parties grew hand in hand with the early expansion of the electorate in the United States. Comparable parties did not develop in Great Britain until the 1870s, after laws were passed to further expand the adult male electorate.

The Golden Age of the Parties

Just as the parties were reaching their maturity, they, and American politics, received another massive infusion of voters from a new source: European immigrants. Hundreds of thousands of Europeans, the majority from Ireland and Germany, immigrated to the United States before the Civil War. So many arrived, in fact, that their entry into American politics prompted controversy. The newcomers found a ready home in the Democratic Party, and an anti-immigrant third party, the American Party (the so-called Know-Nothing Party), sprang up in response in the 1850s.

The tide of immigration was halted only temporarily by the Civil War. After the war ended, new nationalities came in a virtually uninterrupted flow from 1870 until Congress closed the door to mass immigration in the 1920s. More than five million immigrants arrived in the 1880s (equal to one-tenth of the 1880 resident population), and 10 million more came between 1905 and 1914 (one-eighth of the 1900 resident population).

The political parties played an important role in assimilating these huge waves of immigrants. The newcomers gravitated toward the big cities where industrial jobs were available. It was in the cities that a new kind of party organization, the city "machine," developed in response to the immigrants' needs and vulnerabilities. The machines were impressively efficient organizations. They became social service systems that helped the new arrivals cope with the challenges of an urban industrial society. They softened the hard edge of poverty, smoothed the way with government and the police, and taught immigrants the customs of their new home.

The political machine in a city was often indistinguishable from the city's government; this was the classic case of "party government" in the American experience. The machines also were the means by which the new urban working class won control of the cities away from the largely Anglo-Saxon, Protestant elites who had prevailed for so long. As the parties again embodied the hopes of new citizens, just as they had in the 1830s, they reached their high point of power and influence in American history.

The American parties, with the party organization now their dominant part, had reached their "golden age" by the beginning of the 1900s. Party organizations now existed in all the states and localities and flourished in the industrial cities. Party discipline was at a record high in Congress and most state legislatures. Parties ran campaigns for public office; they held rallies and torchlight parades, canvassed door-to-door, and brought the voters to the polls. They controlled access to many government jobs ranging from street inspectors to members of the U.S. Senate. They were an important source of information and guidance for a largely uneducated and often illiterate electorate. They rode the crest of an extraordinarily vital American politics; the highest voter turnouts in American presidential history were recorded during the latter half of the 1800s. The parties suited the needs and limitations of the new voters and met the need for creating majorities in the new industrial society.[13]

The Progressive Reforms and Beyond

The drive to democratize American politics continued into the 1900s. With the adoption of the Seventeenth Amendment, U.S. senators came to be elected directly by the voters rather than by the state legislatures. Women and then blacks finally gained the right to vote. As popular democracy expanded, a movement arose that would impose important changes on the parties.

The period that parties saw as their "golden age"—the height of their influence on American politics—did not seem so golden to groups of reformers. To Progressive crusaders, party control of politics had led to rampant corruption and government inefficiency.[14] Because the Progressives saw party power as the culprit, they tried to weaken the control that the parties, and especially the party organizations, had achieved by the late 1800s. The reformers attacked party "boss rule" with the direct primary, which allowed citizens to choose the parties' candidates. Presidential nominations were made more open to the public by establishing presidential primaries in the states. Many state legislatures wrote laws to define and limit party organizations, and activists within the parties reformed their national conventions.

The reforms succeeded; the parties would never regain the exalted position that they had enjoyed in the three decades after the Civil War. But this success had its price. When citizens gained the right to nominate the parties' candidates, they weakened the most important function of party organizations and party leaders. Candidates, who could now appeal directly to primary voters, became more independent of the party organizations. The effect of the Progressive reforms, then, was to undercut the dominance of the party organization within the party as a whole. So the expectations of a democratic society, which first made the parties more public, more decentralized, and more active at the grassroots level, later turned on the party organization, leaving it less and less capable of the important role that it once played in American politics.[15]

More recently, however, the party organizations and their leaders have created new sources of power for themselves. Beginning in the 1970s, first the Republicans and then the Democrats expanded the fund-raising capacity of their national party organizations and used their new money to provide more services to candidates and to increase the capabilities of their state party organizations, and sometimes even the local parties. In the last three decades the Democratic Party, through its national committee and convention, has created rules for state Democratic Parties to follow in the process of nominating a presidential candidate. Both of these changes have strengthened the national party organizations relative to the state and local parties. In fact, the national party organizations probably have more of a presence within the two major parties, relative to the state and local party organizations, now than they have at any other time in American history. (Chapters 3 and 4 have more to say on these changes.)

In short, the parties have changed dramatically and continue to change. Yet they remain the leading organizations of popular democracy. They developed and grew with the expansion of the right to vote and the growing role of citizens in electoral politics. They are the channel through which ambitious people try to move into positions of power and large numbers of voters come together to choose their representatives. They help to clarify the alternatives in dealing with such challenging issues as abortion, taxes, and national defense. They amplify the voices of some groups in making demands on public policy and dampen the voices of others.

WHAT DO THE PARTIES STAND FOR?

There have been many changes over time as well in the parties' positions on issues, even major issues. Both the Democrats and the Republicans, for example, have shifted their positions dramatically over the years on the question of civil rights for black Americans. The traditional decentralization of the American parties (discussed in the next chapter) has meant that party organizations in some states or local communities have taken stands different from organizations of the same party in other areas.

Yet there have often been times of clear party differences on big policy questions. The current period is one of those times. Although some would argue that the parties' issue stands are simply a means to attract votes, the ongoing competition between the Democrats and Republicans, and the nature of the American party system, has always been more than just a story of raw ambition. Ever since the parties began as groups of leaders in Congress, they have organized not just to gain power but to do so to achieve particular goals. Changes in the electorate and the growing strength of the national party organizations in the past three decades have encouraged the definition of clearer policy stands within both parties, as well as sharper differences between them in the sources of their leadership and core supporters.

If you explore the Republican National Committee's website, the party platform, or the votes of Republicans in Congress, you will find that the Republican Party has long believed in a strong business sector and distrusted the power of government to remedy individual inequalities by creating welfare programs or redistributing income. President Bush refers to the Republican vision as an "ownership society," in which individuals will have more opportunities to build up their own wealth and to steadily free themselves from the heavy yoke of government intervention.

These principles can be seen in the party's positions on many current issues (see Table 1.1). Tax cuts for individuals and businesses are high on the party's agenda in the early 2000s; lower taxes shrink the government's revenue and, therefore, its ability to create new programs—a strategy that some conservatives call "starving the beast" (government). The tax cuts should favor those who are better off, many Republicans would argue, because that helps the economy grow. The party has traditionally argued for protecting property rights, which also limits the government's ability to interfere in the economic decisions of its citizens.

Republican positions on other policy questions also demonstrate these commitments to private rather than governmental solutions to problems and to state and local rather than national and international authority. In education, for example, the party argues for local control over schools and proposes that parents receive tax breaks for sending their children to private schools. In the area of defense, the Republican tradition defines a strong national defense as requiring a powerful military rather than as giving priority to international agreements on arms control and other matters.

Over time, Republicans have been more likely than Democrats to draw their party leaders and candidates from the business sector. Consistent with that, the party's relationship with labor unions has long been somewhere between strained and nonexistent. Core groups of Republican supporters include conservatives (conservative Christians in particular), white southerners, and people with higher incomes.

The Democratic Party represents a different tradition. To Democratic activists, government is a valuable means of redressing the inequalities that the marketplace can cause.

TABLE 1.1   Party Differences in the Early 2000s: Issues and Core Supporters

Democrats	Republicans
Core belief	
A strong government provides needed services and remedies inequalities	A strong government interferes with business and threatens freedom
Biggest exception	
Government should stay out of people's moral decisions on abortion, homosexuality, etc.	Government should regulate people's moral decisions on abortion, homosexuality, etc.
Issue agenda	
Education, health, social services	Strong military, tax cuts
Environmental protection	Property rights
Emphasizes	
Fairness, especially for disadvantaged groups	Individual success, not group rights
Relations with labor unions	
Close and supportive	Distant and hostile
Core supporters	
Lower-income people	Higher-income people
East and West Coasts	South, Mountain West
Minority groups	Caucasians
Secular individuals	Conservative Christians
Teachers, trial lawyers	Businesspeople

Source: Compiled by the author from materials including the 2004 Democratic and Republican platforms and the American National Election Studies 2004 *Guide to Public Opinion and Electoral Behavior* (at http://www.umich.edu/~nes).

These activists believe that needed social services should be public, provided by government, rather than privatized. Tax cuts, they argue, limit the ability of government to provide these needed services. If a tax cut is needed, they say, it should be directed toward helping the needy rather than those who are more affluent. Whereas Republicans believe that the point of government is to promote greater individual economic achievement, even at the cost of economic inequality, Democrats are willing to accept economic inefficiency as long as government provides a safety net to those who need it.

During the past half-century, the national Democratic Party has favored using government to enforce civil rights for black Americans, and during the past 20 years has been the party of abortion rights and environmental action. If property rights get in the way of environmental protection, Democratic activists contend, then property rights must usually give way. The party's stand on education, similarly, stresses the need for investment in public schools and equality of opportunity. That is one reason why the Democrats are more likely to draw their candidates and activists from among teachers and trial lawyers. The core of Democratic support comes from lower-income people, those living on the East and West Coasts, minorities, and organized labor.

Yet, even today, neither party is a model of consistency on issues. In particular, as Table 1.1 shows, the parties seem to switch core beliefs on some issues of individual morality. The Republican Party, which usually opposes government interference, asks for government action to limit abortions and homosexual behavior and to support conservative family values. And the Democrats, the party that sees government as an ally for the needy, wants government to stay out of individuals' lives on issues such as abortion and homosexuality.

This party switch on so-called "moral issues" could be seen in a dramatic series of events in 2005. Terri Schiavo, a seriously brain-damaged woman in a persistent vegetative state, had been kept alive by a feeding tube for 15 years. Her husband intended to have the feeding tube disconnected, saying that his wife had expressed a desire not to be kept alive by extraordinary means. Her parents disagreed and, with the support of pro-life groups, sought to have the feeding tube reconnected. After several state judges sided with the husband, national Republican leaders pushed hard for federal authority to override the state courts, citing the need for a "culture of life." The Republican efforts failed and Schiavo died, but the scenario of Republicans arguing for federal intervention and Democrats opposing it brought this inconsistency in the parties' stands into sharp relief.

These twists and turns in party principles can sometimes stem from a party's efforts to pick up additional support. In the case of the "moral issues," for example, some conservative Republicans in the 1970s became aware that the pro-life and anti-gay rights stands of the Christian Right were much more engaging to swing groups of voters than were some of the conservative wing's economic proposals.

They also grow out of the powerful impact of their environment on the parties' development. The Republican Party could begin life as a party of both business interests and big government because the expanding businesses of the 1800s needed government help. The building of roads and other means of transporting goods, large-scale communications networks, and high tariffs to protect American-made goods could be done much more efficiently by the national government than by the states or the businesses themselves. Once American business became well established and the needed infrastructure was in place, however, a strong national government could become a threat to businesses—as it did in responding to the Depression of the 1930s—because it could regulate their operations and raise their taxes to help fund social programs.

PARTIES ARE SHAPED BY THEIR ENVIRONMENT

Throughout their history, then, the nature of the parties' activities, their issue positions, and even their organizational form have been influenced by forces in their environment, and they have affected that environment in return. One of the most important of these forces has been the nature of the electorate: who has the right to vote?

Voters and Elections

As we have seen, the expansion of the right to vote has helped shape the parties' development. Each new group of voters entering the electorate challenges the parties to readjust their appeals. As they compete for the support of these new voters, the parties must rethink their strategies for building coalitions that can win elections. Parties in states where black citizens finally gained the right to vote, for example, learned to campaign differently from the days when they needed to appeal to an all-white clientele.

The parties' fortunes are also bound up with the *nature* of American elections. The move from indirect to direct election of U.S. senators, for instance, transformed both the contesting of these elections and the parties that contested them. If the Electoral College system is ever abolished and American presidents are chosen by direct popular vote, that change, too, would affect the parties.

A state's election rules have great impact on the parties' activities as well. If you were a party leader in a state where conventions of party activists used to nominate state and congressional candidates, imagine the changes that you would face when your state switched to the direct primary and voters gained the power to choose these candidates. Even relatively minor differences in primary laws from state to state, such as differences in the form of the ballot or the timing of the primary, affect the parties. The electoral institutions of the nation and the states set the rules within which the parties compete for votes, and thus influence parties' activities and organization.

Political Institutions

The two main "rules" of American politics, federalism and the separation of powers, affect the parties profoundly. Consider, for example, the impact of the separation of powers. Nationally and in the states, American legislators and executives are elected independently of one another. That makes it possible and, in recent decades very likely, for the legislature and the governorship or the presidency to be controlled by different parties. Most other democracies, in contrast, have parliamentary systems in which the legislative majority chooses the officials of the executive branch from among its own members. When that parliamentary majority can no longer hold, a new government must be formed. An important result of the separation of powers is that American legislative parties can rarely achieve the degree of party discipline and cohesion that is common in parliamentary systems.

In addition, because the American chief executive and the cabinet secretaries are not legislative party leaders, as they would be in a parliamentary system, there is a greater opportunity for conflict between executives and legislators of their own party. This conflict is even more likely because, in a system with separated powers, legislators can vote against a president or governor of their party on key issues without fearing that they will bring down the entire government and force new elections. So support for and opposition to executive programs can cut across party lines in Congress and state legislatures to a degree rarely found in parliamentary democracies.

The federal system, in which states have a number of independent powers (rather than being "branch offices" of the national government) has also left an imprint on the American parties. It has permitted the survival of local political loyalties and traditions. It has spawned an awesome range of public offices to fill, creating a system of elections that dwarfs that of all other democracies in size and diversity. These local traditions and loyalties have nurtured a large set of semi-independent local parties within the two national parties.

Laws Governing Parties

No other parties among the world's democracies are as entangled in legal regulations as are the American parties. It was not always this way. Before the Progressive reforms a century ago, American parties were self-governing organizations, almost unrestrained by state or federal law. For most of the 1800s, for example, the parties printed, distributed, and often—with a wary eye on one another—even counted the ballots. The "Australian" (or secret) ballot changed all of this, giving the responsibility for running elections to government, where it has remained ever since. During their "golden age," as noted earlier, the parties made their own rules for nominating candidates. But the arrival of the direct primary in the early 1900s and recent reforms of the presidential nominating process have severely limited the parties' autonomy. Civil service reform and court action have also largely stopped the parties from hiring workers for government jobs, a practice that was common in the late 1800s.

The existence of 50 different sets of state laws governing the parties has produced 50 different varieties of political parties. State laws control the forms of their organization and even define the parties themselves, often by defining the right to place candidates on the ballot. Most states try to regulate party activities; many, for example, regulate party finances, and most place some limits on their campaign practices. More recently, the federal government has added burdens of its own, including regulating parties' campaign practices and finances.[16]

Political Culture

A nation's political culture is the set of political values and expectations held by its people. It deals with the public's view of how the political system works, how it ought to work, and what roles individual citizens can play in politics and government. One of the most persistent components of the American political culture is the feeling that party politics is an underhanded, dirty business. A 2004 survey, for example, demonstrated that enthusiasm for the two parties was so limited that, when given a "feeling thermometer" ranging from 0 to 100 degrees on which to indicate their level of positive feeling, respondents could muster no more than an average rating of 56 for the Democrats and the Republicans—a chilly temperature in which to live.[17]

These and other elements of the political culture help shape what the parties can be. Public distrust of parties encourages candidates to campaign as individuals rather than as members of a party team and even to avoid mentioning their party in campaign ads. The widespread view that legislators ought to vote based on their local district's interests, for example, can make it harder to achieve party discipline in Congress and state legislatures. Even the question of what we regard as fair campaigning simply reflects the values and expectations of large numbers of Americans. Whether a strongly worded campaign ad is seen as "negative" or as "hard-hitting and informative" depends on cultural values, not on some set of universal standards. These cultural values affect citizens' feelings about the parties' behavior and, as a result, they influence the behavior itself.

The Broader Environment

Parties' environment is broader than their *political* environment. Perhaps no force has been more important for party politics than the emergence of the modern mass media, especially television and the Internet. Because the media can provide so much information about politics and candidates, voters need not depend on the parties to learn about elections and issues. Just as important, candidates can contact voters directly through the media rather than having to depend on the parties to carry the message for them. That has weakened party control over candidates' campaigns. To add insult to injury, media coverage tends not to pay much attention to the parties themselves. Television attaches great importance to visual images, of course, so it is much more likely to cover individuals—candidates and public officials—than to cover institutions, such as parties, that do not have a "face."

Economic trends can also have a strong and often disruptive impact on the parties. When an economic recession occurs, for example, parties will find it harder to raise money. If the crisis is especially severe, as was the Great Depression of the 1930s, it may even fracture and reorganize the pattern of citizens' party loyalties, end the careers of prominent party leaders, and make a majority party into a weakened minority.

In this chapter, we have explored the nature of parties, what they do, and how they have developed in and been shaped by their environment. These themes will continue to guide us throughout the book. The next chapter tackles one of the biggest puzzles that students of parties face when comparing the American parties with those in other nations: Why does the United States have two major parties, rather than several, or only one?

Chapter 2

The American
Two-Party System

Red states and blue states. Democrats and Republicans. Liberals and conservatives. Many Americans think about partisan politics the same way Noah envisioned his ark: There ought to be two of everything. It is an understandable assumption; media coverage focuses on the two-party system so fully that it seems obvious that a democracy needs two major parties in order to survive.

Except that it doesn't. The United States is one of the few democracies with a two-party system. Some democratic nations, such as Mexico, have had extended periods of one-party rule. Many more democracies, including most of those in Europe, have long supported multiparty systems with three, four, or even more parties. In these nations, one single party is often unable to win a majority of the votes, so two or more parties put together a coalition in order to govern.[1]

One-party and multiparty systems have been part of the American experience as well. Some states and cities have had a long tradition of one-party rule; in other areas, several parties have flourished at certain times. Minor or third parties and independent candidates continue to leave their mark on American politics. Green Party candidate Ralph Nader probably took just enough votes from the Democrats in 2000 to tip the presidential election to Republican George W. Bush.[2] Ross Perot's independent presidential campaign in 1992 won the support of almost 20 million Americans—the third highest percentage of the popular vote for a minor-party candidate in U.S. history. At the state level, reporters were captivated by the spectacle of a former professional wrestler named Jesse "The Body" Ventura winning the governorship of Minnesota in 1998 as the Reform Party candidate.

These campaigns are fun to watch; not many governors have worn a pink feather boa into a public arena or moonlighted as color commentators for the XFL (the late Extreme Football League). For better or for worse, however, they are rare. For most of American history, only two parties have had a realistic chance of winning any given election and of governing. Even the rapid rise of the most successful third party in American history, the Republican Party, shows the power of two-party politics in the United States. The party was founded in 1854, but instead of competing with the existing

Democrats and Whigs, it replaced the Whig Party within two short years. Ever since the Era of Good Feelings ended in the 1820s, then, the United States has had a two-party system in national party competition.

Why has American politics remained a two-party system for so long, when most other democracies have more than two competitive national parties? In this chapter, we look at the level of competition between the parties, the major theories as to how the two-party system developed, and the efforts by third parties and independent candidates to break the two-party mold.

THE NATIONAL PARTY SYSTEM

Throughout this remarkably long period of two-party politics, the two major parties have been very close competitors, at least at the national level. Consider the record of presidential elections. Since 1868, the great majority of these elections (29 out of 35) have been so close that a shift of 10 percent of the vote or less would have given the White House to the other party's candidate instead. Almost half (16) were decided by a spread of less than 7 percent of the popular vote. Some of the closest presidential contests in American history have taken place in the past decade. The 2000 election was a virtual tie, and in 2004 President Bush's margin of victory was the smallest ever achieved by an incumbent president.

In the aggregate, elections to the House of Representatives have been even closer. Overall, during the past 70 years, the percentage of the two-party vote cast for all Democratic candidates in a given election has not differed much from the vote cast for Republicans (see Table 2.1). Even in what was often called a Republican sweep in 2004, when the party won its largest House majority since 1949, Republican House candidates received just 51.3 percent of the national two-party House vote, and the majority

TABLE 2.1 Percentage of the Two-Party Vote Won by Republican Candidates for President and House of Representatives: 1940–2004

Decade Average	Presidential Elections		House Elections	
	% Republican of Two-Party Vote	% Difference Between Republican and Democratic Vote	% Republican of Two-Party Vote	% Difference Between Republican and Democratic Vote
1940s	46.3	7.3	49.8	5.9
1950s	56.6	13.1	48.1	4.2
1960s	46.3	7.8	46.7	6.7
1970s	55.4	12.6	44.5	10.7
1980s	56.1	11.9	46.1	7.6
1990s	45.9	7.1	49.5	4.3
2000s	50.4	1.4	51.5	3.0

Sources: Calculated from Harold W. Stanley and Richard G. Niemi, *Vital Statistics on American Politics 1999–2000* (Washington, DC: CQ Press, 2000), Tables 1–7 and 1–12. Data for 2000 House races were calculated from U.S. Census Bureau, *Statistical Abstract of the United States: 2001* (Washington, DC: Government Printing Office, 2001), p. 239, and for 2002 and 2004 House races from *CQ Weekly* postelection issues.

Republicans gained only 53 percent of House seats and 55 percent of the Senate. We see the same pattern of close party competition in the states as a whole. In 2005, Republicans controlled 49 of the state legislative chambers that have partisan elections, Democrats held 47, and two were tied. (The remaining state legislature, Nebraska's, is unicameral and nonpartisan.) The number of Democratic state legislators across the nation was almost exactly equal to the number of Republican legislators.

Although the national party system hasn't always been this competitive, the two major parties have been extremely resilient over time. Media coverage may suggest otherwise because it tends to trumpet the events of the moment. However, whenever one party has taken a big advantage, in the long run the other party has been able to restore the balance. Although the Democrats seemed to be on the ropes after the Reagan victories of the 1980s and the Republican congressional sweep of 1994, they recovered quickly enough to keep the presidency in 1996 and to continue gaining seats in Congress in 2000. By the same token, the GOP (or Grand Old Party, a nickname the Republican Party developed in the late 1800s) confounded the pessimists by springing back from the Roosevelt victories of the 1930s, landslide defeat in 1964, and the Watergate-related setbacks of the mid-1970s. And in current politics, the opportunities for sweeping gains by either party have been limited by the development of safer seats.

THE 50 STATE PARTY SYSTEMS

This pattern of close competition at the national level is an important part of the story, but, interestingly enough, it has coexisted for a long time with one-party dominance in many states and localities. Georgia, for example, chose Democratic governors in 50 consecutive gubernatorial elections, starting before the end of Reconstruction, before finally electing a Republican in 2002.[3]

How can we measure the level of competition in the 50 state party systems? There are many questions to answer in building a measure. Which offices should we look at: the vote for president, governor, senator, statewide officials, state legislators, or some combination of these? The competitiveness of a state's U.S. Senate seats may be strikingly different from that of its state legislative races. Should we count the candidates' vote totals, the number of offices that each party wins, or something else?

Measuring State Party Competition

The approach used most often to measure interparty competition at the state level is an index originated by Austin Ranney.[4] The Ranney index averages three indicators of party success during a particular time period: the percentage of the popular vote for the parties' gubernatorial candidates, the percentage of seats held by the parties in each house of the legislature, and the length of time plus the percentage of the time that the parties held both the governorship and a majority in the state legislature. The resulting scores range from 1.00 (complete Democratic success) through 0.50 (close competition between the parties) to 0.00 (complete Republican success).

Like any other summary measure, the Ranney index picks up some trends more fully than others. One reason is that it is based wholly on state elections. This protects the measure from being distorted by landslide victories and other unusual events at the national

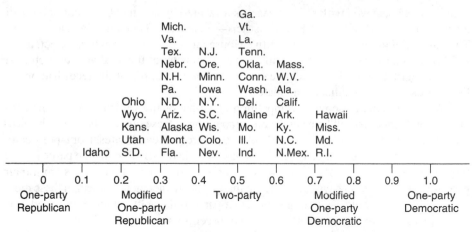

FIGURE 2.1 **Interparty Competition in the States, 1999–2003.**
Source: John F. Bibby and Thomas M. Holbrook, "Parties and Elections," in Virginia Gray and Russell L. Hanson, eds., *Politics in the American States*, 8th ed. (Washington, DC: CQ Press, 2003), p. 88.

level. Yet those national events may foreshadow what will happen in voting for state offices. In the South, for example, growing GOP strength appeared first in competition for national offices and only later worked its way down to the state and local level. In these states, for a time the Ranney index showed less interparty competition than really existed. A second problem is that the dividing lines between categories are purely arbitrary. There is no magic threshold that separates the category "modified one-party" from that of "competitive." Finally, any index score will vary, of course, depending on the years and the offices that it covers. Nevertheless, its findings provide an interesting picture of state party competition.

Figure 2.1 presents the calculations for the Ranney index through the 2002 elections. It shows more balanced party competition at the state level than had appeared in these calculations earlier in the years since World War II. Note especially that no states are classified as fully one-party. The driving force in this change was the development of two-party competition in the southern states, which used to be one-party Democratic, and also in formerly one-party Republican states in the Northeast and Midwest.[5]

There is reason to think that this may be a transitional period, however. The Ranney index has shown a shift toward Republican success in the states more generally, with the tipping point coming at the time of the 1994 elections. Because the Democrats had dominated so many states in earlier years, the result was a period of greater competition between the two parties throughout the 50 states than had existed before. But if the Republican trend in the South continues, as is very likely, then we may see a less balanced pattern in the figure, with states such as Georgia and South Carolina moving from "competitive" to "modified one-party Republican."

Limits on Competitiveness: Incumbency

Below the state level, the decline in party competition is more marked. For example, although the House of Representatives as a whole is closely divided, most House candidates are elected with a comfortable margin of victory. In 2004, for example, the winning candidate won with relative ease, as measured by getting 60 percent or more of the total vote, in 341 of the 435 House districts—more than 78 percent of all House seats. The number of these not-very-competitive House races has been growing. In fact, in the 2004 races almost a quarter of the winners got 75 percent of the total vote or more.[6] At the state legislative level, in recent years, fewer than two-thirds of the races had both a Democratic and a Republican candidate.[7]

What keeps the close party competition at the national level from infiltrating congressional districts as well? One brake on competition in these districts has been the electoral value of incumbency. In the 1800s, the fates of candidates from politically competitive areas depended on the national or statewide forces affecting the parties. Even though American candidates have been better able to insulate themselves from their party's misfortunes than have candidates in many other democracies, voters in these more competitive areas could easily turn to the other party as the political winds changed. The result was a lot of party turnover in seats and insecurity for many candidates.

But especially since the 1950s, members of Congress have had greater electoral security, mainly because incumbency became so valuable a political resource. From 1954 through 1988, for example, the average success rates for incumbents seeking reelection were 93 percent in the U.S. House of Representatives and 81 percent in the Senate. These rates peaked in 1988 for the House when more than 98 percent of the incumbents who ran for reelection won, and in 1990 when all but one of the senators running for reelection won. (A congressional incumbent in these years probably stood a greater chance of being hit by an SUV in Washington, DC, traffic than of losing reelection.)

That job security seemed to be at risk in the early 1990s. A well-reported scandal and a resulting crop of especially strong challengers, followed by an effective national Republican House campaign in 1994, dropped the success rate of House incumbents to "only" between 88 and 90 percent. In addition, a larger than usual number of incumbents retired from the House during this time, due in part to special incentives for retirement in 1990 and in part to avoid a likely defeat. But the House reelection rate returned to 98 percent in each election between 1998 and 2004.[8] Incumbents in most state legislatures were just as likely to keep their jobs.[9] In fact, this incumbency advantage increased in elections for all types of executive and legislative offices.[10]

There are many reasons why incumbency came to be such a valuable resource in congressional elections. Incumbents learned how to benefit from the "perks" of holding office—their name recognition and the attention that they receive from the media, the services they can provide to constituents, the relative ease with which they can raise campaign money, and their experience in having run previous successful campaigns, all of which discourage potentially effective candidates from running against them. These add up to what can be called the *personal* incumbency advantage.[11]

... and Other Reasons for Declining Competitiveness

Researchers have found, however, that although there are larger numbers of safe House seats now than in the early 1990s, the *size* of the average House incumbent's advantage in winning reelection has declined since that time. So the personal incumbency advantage can't fully explain why congressional races are getting less competitive.

Another possible explanation is that during the last decade, state legislators have been able to use very sophisticated computerized techniques to redraw legislative district lines for themselves and for U.S. House members, and to make their districts safer by "choosing their own voters"; we'll look more closely at this in later chapters. Redistricting after the 2000 Census reduced the number of competitive House seats by making three-fourths of these districts safer for one party.[12] Yet again, redistricting can't be the only reason for safer districts because incumbents are doing better in elections for offices that are not redistricted as well, such as local and statewide offices.

Bruce Oppenheimer and Alan Abramowitz have suggested an alternative: that new patterns of residential mobility are a major cause of declining party competition. As people have become more likely to move away from their home towns, they are increasingly able, and likely, to move to areas where like-minded people live. As a result, areas become more homogeneous—and, thus, congressional districts are more likely to be dominated by one party.[13] A recent analysis found that although the 2000 and 1976 presidential elections were both won by very narrow margins, almost twice as many of the voters in 2000 lived in counties where one candidate or the other won by a landslide, suggesting that there has been a "voluntary political segregation" in the United States.[14]

Whatever its cause, the reality is that beneath the lively competition that exists at the national level, there are large numbers of fairly safe electoral districts. One analyst called the 2004 U.S. House elections "the least competitive in history."[15] So ironically, the increased party competition that we see in the nation as a whole is built not on large numbers of highly competitive House, state legislative, and other districts, but rather on the fact that the large number of fairly (and increasingly) safe districts for one party is closely matched by the number of fairly safe districts for the other party.

Political competition is vitally important in a democracy. When an officeholder expects to win reelection easily, he or she has less incentive to pay close attention to voters' needs. In particular, the needs of disadvantaged citizens are more likely to be ignored (because advantaged citizens have other means, in addition to voting, to make their voices heard in government). The increase in safe seats, then, is a cause for concern in the study of parties.

WHAT CAUSES A TWO-PARTY SYSTEM?

We have seen that the American parties are durable and, at least at the aggregate level, closely competitive with one another. Why have we had a two-party system for so long, when most other democracies do not? There are several possible explanations.

Institutional Forces

The most frequent explanation of the two-party system ties it to the nature of American electoral institutions. Called Duverger's law,[16] it argues that single-member districts with plurality elections tend to produce two-party systems. Plurality election in a single-member district means simply that one candidate is elected to each office and that the winner is the person who receives the largest number of votes, even if not a majority. Finishing a close second, or third or fourth, brings no rewards. The American election system is, for most offices, a single-member district system with plurality election; it offers the reward of winning an office only to the one candidate who gets the most votes. So the theory suggests that minor parties will see no point in running candidates if they don't have a shot at winning.

PLURALITY VERSUS PROPORTIONAL REPRESENTATION: HOW IT WORKS IN PRACTICE

Does it matter whether an election uses plurality or proportional representation (PR) rules to count the votes? To find out, let us compare the results of one type of American election in which both rules are used. In presidential primaries—the elections in which party voters choose delegates to the national parties' nominating conventions—the Democrats use PR to select delegates (with at least 15 percent of the vote needed for a candidate to win delegates) and the Republicans generally use plurality election (also called winner-take-all).

Imagine a congressional district that can elect four delegates to the convention, in which candidates A, B, C, and D get the following percentages of the vote. The candidates would win the following numbers of delegates, depending on whether the plurality or PR rule was used:

		Delegates Won	
	% of vote	PR	Plurality
Candidate A	40%	2	4
Candidate B	30%	1	0
Candidate C	20%	1	0
Candidate D	10%	0	0

As you can see, the **plurality** rule increases the delegate strength of the leading candidate (candidate A) at the expense of the other three. The other three candidates run in the hope of getting a plurality, but in the end, the second-place candidate wins nothing. Under PR rules, in contrast, *three* candidates win delegates in rough proportion to their popular support. So in a typical Democratic primary, the less successful candidates (such as candidate C) are encouraged to stay in the nomination race longer because the PR rules permit them to keep winning at least a few delegates. In a typical Republican primary, only the front-runner will win delegates, so the less successful candidates will probably drop out quickly.

The contrast is even clearer when we compare British elections with the multi-member district systems of most European legislative elections. The use of PR in the European elections promotes multiparty politics and coalition governments in which two or more different parties often share control of the executive. In the British parliamentary system, on the other hand, single-member districts operating under plurality rules typically produce a parliamentary majority for one party, giving it sole control of the executive, even if it does not win a majority of the popular vote.

The flip side of Duverger's law is that multimember constituencies and proportional representation result in multiparty systems. A system with multimember constituencies is one in which a particular legislative district will be represented by, say, three or four elected legislators.[17] Each party prepares a slate of candidates for these positions, and the number of party candidates who win is proportional to the overall percentage of the vote won by the party slate (see box above). Because a party may be able to elect a candidate with only 15 or 20 percent of the votes, depending on the system's rules, smaller parties are encouraged to keep competing.

However, a puzzle remains. Single-member district systems with plurality elections exist in some other democracies that support more than two parties. Shouldn't the United States, with its great diversity, do the same? To some analysts, the nature of the American presidency is enough to sustain Duverger's law. The presidency is the most visible single-member district in the United States. It is the main prize of American politics, and only one person is elected to that office at a time. Many other democracies, using a parliamentary system, select a governing "cabinet" as the executive authority. This cabinet is made up of a number of officeholders, so it can be a coalition that includes representatives of several parties, including smaller parties.

In a system with a single executive, minor parties will be weakened because they do not have a realistic chance to compete for the presidency.[18] Even local and regional parties strong enough to elect candidates in their own localities typically find it unrealistic to run a candidate for president. That, in turn, denies a minor party a number of other important opportunities. Without a presidential candidate, a party is not likely to gain the national attention that major parties get. Add to that the uniquely American institution of the Electoral College. To win, a presidential candidate must get a plurality of electoral votes—so far, at least, an impossible task for a minor-party candidate. Because the presidency is so prominent in American politics, the argument goes, it shapes the politics of the system as a whole. Because third parties have no chance of winning the presidency, they will not thrive.[19]

Of course, some minor parties try for the presidency anyway. In 1996, the Reform Party focused primarily on the presidential race. But its candidate, Ross Perot, a billionaire willing to spend tens of millions on his campaign, is clearly not typical of most minor parties, no matter how much they may dream of such an opportunity. So the importance of the single, indivisible executive office in the American system strengthens the tendency toward two-party politics.

Political scientist Leon Epstein has identified another institutional factor, the direct primary, as a force that prevented the development of third parties in areas dominated by one party.[20] Primaries, which allow voters to choose the parties' nominees, have become the main method of selecting party candidates. When disgruntled groups have the opportunity to make their voices heard within the dominant party through a primary and may even succeed in getting a candidate nominated, the resulting taste of power will probably discourage them from breaking away to pursue a third-party course. Thus, in the one-party Democratic South of an earlier era, where traditional animosities kept most people from voting Republican, factional disputes that under other conditions would have led to third-party development were contained within the Democratic Party by the existence of primary elections.

"Dualist" Theories

Some theorists believe that there is a basic duality of interests in American society that has sustained the two-party system. V. O. Key, Jr. argued that tension between the eastern financial and commercial interests and the western frontiersmen stamped itself on the parties as they were forming and fostered two-party competition. Later, the dualism shifted to North-South conflict over the issue of slavery and the Civil War and then to urban-rural and socioeconomic divisions.[21] A related line of argument suggests that there is a natural dualism within democratic institutions: government versus opposition, those favoring and opposing the status quo, and even the ideological dualism of liberal and conservative. Therefore, social and economic interests, or the very processes of a democratic politics, tend to reduce the contestants to two great camps, and that dualism gives rise to two political parties.

We can see tendencies toward dualism even in multiparty systems, in that some parties will succeed in constructing a governing coalition that pulls them together and the other parties will find themselves in opposition. In France and Italy, for example, the Socialists and other parties of the left, or the various parties of the right and center, often compete against one another in elections but then come together along largely ideological lines to contest runoff elections or to form a government. What distinguishes two-party from multiparty systems, in short, may be whether this basic tendency toward dualism is expressed in every aspect of the electoral process or only in the creation and functioning of a government.

Social Consensus Theories

Another possible explanation for the American two-party system is that it reflects a broad consensus on values in American society. Despite their very diverse social and cultural heritage, early on Americans reached a consensus on the fundamentals that divide other societies. Almost all Americans have traditionally accepted the prevailing social, economic, and political institutions. They accepted the Constitution and its governmental structure, a regulated but free enterprise economy, and (perhaps to a lesser extent) American patterns of social class and status.

In traditional multiparty countries, such as France and Italy, noticeable segments of the public have favored radical changes in those and other basic institutions. They have supported fundamental constitutional change, the socialization of the economy, or the disestablishment of the national church. Perhaps American politics escaped these divisions on the essentials because Americans did not have a history of the rigid class structure of feudalism. Perhaps the early expansion of the right to vote made it unnecessary for workers and other economically disadvantaged citizens to organize in order to gain some political power. Perhaps it was the expanding economic and geographic frontiers that allowed Americans to concentrate on claiming a piece of a growing pie rather than on battling one another. Because the matters that divide Americans are secondary, the argument goes, the compromises needed to bring them into one of two major parties are easier to make.[22]

Party Self-Protection (The Best Defense Is a Good Offense)

Once a two-party system has developed, the two dominant parties have a strong motivation to protect it. The two major parties will choose and keep election systems (such as single-member districts) that make it hard for minor parties to do well. Through their control of Congress and state legislatures, the Democrats and Republicans have manipulated the rules for third parties to qualify for the ballot and for third-party candidates to receive public funding. The major parties have no interest in leveling the playing field so that their minor-party competitors can take a shot at replacing them.[23] Further, after the two-party system was launched, it created deep loyalties within the American public to one party or the other and attachments to the two-party system itself.

In addition, the two parties' openness to new groups and their adaptability to changing conditions—qualities rare among democratic parties—have undermined the development of strong third parties. Just when a third party rides the crest of a new issue to the point where it can challenge the two-party monopoly, one or both of the major parties is likely to absorb the new movement. In the 2004 campaign, for example, the Democrats worked hard to appeal to the nearly 3 million voters who supported Ralph Nader's Green Party candidacy in 2000.

Among all these possible reasons for a two-party system, the most important cause is the institutional arrangement of American electoral politics. Without single-member districts, plurality elections, the Electoral College, and an indivisible executive, it would have been much easier for third parties to break the near-monopoly enjoyed by the two major parties. The other Anglo-American democracies, such as Britain and Canada, which share the American institutional arrangements, also tend to be dominated by two parties, although third parties are not as hobbled in these nations as in the American party system.

EXCEPTIONS TO THE TWO-PARTY PATTERN

As we have seen, the American two-party system can harbor pockets of one-party politics within states and localities. There have been other deviations from the two-party pattern. Some areas have developed a uniquely American brand of no-party politics. Third parties or independent candidates have occasionally made their presence felt, as in recent presidential elections. Where do we find these exceptions to two-party politics?

Nonpartisan Elections

One of the crowning achievements of the Progressive movement was to restrict the role of parties in elections by removing party labels from many ballots, mostly in local elections. About three-quarters of American towns and cities, including Los Angeles, Chicago, Miami, and Atlanta, conduct their local elections on a nonpartisan basis. Many states elect judges using a nonpartisan ballot.

Removing party labels from the ballot has not usually removed partisan influences where parties are already strong. The nonpartisan ballot did not prevent the development of a powerful Democratic Party machine in Chicago. A resourceful party organization can still select its candidates and persuade voters when party labels are not on the ballot. Even where local elections are nonpartisan, local voters are still affected by the partisan content of state and national elections. But nonpartisanship does add to the parties' burdens; even the strongest local parties have to try much harder to let voters know which candidates are affiliated with their party.

Typically, however, the reform tended to take root in cities and towns that already had weak parties and for offices, such as judgeships and school boards, where the traditional American dislike of party politics is most pronounced. In contrast, most northeastern cities, where strong party machines were the most visible targets of the Progressives, were able to resist the reforms and to continue to hold partisan local elections.

Beyond removing the party label from ballots and adding to the difficulties faced by party organizations, what difference does it make if an election is nonpartisan? Political scientists have found that a move to nonpartisan elections shifts the balance of power in a pro-Republican direction rather than making politics any less partisan or more unbiased. Without party labels on the ballot, the voter is more dependent on other cues. Higher-status candidates usually have more resources and visibility in the community, which can fill the void left by the absence of party. In current American politics, these higher-status candidates are more likely to be Republicans. Similarly, nonpartisan elections have been found to increase incumbents' chances of winning and to reduce voter turnout.[24]

In an ingenious experiment, one group of researchers compared the behavior of state legislators in Nebraska, who are selected in nonpartisan elections, with those in partisan Kansas. They found that legislators' votes on bills are not as clearly structured in Nebraska as they are in Kansas; that makes it harder for voters to be able to predict how their representatives will behave and to hold them accountable. So nonpartisan elections can weaken the policy links between voters and their legislators—a result that would have greatly disappointed the Progressives.[25]

Pockets of One-Party Monopoly

In the past, the states of the Deep South were the country's best-known examples of one-party domination. Today, traces of one-party politics can still be found in thousands of cities, towns, and counties in which a mention of the other party can produce anything from raised eyebrows to raised tempers.

Where do we find these one-party areas? For most of their history, the major parties, especially in national elections, have divided the American voters roughly along socioeconomic lines: by income, education, and job status. (More about this can be found in Chapters 6 and 7.) A local constituency may be too small to contain the wide range of socioeconomic characteristics that leads to competitive politics. Thus, we can find "safe" Democratic congressional districts in the older, poorer, or black neighborhoods of large cities and "safe" Republican districts in the wealthier suburbs. In other words, the less diverse its people are, at least in terms of the characteristics that typically divide Republican voters from Democratic voters, the more likely the district is to foster one-party politics.

Alternatively, there may be some local basis of party loyalty so powerful that it overrides the relationship between socioeconomic status and partisanship. In the classic one-party politics of the American South, regional loyalties and racial fears long overrode the factors that were dividing Americans into two parties in most of the rest of the country. Feelings about the Republicans as the party of abolition, Lincoln, the Civil War, and the hated Reconstruction were so intensely negative that, even generations after the Civil War ended, they overpowered the impact of socioeconomic differences. In other areas, the effects of a serious scandal or a bitter strike may linger, leaving only one party as a socially acceptable choice.

Once one party has established dominance in an area, the weaker party may have a hard time overcoming its disadvantages. These disadvantages begin with stubborn party loyalties. Many voters are not easily moved from their attachments to a party, even though the reasons for the original attachment have long passed. Further, a party trying to become competitive may find itself caught in a vicious circle. Its inability to win elections limits its ability to raise money and recruit attractive candidates because, as a chronic loser, it offers so little chance of achieving political goals. The Republican Party in the South, for example, found for many years that the Democrats had recruited the region's most promising politicians and claimed its most potent appeals. Now, in many parts of the South, it is the Democrats who face this same disadvantage.

In addition, the weaker party's ability to attract voters locally is affected by media coverage of its national party's stance. If the Democratic Party is identified nationally with the hopes of the poor and minority groups, its appeal in an affluent suburb may be limited, no matter how attractive its candidates are. So a nationalized politics may rob the local party organization of the chance to develop strength based on its own issues, personalities, and traditions. To the extent that party loyalties grow out of national politics, as many Democrats in the South have learned in recent years, competitiveness may be beyond the reach of some local party organizations.

And as noted earlier in this chapter, redistricting can keep the weaker party from bouncing back. Majority parties have found remarkably effective ways to redraw legislative district lines that preserve their advantage, so the minority party in an area must often compete in electoral districts drawn by the stronger party. This is why parties are especially concerned with winning state legislative majorities in years when district lines must be redrawn.

Third Parties

Minor parties—often called "third" parties—have a long history in American politics, but they rarely win elections. Only seven minor parties in all of American history have carried even a single state in a presidential election, and only one (the Progressive Party) has done so twice. Theodore Roosevelt and the Progressives, in 1912, were the only minor-party candidacy ever to run ahead of one of the major-party candidates in either electoral or popular votes.

With rare exceptions, third parties have not fared well since that time. The recent high point of third-party strength was Ross Perot's run as the Reform Party candidate for president in 1996. Perot won just over 8 million votes, but this success was fleeting. In 2000, all third-party presidential candidates combined won less than half that number of votes, and in the highly polarized election of 2004, there were fewer than a million third-party voters (plus just under half a million for Ralph Nader, running as an independent; see Table 2.2).

Third-party successes can be found below the presidential level, but they are as rare as they are fascinating. Of more than a thousand governors elected since 1875, fewer than 20 ran solely on a third-party ticket, and another handful ran as independents.[26] Jesse Ventura's successful candidacy in Minnesota in 1998 got enormous media attention precisely because it was so unusual, but he stepped down from the governorship in 2002 after having been largely ignored by the state legislature, and the next candidate of his party attracted only 16 percent of the vote.[27]

Some third-party campaigns were victorious in 2004. Libertarian candidates won a county executive office in Georgia and 18 other local offices, almost half of them in California. For the third consecutive election, Libertarian candidates collectively polled more than a million votes in races for the U.S. House, though none won a seat. The Green Party

TABLE 2.2   Popular Votes Cast for Minor Parties in 2000 and 2004 Presidential Elections

2000		2004	
Parties	Vote	Parties	Vote
Green (Nader)	2,882,955	Nader (Independent)	463,647
Reform (Buchanan)	448,895	Libertarian	397,234
Libertarian	384,431	Constitution	143,609
Constitution	98,020	Green	119,862
Natural Law/Reform	83,714	Peace and Freedom	27,607
Socialist Workers	7,378	Socialist Workers	11,122
Libertarian (Arizona)	5,775	Socialist Party USA	10,822
Socialist	5,602	Christian Freedom (Minnesota)	2,387
Others and Scattered	8,349	Others and Scattered	48,215
Total	3,925,119	Total	1,224,505

Note: Votes for independent and write-in candidates, other than Ralph Nader, are not included.

Sources: Federal Election Commission. On the 2000 election, http://fecweb1.fec.gov/pubrec/2000presgeresults.htm (accessed May 30, 2003); for 2004, http://www.fec.gov/pubrec/fe2004/2004presgenresults.pdf (accessed May 16, 2005).

elected a state legislator in Maine and 34 local officials. One of them, the mayor of tiny New Paltz, New York, stepped out of third-party obscurity in 2004 when he conducted weddings for hundreds of gay couples. And in addition to winning a state legislative seat in Montana, the Constitution Party elected a county surveyor in West Virginia, though the fact that the candidate had no opponent and won with ten write-in votes seems to have done the trick. Also in 2004, six Progressive Party candidates won state legislative seats in Vermont.

Just as significant, in 2002, Libertarian candidates won enough votes to throw the South Dakota Senate race and the Wisconsin governorship to the Democrats, although some Libertarians might consider that a dubious achievement. However, for every example of third-party success in local elections, there are thousands of races with no minor-party challenge. The Democratic and Republican parties have monopolized American electoral politics even more fully in the states and cities than at the national level. (For one minor-party activist's reaction, see "A Day in the Life" on page 39).

Third parties differ in their purposes, origins, and activities. Their variety is as plain as a look at their labels: Socialist Workers, Green Party, Libertarian.[28]

Differences in Scope of Ideological Commitment   Most minor parties are driven by issues and ideologies, but they differ in the nature and scope of that commitment. The Right to Life and the Southern Independence Parties are very specific and targeted: the former in wanting to ban all abortions and the latter in favoring an independent nation of southern states. At the other extreme are socialist parties whose programs demand sweeping changes, including an end to capitalism and class privilege. The Libertarian Party wants government to involve itself only in national defense and criminal law and to turn over all other programs, from Social Security to education, to private efforts.[29] In sharp contrast, Green Parties argue for extensive government programs on behalf of the environment, peace, and social justice.

COMPETING AGAINST THE "BIG GUYS"

The Democrats and the Republicans, Brad Warren says, have a "death grip" on the American political process. Warren, a tax attorney in Indianapolis, is a Libertarian party activist who ran for the U.S. Senate under that party's banner. "If I need a new pair of socks," he points out, "I can go to dozens of stores and pick from several different brands and dozens of colors—for something as insignificant as socks. But when it comes to politics, which has a monopoly on the lawful use of force in our society, we have only two choices. That is tremendously scary! How do you hold them accountable? If you get angry with the incumbents, you can throw them out, only to reelect the nasty incumbents you had thrown out in the previous election. Four years from now, you'll be throwing out the incumbents you elected today. There's no choice."

Third-party activists, such as Warren, find that they are competing against the "big guys"—the two major parties—on an uneven playing field. A major problem for a third party, Warren says, is simply to get its candidates' names on the ballot. In Indiana, the state legislature used to require any minor party to win just half of 1 percent of the vote for secretary of state in order to qualify its candidates to get on the state ballot automatically in later elections. The Libertarians met that goal in 1982. The result? The legislature raised the hurdle to 2 percent. Ballot access requirements differ from state to state, making it difficult for a minor party to appear on the ballot in all 50 states.

"Even once you have ballot access," Warren argues, "you will still be excluded from any *meaningful* participation in the election. In practice, we run elections on money, not on votes, and in presidential elections, the Republicans and Democrats divide up hundreds of millions of federal dollars among themselves."

The worst problem for third parties, Warren feels, is getting noticed after the major primaries hold primary elections. "I got pretty good media coverage up to the primary election. After the primary, I was nobody. Even though the primary doesn't elect anybody to any office, it *seems to*. Primaries are a government-funded means of anointing the two major parties' candidates as the "real" candidates and de-legitimizing all the others. The media say we have no chance to win, so they won't cover any candidates except the [major] party-anointed ones. The debates typically don't include third-party candidates. Why? Because the commissions that decide who's going to be allowed to participate in debates are 'bipartisan' commissions, made up entirely of Republicans and Democrats, just like the legislatures that write the ballot access laws and the judges who interpret them. We understand that it would be confusing to have too many candidates in a debate. But a party that has gotten on the ballot in all 50 states, like the Libertarians, deserves to be heard."

"The two major parties won't give you any choice," Warren contends, and "if you continually vote for the lesser of two evils, what you get is evil." So what is the role of a third party? To Warren, "It's like that of a bee: You rise up, you sting, and then you die."

Difference of Origins   The minor parties differ, too, in their origin. Some were literally imported into the United States. Much of the early Socialist Party strength in the United States came from the freethinkers and radicals who fled Europe after the failed revolutions of 1848. Socialist candidates did well in cities such as Milwaukee, New York, and Cincinnati because of the concentrations of liberal German immigrants there. Other parties, especially the Granger and Populist Parties, were homegrown channels of social protest, born of social inequality and economic hardship in the marginal farmlands of America.

Some minor parties began as splinters or factions of one of the major parties. For example, the Progressives (the Bull Moose Party) of 1912 and the Dixiecrats of 1948 objected so strenuously to the platforms and candidates of their parent parties that they ran their own slates and presented their own programs in presidential elections. In fact, the Dixiecrats, an anti-civil-rights faction within the Democratic Party, substituted their own candidate for the one chosen by the party's national convention as the official Democratic presidential candidate in several southern states.

Differing Purposes   Finally, third parties differ in their intentions. The aim of some of these parties is to educate citizens about their issues; getting votes is merely a sideline. They run candidates because their presence on the ballot brings media attention that they could not otherwise hope to get. Many of these parties serenely accept their election losses because they have chosen not to compromise their principles to win office. The Prohibition Party, for example, has run candidates in most presidential elections since 1872 with unflagging devotion to the cause of banning the sale of alcoholic beverages but without apparent concern for the fact that its highest proportion of the popular vote was 2 percent, and that came in 1892.

Other minor parties are serious about trying to win office. Often, their goal is local, although today they find it difficult to control an American city, as the Socialists once did, or an entire state, like the Progressives. More realistically, they may hope to hold a balance of power in a close election between the major parties, as Ralph Nader did in the 2000 presidential election. Ross Perot even claimed to be looking for an outright victory in both 1992 (as an independent) and 1996.

What Difference Do They Make?   Some argue that minor parties deserve the credit for a number of public policies—programs that were first suggested by a minor party and then adopted by a major party when they reached the threshold of political acceptability. A possible example is the minimum wage, which was advocated by Socialist Party platforms for 20 or 30 years before the minimum wage law was enacted in the 1930s by a Democratic administration. Did the Democrats steal the Socialist Party's idea, or would they have proposed a minimum wage for workers even if there had been no Socialist Party? There is no way to be sure. Major parties usually propose a new policy once a large number of Americans has accepted the idea, so the party can gain votes. However, the major party might have picked up the new proposal from any of a number of sources in addition to a minor party.

If the impact of third parties is so limited, then what attracts some voters to them? Note that there aren't many such voters; the self-fulfilling prophecy that a vote for a third party is a wasted vote is very powerful in American politics.[30] Yet some voters do cast third-party ballots. To Steven Rosenstone and his colleagues, this results from the failure of major parties "to do what the electorate expects of them—reflect the issue preferences of voters, manage the economy, select attractive and acceptable candidates, and build voter loyalty to the parties and the political system."[31] So third parties tend to gain support when they promote attractive ideas that the major parties have ignored, or because of dissatisfaction with the major party candidates, rather than because a lot of voters believe in a multiparty system as a matter of principle.

The Rise of Independent Candidates

In recent elections, dissatisfaction with the two major parties has also produced several notable independent candidacies—those who run as individuals, independent of any party organization, major or minor. The most successful was Ross Perot, who mounted a well-funded independent candidacy for president in 1992 before running as the Reform Party candidate in 1996. The story of Perot's two candidacies, one as an independent and the other as a third-party candidate, helps us understand some of the advantages of running independently.

In his race as an independent presidential candidate in 1992, Perot and his supporters built a remarkably strong national organization. Through its efforts, Perot got on the ballot in all 50 states. He ended the race with 19.7 million votes—a larger share of the popular vote than any "third" candidate in history who was not a former president. In fact, he outdrew the combined total of all his third-party opponents in that race by more than 19 million ballots. The key ingredient in his success was money; Perot invested more than $65 million of his own funds in his campaign. His money financed organizational efforts at the grassroots level and bought large blocks of expensive television time. Even so, Perot failed to win a single state, and much of his support seemed to come from voters who were more dissatisfied with the major-party candidates than they were attracted to a long-lasting commitment to another party or candidate.[32]

Three years later, Perot organized the new Reform Party and sought to qualify it for the ballot in all 50 states. That was much harder than qualifying to run as an independent. In California, which was his toughest challenge, Perot had to get at least 890,000 signatures on a petition by October 1995 to win a place on the state's ballot 13 months later. He failed. Using a different mechanism, Perot finally qualified in California and in all other states but found it difficult to recruit acceptable Reform candidates for other offices. On Election Day, Perot got less than half as many votes as a Reform Party candidate than he had four years earlier as an independent.

Why was his third-party effort less successful? Many factors were at work. One may have been simple familiarity; at times a candidate does not benefit from letting voters get to know him or her better. Perot spent much less of his own money in 1996 than he had four years earlier. States' election laws probably had an important effect; they are often less restrictive for a single or independent candidate than for a new third party. In addition, it is harder for an organization to support many candidates rather than just one. In the 2000 presidential campaign, for example, conflicts among Reform Party activists became so intense that the party's national convention erupted into a fistfight and the party split.

Once a third party has qualified for the ballot, the tables turn. Ralph Nader's experience as a presidential candidate in 2000 and 2004 was just the opposite of Perot's. In 2000, Nader won access to 43 state ballots fairly easily because he ran as the Green Party candidate, which had already qualified for ballot access in those states. In 2004, Nader faced an epic struggle to get on those same ballots as an independent candidate. Democratic activists filed lawsuits to try to keep Nader off state ballots, and Republicans often supported Nader's efforts, because his candidacy was expected to hurt Democrat John Kerry more than Republican George W. Bush.

Even when a third party meets the difficult challenge of maintaining its line on the ballot, it will still face the enormous hurdle of recruiting candidates for offices up and down the ballot, for thousands of state legislative seats and county offices as well as for president. The Greens and the Libertarians have made real efforts since 2000 to establish themselves as organizations that extend beyond a relatively small number of candidates. If history is any guide, however, that is a battle they are likely to lose. The result is that when voters consider alternatives to the major parties, independent candidates (especially if they happen to be billionaires) will continue to have advantages over those who try to form fully elaborated third parties.

WILL THE TWO-PARTY SYSTEM CONTINUE?

This look at two-party politics and its alternatives leads us to two main conclusions. First, in important respects, the two-party system is secure in the United States. Third parties are not gaining ground. Third-party members of Congress, common in the early decades of the two-party system, have been rare throughout the 1900s and especially in recent years (Figure 2.2). Since 1952, only one member of Congress has been elected on a third-party ticket. Three have recently served as independents, but all have aligned themselves with one of the major parties' caucuses. Minor-party candidates have also fared poorly in state legislative contests during this period.

The barriers to ballot access for minor-party and independent candidates are not as high now as they once were. But candidates other than Republicans and Democrats must still jump substantial hurdles to get on state ballots and must still satisfy a patchwork of different state requirements to qualify for the ballot nationwide. Even when courts have overturned laws that discriminate against these candidates, the decisions have been limited, requiring petitioners to mount a challenge in each state.[33] Quirks in local election laws continue to support a few local third parties. The classic instance is New York's minor parties, notably the Liberals and Conservatives. They survive because they can nominate candidates of a major party to run under their parties' own labels as well.[34]

In addition, the financial hurdles faced by independent and third-party candidates remain formidable. Although candidates don't need to be Democrats or Republicans in order to reach voters throughout the United States with television and the Internet, the enormous cost of modern campaigns probably restricts this opportunity to only a few highly visible or personally wealthy individuals. Third-party presidential candidates can receive public funding for their campaign if they win at least 5 percent of the popular vote. But in 30 years, the only campaign to qualify was Perot's Reform Party in 1996. That assured the Reform Party's 2000 presidential candidate of receiving $12 million in federal funds for his campaign. The money no doubt increased the attractiveness of the

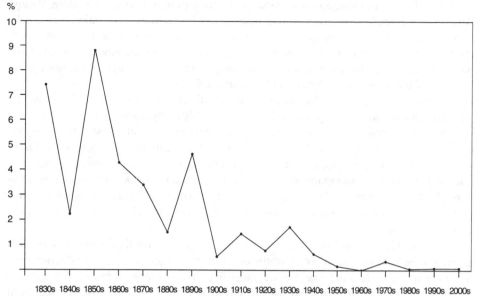

%

FIGURE 2.2   Third-Party and Independent Members of Congress: 1830s–2005.

Note: Figures are percentages of third-party and independent senators and representatives during each decade.

Source: Updated from Norman J. Ornstein, Thomas E. Mann, and Michael J. Malbin, *Vital Statistics on Congress, 2001–2002* (Washington, DC: The AEI Press, 2002), pp. 56–58.

party's presidential nomination; yet the eventual nominee, Patrick Buchanan, earned less than half of 1 percent of the popular vote.

Independent candidates for president and governor have made some elections less predictable. But running by themselves, with no other candidates on their "tickets," they are unlikely to create an enduring challenge to the Democrats and Republicans; they remain no more than periodic threats. To make a sustained challenge that could fundamentally transform the American parties, these independents would need to organize to confront the major parties from the top to the bottom of the ballot. Those who try soon realize that the two-party system may not be greatly beloved but it is very well entrenched.

How would a multiparty system change American politics? Proponents could cite a number of benefits. Voters would have more choices. Smaller parties, speaking for identifiable segments of society, might give citizens in these groups more confidence that their voices are being heard by government. A greater variety of views would be able to find expression through a party platform.

On the other hand, when the threshold for ballot access is lowered, extremist parties are better able to gain a foothold. In a system where the government will probably be a coalition of several parties, voters need to anticipate the compromises that their preferred party will make in order to form a government and perhaps, in order to influence that compromise, vote for a party whose views are more extreme than their own.[35] Votes are more directly translated into leadership in a majoritarian two-party system, though American politics, with its separation of powers, limits that direct translation now. Coalition governments can be unstable. And a multiparty system would likely require major changes in American electoral institutions, such as the single-member presidency and winner-take-all election rules. But these advantages and disadvantages are a moot point, because of the durability of American two-party politics.

The second major trend that we have seen in this chapter is an especially intriguing one. The Democratic and Republican Parties are highly competitive at the national level; presidential elections are won by small margins and there are relatively slim party majorities in both the U.S. House and Senate. When we look beneath the aggregate level at individual House and state legislative districts, however, the close competition vanishes. The intense party competition at the national level is built on the backs of fairly equal numbers of safe Democratic and safe Republican congressional and lower-level seats. Fewer House districts are competitive enough to switch party control now than has been the case in decades.[36]

Officeholders elected in districts that are relatively safe for their party may not feel as great a need to appeal to voters of the other party as they would if the district were more competitive. Incumbents in noncompetitive districts face more of a threat in the primary election than from the other party, and these primary threats usually come from the ideological extremes of their party. As we will discuss in Chapter 13, then, the increasing number of safe incumbents can take more partisan stands and behave in office in a more partisan or even a more extremist manner, knowing that they may be able to ward off a primary challenger that way and are not likely to suffer for it in the general election. Party polarization in Congress, state legislatures, and among politically involved citizens has accompanied this process. Even in a relatively stable two-party system such as that in the United States, moderation in political debate can be in short supply.

PART TWO

The Political Party as an Organization

There is much more to the American political parties than most of us see. A major party is a network of organizations that exists at all the levels at which Americans elect public officials: precincts, townships, wards, cities, counties, congressional districts, states, and the nation itself. The next three chapters examine these organizations and the activists and leaders who give them life.

We will focus in these chapters on the "private life" of the party organization, as opposed to its "public life" in campaigns and in government. In particular, we explore these questions: How do the party organizations work and how have they changed over time? What do they do well and what don't they do at all? Where does the power lie in the party organizations? What kinds of people become party activists? These internal characteristics of the party influence its ability to act effectively in the larger political system.

American party organizations vary tremendously. Parties in various parts of the nation have ranged from powerful and elaborate organizations to empty shells. Overall, however, by the standards of most western democracies, the American party organizations would be considered to be fairly weak. Shackled by state laws, the party organizations have rarely been able to exercise much influence over the other two parts of the party: its candidates and officeholders (the party in government) and the party in the electorate.

The three parts of any party differ in their goals. At election time, for instance, the party organization wants to see the maximum number of its candidates win, whereas individual candidates aim to satisfy their own ambitions, and party voters are concerned mainly with taxes, gay marriage, or getting some reassurance against terrorism. Each seeks control of the party to achieve its own ends. In the American system, the party organizations find it difficult to hold their own in this competition and to get the resources they need to influence elections and promote policies. American party organizations must depend on the members of their party in government to vote for the proposals contained in the organization's platform and pass them into law. Party organizations must also work hard to court and mobilize the party electorate, who are not formally party members or, in many cases, even especially loyal to the party in their voting.

This lack of integration among the party's three sectors is typical of *cadre parties*— one of two terms often used to describe the nature of party organizations. Imagine that party organizations are arranged along a continuum. At one end of this continuum is the cadre party, in which the organization is run by a relatively small number of leaders and activists with little or no broader public participation. These officials and activists make the organization's decisions, choose its candidates, and select the strategies they believe voters will find appealing. They focus mainly on electing party candidates rather than on issues and ideology. For this reason, the party's activities gear up mainly at election time, when candidates need their party organization's help the most. The cadre party, then, is a coalition of people and interests brought together temporarily to win elections, only to wither to a smaller core once the elections are over.

At the other end of this scale is the ***mass-membership party***, a highly participatory organization in which all three parts of the party are closely intertwined. In this type of party, large numbers of voters become dues-paying members of the party organization and take part in its activities throughout the year, not just during campaigns. A mass-membership party concentrates on promoting an ideology and educating the public as well as on winning elections. Its members decide what the party's policies should be as well as choose its organizational leaders. Members of the party in the electorate are so integral to the party organization that the party may even provide them with such non-political benefits as insurance and leisure-time activities. Because the membership-based party organization has great power over candidate selection (it does not need to give less involved voters the right to choose party candidates, as happens in a primary election), it can also exercise much greater control over the party in government.

In important ways, the major American parties can be considered cadre parties. Most local and state party leaders and activists are not paid professionals but volunteers, whose party activities ramp up around election time. These organization leaders do not try hard to control the party's candidates and elected officials, nor are they likely to succeed. Most of the American parties' sympathizers in the public are not involved at all in the party organization.

They do not fit the cadre mold perfectly; in practice, parties have a tendency to slither out of precise definitions.[1] For example, in the days before television dominated American life, parties engaged lots of volunteers in campaign work, although these activists never gained much power in the party. Now, voters rather than party leaders get to choose the party's candidates. Party leaders make contact with their supporters in the electorate more frequently. And the state and national party organizations are active year-round and employ full-time professional staffers.

Nevertheless, these changes have not made the major American parties into mass-membership organizations. The major parties concentrate on electing candidates more than on educating voters on issues. Also in contrast to mass-membership parties, the American parties do not monopolize the organization of political interests in the nation; rather, they compete in a political system in which voters are already organized by large numbers of interest groups and other organizations.

Why does it matter whether party organizations are strong or weak, cadre or mass membership? Because party organizations are at the very center of the political parties; they are the sector of the parties that can provide the continuity, even as the party's candidates, elected officials, and citizen enthusiasts come and go. A strong party organization can hunt for the resources needed for long-term election success and can present a unified, persuasive approach to issues. So the development of a stronger party organization can change the character of politics and elections. In fact, as American party organizations have become more robust in recent years, they have altered our politics in ways ranging from campaign fund-raising practices to the nature of political debate. Chapter 3 begins with an exploration of the party organizations closest to home: state and local parties.

Chapter 3

The State and Local Party Organizations

On a narrow street near City Hall, a white storefront bears a name neatly stenciled in silver script, "Monroe County Democratic Party." Yet on this spring afternoon, a quick look shows that the office is empty; desks and phones are gone, and only an overturned table bears witness to the fact that in the months before the 2004 election, this headquarters was alive with activity.

Headquarters like these have been the focus of wildly differing claims about the power of local and state party organizations in the United States. During the late 1800s and early 1900s, local parties were frequently described as "machines," with fearsome power to control city governments and mobilize vast armies of activists. Even so, many American local parties at this time were much less powerful. Later in the mid-1900s, most party organizations at the state and local levels were thought to be so weak that they could be justifiably overlooked. That has changed as well. Party organizations in the United States have undergone remarkable transformations in the past century.

What difference does it make if a party organization is vibrant or sickly? As the Introduction noted, in many ways the party organization is the backbone of a political party. It gives the party a way to endure, despite a changing cast of candidates and elected officeholders. More than the party in government or the party identifiers, the party organizations are the keepers of the parties' symbols—the unifying labels or ideas that give candidates a shortcut in identifying themselves to voters and that give voters a means to choose among candidates. Without this organization, a party becomes nothing more than an unstable alliance of convenience among candidates, and between candidates and groups of voters—too changeable to accomplish the important work that parties can perform in a democracy.

In this chapter, after considering how to measure "party strength," we will explore the reality of state and local party organizations by viewing them in their environment—in particular, the environment of rules that have been enforced on them by state law. Next, we will turn to the local party organizations, tracing their path from the fabled "political machines" that dominated a number of eastern and midwestern cities beginning in the late 1800s, to the fall and rise of local parties more recently. Finally, we will see how the state parties grew from weakness to greater strength in the closing decades of the twentieth century.

WHAT IS A "STRONG" PARTY?

Before looking at the state and local parties as organizations, we need to determine how a "strong" party could be defined. Many researchers measure a party's vigor by examining its organizational features, such as the size of its budget and staff and whether its workers are full-time professionals or occasional volunteers. Stronger parties would have larger budgets and more full-time, paid staff members. That can be termed party *organizational* strength.

There are other ways to measure party strength. A strong party would work effectively to register voters, tell them about party candidates, and get them to the polls on Election Day. It would be successful in filling its ticket with attractive candidates. Its candidates would win more races than they lose. We could even measure whether the party is able to get its platform enacted into law (and we will, but not until Chapter 15).

In order for a party to do these things, especially to register voters, canvass, and get out the vote, it needs money, staff, and other forms of organizational strength. We will look at most of these measures of party strength in this chapter but focus mainly on party organizational strength.

THE LEGAL ENVIRONMENT OF THE PARTIES

Americans' traditional suspicion of political parties has led most states to pass large numbers of laws intended to control their party organizations, much of it during the Progressive Era of the late 1800s and early 1900s. In some states, the parties have been kept on a long leash; party committees are regulated "lightly" in 17 states, most of them in the South, Plains states, and upper Midwest.[1] At the other extreme, in 15 states—including California, New Jersey, and Ohio—lawmakers have thought it necessary to tell the state parties everything from the dates on which their central committees must meet to the types of public buildings in which they must hold their conventions.

These extensive state rules have not necessarily weakened the parties; some of the strongest party organizations in the nation are also the most tightly regulated. In fact, all these state laws help prop up the Democratic and Republican Parties against competition from third parties. However, they do give state governments a set of tools for keeping an eye on their parties. They also indicate that state law does not view the parties simply as private groups. As Leon Epstein has put it, the parties are seen as public utilities that can be subject to a great deal of state direction.[2]

The party organizations do not face similar kinds of regulations from the federal government. The U.S. Constitution makes no mention of parties, nor has Congress tried very often to define or regulate party organizations. Only in the 1970s legislation on campaign finance and its later revisions is there a substantial body of national law that affects the parties in important ways.

States do not have complete freedom to decide how to regulate the parties. Over the years, federal courts have frequently stepped in to protect citizens' voting rights (in cases to be discussed in Chapter 8) and to keep the states from unreasonably limiting third-party and independent candidates' access to the ballot (see Chapter 2). In some cases, courts have even begun to dismantle some state regulation of party organizational practices. In the 1980s, for example, the Supreme Court ruled that the state of Connecticut could not prevent the Republican Party from opening up its primary to independents if it wanted to. Soon after, the Court threw out a California law saying, among other things, that parties could not endorse candidates in primary elections.[3] And as we'll see in Chapter 9, a 2000 Supreme Court decision overturned a California state initiative setting up a "blanket primary" on the ground that it violated the party organization's First Amendment right to decide who votes in its primaries. Nevertheless, American party organizations are more heavily regulated than are their counterparts in other democracies.

LEVELS OF PARTY ORGANIZATION

Although state laws vary, the party organizations created by the states follow a common pattern. Their structure corresponds to the levels of government at which voters elect officeholders. This structure is often pictured as a pyramid based in the grassroots and stretching up to the statewide organization. A pyramid, however, gives the misleading impression that the layer at the top can give orders to the layers below. So picture these party organizations, instead, as they fit into a geographic map (Figure 3.1).

In a typical state, the smallest voting district of the state—the precinct, ward, or township—will have its own party organization composed of men and women elected to

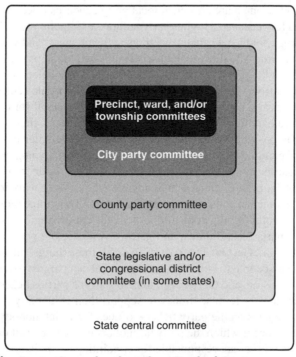

FIGURE 3.1 The Party Organizations in a Typical State.

the party's local committee (and called committeemen and committeewomen). Then come a series of party committees at the city, county, and sometimes even the state legislative, judicial, and congressional district levels. Finally, a state central committee represents the state party as a whole. State laws usually prescribe the smallest and the largest of these levels, but the parties themselves may determine the middle levels.

Local Party Committees

The county is the main unit of local party organization in most states. That is because large numbers of important local officials are elected at the county level, and usually in partisan elections: sheriffs, prosecutors, county attorneys, judges, commissioners and council members, county clerks, treasurers, assessors, auditors, surveyors, coroners, and more. These officials control vital functions ranging from policing the area and prosecuting those accused of crime to assessing and collecting property taxes. Party organizations exist in almost all of the nation's counties to at least some degree. These are the parties' "grassroots," where a lot of the activity of party volunteers takes place.

In most areas, counties are divided into smaller units called precincts. Each precinct (or town, township, or ward, in some areas) in theory has a party leader—a committeeman and/or committeewoman—to conduct the party's activities in that area. Because there are about 193,000 precincts in the United States, it would be easy to imagine a vibrant party base made up of at least 200,000 committed men and women. However, this exists only in the dreams of party leaders; in reality, many of these local committee positions are vacant because nobody wants to serve in them.

When these positions do get filled, it generally happens in one of three ways. Most committeemen and -women are chosen at local party caucuses (meetings) or in primary elections, but in a few instances, higher party authorities appoint them. In the states that use caucuses, parties hold local caucus meetings in the precincts and wards that are open to any voters of the area who declare themselves attached to the party. These local party supporters then elect the precinct committee leaders and often elect delegates to county and/or state conventions as well. In states that choose precinct committeemen and -women in the primaries, any voter may nominate him- or herself for the job by filing a petition signed by a handful of local voters. If, as often happens, there are no nominees, the committeeman or -woman may be elected by an even smaller handful of write-in votes. These local committee positions, in short, are not normally in great demand, especially in the weaker party in an area. So the local parties are far from being exclusive clubs; their "front doors" are often open to anyone who cares to walk in.

What do these precinct and county party leaders do? Their three most important jobs are registering new voters, going door-to-door (called "canvassing") to tell potential supporters about the party's candidates, and getting voters to the polls on Election Day (known as "GOTV," or "Get Out The Vote"). To do all these things, the local parties need to recruit volunteers: people to help with local political campaigns; to carry out the tasks of registering, canvassing, and GOTV; and to help staff the party's headquarters. County party leaders may also try to raise money to support their local party's candidates. And when there are vacancies on the party ticket—offices for which nobody chose to run in the primary election or for which the party has not been able to recruit candidates—then the local party committees are responsible for appointing a candidate to run. In the less active local parties, the committeemen and -women may do little more than show up at an occasional meeting and campaign for a party candidate or two.

The precinct committeemen and -women usually come together to make up the next level of local party organization, or they elect the delegates who do. In some states the next level is the city party committee; in others it may be the town, county, or state legislative and congressional district committees. Usually, however, there is greater activity at the county level than in any other layer of the local party.

State Central Committees

At the state level, the party organization is usually called the state central committee. The state parties typically help to recruit candidates for statewide office (for instance, state treasurer or attorney general) and state legislative seats, assist in training them, and raise money to support their campaigns. Increasingly they also work with the local parties on the crucial tasks of voter registration, canvassing, and GOTV.

State law commonly gives party central committees a number of other important powers: the responsibility for calling and organizing party conventions, drafting party platforms, supervising the spending of party campaign funds, and selecting the party's presidential electors, representatives to the national committee, and at least some of the national convention delegates and alternates. Some other states give these powers to the party's statewide convention instead. In a few states, such as Indiana, the party's state convention actually nominates candidates for some statewide offices, a reminder of the power that the party conventions had in the days before the direct primary.

The increasing importance of the state parties, as we will see later in this chapter, has made them more attractive to a variety of other political groups. A dramatic example unfolded in 2001 when the former Executive Director of the Christian Coalition, Ralph Reed, became a candidate for chair of the Georgia State Republican Party. Reed campaigned on the basis of his party-building experience, promising that he would set up or help sustain a fully staffed GOP organization in every county of the state. His rivals for the position claimed that Reed's right-wing image would scare off moderate voters. Reed won the job. Soon after, he organized an intensive statewide canvass just before the 2002 elections and got much of the credit when Georgia voters elected a Republican governor and unseated a Democratic U.S. Senator and the Democratic leaders of both houses of the state legislature. As the state parties gain strength, their leadership positions become much more desirable to groups in the party's constituency.

These are the formal organizational structures that state law creates for the state and local parties. From them, we can draw three important conclusions. First, the levels of party organization have been set up to correspond to the voting districts in which citizens choose public officials in that state (for example, city, county, and congressional districts), and the main responsibility of these organizations under state law is to contest elections. State laws, then, see the party organizations as helpers in the state's task of conducting nominations and elections—tasks that before the turn of the twentieth century belonged almost entirely to the parties alone.

Second, the laws indicate that state legislators are ambivalent about what constitutes a party organization. Many of these laws treat the parties as cadre organizations (see page 45) run by a small number of party officials. Yet when they specify that the party's own officials, including local committeemen and -women, must be chosen in a primary election, this gives party voters—and potentially, any voters—a vital, quasi-membership role in the party organization. So state laws help to create a party that is semipublic, rather than a genuinely private group whose active members choose its leaders and set its direction.

Finally, the relationships among these state and local party organizations are not those of a hierarchy, in which the "lower" levels take their orders from the higher levels. Instead, through much of their history, the parties were best described as "a system of layers of organization"[4] or as a "stratarchy,"[5] in which each of the levels has some independent power. In fact, power has traditionally flowed from bottom to top in the local and state parties, as opposed to a hierarchy, where power would be centralized at the top.[6] Party organization is a system of party committees close to, and growing from, the political grassroots. The result is that the party organizations remain fairly decentralized and rooted in local politics, even in the face of recent trends toward stronger state and national committees.

THE LEGENDARY PARTY MACHINES

Perhaps the high point of local party organizational strength in the United States occurred during the heyday of the urban political "machine." Machine politics reached its peak in the late 1800s and early 1900s when, by one account, a large majority of American cities were governed by machines.[7] The party machine, historians tell us, was a durable, disciplined organization that controlled the nominations to elective office. It had the hierarchical structure that today's local parties lack. It relied on material incentives—jobs and favors—to build support among voters. Above all, it controlled the government in a city or county.[8]

Yet, for all their power in shaping how we think of party organizations, the great urban machines were not found in all cities, and, like the dinosaurs, they have disappeared. The last of the great party machines was Chicago's, and it declined after the death of Mayor Richard J. Daley (the father of the current mayor) in 1976. These dinosaurs were brought down by a number of forces. Some party machines, such as those in Pittsburgh and New York, never recovered from election upsets by middle-class reformers. Others, including those in Philadelphia and Gary, Indiana, lost power when racial tensions overshadowed the old ethnic politics.[9]

How the Party Machines Developed

In the late 1800s, large numbers of the immigrants arriving in major American cities had urgent economic and social needs. These newcomers were poor, often spoke no English, and faced a difficult adjustment to their new urban environment. Party leaders in many of these cities—usually Democrats, reflecting that party's history of openness to immigrants—saw the opportunity for a clever and mutually beneficial exchange. The populations of immigrants needed jobs, social services, and other benefits that a city government could provide. The party leaders needed large numbers of votes in order to gain control of city government. If the party could register these new arrivals to vote, their votes could put the party in power. In return, the party would then control the many resources that the government had available and could give the new voters the help they needed so desperately.

Jobs ranked high among the newcomers' needs. So the most visible of the benefits offered by party machines were *patronage* jobs in the city government—those awarded on the basis of party loyalty rather than other qualifications. During the glory days of the machine, thousands of these patronage positions were at the machine's disposal. By giving patronage jobs to party supporters, the party's leaders could be assured that city workers would remain loyal to the machine and would work to help it win elections by delivering not only their own votes but those of their friends, family, and neighbors as well.

For example, in its prime, the Chicago Democratic machine controlled an estimated 35,000 patronage jobs in government and influenced hiring for another 10,000 jobs in the private economy. Adding the families and friends of these job holders, the party machine could deliver 350,000 motivated voters at election time. Local party workers also won voter loyalties by finding social welfare agencies for the troubled or by providing Christmas baskets or deliveries of coal. Machine leaders, called "bosses," attended weddings and wakes, listened to job seekers and business executives, bailed out drunks, and helped the hungry and homeless.

The machine had favors to offer to local businesses as well. Governments purchase many goods and services from the private sector. If a bank wanted to win the city's deposits, it could expect to compete more effectively for the city's business if it were willing to contribute to the party machine. Insurance agents who hoped to write city policies, lawyers who wanted the city's business, newspapers that printed city notices, even suppliers of soap to city bathrooms, all were motivated to donate money or services to the party machine. In addition, city governments regularly make decisions on matters that affect individuals' and businesses' economic standing, such as building permits and health inspections. If you were helped by one of these decisions, you could expect the machine to ask for your thanks in the form of contributions and votes. A political leadership intent on winning support in exchange for these so-called "preferments" can use them ruthlessly and effectively to build its political power.

How Machines Held On to Power

The classic urban machine, then, was not just a party organization but also an "informal government," a social service agency, and a ladder for upward social and economic mobility. In some ways, it looked like the local organization of a European mass-membership party, except that the American machine had little or no concern with ideology. Its world was the city; it focused on the immediate needs of its constituents, and its politics were almost completely divorced from the issues that animated national politics.

An important source of the machines' strength was their ability to appeal to ethnic loyalties. The rise and fall of the American political machine is closely linked to changes in ethnic-group migration to the big cities. The machine was a method by which ethnic groups, especially the Irish, gained a foothold in American politics.[10]

The machines were capable of creating a "designer electorate" by using force and intimidation to keep their opponents from voting. Because the party machines controlled the election process, it was possible, in a pinch, to change the election rules and even to count the votes in a creative manner. One of the indispensable tools of rival party work-ers in Indianapolis, for example, was a flashlight—to locate ballots that did not support the dominant party's candidates and happened to fly out of the window at vote-counting headquarters in the dark of night.

We think of machine politics as flourishing in the big cities, but American party machines took root in other areas as well. The conditions that led to the development of machines, especially a large, parochially oriented population with short-term economic needs, were also found in small southern and one-company towns. Even some well-to-do suburbs have spawned strong machine-style party organizations. In the affluent Long Island suburbs of New York City, for example, a Republican Nassau County political machine developed that controlled local government and politics "with a local party oper-ation that in terms of patronage and party loyalty rivals the machine of the famed Demo-cratic mayor of Chicago, Richard J. Daley."[11] The Nassau machine, which was generations old, was dominated by Italian-Americans and provided jobs just like the big-city machines of old, before losing its dominance in the 1990s. But in nearby Queens, the local Democratic organization rebounded from scandal and continues to elect can-didates, fill judgeships, and control primaries.

We cannot be sure how powerful the party machines really were, even at their strongest. A Chicago study found, for example, that in 1967 and 1977, the party machine distributed public services mainly on the basis of historical factors and bureaucratic deci-sion rules rather than to reward its political supporters.[12] In New Haven, researchers reported that ethnic loyalties seemed more important to a party machine than even its own maintenance and expansion. The machine, led by Italian-Americans, distributed summer jobs disproportionately to Italian kids from nonmachine wards, who rarely took part in later political work, and not to kids from strong machine areas.[13]

Regardless of how well they functioned, there is no doubt that the conditions that helped sustain party machines have been undercut. Economic change and political reform took away the machine's most important resources. Most city jobs are now covered by civil service protection, so the number of patronage jobs that can be used to reward the party faithful has been greatly reduced. Federal entitlement programs, such as welfare and Social Security, have reduced the need for the favors that party machines could pro-vide. Economic growth has boosted many Americans' income levels and reduced the attractiveness of the remaining patronage jobs; the chance to work in the sewer system or on garbage pickup just doesn't have the allure that it once may have had. Higher edu-cation levels have increased people's ability to fend for themselves in a complex bureau-cratic society. And in many areas, racial divisions have overwhelmed the machine's ability to balance competing ethnic groups.

LOCAL PARTY ORGANIZATIONS DECLINED AND THEN REBUILT

After the machines failed, local parties' organizational strength dropped dramatically in many areas. By the mid-1900s, many city and county parties were starved for leadership, money, and volunteers. Then the rebuilding and restructuring began.

Local Parties in the 1970s

We got the first comprehensive look at the nature of local party organizations in a 1979–1980 survey of several thousand county leaders (see Table 3.1).[14] The results showed the distinctive fingerprints of cadre parties, and fairly weak ones at that. The researchers found that most county organizations were headed by a volunteer party chair and executive committee; almost none received salaries for their efforts; and only a few had a paid staff to assist them. They had few resources to work with; not many of these local party leaders enjoyed the most basic forms of organizational support, such as a regular budget, a year-round office, or even a telephone listing. They did meet regularly, had formal rules to govern their work, and, together with a few other activists, raised funds and sought out and screened candidates. However, their activity was not constant; it peaked during campaigns.

Democratic local parties didn't differ much from Republican local parties in terms of the overall strength of their organizations during the 1970s. States differed a great deal, however, in the organizational strength of their local parties. Some states in the East and Midwest had relatively strong local organizations in both parties, while others— Louisiana, Georgia, Alabama, Kentucky, Texas, and Nebraska—had relatively weak parties at the county level. In a few states, such as Arizona and Florida, one party was

TABLE 3.1 Changes in Local Parties' Organizational Strength, 1979/1980–1996

	Democrats		Republicans	
The local party organization has (in percent)	1996	1979–1980	1996	1979–1980
A complete or nearly complete set of officers	95	90	96	81
A year-round office	17	12	25	14
A telephone listing	27	11	30	16
Some paid staff members				
Full-time	4	3	4	4
Part-time	6	5	7	6
A regular annual budget	26	20	34	31
A campaign headquarters	60	55	60	60
Campaign activities				
Organized door-to-door canvassing	55	49	57	48
Organized campaign events	81	68	82	65
Arranged fund-raising events	74	71	76	68
Contributed money to candidates	75	62	78	70
Distributed posters or lawn signs	93	59	93	62
Used public opinion surveys	13	11	15	16

Note: The 1979–1980 figures are based on responses from a total of 2,021 Democratic and 1,980 Republican organizations to a mail survey; the 1996 figures are based on mail surveys of all county party chairs in nine states (Arizona, Colorado, Florida, Illinois, Missouri, Ohio, South Carolina, Washington, and Wisconsin), with responses from 340 Democrats and 335 Republicans.

Source: John Frendreis and Alan R. Gitelson, "Local Parties in the 1990s," in John C. Green and Daniel M. Shea, *The State of the Parties*, 3rd ed. (Lanham, MD: Rowman & Littlefield, 1999), pp. 138–139.

considerably stronger at the local level than the other party. Most often, strong organizations of one party were matched with strong organizations in the other party.[15]

There is persuasive evidence, however, that the county party organizations in 1980 were in the middle of a growth spurt. By asking 1980 county party chairs about the changes in their parties since 1964, researchers found that, on average, local parties had become much more involved in the nuts-and-bolts activities of registering voters, raising money, and publicizing candidates. When the researchers checked in again with these county organizations in 1984, they saw further development, and a national survey in 1988 indicated even higher levels of local party activity. Similar trends were reported in studies over time of local party organizations in Detroit and Los Angeles.[16]

Local Parties Today: Richer and More Active

By the early 2000s, although local parties continued to depend on volunteer effort, they were enjoying more of the benefits that money could buy. A study of the county party organizations in nine states during the 1996 presidential election found that the basic ingredients for a viable party organization (a permanent office, a budget, a telephone listing, a staff) were more widespread than they had been in 1980.[17] Most of these county parties were organizing campaign activities, arranging fund-raising events, donating money to candidates, sending out mailings, telephoning voters to urge them to support the party ticket, distributing yard signs, and running get-out-the-vote drives, and again, more local parties reported conducting these activities in 1996 than in 1980.

Other forms of campaigning, such as using public opinion polls, buying radio or TV time for candidates, and coordinating the activities of interest groups' political action committees in campaigns were not common in either year. But it seems clear that more money has been flowing to local party organizations in recent years, and the result has been more energized local parties.

For an example of this increase in party organizational strength, consider party politics in Michigan. Michigan Democrats, long the minority party, were in sorry shape for the first half of the 1900s, after machine politics had faded. By the end of the 1940s, more than half of the state's counties had no Democratic county committees. Then, labor unions, led by the United Auto Workers, stepped in to bring volunteer and financial support to the Democrats. Within two years, there was a Democratic Party organization in almost every county in the state. After internal conflicts took their toll in both parties during the 1960s and 1970s, organized labor moved again to rebuild the Democratic organization. By the late 1990s, the great majority of Democratic local party organizations were raising money and donating it to candidates, buying ads, and distributing literature. The county organizations have now become the backbone of the state Democratic Party.[18]

Local party leaders in many areas of the country have recently stepped up their efforts in two areas. The first is absentee and early voting. Since 2000 most states have relaxed their formerly strict requirements for casting an absentee vote, so large numbers of registered voters are now allowed to cast their ballots by mail in advance of the election or even to vote in person before Election Day. To take advantage of these changes in requirements, many local parties—those in the state of Washington, for example—are mailing absentee ballot requests to all known party voters. By using this means of "banking" as many loyalists' votes as possible, the party organization doesn't need to worry

TAKING OVER A STATE PARTY, ONE COUNTY AT A TIME

County governments make decisions that hit Americans where they live, on matters ranging from education to taxes. In many parts of the country, county party organizations can become attractive beachheads from which to try to change local policies. In the lead-up to the 2006 elections, a group of Christian conservatives has created the Ohio Restoration Project, with the aim of taking control of all 88 Republican county party organizations in the state. The Project hopes to mobilize 2,000 "Patriot Pastors" among evangelicals, Baptists, Pentecostals, and Roman Catholics; their purpose is to return Christian morals to the public schools and to oppose gay marriage and abortion. By using the local party machinery to recruit activists, train candidates, raise money, and register at least half a million new voters, they intend to elect city councils and school boards as well as a candidate for the state governorship, J. Kenneth Blackwell.

The project's organizer, Pastor Russell Johnson, claims that the current "establishment of the Ohio Republican Party is out of touch with its base. It acts as if it lives in Boston, Mass." The existing Republican organizations, he charges, have "their little political gatherings and cocktail meetings at the country club," but they have lost the ability to light a fire under the party's base. Evangelicals and other conservative Christians, he argues, can bring tremendous energy and organization as well as money and votes to local parties. In contrast, the mainstream county parties "can't build that kind of loyalty. They can't spend millions to buy what our people will give for free."

State Republican Party chair Robert T. Bennett has been watching the struggle intently. If the local parties move too far to the right, he cautions, they might undermine the Republican dominance of the state. Some other states and counties have experienced what has been called a "three-party system"—a division among Democrats, traditional Republicans, and evangelical Republican conservatives—in which Democrats have been able to eke out a plurality of votes. The Restorationists, however, have no such fears. Blackwell described the movement as "a struggle for the heart and soul of the Republican Party. And that's healthy."

Source: James Dao, "Movement in the Pews Tries to Jolt Ohio," *New York Times,* March 27, 2005, p. 14.

that last-minute campaign surprises or Election Day thunderstorms will depress the party vote. In addition, it allows local parties to spread out their GOTV drives over several weeks and then focus their Election Day activities on a smaller segment of less highly committed voters. The downside is that because absentee voting is much harder to monitor than voting at the polls, parties need to find ways to prevent the other party from delivering batches of absentee ballots that have been filled out illegally or with "help" from overzealous party workers.

The second area in which local parties are expanding their efforts is candidate recruitment. One study found that more than a third of people regarded as potentially strong candidates for Congress in 1998 had, in fact, been contacted by local party leaders and that those contacted were more likely to run.[19] In another study, almost half of all state legislative candidates reported that local party leaders had encouraged them to run.[20] County party leaders can improve their chances of recruiting candidates when, as in Ohio, they can endorse candidates in primaries and fill vacancies in elections. Keep in mind, however, that it is not yet clear whether being recruited by a local party organization, as opposed to being a "self-starter," helps a candidate win the general election.

In sum, we have good evidence that county party organizations were stronger and more active in the 1990s and early 2000s than they had been a generation earlier. Because there are so few reliable records prior to the 1960s, it is hard to determine whether these local organizations are as effective organizationally as they were thought to have been a century ago. Even the most active local parties today are probably no match for a powerful urban machine. Nevertheless, not many of these local parties are completely dead either. So many counties may now have more robust party organizations than they have ever had.

What accounts for the growing strength of the county parties? The short answer is money. Party organizations at all levels have developed more effective tools for raising money than they have had for some time. Local parties have benefited, in particular, from the willingness of the increasingly well-heeled state parties to share the wealth. At the same time, however, the nature of the local parties has changed. From organizations that once were at the very center of election activity, the county parties have become service providers to candidates who often have several other sources of services. So the challenge for the local parties is this: In an age of largely candidate-centered campaigns, does this growing county organizational presence matter as much as it would have a few decades ago?[21]

THE STATE PARTIES: NEWFOUND PROSPERITY

State parties have always been the poor relations of American party politics. Throughout the parties' history, the state committee rarely had significant power within the party organizations. There have been exceptions, of course. Some powerful, patronage-rich state party organizations developed in the industrial heartland in the late 1900s.[22] But in most states, most of the time, the party's state committee has not been the site of the party's main organizational authority.

In recent years, however, state parties have grown in importance. They are richer, more professional, and more active now than they have ever been before. There has been some centralization of activity throughout the party structure. Let us start the story in the years before this change began.

Traditional Weakness

There are many reasons why the state party organizations were traditionally weak. They began as loose federations of semi-independent local party chairs. These local parties within a state differed from one another in many ways; there were rural/urban and regional differences, ethnic and religious differences, loyalties to local leaders, and, especially, conflicts between more liberal and more conservative interests. If one of these factions gained control over the state party organization, the others would be seriously threatened. So this threat was often avoided, in the past, by keeping most of the party's resources out of the hands of the state organization. Power, in other words, was decentralized, collecting in the most effective of the local organizations.

Other forces also weakened the state party organizations. Progressive reforms early in the 1900s, most importantly the introduction of the direct primary (see Chapters 9 and 10), sapped the influence of state parties over nomination and election campaigns for state offices. Due in part to these reforms, candidates could win party nominations in primary elections without party organization support, raise money for their own campaigns and, thus, run them without party help. The Populist and Progressive influence can be seen even now, in that it is the states where the Populists had greatest strength—the western states, especially the more rural ones—where we still find relatively weak state party organizations.[23]

Beginning in the late 1960s, the national Democratic Party adopted reforms that greatly increased the number of primaries in the presidential nominating process. That weakened the state party's role in selecting a presidential candidate. It is the voters, rather than the state party organization, who choose convention delegates now; most of the delegates come to the convention pledged to a particular candidate for the nomination rather than controlled by state party leaders. Further, extensions of civil service protections and growing unionization eroded the patronage base for many state parties. In what may have been the final indignity for patronage politics, some courts have even prevented the firing of patronage workers when the governing party changes.

The existence of one-party dominance in several states during the first half of the 1900s also kept a number of state parties weak and conflict-ridden. Southern Democratic Parties were a notable example (and southern Republican Parties were all but nonexistent). When a single party dominates a state's politics, the diverse forces within the state are likely to compete as factions within that party; the state party organization has neither the incentive nor the ability to unify, as it might if it faced a threat from a viable opposition party. For all these reasons, many state party organizations were described as "empty shells" in the 1940s and 1950s.[24]

Increasing Strength in Recent Years

Since the 1960s, however, state party organizations have become stronger and more active. The state parties began to institutionalize—to become enduring, specialized, well-bounded organizations—during the 1960s and 1970s. In the early 1960s, for example, only 50 percent of a sample of state organizations had permanent state headquarters; two decades later, in 1979–1980, that was true of 91 percent. The number of full-time, salaried state party chairs doubled during this time, as did the number of full-time staff employed by the parties in nonelection years. These resources—full-time leaders and a stable location—are vital to the development of parties as organizations.[25]

As with local parties, the state organizations have continued to expand since then. By 1999, more than half of the state parties surveyed in a research study had full-time party chairs, research staff, and public relations directors. Three-quarters had a field staff, and 91 percent employed a full-time executive director, perhaps the most crucial position in a state party organization. A number of state parties, especially Republicans, have created internship programs for college students; the Mississippi Republican Party is a good example. The empty shells are being filled. Interestingly, southern parties, long among the weakest and most faction-ridden, have become some of the strongest state party organizations in the past two decades.[26]

Fund-raising   State parties have put special effort into developing fund-raising capabilities in recent years. By 1999, according to a study by John H. Aldrich (see Table 3.2), 98 percent of the state parties surveyed held fund-raising events, and the same percentage had direct mail fund-raising programs. State parties used the money to support a variety of races; party candidates for governor, state legislature, and the U.S. Senate and House received contributions from more than four-fifths of these parties. Over 90 percent of the parties surveyed by Aldrich had recruited a full slate of candidates for state races; the parties' new fund-raising skills can be very useful in convincing attractive prospects to run for an office.[27]

The parties are especially active in recruiting and helping fund candidates for the state legislature, to a greater extent than the national or local parties do.[28] These candidates get additional help from the legislative parties; state legislative campaign committees have come to play an increasingly important role in legislative campaigns.[29] Candidates for the state legislature often rely on different levels of party committees for different kinds of help. In some states, the candidates see the legislative parties as at least somewhat helpful in fund-raising and hiring consultants, whereas the local parties are thought to be more helpful in traditional grassroots activities such as get-out-the-vote drives.[30]

The increase in election-year fund-raising by the state parties between 1980 and 1999 fairly leaps off the page in Table 3.2. This was augmented by a big increase in money transferred from national party committees to the state parties and candidates. Although most of the funds moved directly into campaign advertising in competitive races, in 2000, the national party organizations transferred a whopping $430 million to parties and candidates at the state level, many times the amounts that the national parties infused into the state organizations just a few years earlier.[31] Collectively, the state parties were able to spend $53 million raised in large sums, called "soft money" (funds that are not raised under federal regulations; see Chapter 12), on voter mobilization and GOTV activity in the 2000 campaigns.[32]

TABLE 3.2   Increasing Organizational Strength Among the State Parties

Party Strength and Activity	1999	1979–1980	Difference
Typical election-year budget	$2.8 mil.	$340 K	+$2.46 mil.
Typical election-year full-time staff	9.2	7.7	+1.5
Conducted campaign seminars	95%	89%	+6%
Recruited a full slate of candidates	91%	—	—
Operated voter ID programs	94%	70%	+24%
Conducted public opinion surveys	78%	32%	+46%
Held fund-raising event	98%	19%	+77%
Contributed to governor candidate	89%	47%	+42%
Contributed to state legislator	92%	47%	+45%
Contributed to state senator	85%	25%	+60%
Contributed to U.S. congressional	85%	48%	+37%
Contributed to local candidate	70%	—	—

Note: Data for 1999 come from a mail survey conducted by John H. Aldrich and associates of 65 state party chairs (39 Democrats, 26 Republicans). Data for 1979–1980 are from a mail survey of state parties.

Source: For the 1999 data, see Aldrich's "Southern Parties in State and Nation," *Journal of Politics* 62 (2000): 659. The 1979–1980 data are from James L. Gibson, Cornelius P. Cotter, and John F. Bibby, "Assessing Party Organizational Strength," *American Journal of Political Science* 27 (1983): 193–222.

Just as important for the development of strong party organizations, fund-raising during nonelection years was growing as well. The nonelection-year budgets of the state parties climbed from an average (in absolute dollars) of under $200,000 in 1960–1964 to $340,667 in 1979–1980, then to $424,700 by the mid-1980s, and to $900,000 by 1999. The result is that "most state parties are multimillion-dollar organizations with experienced executive directors and knowledgeable staffs." [33]

Passage of new campaign finance legislation in 2002 (the Bipartisan Campaign Reform Act, or BCRA, discussed in Chapter 12) took away the national parties' ability to transfer soft money to the state parties. Although that raised worries about their financial future, BCRA did allow state parties to spend federally regulated money (which the national parties could transfer to states without limits) on federal campaign activities and to raise a certain amount of soft money themselves (up to $10,000 per donor) for grass-roots mobilization and party-building. These, added to the high stakes of polarized politics, helped the state parties to expand their fund-raising further; in 2003, even after the end of the soft money transfers, state Democratic and Republican Parties raised a total of $189 million—more than they had in 2001.[34] And though the collective state party receipts of $735 million for the 2004 election cycle were somewhat down from 2000, and media buys by state parties did drop sharply, spending in some states, including Missouri and Indiana, went up considerably.[35] State parties, then, have become effective fund-raisers and most have learned to cope with the BCRA reform rules.

Campaign Services   Now that many state legislative and statewide candidates—even local candidates in some states—need consultants, voter lists, and computers to run a competitive campaign, they turn to the state party organizations to provide these expensive services. With their increased organizational and financial resources, the state parties have been able to comply. All the parties in Aldrich's sample operated voter identification programs to determine which voters were most likely to support their party's candidates. They also took part in get-out-the-vote drives as well as joint fund-raising with county party organizations. Most provided campaign training seminars, and almost four-fifths conducted public opinion polls in the late 1990s.[36] Coordinated campaigns (called "victory plans" by the Republicans), emphasizing the sharing of campaign services among a variety of candidates, could be run through the state party organizations, though the BCRA rules have greatly reduced these shared efforts since 2002.

Republican Advantage   Unlike the situation at the county level, Republican state organizations are considerably stronger now than their Democratic counterparts. The Republican parties surveyed by Aldrich had much larger budgets and larger and more specialized staffs. Because they are bigger and richer, they can provide more services to their candidates and local parties. For example, Republican state parties are more likely to conduct polls, employ a field staff and researchers, and contribute to local parties than the Democrats are.[37] This GOP advantage stemmed in part from the extensive subsidies the national party provided to all the state parties.

Allied Groups   State Democratic parties, however, hold an important counterweight. Labor unions, especially teachers' and government employees' unions, have worked closely with their state Democratic Party organizations to provide money, volunteer help, and other services to party candidates, though this, too, has become more difficult since BCRA was passed. In states such as Alabama and Indiana, the state teachers' union is so closely connected with the state party that critics might find it difficult to tell where one stops and the other begins. State Republican Parties have close ties to allied groups as well. Small business groups, manufacturing associations, pro-life groups, and Christian conservative organizations often provide services to Republican candidates.

Because of the close association between parties and these allied groups, it is possible to think of the parties as networks of organizations, which include the citizen groups, issue organizations, polling and other consulting firms, and "think tanks" (research groups) that offer their resources and expertise to a party.[38] For party leaders, these allied groups can be a mixed blessing, of course; labor unions and business groups have their own agendas, and they can be as likely to try to push the party into locally unpopular stands as to help in the effort to elect party candidates.

It is not easy to build a powerful state party organization. It requires having to overcome both the localism of American politics and the widespread hostility toward party discipline. Strong and skillful personal leadership by a governor, a senator, or a state chairman helps.[39] So does a state tradition or culture that accepts the notion of a unified and effective party. State law makes a difference as well. More centralized party organization has flourished in the states that make less use of primary elections, so the party organization has more control over who the statewide and congressional candidates will be. Good examples include both Pennsylvania parties, the Ohio Republican Party, and the North Dakota Democratic organization.

The Special Case of the South   The most striking case of party organizational development has occurred in the South. Here, several forces—notably southerners' reaction to the civil rights movement and the resulting development of two-party competition at the state level—have spurred the development of much stronger state parties. As the national Democratic Party showed greater concern for the rights of African Americans in the 1960s and 1970s, and particularly as the Voting Rights Acts greatly increased the proportion of African-American voters in southern states, conservative southern Democrats became increasingly estranged from their national party. Southern support for Republican candidates grew, first in presidential elections, later in statewide and U.S. Senate races.

In the 1980s, state legislative candidates could sense the opportunity to run and win as Republicans. By 1994, Republicans were contesting almost one-third of the state legislative seats in the South and winning two-thirds of those seats. Between 1994 and 2005, Republicans won the governorship of all but one southern state at least once, and they won a majority in at least one house of the state legislature in most of these states. Republicans, in short, are rapidly surpassing Democrats in state elections—this in a region where, just a few decades before, it was often more socially acceptable to admit to having an alcoholic than a Republican in the family.[40]

Along with these electoral gains, southern Republican Parties grew stronger organizationally. North Carolina's state Republican Party, for example, was only minimally organized in the early 1970s. But it started in earnest to recruit state legislative candidates during the mid-1980s. By the 1990s, with a much expanded budget and staff, the party focused on attracting experienced candidates for targeted districts, producing direct mail and radio ads, and helping candidates with training and research. Even the Florida

Republicans, still not very strong organizationally, have come a long way since the years when state party chairs had "portable offices" in their homes or businesses.[41] As a result, each of the southern states now has two active party organizations, and the strength of these organizations has been increasing since the 1990s.[42]

National Party Money One important ingredient in strengthening the state party organizations has been the national parties' party-building efforts. The full story of these efforts is told in Chapter 4, but the central point is that the national parties, with more energetic leadership and more lavish financial resources than ever before, have infused a great deal of money into the state parties, and at least some of the money has been directed toward helping build the state parties' organizational capacity. State parties have also become major fund-raisers in their own right, raising money for both state and federal campaigns, and the BCRA rules have spurred them into even greater activity. Thus the state parties, so recently the poor relations of the party organizations, have come into money.

SUMMING UP: HOW THE STATE AND LOCAL PARTY ORGANIZATIONS HAVE TRANSFORMED

There have been dramatic changes in party organizational strength at the state and local levels. The high point of *local* party organizations was probably reached a hundred years ago, when some parties could be described as "armies drawn up for combat" with an "elaborate, well-staffed, and strongly motivated organizational structure."[43] Although this description did not apply to party organizations throughout the nation even then, it would be hard to find a local party organization that could be described in these terms today.

Local parties were buffeted by a variety of forces since then. Progressive reforms adopted in the early 1900s undermined party organizations by limiting their control over nominations and general elections as well as over their valued patronage resources. A number of other factors—federal social service programs, economic growth, a more educated electorate, and even racial conflict—also undercut the effectiveness of the local parties.[44]

Yet local parties have come a long way toward adapting to these changes. County parties have moved to fill at least some of the void created by the decline of the urban machines. New sources of funding are enabling these county parties to expand their activities. Local party organizations, in short, are demonstrating again their ability to meet the new challenges posed by a changing environment—a resilience that has kept them alive throughout most of American history.

The state party organizations have followed a different route. Traditionally weak in all but a handful of states, the state parties were little more than vessels that could barely contain conflicting local parties. State party organizations have grown much more robust and professional in recent years. They are providing campaign and organizational services to local parties and candidates who, in an earlier era, would not have dreamed of looking to their state headquarters for help.

In fact, the recent flow of money, resources, and leadership from the national party to the state party, and in turn from the state to the local parties, has helped to modify the traditional flow of party power. Through most of their lives, the American parties have been highly decentralized, with power and influence lodged at the grassroots. The parties were hollow at the top, depending on the base for whatever influence and resources they had. Because of the death of urban machines and the birth of vigorous state and national party organizations, we no longer see this extreme form of decentralization. The nationalization of American society and politics has affected the party organizations as well, leading to more of a balance of power among party organizations at different levels.

Yet ironically, even though they are much stronger now, the state and local party organizations probably have less impact on our politics than they once did. One reason is that they have much more competition for the attention of voters, candidates, and the media. The party organizations are part of a campaign environment consisting of other groups ranging from independent consultants to organized interests. The campaign communications sent out by the parties merge into a flood of direct mail fund-raising and advertising by citizen groups, corporate and labor political action committees, and nonprofit groups, all of whom try to influence voters' choices. Many of these groups encourage individuals to run for office. They can offer candidates money and a means to reach voters independent of the party organization. They have campaign expertise rivaling that of the party's experts.

Second, although most state parties have become much more able fund-raisers, the party's resources are still dwarfed by those of other actors in elections. In state legislative campaigns, for example, this new party money has accounted for only about 5–10 percent of the funds received by most candidates. Campaigners are happy for every dollar, of course, but these relatively small sums, even with the helpful services that accompany them, may not be enough to entice candidates to listen carefully to the party on legislative matters or any other concerns.

So the increasing organizational strength of the state and local parties has helped them adopt modern campaign skills and recapture a role in candidates' campaigns. However, it is not a *dominant* role—not in the way it could have been if party organizations, rather than voters in primaries, selected party candidates. Party organizations rarely *run* the campaigns; instead, their new resources give them more of a chance to compete for the attention of those who do—the candidates—at a time when other competitors (organized interests, consultants, and others) have become more effective as well.

Does this mean that the increases in party organizational strength are unimportant? Clearly not. In a very competitive political environment, there is little doubt that it is better to have a stronger organization than a weaker one and to have more resources rather than fewer. Further, strong and competitive party organizations are likely to be motivated to serve the needs of citizens in their area, which might enhance the status of parties in people's eyes.

In the end, despite all the changes in party organization during the past few decades, their most basic structural features have not changed. The American state and local parties remain cadre organizations run by a small number of activists; they involve the bulk of their supporters mainly at election time. By the standards of parties in other democratic nations, American state and local party organizations are still weaker—more limited in their activities and authority and more easily dominated by a handful of activists and elected officials. But by the standards of American politics, the state and local organizations are more visible and active than they have been in some time.

Chapter 4

The Parties'
National
Organizations

Just a few decades ago, if the Democratic National Committee and Republican National Committee had disappeared from the face of the earth, it might have taken weeks for anyone else to notice. At that time, the national committees were poor and transient renters, often moving back and forth between New York and Washington, and active mainly during presidential campaigns. Leading students of the national committees could accurately describe them as "politics without power."[1] The real power in the party system was decentralized, collected in the local party organizations.

There is good reason why the parties have long been decentralized, as Chapter 3 indicated. Virtually all American public officials are chosen in state and local elections; even the voting for president is conducted mainly under state election laws. In years past, most of the incentives parties had to offer, such as preferments and patronage jobs, were available at the state and local levels, and the state governments have been the chief regulators of parties. All these forces have given the parties a powerful state and local focus that can restrain any shift in power within the party organizations. So state and local party organizations have chosen their officers, attended to the nomination of their own candidates, taken their own stands on issues, and raised and spent their own funds, usually without much interference from the national party.

Yet powerful nationalizing forces have long since affected most other aspects of American politics. Government in the federal system became more centered in Washington beginning in the 1930s. Party voters now respond to national issues, national candidates, and increasingly to national party labels. The party organizations adapted more slowly to these nationalizing forces. Since the 1970s, however, the two parties have responded to a series of crises by infusing life into their national committees. Their resources and staffs have grown. They have taken on new roles, activities, and influence. They have been able to limit the independence of state and local organizations in selecting delegates to the parties' national conventions.

The change has been remarkable. Only in the earliest years of the American parties, when presidential candidates were nominated by the congressional caucus, were the national parties as important in American politics. Although the state and local pull remains strong, the national organizations are an increasingly powerful presence in the parties. The parties are still not controlled from the top down, but the distribution of power among the national, state, and local parties is now more balanced than ever before.

How has this expansion of national party power affected the workings of American politics? What are its benefits and its costs? To start exploring these questions, let us examine what the national parties are and what they can do.

THE NATIONAL PARTIES

What is the national party? Officially, each major party's supreme national authority is the convention it holds every four years to nominate a candidate for the presidency. But the convention rarely does more than select the presidential and vice-presidential candidates and approve the party's platform and rules. So in practice, between conventions, the two parties' main governing bodies are their national committees.

The National Committees

Each party's *national committee* is a gathering of representatives from all its state parties; its leaders run the national party on a daily basis. Their main focus is to help elect the party's presidential candidate and also to promote the party's issue agenda, aid state parties, and assist in some other races, such as major gubernatorial campaigns. Both national committees have a long history: the Democrats created theirs in 1848 and the Republicans in 1856. For years, every state (and some territories, such as Samoa and Guam) was represented equally on both national committees, regardless of its voting population or the extent of its party support. California and Wyoming, then, had equal-sized delegations to the national party committees, just as they do in the U.S. Senate, even though California has a population of 36 million and Wyoming's is 500,000. That system overrepresented the smaller states and also gave roughly equal weight in the national committees to the winning and the losing parts of the party. In practice, this strengthened the southern and western segments of each party, which tended to be more conservative.

Since 1972, when the Democrats greatly changed the makeup of their national committee, the parties have structured their committees differently. After briefly experimenting with unequal state representation in the 1950s, the Republicans have kept their traditional confederational structure by giving each of the state and territorial parties three seats on the Republican National Committee (RNC). In contrast, the Democratic National Committee (DNC), now almost three times the size of its Republican counterpart, gives weight both to population and to party support in representing the states. California, for example, has 21 seats on the DNC, and Wyoming has 4. This change reduced the influence of conservatives and moderates within the DNC.

The two national committees also differ in that the Democrats give national committee seats to representatives of groups especially likely to support Democratic candidates, such as blacks, women, and labor unions—a decision that shows the importance of these groups to the party—as well as to associations of elected officials, such as the National Conference of Democratic Mayors. National committee members in both parties are chosen by the state parties and, for the Democrats, by these other groups as well.

THE NATIONAL PARTY CHAIRS: FUND-RAISERS ABOVE ALL

Although Howard Dean didn't win the Democratic presidential nomination in 2004, his campaign created a network of millions of small donors in what was regarded as a masterful job of Internet fund-raising. Even so, when the former Vermont governor was elected Democratic National Committee Chair, Dean had very big shoes to fill. His predecessor, Terry McAuliffe, had raised hundreds of millions of dollars for the Democratic Party. McAuliffe tried to make sure that the money was invested strategically; he pressed state party chairs to share their voter lists with the national party so that it could, as the GOP had, develop a database with information on more than 170 million voters. When McAuliffe's term ended in 2005, Dean won the DNC job partly on the strength of his campaign's ability to generate energy at the grassroots. But his candidacy was initially opposed by some party moderates, who feared that his selection would signal a party move to the left.

There was no internal party dispute about the Republican National Committee's top job. President George W. Bush chose the campaign manager for his successful 2004 reelection race, Ken Mehlman, as RNC chair right after the campaign ended. Mehlman stepped into a wealthy and well-organized RNC. The committee's "72-Hour Task Force," a national program to mobilize votes for Republican candidates during the weekend before the 2002 congressional elections, was considered to have been highly successful in 2004 as well, and Mehlman promised to make it a permanent feature of the RNC's campaign work. Mehlman, who is closely associated with the party's conservative base, pledged to attract voters who support a "culture of life," gun rights, and traditional marriage. Both parties' national committees, then, approached 2008 with national chairs who appealed to their party's base—Dean to liberals, Mehlman to conservatives—but whose first priority would be raising as much money as possible.

Sources: Dan Balz, "State Chairs Endorse Dean for DNC Chief," *Washington Post,* February 1, 2005, p. A4; Thomas B. Edsall, "Bush Taps Campaign Manager to Lead Party," *Washington Post,* November 16, 2004, p. A3.

National Party Officers

The national committees have the power to choose their own leaders. By tradition, however, the parties' presidential candidates can name their party's national chair for the duration of the presidential campaign, and the committees ratify their choices without question. The national chair chosen by the winning presidential candidate usually keeps his or her job after the election. In 2004, for example, President Bush picked the manager of his reelection campaign, Ken Mehlman, to become RNC Chair. So in practice, only the "out" party's national committee actually chooses its own national chair, as the DNC did in selecting Howard Dean in 2005 (see box above).[2]

The chairs, together with the national committees' permanent staffs, dominate these organizations. The members of the full national committees come together only two or three times a year, largely to call media attention to the party and its candidates. So the national chair, with a permanent staff that he or she has chosen, has, in effect, been the heart of the national party organization.

Presidents and Their National Parties

The national committees' role, and that of their chairs, depends on whether the president is from their party. When their party does not hold the presidency, the resulting power vacuum is likely to draw the national chair and committee into some degree of national leadership. They will bear the responsibility for helping pay debts from the losing campaign, raising new money, and energizing the party organization around the country. The "out" party's national chair may speak for the party and the alternatives it proposes (as will prominent elected officials, such as the most visible of the party's senators). So the national chair and committee play more influential roles, by default, when their party has less control over the national government.

With a party colleague in the White House, on the other hand, the national committee's role is whatever the president wants it to be. Presidents came to dominate their national committees early in the twentieth century and especially since the 1960s and 1970s. James W. Ceaser cites the example of Robert Dole, RNC chair from 1971 to 1973, who was quickly fired by the president when Dole tried to put a little distance between the party and the president's involvement in Watergate: "I had a nice chat with the President . . . while the other fellows went out to get the rope."[3] Some presidents have turned their national committees into little more than managers of the president's campaigns and builders of the president's political support between campaigns. Other presidents, such as George W. Bush, have used their control to build up the national committees to achieve party, not just presidential, goals.

In the president's party, the national chair must be agreeable to and willing to be loyal primarily to the president. Within the opposition party, the chair needs to get along with or at least be trusted by the various segments of the party. Experience in running a complex campaign is also desirable; because of changes in campaign finance rules, the national committee's work in presidential elections has had to become more independent of the presidential candidate's own campaign organization. With a close and expensive race expected in 2008, it is understandable that both parties have chosen national chairs with a great deal of fund-raising and campaigning experience.

OTHER NATIONAL PARTY GROUPS

Several other party organizations are closely related to the two parties' national committees and are normally included in the term "the national party."

Congressional Campaign ("Hill") Committees

The most important of these related groups are each party's *House and Senate campaign committees* (called the "Hill committees" because they used to be housed on Capitol Hill). The House committees were founded in the immediate aftermath of the Civil War; the Senate committees came into being when senators began to be popularly elected in 1913. The Democratic Congressional Campaign Committee (DCCC), the National Republican Congressional Committee (NRCC), the Democratic Senatorial Campaign Committee (DSCC), and the National Republican Senatorial Committee (NRSC) are organized to promote the reelection of their members and the success of other congressional candidates of their party.

Although incumbent House and Senate members control these committees, they have resisted the pressures to work only on behalf of incumbents' campaigns; they also support their party's candidates for open seats and challengers who have a good chance of winning. In short, they concentrate their money where they think they are likely to get the biggest payoff in increasing their party's representation in Congress. During the past three decades, the congressional campaign committees have developed their own fund-raising and service functions. They provide party candidates with an impressive range of campaign help, from get-out-the-vote efforts to hard cash (see box on page 70). They also work to channel money from political action committees to the party's candidates. For House and Senate candidates, the Hill committees are more influential than their parties' national committees.

Women's and Youth Groups

For a long time, both the Democrats and Republicans have had women's divisions associated with their national committees.[4] Both have also had national federations of state and local women's groups: the National Federation of Democratic Women and the National Federation of Republican Women. The importance of these women's divisions has declined markedly in the past 30 years as women have entered regular leadership positions in the parties.

On campuses, the College Republican National Committee (the CRs) and the College Democrats (whose web log or "blog" is named Smart Ass, in honor of the party's donkey mascot) have experienced big increases in membership and numbers of chapters in the early 2000s. The CRs train field representatives to organize other college Republicans in states with important races, and have been closely associated with a number of conservative nonparty groups. Their Democratic counterparts similarly recruit volunteers for campaigns at all levels. The Young Democrats of America and the Young Republican National Federation also work actively in a variety of locations among high school and college students as well as young adults.

Democratic and Republican Governors' Associations

State governors have long had a powerful voice in their national parties, for several reasons. They hold prestigious offices, earned by winning statewide elections. Many lead or, at least, are supported by their state party organization, and some will probably be considered potential candidates for president; think, for example, of Jeb Bush for the Republicans and Tom Vilsack for the Democrats. By the late 1970s and early 1980s, the governors of both parties had Washington offices and staffs. When their party won control of Congress in 1994, Republican governors played a big role in advising on policy positions, and after the 2004 elections they lobbied their colleagues in Congress and the White House to pay more attention to issues of special concern to state governments, such as the high costs of Medicaid to state taxpayers.[5] Governors' organizational influence in the national parties, however, tends to be greatest, like that of the national committee chair, when their party is out of power.

State legislators and local officials in both parties are organized as well and are formally represented on the Democratic National Committee, although they do not have much influence on either party's national operations. A more influential group is the

HOW TO TARGET A CONGRESSIONAL CAMPAIGN

The parties' "Hill committees" try to support all their congressional candidates to at least some degree, and they target a few candidates for much more intensive help. The most important criteria for choosing which campaigns to target are the competitiveness of the district and candidate quality, as measured by the amount of money the candidate has been able to raise (or contribute to his or her own campaign) by midsummer of the election year. Candidates, then, try to hold on to as much of their campaign money as possible until midsummer (more precisely, until June 30, the Federal Election Commission's reporting deadline for second-quarter fund-raising) in order to impress the party operatives. Hill committee targeters also ask: Is the candidate's organization capable of spending the money effectively? How expensive are the district's media? How much support does the opponent have?

Each party in 2004 focused the bulk of its resources on about a dozen congressional races. Another dozen or more candidates became "secondary targets," who could move on or off their party's list quickly, depending on the parties' financial situation and the candidates' poll numbers.

Once they have chosen their target list of candidates, the Hill committees can offer these services:

- Help with hiring and training campaign staff, choosing consultants, and making strategic decisions
- Information about issues relevant to their campaigns and "oppo" research on the opponent's strengths and weaknesses
- Advice and, when needed, television and radio production facilities to help candidates make effective ads at low cost (though the production is done mainly by party-related private consultants)
- Poll data to gauge the campaign's progress and measure responses to particular issues and messages
- Contributor lists given to selected candidates on the condition that these candidates give their own contributor lists to the party after the election
- Party fund-raising events in Washington and party leaders' visits to candidate events, live and via satellite uplink, to help candidates raise money and attract votes
- "Hard-money" direct contributions to campaigns*
- "Coordinated spending" to buy polls, media ads, or research for a candidate*
- Independent spending on ads in the candidate's district* and help in raising money from political action committees (PACs), other political groups, and individuals

*Explained in Chapter 12.

Sources: Paul S. Herrnson, *Congressional Elections*, 4th ed. (Washington, DC: CQ Press, 2004), pp. 90-128; and Victoria A. Farrar-Myers and Diana Dwyre, "Parties and Campaign Finance," in Jeffrey E. Cohen, Richard Fleisher, and Paul Kantor, eds., *American Political Parties: Decline or Resurgence?* (Washington, DC: CQ Press, 2001), pp. 143–146.

Democratic Leadership Council (DLC). Founded in 1985, it brings together Democratic elected officials, led by influential members of Congress and governors and some prospective candidates for president. The DLC represents the moderate wing of the party and works to make the Democrats more appealing to southern and western voters. On the Republican side, groups such as the Republican Liberty Caucus and the conservative Heritage Foundation also try to affect party policy.

TWO PATHS TO POWER

The two national parties have traveled two different roads to reach these new levels of effectiveness. The Republicans have followed a service path by building a muscular fund-raising operation in order to provide needed services to their candidates and state parties. The Democrats, in contrast, first followed a procedural path, strengthening their national party's authority over the state parties in the selection of a presidential nominee.

The central element in both national parties' development, however, was their ability to attract thousands of small contributions through mass mailings to likely party supporters. This gave the national parties, which formerly depended on assessments provided by the state parties, an independent financial base. Ironically, then, at a time when some were warning that the parties were in decline, the national party organizations were reaching levels of strength that had never been seen before in American politics.

The Service Party Path

The *service party* was born during the 1960s, when a quiet revolution began in the Republican National Committee. The committee's chairman at the time, Ray Bliss, involved the committee more and more in helping state and local parties with the practical aspects of party organizational work. Chairman William Brock continued this effort in the mid- to late 1970s as a means of reviving the party's election prospects after the Republican losses of the post-Watergate years. Under Brock, the RNC helped to provide salaries for the executive directors of all 50 state Republican Parties; offered expert assistance to the state parties in organizing, strategizing, and fund-raising; and also gave financial help to more than 4,000 state legislative candidates. Bliss and Brock fashioned a new role for the RNC by making it into an exceptionally effective service organization for the state and local parties.[6]

There were two keys to success in performing the new service role: money and mastery of the new campaign technologies. Using the new ability to generate computer-based mailing lists, the Republicans began a program of direct-mail appeals that brought in ever-higher levels of income, as you can see in Table 4.1. The RNC succeeded in raising $105.9 million in "hard money" (contributions regulated by federal law; these terms are explained in Chapter 12) in the 1983–1984 election cycle—a record for national committee fund-raising that wasn't broken until 1995. The national Republican committees used the money, as Bliss and Brock had, to provide a broad array of services to candidates and to state and local party organizations, including candidate recruitment and training, research, public opinion polling, data processing, computer networking and software development, production of radio and television ads, direct mailing, expert consultants, and legal services. State party leaders were glad to accept the help; as the party more

TABLE 4.1   Party "Hard Money" Receipts: 1975–1976 to 2003–2004 (in millions)

Democratic Committees	National	Senate	House	State/Local	Total
1975–1976	$13.1	1.0	0.9	0.0	15.0
1977–1978	$11.3	0.3	2.8	8.7	26.4
1979–1980	$15.1	1.7	2.1	11.7	37.2
1981–1982	$16.4	5.6	6.5	10.6	39.3
1983–1984	$46.6	8.9	10.4	18.5	98.5
1985–1986	$17.2	13.4	12.3	14.1	64.8
1987–1988	$52.3	16.3	12.5	44.7	113.8
1989–1990	$14.5	17.5	9.1	44.7	78.5
1991–1992	$65.8	25.5	12.8	73.7	163.3
1993–1994	$41.8	26.4	19.4	55.6	132.8
1995–1996	$108.4	30.8	26.6	93.2	221.6
1997–1998	$64.8	35.6	25.2	63.4	160.0
1999–2000	$124.0	40.5	48.4	149.3	275.2
2001–2002	$67.5	48.4	46.4	114.2	217.2
2003–2004	$311.5	88.7	93.2	191.6	685.0

Republican Committees					
1975–1976	$29.1	12.2	1.8	0.0	43.1
1977–1978	$34.2	10.9	14.1	20.9	84.5
1979–1980	$76.2	23.3	28.6	33.8	169.5
1981–1982	$83.5	48.9	58.0	24.0	215.0
1983–1984	$105.9	81.7	58.3	43.1	297.9
1985–1986	$83.8	84.4	39.8	47.2	255.2
1987–1988	$91.0	65.9	34.7	66.0	251.3
1989–1990	$68.7	65.1	33.2	39.3	202.0
1991–1992	$85.4	73.8	35.3	72.8	264.9
1993–1994	$87.4	65.3	26.7	75.0	244.1
1995–1996	$193.0	64.5	74.2	128.4	416.5
1997–1998	$104.0	53.4	72.7	89.4	285.0
1999–2000	$212.8	51.5	97.3	176.6	465.8
2001–2002	$170.1	59.2	123.6	132.5	424.1
2003–2004	$392.4	79.0	185.7	202.3	859.4

Note: Beginning with 1987–1988, total receipts do not include monies transferred among the listed committees.

Source: Federal Election Commission at http://www.fec.gov/press/press2005/20050302party/Party2004final.html, as amended at http://www.fec.gov/finance/disclosure/srssea.shtml (accessed June 10, 2005). State and local figures are from Raymond J. LaRaja, "State and Local Political Parties," in Michael J. Malbin, ed., *The Election After Reform* (Lanham, MD: Rowman & Littlefield, 2006).

closely identified with the business community, Republicans felt comfortable with these marketing innovations.

The Democrats' Procedural-Reform Path

At about the same time, the national Democrats had begun to expand the power of the national party organization for other reasons. Reformers supporting the civil rights movement and opposing American involvement in the Vietnam War pressed for change in the Democratic Party's positions on these issues. The reformers focused on changing the rules for selecting presidential candidates. Their aim was to make the nominating process more open and democratic and, in particular, more representative of the concerns of people like themselves: blacks, women, and young people.

In the mid-1960s, these reforms began with efforts to prevent southern states from sending all-white delegations to the national convention. After the 1968 election, the first of a series of reform commissions dramatically overhauled the party's rules for nominating presidential candidates. (This story is told in more detail in Chapter 10.) In doing so, the Democrats limited the autonomy of the state parties and the authority of state law in determining how convention delegates were to be selected, thus giving the national party the authority over the presidential nominating process.[7] Key court decisions upheld these actions, further solidifying the newfound power of the national party.

Why would the state party leaders have been willing to go along with this erosion of their independence? Some may still be asking themselves that question. The reformers' success indicates that state Democratic leaders were not sufficiently aware of the threat posed by the reforms; it also reflects the unusual politics of that time and the existence of a power vacuum at the top of the Democratic Party in the 1960s. This change was limited to the Democrats, however. Republican leaders, consistent with their party's commitment to states' rights, did not want to centralize power in their own party organization.[8] Yet the GOP was still affected by the tide of Democratic Party reform because the bills passed by state legislatures to implement the reforms applied to both parties.

In the early 1980s, the Democrats took stock of the reforms and did not like what they saw. The newly centralized authority in nominating a presidential candidate and the increased grassroots participation in the nominating process had done little to win elections. Further, it had divided the party and alienated much of the Democratic Party in government, many of whom stayed home from party conventions in the 1970s. So the national Democrats decided to soft-pedal procedural reforms and move toward the Republican service model. The party rushed to broaden the base of its fund-raising and to provide the means and know-how to recruit candidates and revitalize local parties. When the dust from all this effort settled, authority over party rules had been nationalized, and what had been two models for strengthening the national party were rapidly converging into one.[9]

Both Parties Take the Service Path

The good news for the Democrats in the 1980s was that they were dramatically improving their fund-raising, reducing their long-standing debt, and increasing their activities in the states and localities. The bad news was that the Republicans were far ahead of them to begin with and were continuing to break new ground. The national Democrats made no secret of their effort to imitate the Republican success in raising money and using it to buy services. Slowly, they began to catch up; what began as a three-to-one and even five-to-one financial advantage for the Republicans was later cut by more than half (see Figure 4.1).

One reason was the party's increasing reliance on what was called "soft money" (see Chapter 12)—funds exempted from federal campaign finance rules, which were raised in unlimited amounts, most often from labor unions, business interests, and wealthy individuals. Major contributions from labor unions made it easier for the Democrats to compete with Republicans in soft money than they could in raising hard money. Both national

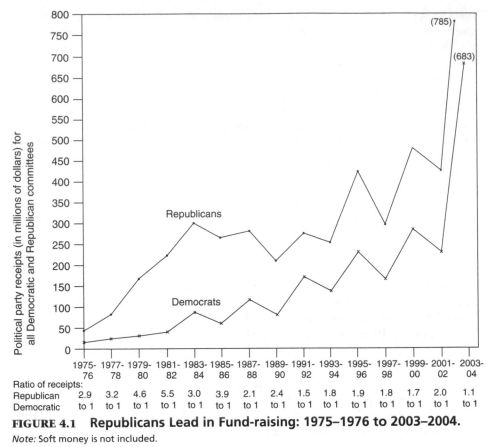

Ratio of receipts:

	1975-76	1977-78	1979-80	1981-82	1983-84	1985-86	1987-88	1989-90	1991-92	1993-94	1995-96	1997-98	1999-00	2001-02	2003-04
Republican	2.9	3.2	4.6	5.5	3.0	3.9	2.1	2.4	1.5	1.8	1.9	1.8	1.7	2.0	1.1
Democratic	to 1	to 1	to 1	to 1	to 1	to 1	to 1	to 1	to 1	to 1	to 1	to 1	to 1	to 1	to 1

FIGURE 4.1   Republicans Lead in Fund-raising: 1975–1976 to 2003–2004.

Note: Soft money is not included.

Source: Same as Table 4.1.

parties' committees began to take advantage of the development of unrestricted soft money starting in the early 1990s. In 2000, for example, the national Republicans established the "Republican Regents" program for individuals and corporations who gave at least $250,000 in soft money to the party during a two-year period, which helped produce record soft-money donations, and the Democratic "Jefferson Trust" honored givers of at least $100,000.[10] By that year, almost half of the national parties' fund-raising came in the form of soft money.

Some of the money went into building up the state and even the local parties. In the 2002 election cycle, for example, the RNC and the Republican Hill committees transferred $145.6 million to their state and local organizations and the three Democratic committees transferred $158.6 million.[11] Most of this was soft money, which could be used for campaign advertising as long as it did not use words such as "elect" or "defeat" in connection with a candidate. But at least some of the money went into voter mobilization drives that could help the state party more generally.

A much larger portion of the national parties' money has gone into races for the U.S. House and Senate. Since the mid-1980s, both parties have provided increasing levels of aid to selected candidates. The Republican committees have taken the lead; the stunning success of GOP candidates in the 1994 congressional elections, for example, was due in part to aggressive fund-raising as well as candidate recruitment by their Hill committees.

Campaign finance reform passed in 2002 (the Bipartisan Campaign Reform Act, or BCRA, discussed in Chapter 12) mandated that the national committees would no longer be able to collect soft money after the 2002 congressional elections. Both national parties stepped up the pace to pull in every possible dollar before the deadline. The Democrats saw the coming ban on national party soft money as a particular threat to their competitive standing because their soft-money collections had been flourishing, but their hard-money fund-raising had expanded only gradually. In 2002 the Democratic Hill committees did outraise their Republican counterparts in soft money by $151 million to $136 million. But the Republican two-to-one advantage in hard money helped ensure Republican control of both houses of Congress.

Rising to the Challenge of New Campaign Finance Rules

Once the BCRA rules came into effect in the 2004 campaigns, many observers felt sure that the loss of soft money would seriously weaken the national parties, and especially the Democrats. The new fund-raising rules did challenge both parties. For example, national party committees could now transfer only hard money to state and local party committees, so these transfers dropped to $50.5 million for the Republicans and $66.1 million for the Democrats. Most state parties (see box on page 76) got much less from their national party in the 2004 campaigns than they had in 2002. The national parties concentrated much of their money instead on running their own advertising directly in House and Senate campaigns ("independent spending"), which by law had to be strictly separated from that of the candidates' own efforts. So the Senate and House candidates whom the national party committees targeted in 2004 got several times more national party money and advertising than had the best-funded congressional races in 2002.

Overall, both national parties adapted very successfully to the new rules. They helped make up for the lost soft money by putting new emphasis on grassroots fund-raising, harvesting many more small, hard-money donations from individual contributors. For example, the DNC greatly expanded its direct mail fund-raising program, which had been minimal during the 1990s, and reaped millions of new donors in return. In the 2004 election cycle, the DNC raised $166 million in contributions of less than $200, which accounted for more than 40 percent of the DNC's fund-raising. In all, the two national parties raised even more money in 2003–2004 than ever before. The DNC collected almost five times as much hard money in 2004 as it had in 2002—$312 million compared with $67 million. The DCCC and the RNC both doubled their hard-money fund-raising in 2004, and the DSCC came close to doing so. The Republicans, as well as the Bush campaign, also encouraged big hard-money donors (those able to give the federally allowed maximum of $2,000) to solicit similar contributions from their friends and colleagues and to "bundle" these donations to reach totals of $100,000 or $200,000, in return for recognition from the campaign.

With all these adjustments, the national parties broke all fund-raising records in the early 2000s. In the period leading up to the 2002 elections, the six national party committees had collectively raised almost $1 *billion*—substantially more than in any previous midterm race and almost as much as the two parties had raised in the 2000 general

WHO GOT THE MOST NATIONAL PARTY MONEY IN 2001–2002 AND 2003–2004?

State parties

2001–2002	**2003–2004**
Texas Democratic Party $15.3 million	Florida Republican Party $11.4 million
Minnesota Republican Party $12.2 million	Florida Democratic Party $6.4 million
Florida Republican Party $12.2 million	Ohio Democratic Party $5.6 million
Minnesota Democratic Party $11.6 million	Pennsylvania Democratic Party $5.3 million

Senate candidates (including party direct contributions, coordinated spending, and party independent spending for the candidate and against his/her opponent)

John Cornyn, Texas Republican (open seat—won) $2.2 million	Mel Martinez, Florida Republican (open seat—won) $ 6.2 million
Suzanne Haik Terrell, Louisiana Republican (challenger—lost) $1.5 million	Betty Castor, Florida Democrat (open seat—lost) $5.7 million
Doug Forrester, New Jersey Republican (open seat—lost) $1.0 million	Erskine Bowles, North Carolina Democrat (open seat—lost) $4.4 million
Saxby Chambliss, Georgia Republican (challenger—won) $0.9 million	Inez Tenenbaum, South Carolina Democrat (open seat—lost) $4.1 million

House candidates

John Swallow, Utah Republican (challenger—lost), $0.5 million	Dave Reichert, Washington Republican (open seat—won) $3.8 million
Steve Pearce, New Mexico Republican (open seat—won), $0.2 million	Gregory Walcher, Colorado Republican (open seat—lost) $3.7 million

Note: National party money includes money transferred by all six national party committees (DNC, RNC, NRSC, DSCC, NRCC, DCCC).

Sources: Federal Election Commission data on the Internet at http://www.fec.gov/press/20030320party/20030103party.html and http://www.fec.gov/press/press2005/20050302party/Party2004final.html

election, when they had a presidential candidate to support. In 2004, even with the BCRA reforms, the two parties' national committees came up with an eye-popping $1.2 billion. And although the totals for Democratic committees still fell short of the Republicans', the most remarkable fact was that the Democrats almost matched the Republicans' collections for the first time in the 30 years that federal fund-raising records have been kept.

Both national parties also tapped their congressional incumbents and even their candidates as contributors. In 2002, the NRSC required each Senate Republican to donate or raise the impressive sum of $500,000 in soft or hard money so that the committee could redirect campaign funds from those who could most easily raise the money to those who needed it. The Republican chair of the House Ways and Means Committee, Bill Thomas, gave $1 million from his campaign account to the NRCC in that year and Democratic Senator Charles Schumer transferred $2.5 million to the DSCC in 2004 from his personal campaign committee.[12] Looking toward the 2006 elections, each Republican

House member was required to raise at least $50,000 for the national party in 2005, and a network of congressional "team captains" was assigned to track each member's progress, just as party whips track legislative votes. As one incumbent put it, "This is the hardest part of being a member, and we all get weary of it," but Senate and House Republicans expected to reach their goal of raising $23 million for the national party by the end of the year from lobbyists, trade associations, and wealthy constituents.[13] The parties' success in getting incumbents to hand over their funds and to put their fund-raising skill in the service of other party candidates demonstrated the extent to which the congressional parties have become important instruments of collective power for their members.

Over time, all these fund-raising advances have permitted both national parties to hire increasing numbers of professional staff members, who in turn have been able to put new campaign technologies into practice. The numbers vary from month to month, but all six national party committees have many times more staffers than they did three decades ago. Since the mid-1980s, then, both national parties have become institutionalized as active, well-staffed "service parties" working to support party candidates and state and local organizations, not only through direct contributions but also through investments in voter identification, registration, and database management.[14]

WHAT IS THE IMPACT OF THESE STRONGER NATIONAL PARTIES?

These dramatic changes in the national parties have helped to beef up the parties' roles in nominating and electing candidates, roles that had been seriously undercut a century ago with the advent of the direct primary. To an important degree, the national and state parties (especially the Republicans) are now actively involved in the campaign support functions that private campaign consultants and other political groups had monopolized just a few years ago. It is not likely that party organizations can displace consultants and other sources of campaign expertise, but the money and services provided by the national parties have helped to raise their profiles in the eyes of candidates. The increasing strength of the national partics has also altered the relationships within the parties.

Effects on Candidates' Campaigns

The strengthened national parties perform a number of vital functions in presidential campaigns. Both national committees research the issues, study the opponent's record and background, and search for their own candidate's weak points and ways to thwart attacks. They train state party staff and field directors and maintain relationships with important groups in the party's constituency: organized labor, minority groups, women, and environmentalists for the Democrats, evangelical and other conservative Christian groups, and business organizations for the Republicans.

Both parties also maintain huge databases on likely party voters; they plug the information gleaned from party canvassers into state and national party computers so that, just as businesses do, they can make predictions as to how particular sets of voters are likely to behave. This "database targeting," used extensively by both parties for the first time in the 2004 election, helps both parties improve the efficiency of their fund-raising and get-out-the-vote operations. A voter identified by a Democratic canvasser as interested in education can be scheduled for a later visit from a teacher who promotes the

Democratic candidate's ideas on education.[15] Information-gathering of this magnitude requires funding and computer facilities on a scale that the national party organizations have become capable of providing.

In Senate and House campaigns, however, the national party's newfound strength is increasingly concentrated in a few states and districts. In the 1980s and 1990s, the national party committees supported a wide range of viable candidates. The committees tended to protect their incumbents when they expected a lean election year and invested in challengers and open seats when a big victory looked likely. But by the early 2000s, the two parties were so evenly matched in the House and Senate and the number of truly competitive seats had shrunk so dramatically that both parties' congressional committees were pouring the great majority of their money and help into those few competitive races.[16]

The volume of party funds and field staff coming into the small number of competitive campaigns was unprecedented. In one of the most visible cases, a runoff for a Louisiana Senate seat in 2002 offered the GOP the chance to expand the razor-thin edge that it had won in the Senate on Election Day. National Republican committees, free from their responsibilities in all the other races, ran the Republican challenger's runoff campaign from party headquarters in Washington, DC, and the state capital. The challenger, Suzanne Haik Terrell, had been recruited to run by the White House. The national party designed her message and spent $500,000 on get-out-the-vote efforts. The NRSC made and funded ads on her behalf. "The result," according to a reporter, "is that Terrell's tiny headquarters in Baton Rouge is oddly quiet."[17]

When the candidate's headquarters is quiet and the national party committees in Washington are humming, we have an indicator that at least in these few targeted races, the national party committees' money and other resources have given them real power over the campaign. For instance, in 2002, the national parties spent more in a closely fought Colorado congressional race than the candidates' own campaigns did, and the national party committees specified exactly what the campaigns were to do with the party money. The race, the candidates acknowledged, was in large part under the parties' control, not their own. The Democratic candidate's campaign manager probably spoke for both candidates in his exasperation at the national party's micromanaging: "They crawl up our ass on a daily basis."[18]

In another stressful confrontation between Hill committees and congressional campaigns, NRCC strategists in 2002 strongly disapproved of the reelection campaign of Rep. Jim Leach, a longtime Iowa Republican, calling it "perhaps the worst incumbent campaign in the country." Leach was facing a wealthy Democratic challenger in a district that had been redrawn to favor a Democrat. The NRCC, fearing the loss of its House majority if the Iowa seat changed hands, poured $1.2 million into the race. Some of the money was used for attack ads, an approach with which Leach strongly disagreed.[19] The national parties' heavy investment in campaigns, then, can lead to conflicts as well as to cooperation with party candidates. That can happen on occasion even in presidential races, as in the run-up to the 2004 campaign when the RNC ran TV spots portraying President Bush as committed to preemptive action to defend the United States just at a time when the president was giving speeches emphasizing his concern with alliance-building and collaborative action.

The Leach and Terrell campaigns are unusual, however. In most congressional races, the national party committees have not put in enough money or other resources to attract even some attention, much less power, over the candidates and their staffs.

National party involvement in the targeted House and Senate races in 2002 and 2004 shows the potential for greater party impact on campaigns, but the potential is far from being realized.

Effects on State and Local Parties

More generally, have the increasing visibility and resources of the national parties led to a transfer of power from the state and local to the national party organizations—to centralization rather than decentralization of the parties? Probably not. The forces that encourage a state and local party focus remain strong.

But it is clear that the national parties' new strength has lessened the *de*centralization of the party organizations. When the national parties have a lot of money and services to give, their power and influence grows. The RNC in particular has used its hard money resources in 2004 to build up Republican state party organizations as an investment in future election efforts. In a number of cases, national party committees have made their funding or other help contingent on the campaign's or state party's acceptance of certain requirements: that they hire particular staffers or consultants or use particular campaign techniques. The result can be more of a national imprint on the issues discussed in state and even local campaigns, the kinds of candidates recruited, and the ways in which the parties are organized. Is this a good thing for American politics? "Which Would You Choose?" on page 80 gives you arguments on both sides of this question.

This increased national influence can produce some interesting strains among party organizations at different levels of government, just as it has produced strains between the parties and some candidates. One of the areas of greatest conflict between the national parties and their state and local brethren centers on national party involvement in primaries. It is always a temptation for national party officials to try to select and groom the candidate they think will have the best odds of winning in a district. The House and Senate campaign committees, whose chance for a majority in Congress depends on the effectiveness of candidates in competitive races, find it very frustrating to watch a less capable candidate win their party's primary and go on to run a less-than-professional campaign for the seat.

Yet there are big risks involved when a national party organization tries to endorse a candidate in a primary. If the party organization backs a candidate who later loses the primary, then the party alienates the winning candidate, perhaps splits the state party in the process, and makes itself look weak to boot. The DCCC provided a textbook example of these hazards when it decided to endorse four congressional candidates in the 2000 primaries. Two of the four lost, and the effort caused intraparty fighting that became a public embarrassment to the national Democrats.

National Democratic committees stayed out of party primaries in the 2002 election, but the national Republicans chose to wade boldly into this thicket and came out relatively unscathed. Anxious to regain control of the Senate in 2002, the NRSC focused early on 10 states that it considered winnable for a strong Republican candidate. Using public opinion polls to measure the favorability ratings of various possible candidates, NRSC strategists identified the strongest prospective contenders and, with President Bush, worked to persuade these people to run. The NRCC did the same in some key House races. All three national Republican committees then raised record amounts of money to pour into the closest races.[20]

COULD A STRONGER NATIONAL PARTY HELP YOU?

YES! Political parties offer you a valuable shortcut. Government decisions affect almost everything you do, but you may not have time to research dozens of complicated issues (health care, energy prices) and candidates in order to vote for those who will act in your interest. A party can do the research for you. If you generally agree with, say, the Republican Party, it can offer you a set of recommended candidates with no effort on your part. But if each state and local Republican organization can act independently, and if some of these organizations are moderate and others are conservative, then how can you be sure that your state and local Republican candidates will support the positions that drew you to the party? A strong national party could help recruit candidates whose views are consistent with the party's philosophy and help them get elected. Besides, who would you rather have raising campaign money: the national party or the individual candidates who will soon be voting on bills affecting the donors' interests?

NO! The United States is very diverse; the concerns of Democrats in Omaha may well be different from those in San Francisco, New Hampshire, and the Florida Panhandle. If a national party is strong enough to promote a clear set of ideas on what government should be doing, then whose ideas should it promote: those of the Omaha Democrats or those of the San Francisco Democrats? If a national party is strong enough to elect its candidates, wouldn't it be capable of telling them how to vote in Congress, whether or not their constituents agreed? Even if a national party organization confines itself to raising money and giving it to candidates, doesn't that give the national organization a great deal of influence over state and even local candidates? In a nation with a tradition of hostility to "boss rule," couldn't a strong national party raise those fears again?

The Republican Hill committees were able to recruit many of those on their wish list and to win enough races to capture the Senate. Yet this national intervention, according to one reporter, "infuriated" several state Republican Party leaders when the NRCC chair campaigned in their states for the national party's preferred candidates.[21] When the national party committees use their money to affect the choice of candidates or the direction of a campaign, it is likely that there will be ruffled feathers within the state party and the campaign, who feel that they are better judges of what works in the district.

By 2004 and 2006, however, state parties had gotten more accustomed to national party intervention. Hill committees and the Bush administration worked actively in several Senate primaries in both years to promote the candidates they felt had the best chance of winning. The most interesting races were in Pennsylvania; in 2004 the national Republican Party aligned itself with moderate incumbent Arlen Specter, even though he opposed the Bush administration's stands on abortion and other issues, because the administration considered him better able to hold the seat than a more conservative challenger. Then in 2006, the DSCC backed Bob Casey as the strongest primary candidate, even though Casey is pro-life and his challenger supported the Democratic Party's pro-choice stand. When faced with a choice between victory and ideology, both national parties chose victory.

Effects on the Presidency

Is a stronger national party likely to compete with the president's power or to add to it? Clearly, the increasing resources of the national committees give them the opportunity for a more independent political role. This independence has been developing since the 1980s, when the Republican National Committee came into its own as an important actor in party politics. Federal funding of presidential campaigns, with its strict limits on party spending for presidential races, freed the national committees from their traditional concentration on presidential elections and allowed them to dedicate at least some of their resources to party-building at the state and local level. At the same time, the party committees carved out new roles in raising soft money for the presidential campaign and channeling this money to the state and local parties for grassroots voter mobilization.

On the other hand, these new capabilities make the national committee an even more attractive resource for presidents. Naturally, presidents want the new party power to be at their service, and every president in recent memory has kept his party's national committee on a short leash. RNC Chair Jim Gilmore was edged out in late 2001, for example, because he clashed with the White House over control of the committee. Presidents will certainly want the party committees to mobilize all those members of Congress whom they recruited, trained, financed, and helped elect to support the president's program. Also, presidents in their first term will want to draw on the assets of the national party for their reelection campaigns, as much as campaign finance rules permit. So there is considerable pressure on these stronger national parties to put their capabilities at the service of presidential goals.

Effects on Congress

At around the time that the Hill committees have become much more active in recruiting and supporting party candidates, Congress members have become more likely to cast legislative votes with the majority of their party (as Chapter 13 shows). Did these new campaign resources help convince Congress members to support their party's positions on bills? To this point, the party committees have not given out campaign money and services on the basis of a candidate's support for the party's program. As the case of the Pennsylvania primaries shows, their support goes to competitive races rather than to candidates who are ideologically "pure."[22]

However, the committees have not been bashful in reminding members, especially newly elected members, that the party played some role in their election success. Party campaign help is only one part of the story of party support in Congress, but the remarkable cohesion of the post-1994 Republican majority in the House has surely been bolstered by the party leadership's financial and other support for Republican candidates. Constituency pressures will always come first in Congress, but the more senators and representatives can count on campaign support from the congressional party, the more open they will be to party-based appeals.

Relationships within the National Party

For years, the three national committees of each party—the DNC or RNC and the party's Hill committees—had a number of reasons to cooperate with one another. All three committees benefit from voter registration and get-out-the-vote drives, and it is often

WHEN PARTY COMMITTEES COMPETE FOR A CANDIDATE

At a time when U.S. House races are less and less competitive, Lisa Boscola lived in a district that was up for grabs. The incumbent was retiring in 2004, and the district was closely divided by party. Boscola, the 41-year-old daughter of a steelworker, was halfway through her four-year term as a Democratic state senator in Pennsylvania; if she ran for Congress and lost, she'd still have her state Senate seat.

Rep. Steny Hoyer, the House Democratic whip, heard that Sen. Boscola would be a very attractive candidate for Congress and came to Pennsylvania to meet her. Soon after, the longest-serving House Democrat from the state also urged her to run and invited her to dinner with the rest of the Pennsylvania Democratic delegation in Washington. It was heady stuff. She left the meeting with Hoyer flattered and impressed, sure that she would run for the House.

That did not make Ed Rendell happy. Rendell, Pennsylvania's Democratic governor, asked Boscola to come to the governor's residence for a private dinner to convince her that he needed her to remain in the Republican-controlled state senate. In the end, Rendell proved to be persuasive, and Boscola stayed in the Pennsylvania Senate.

As the number of competitive legislative races shrinks, party committees at different levels, trying to recruit the strongest possible candidates in order to gain or retain seats, are wooing the same small group of likely prospects. The demands of fund-raising, the harsh and polarized atmosphere of modern campaigns, and the pressures of a political career on family life are shrinking the pool of prospective candidates for whom party committees compete.

Source: Sheryl Gay Stolberg, "Wooed for Congress, Fewer Will Say, 'I Do,'" *New York Times,* October 13, 2003, p. A20.

cost-effective for them to work together on candidate recruitment and campaigns. A good example was the coordinated campaign conducted by DNC, the DSCC, and the Iowa Democratic Party in 2002, where Senator Tom Harkin and Governor Tom Vilsack were both facing close races for reelection. With money provided by the campaigns and the national Democratic organizations, the state party and labor unions assembled large numbers of volunteers and paid staff. These staffers then contacted 250,000 homes in Iowa to identify likely Democratic supporters, create a database of their concerns, and deliver absentee ballot requests. The result was a substantial harvest of absentee ballots in races that Harkin and Vilsack narrowly won.[23]

The requirements of the new campaign finance rules, first felt in 2004, now discourage these cooperative efforts among party committees on any activities paid for by soft money. In addition, the party committees compete with one another in several ways, and especially in raising money. They and the state parties seek financial support from the same contributors (and jealously guard their contributor lists) and recruit political talent from the same limited pool (see box on this page). Resources are scarce in party organizing, so it is not surprising that different organizations from the same party will struggle over them.

THE LIMITS OF PARTY ORGANIZATION

In sum, the national party organizations have recently generated remarkable amounts of new money and other resources. They have used these resources, expertise, and energy to become major players relative to the state and local parties and major influences on the lives of many federal and even state-level candidates. Organizations capable of raising and spending a billion dollars during a two-year period are not easily ignored.

This impressive increase in strength has not come at the expense of the state and local parties; in fact, the national parties have used at least some of their resources to build the capabilities of these party organizations. Nor has the national parties' new strength made the local and state party organizations into branch offices of their national parties, following their orders in developing campaign strategy and taking stands on public policy. There are still too many forces in American politics encouraging independence, especially in the local parties, to permit the two major parties to centralize their organization and power. The federal system, in which most public officials are elected at the local level, the effects of the separation of powers, variations among states and local areas in public attitudes and regulation of the parties, and the new BCRA rules that discourage cooperative campaigns between federal and nonfederal candidates all work against a centralized party system.

So as resource-rich as they have become, the American party organizations remain fairly decentralized by international standards. At a time when Americans can be assured of getting the same Big Mac in Cincinnati as they can in San Diego, the American parties lack the top-down control and efficiency, the unified setting of priorities, and the central responsibility that we often find in other nations' parties. Where the party organizations of many other western democracies have had permanent, highly professional leadership and large party bureaucracies, most American party organizations, especially at the local level, are still in the hands of part-time activists and inexperienced professionals. This may indicate that the activities of most American local party organizations do not normally require much specialization or professionalism.[24]

In addition, even the strengthening of the national parties may not be enough to elevate the party organizations into positions of prominence in most Americans' thinking about politics. The parties have increased their emphasis on grassroots campaigning in the form of canvassing and phone banks and have used the information to develop microtargeting that can let them aim specific messages at individuals known to be receptive to those messages. Yet the messages focus on the candidates rather than on the party itself. More professional, service-oriented parties may be better at helping candidates run for office than in expanding the role of the party organization in citizens' political thinking.[25] There is little in American political values that would welcome strong and centralized party organizations with more power in American political life.

The American party organizations are fundamentally flexible and election oriented. Their purpose is to support candidates for office and to make the adjustments necessary to do well in a pragmatic political system. As a result, they have long been led by candidates and officeholders, not by career party bureaucrats. As the political system grows more polarized, the party organizations have taken the opportunity to expand their roles and to add to the polarization. But at least to this point, even though the national party committees now have unprecedented levels of funding and activity, they remain candidate-centered organizations in a candidate-centered political world.

Chapter 5

Party Activists

If you have ever done volunteer work, then you have probably spent time in an animal shelter, a food bank, or a homeless shelter. Volunteering in a political party headquarters is not nearly as common. Yet hundreds of thousands of Americans have devoted hours and sometimes even weeks or months of their time to a political party or its candidates. They have made phone calls, written checks, knocked on doors, contacted reporters, and written more checks. They have driven through the snow to party caucuses, gotten doors slammed in their faces while canvassing, and felt the exhilaration of celebrating a victory (or dreamed of doing so) with others who share their views. These party activists are the lifeblood of the parties; they vote in their party's primary, often contribute to its candidates, influence its issue positions, and affect its culture and performance.

Why would people spend their precious free time on volunteer work for a political party? Most likely because they feel that they get something in return. People who become active in a party organization have some reasons—seek some payoffs—for devoting their time to the party's activities rather than to their television programs, their church, or their tennis game. The party organization, of course, has goals of its own. So the party has to be able to work toward its aims—winning elections, educating the public, and governing—while at the same time allowing its volunteers and leaders to achieve theirs. How it meets this tricky challenge (and whether it does) is determined by the ways it recruits party activists and mobilizes them for action.

WHAT DRAWS PEOPLE INTO PARTY ACTIVITY?

The American political parties have never operated primarily in a cash economy. They have rarely bought or hired more than a small proportion of the millions of labor hours they need. Today, although national and state party headquarters employ growing numbers of professional staff members, most Americans who volunteer in their local parties get no cash in return for their considerable time and skills. Even the old customs of paying precinct workers on Election Day or using government employees as the party's workers at election time are vanishing. What, then, induces all these people to donate their time and effort to try to meet their party's goals?

In their seminal theory, Peter B. Clark and James Q. Wilson identified three types of reasons why individuals become active in organizations of all kinds. *Material incentives* are tangible rewards for activity—direct cash payments or other concrete rewards for one's work. *Solidary incentives* are the intangible, social benefits that people can gain from associating with others, from networking and being part of a group. *Purposive incentives* are intangible rewards of a different kind, based on the sense of satisfaction that comes when people are promoting an issue or principle that matters to them. By exploring these three types of incentives, we can learn a lot about people's motives for becoming and staying involved in party work and about the functioning of party organizations as well.[1]

Material Incentives

Over time, the main material, or tangible, reason why people became involved in party activity was the opportunity to share in the "spoils" gained when a party controlled the government. These "spoils" came in the form of patronage and preferments. *Patronage* is the appointment of an individual to a government job as a reward for party work. Although patronage is very limited today, the party can still provide loyal workers with a base of support if they seek elected office. *Preferments* involve, more generally, granting the favors of government to party supporters. Patronage, access to elected office, and preferments have all played important roles in building and sustaining the American party organizations.

Patronage   Early in the life of the Republic and for many decades afterward, Americans were attracted to party work by the prospect of being rewarded with government jobs. Patronage has been used in other nations as well, but no other party system has relied on patronage as fully and for as long as the American system. When political machines controlled many cities, city governments were staffed almost entirely by loyalists of the party in power.[2] As the price to be paid for their jobs, patronage appointees traditionally "volunteered" their time, energy, and often even a part of their salary to the party organization.

Campaign help was especially expected; American party politics is rich with tales of the entire staff of certain government departments being put to work in support of their boss's reelection. Patronage workers were often called upon to "invest" in the party that gave them their jobs. Even now, when such practices are usually frowned on and sometimes illegal, government employees can still face a lot of pressure to contribute time or money to their party.

But at the same time as government employment was growing, the number of patronage jobs available to the parties was shrinking dramatically. Most government employees are now hired under civil service and merit systems, in which applicants get jobs based on their scores on competitive exams. The number of full-time federal positions filled by political appointees has dwindled over the years to fewer than 10,000 today, many of them high-level policy-making positions. States and cities have followed the same path, though more slowly.

The Supreme Court has helped to dismantle patronage at the state and local levels. In 1976 and 1980, the Court ruled that some county political employees could not be fired simply because of a change of the party in power. The Court went further in a 1990 Illinois case, determining that politically based hiring and promotion violated the First Amendment freedoms of speech and association. In each case, the Court agreed that party affiliation might be a relevant qualification in filling policy-making positions, but not in lower level offices.[3] Even where patronage positions remain, it has gotten harder for parties to use them as incentives for *party* activity. In an age of candidate-centered politics, elected executives are more interested in using patronage to build their own political followings than to strengthen the party organization.

Yet some patronage is likely to survive as long as it is attractive to both political leaders and their followers. Mayors, governors, and presidents will continue to reserve top policy-making positions for their loyal supporters. Legislatures will remain reluctant to bring their staff members under the protection of civil service systems. Civil service rules for governmental employees can be bypassed by hiring politically loyal, "temporary" workers outside of the civil service system, or by channeling party loyalists into jobs in private firms that depend on government business. A few big campaign contributors will continue to be named ambassadors to small and peaceful countries. Wherever political leaders retain discretion over personnel appointments, in short, they will find a way to award them to their trusted political supporters, and these opportunities will attract at least some people to political activity.

Keep in mind that some observers are sorry to lose the practice of patronage (as unsavory as it now seems). The use of patronage was promoted by President Andrew Jackson as a means of encouraging a more democratic and less elitist government.[4] When government jobs are filled (and then protected) only by civil service procedures, it becomes almost impossible for reform-minded leaders to replace a sluggish or ineffective bureaucrat with a more efficient worker. Patronage was also thought to be a means of keeping party organizations strong as instruments of democracy. Material incentives can be very effective in attracting workers. Those who participate for reasons other than material rewards may make other demands, for example, for the party to take an ideological stand that might alienate moderate voters. That could undermine the ability of a party organization to act pragmatically and inclusively.

Patronage jobs in government are not the only employment opportunities a party can offer. Party organizations at the state and national levels now hire hundreds of professional campaign workers, as do consulting firms associated with the parties. To provide services to their candidates, party organizations need computer specialists, pollsters, media production experts, field directors, researchers, fund-raisers, strategists, webmasters, direct mail specialists, and other experts in campaign techniques. Some activists are drawn to party work by the chance of landing these jobs, but in general, patronage is no longer an important force in motivating activists.

Elected Office   Some women and men become party activists because they see party work as a first step toward running for office. This has been true for a long time; about 40 percent of the county chairs interviewed in a 1979–1980 national survey hoped to hold public office, and an earlier study found that one-third of all state party chairs became candidates for elective office after serving the party.[5] Because of primary elections, of course, very few party organizations can simply "give" nominations to public office to loyal party activists. It is far more common for candidates to see the party as one of the bases of support for winning votes and, in some areas, as the most important one. Candidates need advice, know-how, people (staff and volunteers), and money, and the party remains a likely source of all of these. So the lure of party support in a later campaign for elected office may bring some people into party work.

Preferments   Party activity can bring tangible rewards for some people, other than elective or appointive office. Because public officials can use at least some discretion in distributing government services and in granting government contracts, there is the potential for political favoritism. Some people make contributions of money or time to their party in the hope of attracting these favors. A big giver might, for example, be hoping to win a government contract to build a new school or library. It is no accident that leaders of the construction industry are so active politically in states and localities that spend millions every year on roads and public buildings.

There are other forms of preference as well. Potential activists may hope for special treatment such as tolerant inspection of their restaurant by the health department, faster than usual snow removal in front of their place of business, or admission to a crowded state university. It may also involve the granting of scarce opportunities, such as liquor licenses or cable television franchises, in return for some form of political support.

Reformers have promoted a number of safeguards over the years to limit government's discretion in giving out benefits and buying goods and services from private firms. Examples are competitive and sealed bidding, conflict of interest statutes, and even affirmative action. Yet, because the potential benefits are so great for both sides, there always seem to be ways of evading even the tightest controls. Even many reformers don't want to eliminate *all* government discretion in the awarding of contracts just in order to stamp out *political* discretion. The result is that preferments may have taken the place of patronage as the main material incentive for political activity. Unfortunately for party leaders, however, now it is elected officials who grant the preferments, not the party leaders themselves.

Solidary (Social) Incentives

Many more people are drawn to party work by the social contact that it provides. In an age when some people's closest relationship is with their computer or their television, the face-to-face contact found at a party headquarters or caucus provides a chance to meet like-minded people and to be a part of an active group. Family traditions may lead some young adults to go to party activities looking for social life, just as others may look to a softball league or a bar. Some find it exciting to meet local officials or others who appear on the news. For whatever reason, researchers find that a large number of party activists cite the social life of party politics as a valuable reward.[6] This is especially true for people who involve themselves in campaign activities; those who confine their party activism to writing checks, of course, are not likely to get much social benefit.

These social contacts may produce other rewards as well. Networking has become a standard means of looking for a job and searching for new business. Young lawyers may find potential clients among the activists and elected officials they meet in the party organization. Real estate agents can learn about prospective home sellers and buyers in party activities. More generally, involvement in a party can help people feel a part of something larger than themselves—a charismatic leader, an important movement, a moment in history. The party can be a small island of excitement in a sea of routine.

Purposive (Issue-Based) Incentives

To an increasing extent, people are led to party activism by their commitment to particular issues or attitudes about the proper role of government. Someone dedicated to abortion rights, for example, might begin by working for a pro-choice Democratic candidate and then come to see the candidate's party as a vehicle for protecting abortion rights. A property rights activist may be attracted to the Republican Party by its statements about the value of private ownership.

Other groups compete for the attention of these activists; the abortion rights supporter, for instance, could also work effectively through organized interests, such as NARAL Pro-Choice America and Planned Parenthood. But the parties hold enough attraction for issue-oriented activists that in recent years, most of those who volunteer for party work seem to be motivated by a desire to use the party as a means to achieve policy goals[7] (see "A Day in the Life," page 89). Although we do not have comparable data on earlier periods, there is reason to believe that this was far less true of party workers a generation or two ago.[8] The energy and passion in party organizations come increasingly from issue-driven activists—those on the right in the Republican Party and those on the left for the Democrats.

Issue-based party activism has played a vital role in shaping politics at all levels. The victories of Ronald Reagan in the 1980s owed a lot to the efforts of Christian fundamentalists in the Republican Party, who backed Reagan in order to legalize school prayer, end pornography and legal abortion, and overturn gay rights laws. Many conservative Christian groups worked for George W. Bush's reelection for the same reasons. As these examples show, an attractive party leader who is seen as taking clear and principled positions on issues can motivate people who share these principles, and who find these leaders compelling, to become more active in their party. Some issues and ideological movements have had enough power to lead activists to switch parties. The abortion and race issues, for example, induced many formerly Democratic pro-lifers and southern conservatives to join the Republican Party beginning in the 1970s, and they soon cemented a set of favored issue positions into the platform of their new party.[9]

A large proportion of these issue-based activists are convinced that their activity has made a difference; in one massive survey, three-quarters of those who reported that they had volunteered in a campaign believed that their involvement had affected at least some votes.[10] So even though it might seem irrational to spend a lot of time on party activity in support of an issue that could be termed a "collective good"—one that, if achieved, will benefit the whole society rather than just the activists who worked hard to achieve it—large numbers of people become active in a party to do just that. Others become party activists out of a more general sense of civic obligation or a belief that citizen participation is essential in a democracy.

PARTIES ON CAMPUS

Two main concerns drew Shane Kennedy into College Republicans (CRs): his feelings about national security and his Christian faith. After graduating from high school in a small Indiana town, Shane joined the army and spent more than three years stationed in Germany. The September 11 attacks took place during his service, as did the early months of the Iraq war. By the time he started college in 2004, he had developed strong feelings about America's national defense and foreign policy, and he wanted to get involved in party politics. But which party? "I see myself as a moderate," he said, "and I really didn't know which to join: the Democrats or Republicans.

"At the time, Mel Gibson's film *The Passion of the Christ* was about to open. I was surprised to see a lot of columns in the campus newspaper and in the national media written by people who labeled themselves as Democrats or left-wingers who were so quick to discredit the movie even before it hit the theatres. They hadn't even seen it yet, but they were criticizing it. That made me really mad, and for the first time opened my eyes to the political agendas that most of the media possess. I believe that this country was built under God; I'm certain of that. So many organizations want a more secular society, but I don't think that's good for the country. So I thought I'd check out the College Republicans. I went to some meetings, attended debates, made friends, and found people I agreed with. During this time I found myself learning a lot from these people, as well as strengthening my feelings about government. I saw how left-wing the campus is and how anti-war it is, and after analyzing it I decided that the Republican Party is definitely the party I want to support.

"Now I'm the Social Director for the College Republicans, throwing parties at which we have a good time together, going bowling, playing golf, and holding many professional events. We're an informal group, but I've been proud of the way we functioned in the last campaign. George W. Bush didn't really need our help in Indiana, but we did help with the Mitch Daniels for Governor campaign, and I was impressed with the amount of effort from all these full-time students in electing the first Republican Governor in Indiana in 16 years.

"Don't get me wrong," he says; "I think both parties have their good points and that having a two-party system is excellent. It is the fabric of our democracy. It's not that I think everything the Democrats do is wrong. Their ideas deserve to be debated and I want to hear and analyze what they have to say. I will be the first to admit when I am wrong, and I dare say, it happens a lot. But during the war in Iraq, it seemed to me that the Kerry campaign was bashing the war for nothing more than political gain. It isn't enough just to support the troops if you don't support the cause for which we're fighting. When I was in Turkey during the beginning months of the war, I read many columns in the papers in which people were against the war. I had a very hard time stomaching this.

"Being 24 years old and at this important point in my life, I am very content with working and supporting the right. I feel as if my ideals are justified and correct and look forward to what the future holds within politics for me. You know the old saying that anybody who isn't a Democrat at 25 has no heart, but anyone who's not a Republican by 40 has no brain? I guess I'm just getting a head start on that whole process."

Mixed Incentives

Most party organizations rely on a variety of incentives. Activists who hope for a political job or some other preferment work together with those motivated by a particular issue and with those who come to party activities for social contact. That can produce conflict among party volunteers who are motivated by different incentives. Someone who became a Democratic activist to work for abortion rights, for instance, is not likely to be satisfied with a party that supports a pro-lifer running on the Democratic label. Others who participate in the party for social reasons may feel that the party ought to be a "big tent," including people who differ in their attitudes toward abortion.

The incentive that recruits people to party work, of course, may not be the incentive that keeps them there. Several studies suggest that activists who come to the party to fight for certain issues are more likely to remain in the party if they come to value the social contact that it gives them. The motive that sustains their party work, in short, tends to shift to solidary incentives: friendships, identification with the party itself, and other social rewards.[11] It may be that committed issue activists simply burn out or that the pragmatic American parties, in their effort to remain flexible enough to win elections, do not always provide the level of ideological dedication needed to sustain party workers whose lives revolve around a set of uncompromising ideals.

Professionals and Amateurs

Drawing on research on these incentives for party work, scholars have classified party activists into two types, based on the role that they play in the organization and the expectations that they have for it. One type of party activist is the ***professional*** (sometimes known as "pragmatist")—the party worker whose first loyalty is to the party itself and whose operating style is pragmatic. These are the party "regulars" who support their party in good times and bad, when it nominates candidates whom they approve of and even when it doesn't. A very different type is the ***amateur*** (or "purist")—the issue-oriented activist, motivated by purposive incentives who sees party activity as only one means of achieving important political goals.[12] (On the differences between these two types, see Table 5.1.)

A party organization populated by amateurs may behave very differently from a party dominated by professionals. Above all, amateur activists are drawn into the party in order to further some issues or principles; for them, the issue is the goal and the party is the means of achieving it. If the party, or its candidates, pulls back on its commitment to their issue, they may pull back on their commitment to the party. So they tend to be less willing to make compromises in their positions in order to win elections. (An example of this is the real-life amateur activism of Martin Sheen, star of television's *The West Wing*; see the box on page 92.) Amateur activists are likely to insist on full participation within the party organization in order to put their issues at the top of the party's agenda. When they come to lead party organizations, they often bring a strong push for reform in both the party's internal business and in the larger political system.

For professionals or pragmatists, on the other hand, the goal is the success of the party in elections; issue positions and candidates are the means of achieving that goal. If they believe that their party is most likely to win by downplaying an issue, moderating a position, or nominating a candidate who is popular but not in lockstep with their views on major issues, then that is the course they are likely to favor. Party leaders, then, must

TABLE 5.1   Comparing Professionals and Amateurs

	Professionals	*Amateurs*
Political style	Pragmatic	Purist
What do they want?	Material rewards (patronage, preferments)	Purposive rewards (issues, ideology)
Their loyalty is to:	Party organization	Officeholders, other political groups
They want the party to focus on:	Candidates, elections	Issues, ideology
The party should choose candidates on the basis of:	Their electability	Their principles
The style of party governance should be:	Hierarchical	Democratic
Their support of party candidates is:	Automatic	Conditional on candidates' principles
They were recruited into politics through:	Party work	Issue or candidate organizations
Their SES level is:	Average to above average	Well above average

find a balance between the demands of the growing numbers of issue-oriented, purist activists and those of their more pragmatic colleagues. It is a common problem in modern society: whether to remain loyal to the group (or the nation) in order to keep it strong and vibrant or to give priority to the principles for which the group was formed.

There is some evidence, however, that this conflict is not as troublesome as it may seem; differences in attitudes between amateurs and professionals do not always show up clearly in their behavior. In a study of delegates to state nominating conventions, amateurs were just as likely as professionals to support candidates who seemed electable rather than those whose ideology they shared.[13] Among county party chairs in 1972, a time when amateurs were thought to hold the upper hand, at least in the Democratic Party, the amateurs did not differ from professionals in their effort to communicate within the party, maintain party morale, or run effective campaigns.[14] And close elections tend to bring out more professional orientations in party activists—a greater willingness to sacrifice ideological purity in order to win. In current politics, the lines between the two groups have been blurred in that the national parties are hiring more strategists and consultants who are dedicated not just to winning races but to achieving a set of ideological goals as well.

HOW DO PARTIES RECRUIT ACTIVISTS?

Like almost all other volunteer groups, party organizations have had an increasingly difficult time attracting willing volunteers. Except at the national level and in some states where there has been an increase in paid positions and exciting professional opportunities, parties often have few effective means of enlisting new activists. To add to the challenge, state laws often take at least part of the recruitment process out of the party's hands. Rules requiring open party caucuses and the election of party officials in primaries limit the party's control over its personnel. This can lead to the takeover of a local (or

MARTIN SHEEN: "AMATEUR" DEMOCRATIC ACTIVIST

Martin Sheen is an activist for social justice in real life, just as he is on television. The actor, who stars as former president Josiah Bartlet on NBC's award-winning series *The West Wing,* first became involved in political activism in the mid-1980s when he rejoined the Catholic Church and became committed to the work of peace activists and priests Philip and Daniel Berrigan. Since that time he has taken part in numerous demonstrations for social justice, including a prayer vigil to protest the war in Iraq in 2003.

His support for environmental protection and gun control, among other issues, has led him to endorse and work for some Democratic candidates. Sheen campaigned for Democratic presidential candidates Al Gore in 2000 and Howard Dean in 2004 and filmed a television ad criticizing candidate George W. Bush's gun control record in Texas; in a media appearance he termed Bush a "moron."

Sheen's political activities are driven primarily by his commitment to a set of ideals, not to individual candidates or to the Democratic Party as a whole. "It doesn't matter if you are a Republican or a Democrat or conservative or independent," he says. "You have no excuse if you are a conservative not to be concerned about the environment. You are equally responsible. Future generations are not going to ask us what political party were you in. They are going to ask what did you do about it, when you knew the glaciers were melting."

His commitment is intense enough that Sheen has been arrested for civil disobedience 64 times at peace and social justice demonstrations. In fact, the continuance of *The West Wing* for some time depended in part on Sheen's political activity; on probation for a previous arrest, he would risk a prison sentence if he were to be arrested again.

Just as Sheen fits the definition of a political "amateur," Robert Strauss is the consummate party "professional." A former Democratic National Committee chair, Strauss has supported both conservative southerners and liberal Democrats. In the 2000 Democratic presidential primaries, he supported Al Gore for the nomination but also donated money to the primary campaign of Gore's rival, Bill Bradley. Why? For Strauss, the important point is the success of the party rather than any specific candidate or issue.

Sources: David Kupfer, "Martin Sheen," *The Progressive,* July 2003; Susan Feeney, "Texans Making Dual Donations in Presidential Race," *Dallas Morning News,* August 22, 1999, p. 1.

even a state) party organization by an intense group of issue activists (see Chapter 3). At the least, it leaves a party vulnerable to shifts in its direction as some leaders and activists move on and new, self-recruited leaders take their places.

Finding Volunteers: Is Anybody Home?

In a much discussed set of writings, political scientist Robert Putnam has shown that Americans' participation in community activities has declined in recent years. Party organizations are not alone in having to search for volunteers; groups ranging from churches to bowling leagues have been starved for participants. Fewer people are involving themselves in the face-to-face activities of politics—attending a political speech or a community meeting—but the lonely activities of check writing and Internet surfing are on the increase. Many culprits have been identified, from the numbers of hours Americans spend watching television to the increasing numbers of dual-career families. The consequences, Putnam argues, are profound: a reduction in "social capital"—the social connections, values, and trust that enable communities to solve their problems more easily.[15]

The lack of participation in party organizations has been carefully documented. One well-designed survey found in the 1990s that only 8 percent of its national sample reported working on a campaign, and just 5 percent said they were involved in a party organization, among the smallest percentages reporting activity in any type of civic organization. Much larger percentages of people say that they take part in charitable groups, sports, and business and professional groups.[16] Similarly grim conclusions come from the American National Election Studies, in which, in each year since 1994, only 5 percent reported going to any political meetings and only 3 percent said they worked for a party or a candidate in 2000.[17] Granted, that is still a lot of people; 3 percent of the adult population would be about 6 million party and campaign activists. But although some of these activists spend a considerable amount of time on political work, mainly at the local level, many others are "checkbook participants" who mail in their contributions but do not volunteer their time and energy.

Party organizations have a constant need for activists of all kinds, so at a time when volunteers are in short supply, the parties are very likely to accept whatever help is available. The nature of that help often varies from one political period to another, depending on the events in the political world at that time. The nature and direction of the Democratic Party were heavily influenced by the influx of liberals activated by the Vietnam War and the civil rights movement in the 1960s and 1970s. Tax revolts in the 1980s and efforts to limit the number of terms that incumbents could serve brought new blood into Republican Party organizations. Currently, activists from the conservative Christian community are bringing their energies and their beliefs into local and state Republican Parties. Because this recruitment process often depends on the presence of magnetic personalities and powerful issues, it tends to take place in spurts rather than continuously. It produces generational differences among party activists in which political outlooks may differ considerably, depending on the time at which individuals became active.[18]

The parties' recruitment system, then, is not very systematic, and it is closely interrelated with the movements and the passions in the larger society at the time. Yet, although the parties have only limited control over their own recruitment, it has major impact on the parties' ability to achieve their goals. A local Democratic Party whose activists come mainly from labor unions will have different concerns and styles from a local Democratic Party dominated by environmental activists, and a Republican organization run by local business leaders can differ from one dominated by the Religious Right. Depending on the nature of the community that these parties are trying to persuade, these local parties may have different levels of success in elections as well.

Means, Motive, and Opportunity

We have seen that there are several incentives for people to become active in a party, but relatively few people do. What influences an individual's decision to try to meet his or her needs through involvement in party politics? Three sets of factors are most important. They include whether the individual has the resources to take part, the attitudes that support involvement, and whether anybody has asked him or her to do so.[19]

The resources—the means—needed to become a party activist include time, money, and civic skills. It takes free time to help plan a party's activities, canvass or call people, and attend other party events. People need money if they plan to make contributions to the party organization or its candidates, and they may need funds as well to get to party conventions and other events. Their educational levels help to determine how much money and time they have available.

Their attitudes toward politics are also important. People are more likely to take part if they are interested in what happens in campaigns and concerned about the workings of government, if they have a feeling of attachment to a party, and if they believe that their involvement could make a difference. Most of these attitudes are related to one's income and education levels and thus add to their impact.

The third important characteristic is quite simple: Has anybody asked them? The parties now have a whole arsenal of tools to contact potential activists: e-mail, regular mail, websites, telemarketing, and in-person canvassing. However, most appeals to take part in campaign work—and especially most *successful* appeals—come from friends or other people known to the potential activist. Over the years, most activists have reported that they first became involved with the party as a result of these informal, personal requests for help.[20] Being asked to participate is a powerful motivator; in a major study, almost half of those who were asked to do campaign work said yes. Most people are never asked, however; only about 12 percent of the respondents in that study reported that anyone had asked them to work on a campaign.[21] That helps to explain why the proportion of party activists is relatively small.

WHAT KINDS OF PEOPLE BECOME PARTY ACTIVISTS?

Who are these party activists who play a wide range of roles in party affairs, from campaigning on behalf of party candidates and serving as delegates to party nominating conventions to answering phones and e-mail at party offices? How representative are they of the rest of the American population?

People from "Political Families"

Although they differ in motivations, American party activists have several characteristics in common that set them apart from the general population. First, they often come from families with a history of party activity. Studies indicate that many party activists had an adult party activist in their immediate family when they were growing up.[22] Consider the case of George W. Bush. His grandfather was a long-time Republican state and national party official and U.S. senator from Connecticut. His dad, a former Republican National Committee chair, had served his party in many other posts as well before becoming president of the United States. Some of his siblings have been involved in Republican politics, including his brother Jeb, who served in the cabinet of a Republican governor and then won the governorship of Florida himself. His nephew, George P. Bush, represented Republicans Abroad in campaigning for his uncle's reelection in 2004. With such a background, politics becomes the family business.

Better Educated and Wealthier than Average

A second distinctive characteristic of party activists is that they tend to have higher incomes, more years of formal education, and higher-status occupations than does the average American. People with incomes over $75,000 are four times more likely to do campaign work as are people whose income is at or below the poverty line. As would be expected, this gap between wealthy and poor is greater among those who contribute money to the parties. Even protest activity is more frequent among the wealthy than among the poor![23]

This tendency for party activists to be better educated and wealthier than the average citizen may seem perfectly natural; people with more money and higher education are more likely to have the means to participate in politics, the interest in political affairs, and the expectation that they would be successful at it. So we might expect this pattern to hold in other democratic nations as well. But that is not the case. Most other democracies have a viable socialist party that recruits many of its activists from the ranks of organized labor. That tends to dampen the relationship between party activism and higher education and wealth.

In fact, it was not always true of American politics either. The urban political machines tended to recruit party workers and leaders who were more representative of the populations with which they worked. For many lower-status Americans, the jobs and favors the machines could provide were probably the crucial reasons for their activism. When patronage and other material incentives dwindled, the social character of these parties changed. A comparison of county committee members from both Pittsburgh parties in 1971, 1976, and 1983 shows that as machine control declined, the education levels of party workers increased.[24] So as issue-based incentives become more common in the American parties, the educational and income differences between party activists and the average citizen tend to grow.

The social characteristics of Democratic activists differ from those of Republicans, just as the social bases of the parties' voters do. Democratic activists are more likely than their Republican counterparts to be black, union members, or Catholic. But differences in education, income, and occupation between the parties' activists have declined in recent years. Although they may come from different backgrounds and certainly hold different political views, the leaders of both parties are drawn especially from the higher-status groups in American society—even more now than in decades past.[25] As a result, it is even more true in the United States than in many other nations that party activism and other forms of active political participation amplify the voices of privileged groups.

Different Agendas

In addition to these differences in income, education, and family background, party activists also differ from other Americans in the types of issues that concern them the most. When one group of researchers asked campaign workers in the 1990s what issues had led to their activism, at the top of their lists were questions of education, abortion, the economy, and human needs (including Social Security and Medicare, jobs, health care, and housing). Almost one in five mentioned abortion, a larger proportion than is usually found in polls of citizens as a whole, and one in four mentioned education. International issues were close to the bottom of the list.[26]

The activists' issue agendas varied according to their levels of income and education. Higher-income activists expressed greater concern about abortion and the environment, whereas lower-income activists' involvement was more likely to have been motivated by a concern about basic human needs.[27] To the extent that higher-income activists are better represented in the parties, issues such as abortion may get more attention in party activities than such issues as housing and health care, at least in recent years.

The types of issues that most clearly divide Democratic from Republican activists have changed over time. In the early 1970s, one of the primary distinctions between the two major parties' activists was the question of social welfare—how much of a role government should have in issues such as welfare and other social services. At that time, there was much greater similarity between the two parties' activists on the abortion issue. Today, in contrast, there are few issues that more clearly divide Democratic from Republican activists than their views on abortion.[28]

More Extreme Views

Most significantly, party activists (and people who take active roles in other areas of politics as well) tend to hold more extreme views on issues than does the average American. In recent decades, there has been a tendency for liberals to become more active as Democrats and for conservatives to dominate activity within the Republican Party, and this gap between the two parties' activists in their issue positions has become more pronounced within the last 15 years.[29] This has been true of Democrats and Republicans in Congress, too, as we will see in Chapter 13.

The widening of the gap seems to be due mainly to the increasing conservatism of Republican activists. Issue-oriented activists have made even more of a mark on Republican Party organizations recently than among Democrats. One study found that since 1994, when Republicans gained a majority in both houses of Congress, Republican activists have been motivated by issues and principles to an even greater extent than Democratic activists have. So now, on most issues, those active in the Republican Party have stood even further to the right of the average voter than Democratic activists have placed themselves to the left of the average voter.[30] This growing issue schism between the two parties' activists can have profound effects on the party's appeals and its candidates.

Fitting all these findings together creates a complicated picture of party activists. The major parties attract men and women with the time and financial resources to afford political activity, the attitudes that make politics a priority to them, and the connections with others who are similarly engaged. These activists also tend to be brought into party activity by controversial issues, are more polarized by party than was the case in the mid-1900s, and are much more polarized in their attitudes than are other citizens. These findings raise an important question: If the parties' volunteers differ from the average American in their income levels, their concern about the issues of current politics, and the intensity and extremism of their views, then how well can they connect their interests and their issue stands with those of the public whom they hope to persuade?

PARTY ACTIVISTS AND DEMOCRACY

We have explored the reasons why people are drawn to party activity, the characteristics of individuals who become activists, their differences from the average American, and the growing gulf between Democratic and Republican activists in their attitudes toward issues. This chapter concludes with three major questions about these findings. Does it matter if party activists are not very representative of other adult Americans? What effects will the increase in issue-oriented, "amateur" activists have on the party organizations? How do the characteristics of Republican and Democratic activists affect party organizational strength?

The Problem of Representation

In comparison with many other democratic nations, as has been just shown, there is a greater difference between American party activists and other citizens in their income and education levels. Other qualities widen the gulf between party activists and the people whom they aim to represent. Activists are more concerned with some types of issues—abortion is a good example—than are most nonactivists, and party activists are often more extreme in their issue positions than are other people who identify with their party. The Democratic Party is led by officeholders, party officials, and volunteers who are typically more liberal than the average Democrat, and the leaders and activists of the Republican Party tend to be more conservative than other Republican identifiers. And the gap between both parties' activists and the average voter has increased since the 1980s.

If party activists do not seem to share the concerns of other citizens, then it is not surprising that many Americans think of the party organizations as alien places. When those most involved in party activities give the appearance of being "true believers" on contentious issues, that might further drive away average citizens. After the 2004 elections, for example, Republican Sen. Arlen Specter of Pennsylvania predicted that the Senate would probably not confirm a Supreme Court nominee who was likely to overturn abortion rights. In response to Specter's prediction, a leader of the Southern Baptist Convention who had become a Republican activist, threatened, "He either gets with the program or we shove him aside."[31]

There is a delicate balance to be achieved in party politics. When the two parties sound too much alike on issues, citizens may not feel that they have clear choices in politics. Democracy can be well served when the major parties take clear and distinctive stands on major policy questions. However, when Republican and Democratic activists take polarized positions, especially on questions that are not central to most Americans' daily lives, and try to marginalize anyone who disagrees, then the parties expose themselves to public distrust, an old problem in American politics.

Amateurs and Pressure for Internal Party Democracy

Another important influence on the party organizations is the increase in the proportion of amateur activists. These activists tend to be not just issue-oriented but also concerned with internal party democracy. In the past four decades, they have come to demand a much louder voice in the party's organization and activity, and their demands have been met. Party leaders depend on activists for many things. So party leaders at various levels work hard to mobilize support within their own organizations and to tolerate at least some degree of internal party democracy in order to retain their volunteers' loyalty.

It could be argued that their success in making the parties—and especially the Democratic Party—more participatory has weakened the discipline of the party organization. Much of the discipline in the classic party machine resulted from the willingness and ability of party leaders to give or withhold material rewards. A disobedient or inefficient party worker sacrificed a patronage job or the hope of one. The newer incentives cannot be given or taken away so easily. A local Republican organization is not likely to punish an errant, ideologically motivated activist by ending the party's support of school prayer. Even if it did, the activist could find many other organizations that may be more effective at pursuing that goal, such as religious lobbies or other organized interests.

On the other hand, a party organization dominated by amateur activists could be strengthened by its commitment to internal democracy. Rank-and-file activists who are contributing their time and effort in the service of a strongly held principle and who feel sure that their views are taken seriously by party leaders may be even more likely to work hard on the party's behalf. Granted, it is easier to imagine a strong and disciplined party organization when it is composed of party professionals who are dedicated to the party's success above all else. But the growing importance of issue-based motives for party activism does not necessarily mean a threat to strong party organizations.

Activists and Party Strength

Strong party organizations, however, have often been considered a threat to American politics. Since the beginning, American political culture has been dominated by a fear that a few people, responsible to no one but themselves, will control the selection of public officials and the choice of policies in "smoke-filled rooms." The result has been a series of efforts to keep the parties from playing too powerful a role in the lives of candidates, elected officials, and voters.

Several characteristics of party activists help to keep the parties decentralized and limited in power. The shortage of volunteers means that party organizations have to pay attention to their activists' concerns; that prevents a centralization of party power (unless, of course, the party activists push for such a centralization, as they sometimes have). The concern of many activists for internally democratic parties also restrains the authority of party leaders at the top. And, in turn, because power in the American parties is diffused through the various levels of party organization, precinct committee members, city leaders, county officials, and activists at all levels are free to define their own political roles and to nourish their separate bases of party power.

The traditional worry about the excesses of party power, then, is probably misplaced. There have been few occasions in American history when the parties have been able to corral the kinds of incentives and resources that they would need in order to flesh out the party organization that they would like or that the state laws detail. The thousands of inactive precinct workers and unfilled precinct positions testify to that. The parties have had no alternative but to try to recruit activists who vary in their backgrounds, styles, and motives, with all the challenges and limits that involves.

PART THREE

The Political Party in the Electorate

If there were a Pollsters' Hall of Fame, surely the first question in it would be: Generally speaking, do you usually think of yourself as a Republican, a Democrat, an independent, or what? The question is meant to classify *party identifiers*—people who feel a sense of psychological attachment to a particular party. If you respond that you do usually think of yourself as a Democrat or a Republican, then you are categorized as belonging to the *party in the electorate*—the second major sector of the American parties. Party identifiers (also called *partisans*) make up the core of the party's support: the people who normally vote for a party's candidates and who are inclined to see politics through a partisan's eyes. They are more apt to vote in their party's primary elections and to volunteer for party candidates than are other citizens. They are, in short, the party organization's, and its candidates', closest friends in the public.

Survey researchers have measured Americans' party loyalty since the 1940s. The dominant measure, just cited, has been used in polls conducted by the University of Michigan, now under the auspices of the American National Election Studies (ANES). After asking whether you consider yourself a Republican or a Democrat, the question continues:

[If Republican or Democrat] Would you call yourself a strong [Republican or Democrat] or a not very strong [Republican or Democrat]? [If independent, no preference, or other party] Do you think of yourself as closer to the Republican Party or to the Democratic Party?

Using these answers, researchers classify people into seven different categories of party identification: strong party identifiers (Democrats or Republicans), weak identifiers (Democrats or Republicans), independent "leaners" (toward the Democrats or Republicans), and pure independents.[1]

Note that this definition is based on people's attitudes, not on their actual voting behavior. Strong party identifiers usually vote for their party's candidates, but the essence of a party identification is an attachment to the idea of the party itself, distinct from feelings about any particular candidates. Someone can remain a committed Republican, for example, even while choosing to vote for the Democratic candidate in a specific race. Given the large number of elective offices in the United States and the value American culture places on independence, we can often find party identifiers who vote for some candidates of the other party. In the same sense, we do not define the party electorate by the official act of registering with a party. Almost half of the states do not have party registration, and in states that do, some voters change their party attachments long before they change their official registration.[2]

The party electorate's relationship with the other two party sectors, the party organization and the party in government, is not always close and cooperative. Although the party cannot survive without the party identifiers' support, party organizations and candidates see their identifiers as a group of customers to be courted at each election but often ignored between elections (except for occasional pleas for contributions). Party identifiers, in turn, seldom feel any obligation to the party organization other than to vote for its candidates, if they choose. Party identifiers are not party "members" in any real sense. In these ways, the American parties resemble cadre parties (see page 45): top-heavy in leaders and activists without any real membership, in contrast to the mass-membership parties that have been such an important part of the European democratic experience.

Despite their independence, party identifiers give the party organization and its candidates a continuing core of voter support; the parties, then, don't have to start from scratch in every campaign. The party in the electorate also largely determines who the party's nominees for office will be by voting in primaries. It is a source of potential activists for the organization. Its members may donate money to the party, or they may work in a specific campaign. They help keep the party alive by transmitting party loyalties to their children. The loyalty that links individuals to their party can be strong enough to affect their reactions to particular candidates and issues. It can be the most significant landmark in an individual's mental map of the political world.

A party in the electorate is not just a collection of individuals; it is a coalition of social groups. Our images of the two parties often spring from the types of people the parties have attracted as identifiers. When people speak of the Democrats as the party of the disadvantaged, or of the Republicans as the party of business, they are probably referring, at least in part, to the party in the electorate. The groups in a party's coalition help to shape its choice of nominees and its stands on issues, and in turn those candidates and appeals help to structure the society's elections and political debate.

The three chapters in Part 3 explore the nature and importance of these parties in the electorate. Chapter 6 looks at the development of party identification and its impact on individuals' political behavior. Chapter 7 examines the parties as coalitions of social groups and traces the changes in those coalitions over time. Chapter 8 focuses on the differences between the people who vote and those who do not. These differences have an important effect on the parties' choices in mobilizing their faithful and recruiting new supporters.

Chapter 6

Party
Identification

Think back to your years in elementary school. If you are like millions of other Americans, by the time you completed sixth grade, you had begun to identify yourself as a Democrat, a Republican, or an independent. This sense of psychological attachment that most Americans develop toward a political party is called a *party identification.*[1] It is an attachment that typically develops early in people's lives and can influence a wide range of political attitudes and behavior. About one-third of Americans call themselves "strong" partisans, and another 28 percent express some party attachment, though not a strong one. Even among those who at first claim to be independents, most admit to some partisan feeling.

Researchers characterize party identification, or party ID, in several ways. Some look at a party attachment as a form of social identity, similar to a religious or ethnic identity. A black college student, for instance, might have a long-standing sense of herself as a Democrat because of the close ties between black Americans and the Democratic Party. Other researchers think of party ID as a perceptual screen—a lasting picture of the political world that, once formed, can filter out any conflicting information the individual may receive. For a third group of researchers, party identification is more changeable; it is like a running tally of an individual's positive or negative experiences with the party's stands or its performance in office. This assessment, which is constantly being updated, can help him or her make efficient voting decisions without bothering to learn much about specific candidates.[2]

These differing perspectives on the nature of party identification can lead us to different conclusions about its stability. But these approaches are not necessarily mutually exclusive; each can help us understand more about the nature of partisanship in American politics. Clearly, a party ID is a form of social identity for large numbers of children and adults; it helps them find their place in the group conflicts that characterize the political world. When this identity is clearly established, it can also serve as a decision-making shortcut. Politics is complicated, even for the political junkies who turn on C-SPAN instead of hip hop or country music. Americans cope with more elections, and therefore more occasions on which they need to make large numbers of political choices, than do citizens of any other democracy. An individual's party ID offers a useful means of cutting through the complexity. It gives the individual a predisposition to support Democratic candidates or Republican candidates without having to do all the research necessary to make a separate decision on each candidate for office or to develop an opinion on each bill the legislature considers.

Just as it can be thought of in several ways, partisanship can be measured in various ways.[3] However we measure it, people's party ID tells us more about their political perceptions and behavior than does any other single piece of information. A party ID will probably be the individual's most enduring political attachment. Where do these party identifications come from?

HOW PEOPLE DEVELOP PARTY IDENTIFICATIONS

Families are the most common source of our first party ID, as they are of so much else in our early lives. People often say that they are Democrats or Republicans because they were brought up that way, just as they may have been raised as a Methodist or a Jew. As children become aware of politics, they absorb their family's judgments about political parties and typically come to think of themselves as sharing their family's partisanship.

Childhood Influences

Party loyalty often develops as early as the elementary grades. Although they do not usually consciously indoctrinate their children into party loyalty, parents are the primary teachers of political orientations in the American culture (see the cartoon on page 103). Their casual conversations and references to political events are enough to convey their party loyalties to their children, just as children learn where their family "belongs" in relation to other social groups. These influences can be powerful enough to last into adulthood, even at times when young adults are pulled toward independence.

This early party ID usually takes hold before children have much information as to what the parties stand for. It is not until the middle-school and high-school years that students begin to associate the parties with general economic interests—with business or labor, the rich or the poor—and thus to have some reasoning to support the party ID that they have already developed. Note the importance of the sequence here. Party loyalty comes first, so it can have a long-lasting impact on attitudes toward politics. Only later do people learn about political issues and events, which may then be filtered, at least in part, through a partisan lens.[4]

Once developed, people's party loyalties are often sustained because their friends, relatives, and coworkers typically share the same partisanship.[5] Some people do leave the party of their parents. Those whose early party loyalty is weak are more likely to change. So are people whose mother and father identified with different parties or who live in a community or work in a setting where the prevailing party influences differ from their own. But when parents share the same party ID, they are more likely to produce strong party identifiers among their children.

Other sources of political learning tend to support a person's inherited party loyalty or at least do not challenge the family's influence. Schools typically avoid partisan politics; they are probably more inclined to teach political independence than partisanship.

THE FAITHFUL REPUBLICANS

During the early and mid-1900s, American churches usually steered clear of partisan conflict even at a time when church-connected political parties existed in Europe. Many churches and other religious groups have become very engaged in politics recently, but they are not likely to lead young people away from their parents' partisan influence. The American parties themselves do very little direct socialization; they do not maintain the large numbers of youth clubs, the social or recreational activities, or the occupational groups that some European parties do.

Influences in Adulthood

These influences on children's and teenagers' political learning are more likely to be challenged beginning in young adulthood, when an individual moves into any of several new environments: college, work, marriage, a new community, and the unexpected honor of paying taxes. At this point in the life cycle, adults can test their childhood party loyalties against their own personal experience with politics. They can see how their favored party performs in matters that concern them, and they can watch the behavior of the other party as well. Their adult experiences may reinforce their early-learned loyalties or may under-mine those loyalties.[6] Or the old loyalties may exist peacefully alongside contradictory new information; people can find out more about candidates and issues, and even change their attitudes toward those political objects, without necessarily changing their party ID.[7]

The longer an individual holds a particular party ID, the more intense it tends to become. Older adults are most likely to hold strong party attachments and least likely to change them. Party ID is more likely to become a habit after decades of political obser-vations and activity. Partisanship may grow stronger across the life cycle because it is so useful a shortcut for simplifying the political decision making of older voters,[8] or because they surround themselves increasingly with others who share their partisan loyalties.

There are times, however, when even committed Democrats and Republicans are driven to change their partisanship. During periods of major party change, when the issue bases of partisanship and the party coalitions themselves are being transformed, some voters desert the partisan tradition of their parents. (We look more fully at the idea of party coalitional change or realignment in the next chapter.) This happened during the social and economic ferment of the New Deal in the 1930s, and we can find more recent examples of the power of major issues to change some people's partisanship. The Bush tax cuts, debate on an abortion bill, and even a local struggle over development can make someone aware that she no longer feels close to the party of her parents. Older adults may be caught up in the excitement of the moment as well, but their partisanship, typi-cally reinforced by years of consistent partisan behavior, resists change much more effec-tively. So when partisan turmoil begins, young adults are more likely than older adults to embrace the change.[9]

PATTERNS OF PARTISANSHIP OVER TIME

Large-scale change in party identifications is the exception, however, and not the rule. Most Americans, once they have developed party loyalties, tend to keep them; partisan-ship becomes a fairly stable anchor in an ever-changing political world. People who do change their party ID normally change only its intensity (for example, from strong to weak identification) rather than convert to the other party.

At the national level, we can see this stability in Americans' responses to the poll question measuring party ID that has been asked in every presidential election year since 1952 by researchers for the American National Election Studies. The data are summa-rized by decade in Figure 6.1; the full data set can be found in Table A.1 in the Appen-dix.[10] The figure shows some change in the overall partisanship of Americans: although Democrats have been in the majority throughout these years, the proportion of Republi-cans has steadily increased. In the 1950s, Democrats outnumbered Republican identi-fiers by a ratio of 1.7 to 1. The gap narrowed decade by decade, and especially beginning in the 1980s, until the two groups of partisans are closer in size today. This increase in Republican support, as we will see in Chapter 7, has been propelled in large part by the gradual movement of white southerners from Democratic to Republican identification.

The change has taken place very slowly, however. In Figure 6.1, look, for example, at the percentage who call themselves strong Republicans (represented by the dark por-tion at the bottom of each Republican column). When summarized by decade, this pro-portion never rises above 14 percent nor drops below 9 percent. The full data set in the

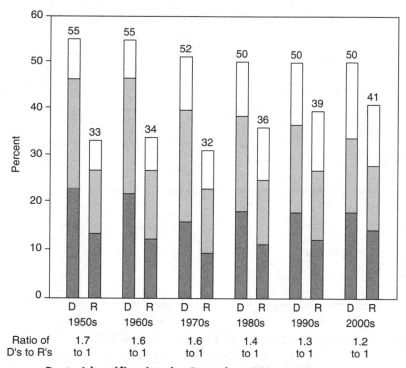

FIGURE 6.1 Party Identification by Decade, 1950s–2000s

Note: Based on surveys of the national electorate conducted immediately before each presidential and congressional election as part of the American National Election Studies program at the University of Michigan. For each party grouping in each decade, the black segment at the base of the bar is the percentage of respondents calling themselves strong Democrats or strong Republicans; in the middle are weak Democrats or Republicans, and at the top is the percentage calling themselves Independents who lean toward the Democratic or the Republican Party. For the full presentation of data for presidential election years, including the "pure" independents, see Table A.1 in the Appendix.

Source: Data made available through the Inter-University Consortium for Political and Social Research.

Appendix shows that over more than 50 years of history, from years when the Republican Party was triumphant to years when it seemed almost dead, the proportion of strong Republicans has stayed within a 7-percentage-point range, between 9 and 16 percent of those surveyed. Overall, the percentage of respondents in each category of partisanship has changed very little from one election year to the next; the biggest change is 7 percent, and the usual difference is just 2 percent.

There is one exception to this story of stable partisanship, and it appears at both the national and individual levels. During an especially turbulent period in recent history—in 1972, 1974, and 1976, a time that included Richard Nixon's landslide reelection as president, the Watergate scandals that caused Nixon to resign, Nixon's subsequent pardon by President Ford, and Ford's own 1976 defeat—researchers interviewed the same set of individuals in three successive surveys. Almost two-thirds of the respondents remained in the same broad category of party identification (44 percent were stable strong/weak Democrats or Republicans, 20 percent stable independents) throughout all

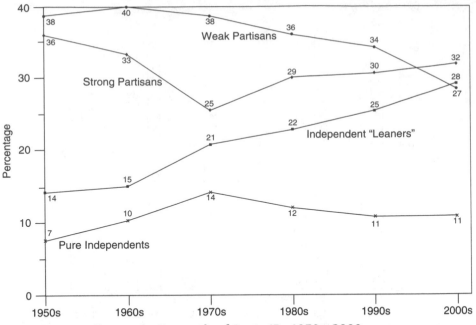

FIGURE 6.2   Change in Strength of Party ID: 1950s–2000s

Note: This is a "folded" party ID scale in which Democrats and Republicans in each category are combined (i.e., the category "Strong Partisans" includes strong Democrats and strong Republicans).

Source: Calculated from American National Election Studies presidential election data and made available through the Inter-University Consortium for Political and Social Research.

three surveys. Only 3 percent actually changed parties.[11] People were more likely to alter their evaluations of prominent politicians and issues than their party ID. Many researchers felt that it would be hard to find better evidence of the stability of party identification than its consistency during these agitated times.[12]

Yet a third of the respondents did change from party identification to independence during these three waves of surveys. In particular (as Figure 6.2 shows), at the national level, there was a big drop in the proportion of respondents calling themselves *strong* partisans (Democrats or Republicans) at this time, and an increase in the percentage of independent "leaners." The three categories of independents grew from 28 percent of the respondents in 1964 to almost 40 percent in 1976. Combined with other events of that time—the political turmoil of the civil rights movement, the protests against American involvement in the Vietnam War, the women's movement, environmental activism—this suggested to a lot of observers that partisanship was fading in the United States.

Has There Been a Decline in Partisanship?

Research in other democracies bolstered the argument that partisanship was in decline. Across the western industrialized world, analysts found a rise in the proportion of independents, a drop in confidence expressed in political parties, and an increase in ***split-ticket*** *voting* (supporting candidates of more than one party).[13] The consequences of this "party decline" would have been profound.[14] What could have caused it? Education levels were rising steadily in democratic nations; perhaps the better educated voters had so much other information available that they didn't need parties as a decision shortcut any more. Maybe candidates were becoming more independent of party ties and influencing other citizens. Perhaps media coverage of politics stressed nonpartisanship or ignored parties.

These explanations produced even more questions, however. If Americans have more information available than ever before, wouldn't they need a device, like a party ID, to help them sift through it? Even though education levels are rising, one of the things we know with greatest certainty about public opinion is that most of us are not very interested in politics, do not know very much about it, and therefore depend on shortcuts with which to make sense of the voting decisions that face us. We may have a wealth of information, but most of us are not motivated to use it. Party ID, then, would probably remain a helpful tool.[15] And among people for whom partisanship is more of a group attachment than a decision-making shortcut, then the increase in information, and even the increase in split-ticket voting, would probably not lead to a long-term decline in partisan feelings.

In fact, indicators of partisanship *have* rebounded since the 1970s. In particular, there has been a resurgence of strong partisanship (see Figure 6.2). The level of strong party identification among voters in 2004 was only five percent lower than it had been in the 1950s, which was considered a very partisan time. At least among those who vote, the decline in party ID has been largely reversed.[16] In fact, in 2004 in some polls, the proportion of voters who considered themselves partisan, and the consistency between partisanship and vote choice, were the highest in more than 20 years.[17] The main changes between the 1950s and today have been a decrease in the proportion of weak partisans combined with a large increase in the numbers of independent "leaners," those who initially call themselves independents but then acknowledge, when probed by poll takers, that they lean toward one party.

Perhaps the revival of party attachment in the 1980s and 1990s was prompted by greater partisanship in Congress and by more partisan political leaders such as President Ronald Reagan and former House Speaker Newt Gingrich. Perhaps partisanship is the normal state of affairs for most Americans, disrupted only temporarily by the ferment of the 1970s. Whatever the reason, party remains an influential political attachment. The evidence of party decline is no longer convincing.

PARTY IDENTIFICATION AND POLITICAL VIEWS

Because of their early development and stability, party loyalties can affect the ways that individuals view politics. Strong partisans often see candidates of their own party as having more attractive characteristics and taking more acceptable issue stands than those of the other party.[18] When a new political candidate begins to get public notice, the reactions of many partisans in the electorate will be colored by their party affiliation. Even when the candidate is well known for other reasons—for instance, when actor Arnold Schwarzenegger first announced his intention to run for governor of California—evaluations of the candidate can quickly divide along party lines once his or her party affiliation becomes known.

Partisanship may influence people's reactions to events as well. Recall the intense controversy after Election Day 2000, when the Supreme Court stopped the recount of votes in some Florida counties and thus decided the presidential election in favor of George W. Bush. In a poll taken two months before the election, 70 percent of Democratic identifiers had said that they approved of the way the Supreme Court was handling its job, and only 18 percent disapproved. A month after the Court's verdict on the presidential race, those numbers had changed markedly. Just 42 percent of Democrats now said they approved of the way the Court was handling its job, and 50 percent said they disapproved. Conversely, approval of the Court among Republicans rose from 60 percent in August 2000 to 80 percent in January 2001. People's reactions to the Court's ruling, then, seem to have been dramatically affected by their party affiliation. Another national poll reported that 60 percent of Democrats described their reaction to the Bush victory as "cheated," compared with 4 percent of Republicans, while 59 percent of Republicans chose the term "thrilled," compared with 6 percent of Democrats.[19]

Party loyalty can affect people's attitudes even when it has to compete with other valued loyalties. Democrat John F. Kennedy was only the second Catholic presidential candidate in American history. Catholics tended to view Kennedy more favorably in that election than Protestants did. Catholic Republicans, however, were not as positive toward Kennedy as were Catholic Democrats. Party ID still made a difference, even among those with the same religious loyalty. Party identification is not the only cause of political attitudes, of course, and people's reactions to particular issues or elected officials may change in the short run, as a result of new information, even as their party ID remains the same. Yet party affiliation helps to condition the way people feel about issues, candidates, and public officials.[20]

PARTY IDENTIFICATION AND VOTING

The most important effect of party attachments is their influence on people's voting behavior. Although party identifiers' support for candidates of their party can't be taken for granted, and the American electoral system discourages faithful party voting—partisans have to fight their way through long ballots, the culture's traditional emphasis on the individual rather than the party, and its distrust of strong parties—party identifiers tend to support their party with a lot of fidelity.

Party Voting

During the past half-century, party identifiers have voted for their party's candidates most of the time. As you can see in Figures 6.3 and 6.4, a majority in each category of partisanship has voted for their party's presidential candidate in every year, except for weak Democrats in 1972 and independent Democrats in 1980 (both GOP landslide years). The most faithful are the strong partisans. Even in the Reagan landslide victory of 1984, when voting Democratic clearly ran against the tide, almost nine out of ten strong Democrats voted for Reagan's Democratic opponent, Walter Mondale, and in the last three presidential elections, at least 96 percent of strong Democrats have supported their party's candidate. However, the prize for party loyalty goes to strong Republicans; only once in 50 years has their support for the GOP presidential candidate dipped below 90 percent,

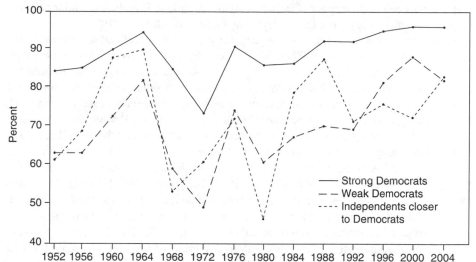

FIGURE 6.3   Percent of Democrats Voting for Their Party's Presidential Candidates, 1952–2004

Note: The numbers for each election year can be found in Table A.2 in the Appendix. Comparable data on voting for the respondent's party's congressional candidates can be found in Table A.3.

Source: American National Election Studies, University of Michigan; data made available by the Inter-University Consortium for Political and Social Research.

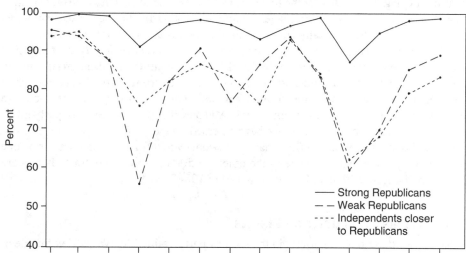

FIGURE 6.4   Percent of Republicans Voting for Their Party's Presidential Candidates, 1952–2004

Note: The numbers for each election year can be found in Table A.2 in the Appendix. Comparable data on voting for the respondent's party's congressional candidates can be found in Table A.3.

Source: American National Election Studies, University of Michigan; data made available by the Inter-University Consortium for Political and Social Research.

and that was due to the appeal of an independent candidate, Ross Perot, who took some Republican votes away from their party's presidential candidate in 1992.

Just as we have seen in the case of party ID, party voting declined somewhat during the late 1960s and early 1970s. There were especially sharp drops in Democratic voting fidelity in 1968 and 1972, as well as during the first Reagan election in 1980. Republican party voting dipped in the 1964 election, in a year when President Lyndon Johnson won a huge victory for the Democrats and in response to Perot's independent candidacy in 1992. During these years, then, strong national electoral trends could pull some groups of partisans away from their party's candidate. But recent studies show that the overall impact of party ID on voting behavior has been on the upswing since the mid-1970s and reached a level by the late 1990s higher than in any other presidential election since the 1950s.[21] Party voting has continued to increase in 2000 and 2004. The polarization of the Republican and Democratic Parties in recent decades has probably helped some voters to clarify their political attachments and to heighten their sense of loyalty to a party and its candidates.

These patterns appear in congressional elections as well. (The data can be found in Table A.3 in the Appendix.) A majority within each group of partisans has voted for their party's congressional candidates in each election, and strong partisans have consistently been the most regular party voters. One key to the Democrats' ability to continue winning congressional majorities in the 1970s and 1980s, at a time when their electoral base was eroding, might have been that they were more faithful than their GOP counterparts in voting for their party's congressional candidates. In 1994, 1996, and 1998, however, Republicans running for Congress got an extra boost in loyalty from their own partisans. This, together with the support of a clear majority of independents, helped them gain control of Congress in 1994 for the first time in 40 years and to keep it in the crucial elections that followed. In a mirror image, Democratic voting fidelity decreased temporarily in the mid-1990s, especially among weak Democrats and Democratic leaners.

Similar results appear in voting at the state and local levels. *Straight-ticket voting*— voting for one party's candidates only—declined among all the partisan groups during the 1960s and 1970s. But most strong Democrats and strong Republicans remained straight-ticket voters. The stronger an individual's party identification was, the more likely he or she was to vote a straight ticket.[22] And as with other indicators of party influence, the decline seems to have stopped and reversed. In the 2004 elections, only 59 congressional districts out of 435 (less than 14 percent) voted for a House member of one party and a presidential candidate of the other—a 50-year low. In contrast, there were 110 such districts in 1996 and as many as 190 in 1984.

Party Versus Candidates and Issues

What causes these ups and downs in the level of party voting? Individuals' voting decisions are affected by the give-and-take of two sets of forces: the strength of their enduring party loyalty (if they have one) and the power of the *short-term forces* operating in a given election. These short-term forces include the attractiveness of particular candidates running that year and the pull of various issues in the campaign. Usually these two sets of forces incline the voter in the same direction; as we have seen, a party ID encourages an individual to see the party's candidates and issue stands in a favorable light.

There are times, however, when an especially attractive candidate or a particularly appealing issue stance—a tax cut or a promise to protect the nation against terrorism—

may lead a voter to desert one or more of his or her party's candidates. At least by some measures, split-ticket voting has been fairly frequent for decades.[23] Voters do not usually split their tickets out of a conscious desire to create a divided government. Rather, voters are more likely to defect from their party ID because they are attracted to a very visible candidate running a well-funded campaign, most often an incumbent of the other party.[24] In the 2004 elections, for example, President Bush won the popular vote in Arkansas by 55 percent, but incumbent Democratic Senator Blanche Lincoln was also reelected with 56 percent of the vote. Typically, those with the weakest party ID or the most ambivalent attitudes about the parties—for example, those who have at least some positive feelings about both parties[25]—are the most likely to defect.

Partisanship as a Two-Way Street

A big challenge in determining the relative importance of party ID, candidate characteristics, and issues in affecting individuals' voting decisions is that these three forces are strongly interrelated. The early studies of party ID in the 1950s assumed that party "came first" in the causal ordering—that it influenced people's feelings about candidates and issues but was not in turn influenced by them. These early studies did not have good measures of how close the voter felt to the candidates on issues.

Since then, with the use of better measures, researchers have shown that there are reciprocal relationships among these three influences. Just as an individual's party loyalty influences the way he or she views politics, feelings about candidates and issues can affect the individual's party ID as well. In particular, there is powerful evidence that reactions to a president's management of the economy (so-called *retrospective evaluations,* in that they refer to past actions rather than hopes for the future) can feed back on party loyalties and weaken or change them. In this way, partisanship can be seen as a kind of "running tally" of party-related evaluations.[26] Even if party ID is usually stable enough to withstand an individual's disappointment in a particular party candidate or in the party's position on an issue or two, an accumulation of these negative experiences can shake or change an individual's partisanship. That is what happened over several decades to the long-standing Democratic loyalties of many conservative white southerners, in response to Democratic administrations' handling of racial and other issues.

In the short run, then, issues and the candidates in a particular election can have a major impact on the outcome, especially now, when the two major parties are so closely matched in numbers of adherents.[27] But party ID has continuing power to influence voters' choices and to affect their feelings about issues and candidates as well. So whether we want to explain the general trends of American voting behavior or the choices of voters in a particular election, party ID plays a prominent role.[28]

PARTY IDENTIFICATION AND POLITICAL ACTIVITY

Another important effect of party ID is that individuals who consider themselves Democrats and Republicans are more involved in political life than are those who call themselves independents. Partisanship is emotionally engaging; it gives partisans a stake in the outcome of political events. So it is the strongest partisans who are the most likely to vote, to pay attention to politics, and to take part in political activities. As in previous

TABLE 6.1 Political Involvement of Partisans and Independents: 2004

	Democrats			Independents	Republicans		
	Strong	Weak	Dem.	Closer to Neither	Rep.	Weak	Strong
Follow public affairs most of the time	40%	23	24	17	23	25	37
Watch programs about campaign on TV	91%	83	88	78	87	83	90
Read about campaign in newspapers	83%	67	64	60	66	63	77
Voted	87%	75	74	54	72	85	95
Tried to influence the vote of others	55%	43	48	35	41	44	65
Displayed button, bumper sticker, sign	35%	15	15	12	11	15	33
Attended rally or meeting	47%	26	25	16	21	20	51
Contributed money to:							
Candidate	16%	5	9	3	3	5	20
Party	13%	4	8	2	2	6	24

Source: 2004 American National Election Study, University of Michigan; data made available by the Inter-University Consortium for Political and Social Research.

years, the 2004 American National Election Studies survey shows that strong Democrats and strong Republicans were more likely than weak identifiers or independents to be interested in politics and to follow reports about public affairs and the campaign on television and in newspapers (Table 6.1).

The strongest partisans are also the most active in other ways. A total of 87 and 95 percent, respectively, of the strong Democrats and Republicans reported having voted in 2004—higher than the turnout levels among weaker partisans or independents.[29] They were also more likely than other citizens to try to persuade other people to vote a certain way, to wear campaign buttons, to display bumper stickers or yard signs, to attend political meetings, and to contribute money to a party or candidate. In fact, strong identifiers were between 15 and 40 percent more likely to attend political meetings and display buttons and signs in 2004 than they were in 2000; the election of 2004 had a powerful impact on strong partisans. The combatants of American electoral politics, in short, come disproportionately from the ranks of the strong Democrats and strong Republicans.

PARTY IDENTIFICATION AND ATTITUDES TOWARD THE PARTIES

Strong party identifiers tend to see a greater contrast between the Republican and Democratic parties than do weak identifiers and independents, both in general and on specific

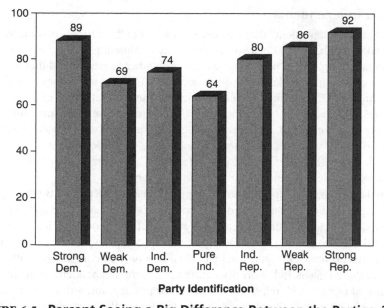

FIGURE 6.5   Percent Seeing a Big Difference Between the Parties: 2004

Source: 2004 American National Election Study, University of Michigan; data made available by the Inter-University Consortium for Political and Social Research.

policy issues (see Figure 6.5). They are more polarized in their evaluations of the two parties' candidates as well as of the parties' ability to govern for the benefit of the nation. Strong partisans are more inclined than weaker partisans and independents to say that their party's president has done his job well and that a president of the opposing party has performed poorly.[30] In the mind of the strong partisan, in short, the political parties are clearly defined and highly polarized along the important dimensions of politics.

These data do not necessarily prove that party ID alone results in greater activity or sharper party images. Other factors also affect people's willingness to become involved in politics. In particular, higher socioeconomic status and the greater political sophistication and easier entry into politics that it often brings can lead people into political activity. The relatively greater involvement of partisans (and, in most years, of Republicans) comes in part from their generally higher socioeconomic status levels as well as from their more ideological commitment to politics.[31] Even so, party ID has a major impact on people's political activity.

THE MYTH OF THE INDEPENDENT

It is intriguing that party loyalties govern so much political behavior in a culture that so warmly celebrates the independent voter. There is clearly a disconnect between the American myth of the high-minded independent—the well-informed citizen who is moved by issues and candidates, not parties—and the reality of widespread partisanship. The problem is with the myth.

Attitudinal Independents

The definition of "independent" that we have used so far in this chapter is someone who tells a poll taker that he or she does not identify with a political party. Studies show that these independents split their tickets more often than other voters do and that they wait longer in the campaign to make their voting decisions. In those ways, they would seem to fit the myth of the thoughtful, deliberative citizen. But they fall short of the mythical picture of the independent in most other ways. They are less well informed than party identifiers are, less concerned about specific elections, and less active politically. They are also less likely to vote. In 2004, as you saw in Table 6.1, independents stayed home from the polls at a higher rate than did party identifiers and scored lower than partisans on virtually every other indicator of political involvement.

Within this group, it is important to distinguish between independents who say they feel closer to one of the two parties (independent leaners) and those who do not ("pure" independents). The independent leaners often turn out to be more politically involved (see Table 6.1) and sometimes even more partisan in voting (especially for president) than weak partisans are (see Figures 6.3 and 6.4). It is only in comparison with strong partisans that these leaners fall short. By contrast, the pure independents typically have the most dismal record, with relatively low levels of political interest and information, turnout, and education. It is the pure independents who are the least involved and least informed of all American citizens.[32]

Behavioral Independents

We can also define independents in terms of their behavior. In his final work, the unparalleled researcher, V. O. Key, Jr., explored the idea of political independence. The picture of the American voter that was emerging from the electoral studies of the 1950s and 1960s was not a pretty one. It showed an electorate whose voting decisions were determined by deeply ingrained party loyalties—an electorate that had not grasped the major political issues and didn't care that it had not.[33]

Key looked for evidence of rational behavior among voters and focused his attention on "party switchers"—those who supported different parties in two consecutive presidential elections—rather than on the self-described independents. In practice, Key's switchers came much closer to the flattering myth of the independent than did the self-styled independents. These party switchers, Key found, expressed at least as much political interest as did the "stand-patters" (those who voted for the same party in both elections). Above all, the switchers showed an issue-related rationality that well fitted the mythical picture of the independent. They agreed on policy issues with the stand-patters toward whose party they had shifted, and they disagreed with the policies of the party from which they had defected.

It is the attitudinal independents, however—those who call themselves independents and express no party preference—who are the subject of the most study. Researchers conclude that they have always been a diverse group containing some who resemble the image of the sophisticated independent but also many of the least involved and informed voters in American politics. The myth that they are a carefully informed and active group of voters who operate above the party fray has withered under the glare of survey research.

Are Independents a Likely Source of Support for Third-Party Candidates?

Even if the attitudinal independents don't know much about politics and don't get involved in much political activity, they still could play an important role in elections. Because they have the weakest ties to the two major parties, they could be more open to the charms of third-party and independent candidates than other citizens are. We can see some evidence of this in presidential elections during the 1990s. One of the biggest stories of the 1992 presidential election was the unprecedented showing of independent candidate Ross Perot. A very rich man, Perot spent millions on a campaign criticizing the two major parties as irresponsible and corrupt. Unlike most independents, Perot flourished rather than faded as the campaign came to an end. He finished with almost 20 million votes, 19 percent of those cast.

On Election Day, Perot did draw most of his votes from self-identified independents and to a lesser extent from independent leaners, as had third-party candidates John Anderson (in 1980) and George Wallace (in 1968) before him.[34] Fully 37 percent of the pure independents said they voted for Perot, compared with only 4 percent of the strong Democrats and 11 percent of the strong Republicans. The same was true of Perot's third-party candidacy in 1996, although the percentages decreased by more than half.[35] In the end, however, there were not enough independents and disgruntled partisans to make a majority for Perot. Even if there were, it would be very hard for any single candidate to construct a winning coalition from a group as diverse as independent voters, who have little in common other than their lack of interest in politics and parties.

This doesn't mean, of course, that independents have no impact. Ralph Nader's well-publicized presidential run in 2000 as a candidate of the Green Parties got enough votes, most of them from independents, to have given the election to Republican George W. Bush. In the very close party competition that has characterized the early 2000s, even a small percentage of independent voters has the power to determine the winner. It is a sobering thought that when an election is close, the voters with the least interest and information about the candidates may be the ones who tip the balance.

CHANGE IN THE IMPACT OF PARTY ID

Party ID, then, is a psychological commitment that is often strong enough to guide other political beliefs and behavior. Democratic and Republican partisans often see issues and candidates through "party-tinted" glasses. They are more likely to vote for their party's candidates and to be active on behalf of the party or its candidates than other citizens are. For those reasons, party ID is a significant force in American politics. Yet partisanship functions in a very different context now than it did a century ago.

A More Candidate-Centered Politics

As we have seen in earlier chapters, American politics has changed in some marked ways in the past century. The great majority of Americans still hold a party ID, at least in the sense that they "lean toward" one of the two major parties. But the parties have faced major challenges to their influence on citizens. About a century ago, states began adopting the direct primary, in which voters had to choose candidates without the useful guidance of a party label. Partisanship remains a helpful shortcut in general elections but does not distinguish one candidate from another in a party's primary. New campaign and fund-raising technologies developed that were harder for the party organizations to monopolize. Candidates with enough money could find ways, using television, direct mail, and other media, to reach voters directly, over the parties' heads.

During the turbulent years of the 1960s and 1970s, as we have seen, the number of self-identified independents grew, and the impact of party ID on people's voting choices declined. Candidates found it helpful to downplay their party label, running instead as individual entrepreneurs. Now, even though party loyalties have regained much of their frequency and influence, candidates still tend to downplay their partisanship as a means of attracting voter support. In addition, other elements of American politics—organized interests, independent campaign consultants, and short-term forces such as candidates' characteristics, issues, and the particular events of the current campaign—have important effects on the strategies that party organizations develop (see box on page 117) and the behavior of citizens. The consequence is that elections have become less party centered and more candidate centered.[36]

What have we lost as a result and what have we gained? A strongly party-identified electorate has a stabilizing influence on politics. When people vote straight-party tickets in election after election, vote outcomes are predictable. Patterns of party support are stable geographically. To the extent that it can be time-consuming and stressful to adapt to political change, predictable elections can be a benefit. When split-ticket voting is more common, we get the patterns of divided party government and more frequent switches in party control of Congress and the presidency that we have seen in recent decades.

The Continuing Significance of Party

Yet we should not underestimate the persistence of party ID. Most Americans—a clear majority if we count only strong and weak identifiers, and almost all Americans if leaners are included as well—still report some degree of attachment to either the Democratic or the Republican Party. Large numbers of Americans are faithful to these loyalties in voting for candidates for office. Voters may stray from the party fold; the abundance of elected offices encourages such defections. But voters continue to perceive candidates, issues, and elections in partisan terms and often vote accordingly.

The 1994 congressional elections were a good example of the strength of party influence. Republican candidates were able to win control of the U.S. House and Senate for the first time since 1954, riding a wave of party voting by Republican identifiers. There was a remarkable level of party voting in 2004, as well as an unprecedented mobilization of strong Democrats and strong Republicans for political activities of all kinds. These elections show that party-dominated contests are still very possible, even in the candidate-centered political world of the early 2000s. Will this continue, or will the instability of modern politics eat away at one or both parties' base of support? The story continues in the next chapter, where we look more closely at the two major parties' supporting coalitions and their changes over time.

PARTY CAMPAIGN STRATEGIES IN THE 2004 PRESIDENTIAL RACE

As a campaign manager, one of your first vital decisions will be whether to focus on mobilizing your base—the types of people who are your core supporters—or whether to try to build up your vote total by appealing to independents and supporters of the other party. If you are running the campaign of the majority party's candidate, you'll win if you can turn out enough of your majority, so you will probably concentrate on rallying your loyalists by appealing to the party's core issues. If your candidate's party is in the minority, then you need to promote those aspects of your candidate's personality that have wide appeal or to raise issues that cross party lines or threaten to split the other party's coalition.

In 2000, the two parties' presidential candidates followed that script. George W. Bush came into the campaign with his party's identifiers in the minority. He stressed that he was a "compassionate conservative" in order to appeal to independents and Democrats who valued such issues as education and health care. Bush also emphasized bipartisanship and an end to "partisan bickering," just as a minority-party candidate would logically do. As would be expected from a majority-party candidate, Democratic Vice President Al Gore emphasized the traditional Democratic core issues of Social Security and Medicare and his concern for "the people, not the powerful."

When Bush ran for reelection in 2004, however, he chose a different approach. Although he continued to appeal to independents and weak Democrats by stressing his leadership and decisiveness in the war on terror, the president's campaign also put major effort into energizing its base. Believing that 4 million conservative Christians had sat out the 2000 election rather than vote for Bush, the president's close adviser Karl Rove used issues such as opposition to gay marriage and abortion rights to bring those core Bush supporters back to the polls in 2004. Democrat John Kerry's campaign, in contrast, behaved like a minority party by opening its campaign with a stress on Kerry's record as a war hero in Vietnam.

Why did the two parties' campaigns seem to switch strategies between 2000 and 2004? The Bush campaign could afford to take the unusual approach of appealing to its base, even though it was not clearly in the majority, for several reasons. One was that the Republican Party's sophisticated campaign apparatus had become better able to locate and turn out its core supporters than the Democrats were, as well as to "cherry-pick" groups of Democratic supporters in key states with specific issue appeals—for instance, peeling off some usually Democratic Latinos by appealing to their religious opposition to gay marriage.

Another was a growing perception that the electorate was changing. When voters are thought to distribute themselves on a bell-shaped curve, with lots of independents and weak partisans in the center and smaller numbers of strong partisans on the left and right, then it makes sense to appeal to the center, especially for the minority party. In 2004, however, commentators were increasingly describing the electorate as polarized, with about 40 to 45 percent steadfastly Republican and another 40 to 45 percent solidly Democratic. If so, then spending scarce resources appealing to the very few in the middle would make less sense, and the Republican strategy was a wise one.

The Bush campaign won with its strategy of energizing its base and cherry-picking additional support. If you were managing the campaign of, say, John McCain in 2008, could you follow the same plan? If you were campaign manager for Hillary Clinton in 2008, how would your choices differ from John Kerry's?

Chapter 7

Party Coalitions and Party Change

California Governor Arnold Schwarzenegger, sometimes known as "The Governator," has a mixed marriage, politically speaking. Schwarzenegger, a wealthy, middle-aged, white man, has owned several businesses. His father was a military officer. The governor's wife, Maria Shriver, is a journalist and comes from a large Catholic family of lawyers and activists for nonprofit groups. Using just the information in this description, would you have been able to tell which member of this couple is a Democrat and which is a Republican?

Party identifications are not distributed randomly among Americans. Some social groups lean heavily toward a Republican identification—business executives and "born-again" white Protestants, for example—and other groups, such as women, African Americans, and Jews, are more likely to consider themselves Democrats. Without any knowledge of their voting history, then, and purely on the basis of their links with certain social groups, we could predict (accurately) that Schwarzenegger is the Republican and Shriver is the Democrat.

The types of people who support a party make up what is called the party's *coalition*—the social, economic, or other groups most inclined to favor that party's candidates through good times and bad. Groups may align with a party for many reasons, but once a group has become associated with a party's coalition, its interests are very likely to affect the stands the party takes on at least some issues and the strategies it follows in campaigns.

The differences between the two parties' coalitions at a particular time are a helpful clue as to which issues dominate the nation's politics at that time. The facts that African Americans have identified so overwhelmingly as Democrats in recent decades, for example, and that southern whites are now dominantly Republican remind us that racial issues continue to be powerful in American elections.[1] At various times in U.S. history, regional conflicts, ethnic and religious divisions, disputes between agriculture and industry, and differences in social class have also helped form the basis for differences between the two parties' coalitions, as they have in other western democracies.

These coalitional changes are not the only important types of change in the party system. There have been changes in the cast of characters themselves, as some parties have been formed (for example, the Republicans, in 1854) and others, such as the early Federalists, have died. The relative dominance of the major parties has changed, when one party's voting strength has surged at the expense of the other party[2]—for instance, the landslide election of Franklin D. Roosevelt in 1932 when the nation cast off its long-time Republican majority in favor of Democratic dominance. We have already examined changes in the nature of the party organizations[3] (in Chapters 3 and 4), including the development of "service parties" whose main focus is to aid candidates rather than to run campaigns themselves.

It is the coalitional changes on which party researchers have lavished the most attention, however. Changes in the alignment of social groups with the parties are especially intriguing because they contribute so much to shaping a nation's politics and policies. In much of this literature, great and enduring changes in the parties' coalitions have been called *party realignments*.[4] The concept of realignment is a controversial one, as you'll see later in the chapter. But that should not keep us from exploring the interesting patterns of group support for the Democrats and Republicans over time and the differences these alignments make.

In this chapter, then, we will look at party change with special attention to the parties' supporting coalitions. We'll examine the development and nature of the coalitions that currently support the Democrats and the Republicans: from what educational backgrounds, occupations, regions, religions, and other social groups do these supporters come, and what interests attract them to one party rather than the other? Finally, we will consider how best to characterize the changes in the parties' coalitions since the New Deal.

THE AMERICAN PARTY SYSTEMS

Many analysts agree that the United States has experienced at least six different electoral eras or party systems. Although some common themes run through all of these eras, each of these party systems has had a distinctive pattern of group support for the parties. Each party system can also be distinguished by the kinds of issue concerns that dominated it and the types of public policies that the government put into effect. (See Table 7.1 for a summary of each party system.) In Chapter 1, we looked at party history to learn about the interrelationships among the three parts of the party. Now let us get a different take on these events, from the perspective of changes in the social group support for the parties.

The First Party System

The initial American party system (from about 1801–1828)[5] emerged out of a serious conflict between opposing groups within the Washington administration: How much power should the national government exercise relative to that of the states? As noted in Chapter 1, the Federalists, led by Alexander Hamilton, wanted to build the new econ-

TABLE 7.1   **Years of Partisan Control of Congress and the Presidency:**
1801–2006

	House		Senate		President	
First party system	*D-R*	*Opp.*	*D-R*	*Opp.*	*D-R*	*Opp.*
(1801–1828)	26	2	26	2	28	0
Second party system	*Dem.*	*Opp.*	*Dem.*	*Opp.*	*Dem.*	*Opp.*
(1829–1860)	24	8	28	4	24	8
Third party system	*Dem.*	*Opp.*	*Dem.*	*Opp.*	*Dem.*	*Opp.*
(1861–1876)	2	14	0	16	0	16
(1877–1896)	14	6	4	16	8	12
Fourth party system						
(1897–1932)	10	26	6	30	8	28
Fifth party system						
(1933–1968)	32	4	32	4	28	8
Sixth party system						
(1969–1980)	12	0	12	0	4	8
(1981–2006)	14	12	9	17	8	18
(1969–2006)	26	12	21	17	12	26

Note: Entries for the first party system are Democratic-Republicans and their opponents; for the second party system, Democrats and their opponents (first Whigs and then Republicans); and for subsequent party systems, Democrats and Republicans. In 2001, Republicans were in the majority in the Senate for the first five months and Democrats for the last seven, so the Senate is counted as being under Democratic control.

omy through the efforts of a strong national government that would collaborate closely with business and industry. A national bank would centralize the state banking systems. This plan would benefit business owners and wealthier citizens, who were concentrated in New England; these groups were the core support for Hamilton's Federalists.

Small farmers and the less well-off, living in the southern and mid-Atlantic states, could see that the Federalists' proposals would hurt them financially; it was the small farmers who would pay the taxes while businesses and speculators would gain. They supported Thomas Jefferson and James Madison's demand for a limited national government, for states' rights, and a more egalitarian vision of the new democracy. The Jeffersonians won the debate; in the hotly contested 1800 election, these Democratic-Republicans, as they came to be called, gained the presidency. The Federalists slowly slipped into a fatal decline, and the party of Jefferson and Madison then enjoyed more than two decades of almost unchallenged dominance.

The Second Party System

The next party system (from approximately 1829–1860) developed when the one-party rule of the Democratic-Republicans could not contain all the conflicts generated by a rapidly changing nation. The party split into two factions on the major issues of the period: how the Union should expand, what the national government's economic powers should be, and, increasingly, how to handle the explosive question of slavery. One faction continued the Jeffersonian tradition of opposition to a strong national government; it included the small farmers of the South and the western frontier as well as the addition of urban workers and their political bosses. Led by Andrew Jackson, it would later call itself the Democratic Party or, at times, "the Democracy." The other, a more elitist and eastern faction represented by John Quincy Adams, referred to itself as the National Republicans and was eventually absorbed into the Whig Party.[6]

This second party system was just as class based as the first; wealthier voters supported the Whigs and the less privileged identified as Democrats. The Democrats dominated, growing as the franchise was extended to more and more Americans and the party system became more mass-based. Democratic rule was interrupted only twice, both times by the election of Whig war heroes to the presidency. As the issues of this period grew more disruptive, however, several minor parties developed and the Whigs began to fracture, especially over the issue of slavery.

The Third Party System

One of these new parties, an antislavery party called the Republicans, was quickly propelled into major party status; it was founded in 1854 and had already replaced the seriously divided Whigs by 1856. Its rapid rise signaled the end of the second party system. The bitter conflict of the Civil War ensured that the new third party system (1861–1896) would have the most clearly defined coalitions of any party system before or since. War and Reconstruction divided the nation roughly along geographic lines: The South became a Democratic bastion after white southerners were permitted to return to the polls in 1876, and the Northeast and Midwest remained a reliable base for Republicans.[7]

So sharp was the sectional division that the Democratic Party's only strongholds in the North were in the cities controlled by Democratic machines (for example, New York City's Tammany Hall) and areas settled by southerners (such as Kentucky, Missouri, and the southern portions of Ohio, Indiana, and Illinois). In the South, GOP support came only from blacks (in response to Republican President Abraham Lincoln's freeing of the slaves) and people from mountain areas originally opposed to the southern states' secession. By 1876, there was close party competition in presidential voting and in the House of Representatives as these sectional monopolies offset one another. Competition was so intense that this period contained two of the four elections in American history in which the winner of the popular vote for President lost the vote in the Electoral College.

This was a time of tremendous industrial expansion. As a result, economic issues, particularly the growth of huge industrial monopolies, were closely related to the sectional party cleavage. The Republicans "were from the beginning the party more identified with moral Puritanism and emerging industrial capitalism."[8] The party worked to support these new American businesses (most of them in the Northeast and, later, the

Midwest) with protective tariffs on imported goods, a railroad system that could haul products from coast to coast, efforts to develop the frontier, and high taxes to pay for all these programs. In contrast, the Democrats represented groups that had been passed over by economic expansion and who were deeply suspicious of capitalism, such as farmers and the working class, as well as the white South.

The Fourth Party System

The imprint of the Civil War continued to shape southern politics for the next century. However, the Civil War party system soon began to fade elsewhere, under the weight of farm and rural protest and the economic panic of 1893. Tensions within the Democratic Party between poor whites and the more conservative party leaders erupted into a fight over the party's leadership in the 1890s. The less wealthy, egalitarian wing won, nominated populist William Jennings Bryan as the Democratic presidential candidate in 1896, and reformed the party's issue stances. Bryan went down to crashing defeat, however, and Republicans began a long domination of American national politics, disrupted only by their own internal split in 1912.

This fourth party system (from approximately 1897–1932) again reflected both regional and economic conflicts. It pitted the eastern business community, which was heavily Republican, against the western and southern rural "periphery," with the South even more Democratic than before. Southern Democrats, out from under the heavy hand of Reconstruction, were able to reinstitute racially discriminatory laws and to prevent blacks from voting in the southern states. The waves of immigrants into the large cities swelled the ranks of both parties, although Catholic immigrants, especially from Europe, tended to be drawn into Democratic Party organizing.

In the 1920s, the Progressive Party made inroads into major party strength early in the decade, and in 1928, Democratic candidate Al Smith, the first Catholic ever nominated for the presidency, brought even more Catholic voters into Democratic ranks in the North and drove many Protestant southerners temporarily into voting Republican.

The Fifth Party System

The shock of the Great Depression of 1929 and the subsequent election of Democrat Franklin Roosevelt produced the fifth, or New Deal, party system. During the 1930s, as a means of pulling the nation out of economic ruin, Roosevelt pushed Congress to enact several large-scale welfare state programs. These Roosevelt "New Deal" programs—Social Security, wages and hours laws, protection for labor unions—strengthened the Democrats' image as the party of the disadvantaged. Even groups such as blacks, long allied with the Republicans, were lured to the Democratic banner; socioeconomic needs were powerful enough to keep both blacks and southern whites as wary allies in the Roosevelt coalition. The costs of the New Deal and the impact of its programs heightened the stakes of the conflict between higher income and lower income groups, so the socio-economic stamp on the party system again became pronounced, as well as the division between business and labor. So by 1936, the new Democratic majority party had become a grand *New Deal coalition* of the less privileged minorities—lower income people, industrial workers (especially union members), poor farmers, Catholics, Jews, blacks—plus the South, where the Democratic loyalty imprinted by the Civil War had become all but genetic.

It is clear from this brief tour of party history that the effects of socioeconomic, racial, and regional divisions have waxed and waned, but all have had a continuing and powerful role in shaping the parties' coalitions over time. What is the nature of the two parties' coalitions today? As we explore the fate of the New Deal coalition, we'll look at the evidence suggesting that it has changed sufficiently to produce a sixth party system in the closing years of the twentieth century.

THE SOCIAL BASES OF PARTY COALITIONS

Socioeconomic Status Divisions

Most democratic party systems reflect divisions along social class lines, even if those divisions may have softened over the years.[9] James Madison, one of the most perceptive observers of human nature among the nation's founders, wrote in the *Federalist Papers* that economic differences are the most common source of factions.[10] The footprints of socioeconomic status (SES) conflict are scattered throughout American history. Social and economic status differences underlay the battle between the wealthy, aristocratic Federalists and the less privileged Democratic-Republicans. These differences were even sharper between the Jacksonian Democrats and the Whigs a few decades later, and again during the fourth and fifth party systems.

The relationship between party and SES can still be seen in American politics today (see Table 7.2, sections A and B). Read across the top row of section A, for instance. You will find that among survey respondents in the lower third of incomes, 17 percent call themselves strong Democrats, 16 percent call themselves weak Democrats, and 17 percent lean toward the Democratic party but, toward the right side of the row, only 11, 10, and 16 percent, respectively, call themselves leaning, weak, or strong Republicans. The next column, titled "Dem. minus Rep.," shows that there are 13 percent more Democrats (counting strong and weak identifiers and Democratic "leaners") than Republicans among these lower income people.

Those with less education are even more likely to call themselves Democrats than lower-income people are (section B). Here, 22 percent of those who didn't finish high school identify as strong Democrats, 16 percent are weak Democrats and 13 percent are Democratic leaners. On the Republican side of the table, there are only 10 percent Republican leaners, 8 percent weak Republicans, and 11 percent strong Republicans among those who didn't finish high school, for an overall Democratic edge ("Dem. minus Rep.") of 22 percent. Why do we see these trends if the impact of social class is diminishing in politics? The overall decline in class voting among whites since the time of the New Deal has been counterbalanced by the very high Democratic identification among blacks, who are predominantly lower income.[11]

Socioeconomic forces, then, continue to leave their mark on American party politics. In fact, some observers argue that outside the South, less affluent voters have become even more supportive of Democrats in recent decades. The substantial gulf between rich and poor in the United States and the differences between the parties' stands on issues of special concern to lower income people (such as government-provided health care and social services) help sustain the relationship between lower SES and Democratic partisanship.

TABLE 7.2   Social Characteristics and Party Identification: 2004

	Democrats		Independents			Republicans		Dem. Minus Rep.	Cases
	Strong	Weak	Closer to Dem.	Closer to Neither	Closer to Rep.	Weak	Strong		
A. Income									
Lower third	17%	16	17	13	11	10	16	13	324
Middle third	18%	15	19	7	12	16	14	10	402
Upper third	16%	14	15	8	11	14	21	−1	322
B. Education									
No high school diploma	22%	16	13	18	10	8	11	22	89
High school grad	18%	16	16	12	13	11	14	12	315
College	15%	14	18	7	11	16	19	1	644
C. Region									
South	19%	18	15	7	10	13	17	12	367
Nonsouth	16%	13	18	10	12	14	17	4	681
D. Religion									
Jews	44%	19	16	0	3	0	3	73	32
Catholics	18%	13	17	12	8	13	19	8	232
Protestants	15%	16	14	9	12	14	19	0	616
White Protestants*	9%	11	11	8	15	18	28	−30	452
E. Race									
Blacks	31%	31	21	12	5	1	1	76	180
Whites	14%	12	16	9	13	16	20	−7	868
F. Gender									
Female	22%	16	16	9	9	12	16	17	637
Male	12%	14	19	11	14	14	16	1	563

* The survey did not ask how many of these white Protestants consider themselves to be fundamentalist or "born again."

Note: Totals add up to approximately 100 percent reading across (with slight variations due to rounding). Dem. minus Rep. is the party difference calculated by subtracting the percentage of strong, weak, and leaning Republicans from the percentage of strong, weak, and leaning Democrats. Negative numbers indicate a Republican advantage in the group.

Source: 2004 American National Election Study, Center for Political Studies, University of Michigan; data made available by the Inter-University Consortium for Political and Social Research.

The result is that, especially in congressional elections, Democrats are even more likely to win in lower income districts now than they were 20 years ago.[12]

Table 7.2 also shows that the current relationship between *higher* SES and party differs in some interesting ways from that of the New Deal coalition. People with a college education are no longer largely Republican; as the doors of higher education open to a wider variety of students, those with college degrees now divide themselves fairly evenly between the parties. Similarly, those with service jobs (which tend to be lower paying) and blue-collar jobs remain more likely to be Democrats, but upper-income people are no longer as distinctively Republican—perhaps because this group now contains fewer business people and more professionals, many of whom are concerned with quality-of-life issues such as the environment and women's rights. The identification of many professionals with the Democratic Party is reflected in the support Democratic candidates receive from teachers' unions and trial lawyers.

The impact of SES should not be overstated. Socioeconomic status has been less important as a basis for party loyalty in the United States than in many other western democracies,[13] and even at the height of the New Deal, the SES differences between the parties were less clear than the parties' rhetoric would suggest. Some groups locate themselves in the "wrong" party from an SES point of view; for example, white fundamentalist Protestants have trended Republican in recent years even though their average income is closer to that of the average Democrat than to the average Republican.[14] Because SES divisions between the Republicans and Democrats can be fuzzy, the parties do not usually promote blatantly class-based appeals; they try to attract votes from a variety of social groups.

Sectional (Regional) Divisions

Historically, the greatest rival to SES as an explanation for American party differences has been sectionalism. Different sections of the country have often had differing political interests. When a political party has championed these distinct interests, it has sometimes united large numbers of voters who may vary in other ways.

The most enduring sectionalism in American party history was the one-party Democratic control of the South. Well before the Civil War, white southerners shared an interest in slavery and an agricultural system geared to export markets. The searing experience of that war and the Reconstruction that followed made the South into the "Solid South" and delivered it to the Democrats for most of the next century. The 11 states of the former Confederacy cast all their electoral votes for Democratic presidential candidates in every election from 1880 through 1924, except for Tennessee's defection in 1920. Al Smith's Catholicism frightened five of these states into the Republican column in 1928, but the New Deal economic programs brought the South back to the Democratic Party for the four Roosevelt elections.

As we will see later in the chapter, however, the civil rights movement was the opening wedge in the slow process that separated the South from its Democratic loyalties. Even now (Table 7.2, section C), southerners are slightly more Democratic in their basic partisan leanings than non-southerners, thanks in large part to the overwhelming Democratic partisanship of southern blacks. But this Democratic edge is much less pronounced than it was until the 1960s, and it appears to be disappearing entirely, as white southerners become more and more likely to vote Republican in federal and state elections. (On the distinction between party identification and voting behavior, see Chapter 6.)

At times, the party system has also reflected the competition between the East, which used to dominate the nation's economy, and the South and West. In the first years of the American republic, the Federalists held to an ever-narrowing base of eastern seaport and financial interests, while the Democratic-Republicans expanded westward with the new settlers. Jackson aimed his party appeals at the men of the frontier, and the protest movements that thrust William Jennings Bryan into the 1896 campaign sprang from the discontent of the western prairies and the South with eastern bankers and eastern capitalism. The geographic distribution of the 1896 presidential vote, with the Democrats winning all but three states in the South and West, but losing all northern and Border States east of the Mississippi River, is a striking example of sectional voting.

Sectional divisions in voting are still present today; Democrat John Kerry, who lost every southern state in 2004, could attest to that. The Mountain West has sometimes acted as a unified bloc in national politics on concerns that these states share, such as protecting the coal deposits and the ranchers in the western states against federal environmental laws. So in recent presidential elections, commentators have referred to the "Republican L," the substantial support for Republican candidates in the Rocky Mountain and Plains states and then across the South.

Religious Divisions

There have always been religious differences between the American party coalitions, just as there are in many other democracies. In the early days of the New Deal, Catholics and Jews were among the most loyal supporters of the Democratic Party, although Catholic support for Democrats has declined in recent years (Table 7.2, section D). Some of the relationship between religion and party loyalty is due to the SES differences among religious groups. Yet religious conviction and group identification also seem to be involved.

Internationalism and concern for social justice, rooted in the religious and ethnic traditions of Judaism, have disposed many Jews toward the Democratic Party as the party of international concern, support for Israel, and social and economic justice.[15] The longstanding ties of Catholics to the Democratic Party reflected the party's greater openness to Catholic participation and political advancement. Most of the national chairmen of the Democratic Party during the past century have been Catholics and the only Catholic presidential nominees of a major party have been Democrats.

Northern white Protestants have trended Republican ever since the party began, but the relationship is complex. In recent years, we have seen a division between mainline Protestant denominations and white evangelicals. According to the Pew Research Center, white evangelical Protestants were evenly divided between Democratic and Republican partisanship as recently as the late 1980s, but by 2003 there were almost twice as many Republicans among this group as Democrats.[16] These evangelical Christians had particular impact on the 2004 elections, when more than 26 million white evangelicals went to the polls, comprising almost a quarter of the electorate, and three-quarters of them voted for President Bush. Increasing support for the Republicans among white "born-again" Protestants, especially in the South, is due in part to the parties' stands on issues such as abortion and school prayer as well as to Republican leaders' social conservatism and emphasis on traditional values.[17]

More generally, voters who consider themselves very religious are now substantially more Republican than Democratic. In fact, the greatest religious difference in voting preferences in the early 2000s, and arguably the best predictor of partisanship more generally, is not the difference between Catholics and Protestants but between those who attend church or other houses of worship regularly and those who attend only rarely or not at all.

Racial Divisions

Decades ago, the Republican Party, which was founded to abolish slavery, was associated with racial equality in the minds of both black and white Americans. Between 1930 and 1960, however, the partisan direction of racial politics turned 180 degrees. It is now the Democratic Party that is viewed as standing for racial equality. As a result, blacks identify as Democrats in overwhelming numbers today, as they have since at least the 1960s, regardless of their SES, region, or other social characteristics (Table 7.2, section E). In a recent poll, two-thirds of blacks interviewed agreed that the Democratic Party is committed to equal opportunity; only three in ten blacks said that about the Republican Party.[18] In 2004, 88 percent of blacks reported voting for Kerry, compared with only 41 percent of whites.[19] There is no closer tie between a social group and a party than that between blacks and the Democrats.[20]

Ethnic Divisions

Latinos are the fastest-growing segment of the U.S. population. The 2000 U.S. Census showed that the Latino population grew by nearly 60 percent in the previous decade to more than 35 million, and then to 41 million by mid-2004. Latinos have surpassed non-Hispanic blacks as the nation's largest minority group. Latinos have long exercised voting strength in states such as California, Texas, and Florida. As their numbers shoot up nationwide, both parties work harder to attract Latino voter support, just as Latinos seek to gain political influence to the same degree achieved by blacks. In fact, a White House pollster warned that unless Republicans steadily increased their share of the Latino vote in 2004 and beyond, Republican candidates would lose those elections.[21]

Yet winning the Latino vote is easier said than done, mainly because Latinos include many different nationalities with differing interests. The Cuban émigrés who settled in Miami after Fidel Castro took power in the 1950s tend to be conservative, strongly anti-Communist, and inclined to vote Republican, whereas the larger Mexican-American population in California leans Democratic. Surveys show that most Latino voters identify themselves as Democrats, but Republican strategists see Latinos as potentially responsive to a socially conservative message.[22] Republican strategists worked hard to deliver that message in the 2004 elections, with efforts ranging from advertising on Spanish-language TV stations to President Bush's proposal to give temporary legal status to undocumented (and often Mexican or Central American) workers. They seem to have succeeded; Latinos divided more evenly between the parties in 2004 than they had in previous elections.

Gender Divisions

For more than two decades, the votes and stands of women have diverged from those of men (see Table 7.2, section F). In 1980, about 6 percent more women voted for Jimmy Carter than men did. The so-called gender gap grew after that. Men rated President Reagan much more positively than women did, and by the mid-1980s, the gender difference had extended to partisanship; men were less likely than women to identify as Democrats. This partisan gender gap increased in the 1990s. It closed a bit in 2004, when President Bush increased his support among women. But the gap opened again in early 2005 as economic concerns replaced war and terrorism on the political agenda.[23] The gender gap has not developed as a result of women becoming more Democratic. Instead, both men and women have become more Republican, but men have done so at a faster pace and to a greater degree.[24]

Why should gender be related to partisanship? Studies of the gender gap suggest that there are differences between men's and women's attitudes on some major issues; on average, women express greater support for social programs and less support for defense spending. These differences correspond with the two parties' issue agendas; the Democratic Party emphasizes education, health care, and other social programs, whereas the Republicans put a priority on military strength and tax cuts. People's attitudes toward gender equality and abortion, in particular, have become more closely correlated with their party identification during the past three decades, and when these and other "women's issues" are stressed by candidates, a gender gap is more likely to appear.[25] The national parties also project some lifestyle differences that may affect men's and women's partisanship. Among members of the U.S. House and Senate first elected in 2002, for instance, 80 percent of those who list their spouse as sharing their last name were Republicans, and almost 70 percent of those whose spouse had a different last name were Democrats.[26]

Single women have become a particularly distinctive Democratic constituency. According to a *Los Angeles Times* national exit poll in 2004, 64 percent of single women (comprising almost one in five voters) supported John Kerry.[27] Single women, and especially single mothers, are probably more economically insecure on average than married women are, and thus could be more likely to see government social programs as an ally.

ISSUES ARE CENTRAL TO THE PARTIES' COALITIONS

As this discussion of the gender gap suggests, the alignment of social groups with parties in modern American politics is closely interrelated with the parties' stands on issues. A group's presence in a party coalition indicates that many of the group's members— white evangelical Christians, for instance—have some shared reactions to major issues and candidates, which have drawn them to one party rather than the other. To keep their support, the party is likely to express solidarity with the group's concerns, to speak its language, and to feature some of the group's leaders in its conventions and campaigns. In the case of evangelical Christians, the Republican Party has incorporated stands against gay marriage and unlimited embryonic stem cell research into its platform and faith-based initiatives into its rhetoric. Thus, exploring the relationships between parties and social groupings can tell us a lot about the views and interests to which each party must respond.

Fortunately, we have a huge arsenal of public opinion polls to examine the attitudes on issues within each party's supporting coalition. Table 7.3 shows the preferences of party identifiers and independents on a range of issues that have been featured prominently in recent presidential campaigns. There are big differences between Democrats and Republicans (seen in the "Dem. minus Rep." column) in attitudes toward welfare state programs. Democrats are much more favorable than are Republicans to maintaining government spending on services and a government role in providing jobs for the unemployed (sections A and B). The recipients of these services and jobs tend to be lower SES people, whose Democratic leanings can be seen in Table 7.2. Note, however, that

TABLE 7.3   Issue Attitudes and Party Identification: 2004

	Democrats		Independents			Republicans			
	Strong	Weak	Closer to Dem.	Closer to Neither	Closer to Rep.	Weak	Strong	Dem. Minus Rep.	Cases
A. Government spending on services									
More	22%	15	16	7	9	12	19	13	302
Same	27%	16	20	8	13	9	6	35	146
Less	14%	22	19	2	16	15	12	12	81
B. Government role in providing jobs and a good standard of living									
Gov. help	29%	17	22	12	9	8	4	47	368
In between	18%	19	24	6	9	14	9	29	224
Help self	7%	11	12	10	15	16	28	−29	502
C. Government role in improving position of blacks									
Gov. help	33%	20	22	9	5	6	5	59	255
In between	16%	20	21	10	10	12	12	23	269
Help self	10%	11	13	9	14	17	25	−22	539
D. Government spending on defense									
Decrease	28%	19	29	9	6	8	2	60	200
Same	20%	21	21	8	9	12	8	33	282
Increase	9%	9	12	10	16	15	27	−28	570
E. Abortion									
Own choice	25%	14	22	9	9	11	10	31	387
In between	12%	15	15	10	14	15	19	−6	511
Illegal	13%	15	7	10	11	16	28	−20	137
F. Ideological self-identification									
Liberal	31%	20	29	6	7	5	3	65	421
Moderate	15%	16	25	16	7	11	9	29	91
Conservative	7%	11	10	10	15	19	26	−32	634

Note: Totals add up to approximately 100 percent reading across (with slight variations due to rounding). Dem. minus Rep. is party difference calculated by subtracting the percentage of strong, weak, and leaning Republicans from the percentage of strong, weak, and leaning Democrats. Negative numbers indicate a Republican advantage in the group. Individuals who were unable to describe themselves in ideological terms were not included in the data in section F.

Source: 2004 American National Election Study, Center for Political Studies, University of Michigan; data made available by the Inter-University Consortium for Political and Social Research.

factors other than an individual's own SES can affect his or her views on these issues. Even more important are people's perceptions of how the economy is doing as a whole.[28]

Party differences are also substantial on non-SES issues, such as civil rights, defense spending, and abortion (see Table 7.3, sections C–E). Since the 1960s, for example, party identifiers have been sharply divided in their attitudes toward racial policy, with Democrats much more likely to favor a government role in helping minorities than Republicans are. (Recall from Table 7.2 the strong tendency for blacks to identify as Democrats.)

In 2004, defense and foreign policy issues and concerns about abortion separated Democrats from Republicans to a significant degree. In their voting choices as well, those who supported abortion rights were twice to three times more likely to vote for Kerry than for Bush in 2004.[29]

Interestingly, the abortion issue had not been related to party identification as recently as 1988. Then, attitudes toward abortion cut across party lines, dividing Democrats from Democrats and Republicans from Republicans.[30] An issue with the power to affect party identification can threaten to rearrange the two parties' coalitions and possibly even create major change in the party system. This did happen to at least some extent; the fact that pro-choice sentiment is now much stronger in the Democratic than the Republican Party suggests that some people changed their partisanship to correspond with the pro-choice position of Democratic leaders or the pro-life stance of Republican leaders.

There is additional evidence that the two parties' coalitions are more sharply divided on many issues than they were a few decades ago and the gap is growing. Look, for example, at the truly striking party difference between those who call themselves liberals and those who identify themselves as conservatives (Table 7.3, section F). As one pollster puts it, "We have two massive, colliding forces. . . . One [the Republican coalition] is rural, Christian, religiously conservative, with guns at home. . . . And we have a second America [the Democratic coalition] that is socially tolerant, pro-choice, secular, living in New England and the Pacific coast, and in affluent suburbs."[31] Party divisions, then, increasingly reflect differences that have been termed "the culture wars."[32]

In short, there is a close and reciprocal relationship between the stands a party takes and the groups that form the party's core support. Parties take positions on issues to maintain the support of the groups in their existing coalition. Sometimes party leaders use issue positions to draw members of other social groups to the party, as both parties are now doing to win the support of Latino voters. At times, it is the group that tries to put its concerns on the party's agenda; pro-lifers did so in the Republican Party as abortion rights activists did with the Democrats. As these newer groups become a larger force within the party coalition, the party's leadership will try to firm up their support with additional commitments on their issues. So there is a dynamic and fascinating interaction between the social groups in a party's coalition and the party's stands on issues.

THE DEVELOPMENT OF THE
SIXTH PARTY SYSTEM

The alignment of social groups with the parties in the early 2000s differs in some significant ways from that of the New Deal coalition. That should not be surprising; the political environment has changed a lot during the past 70 years. Once the Second World War had brought the U.S. out of the Depression, some groups that had benefited from government assistance under Roosevelt moved up into the growing middle class. In return for this economic gain, however, they found themselves paying higher taxes to support those who still needed the assistance; that led many people to reevaluate the costs and benefits of the welfare state in their own lives. At the same time, the issue of race, which had been held in check by Roosevelt's deft maneuvering, was pushed to the top of both parties' agendas by activists hoping to change their parties' stands.

The party system has changed in other important ways since the New Deal as well. Democratic dominance has given way to close competition between the parties. The party organizations do not expect to anoint candidates now, run their campaigns, or hand out patronage jobs. Rather, the party organizations work primarily to help fund and support campaigns that are run by candidates and their paid consultants. And the relationship between party ID and election results has changed. Until 1952, the elections of the New Deal party system had usually been *maintaining elections,* in which the presidential candidate of the majority party—the party with the most identifiers—normally won. Since 1952, most national elections have been *deviating elections*—those in which short-term forces such as candidate characteristics or issues are powerful enough to cause the defeat of the majority party's candidate.

Major Changes in the Parties' Supporting Coalitions

Liberal northern Democrats in the late 1940s pressed their party to deliver on the long-delayed promise of civil rights for blacks. When Democratic administrations responded, and began to use federal power to end the racial segregation of schools and public accommodations such as restaurants and hotels, some conservative white southerners felt betrayed by their national party. They found an alternative in 1964 when Republican presidential candidate Barry Goldwater opposed the Civil Rights Act. Goldwater argued that no matter how much Republicans supported civil rights, the party's commitment to smaller government and states' rights precluded the federal government from forcing integration on reluctant state governments.

Soon after, when the Voting Rights Act restored southern blacks' right to vote, their overwhelmingly Democratic voting patterns led the national Democratic Party to become even more liberal on race and other issues closely linked with race. Both national parties, then, had markedly changed their positions on this issue. The Democrats moved from an acceptance of segregation in the South to a commitment to use government as the means to secure rights for black Americans. The Republicans, with roots in the abolitionist movement, reacted against the big-government programs of the New Deal with a commitment to states' rights and small government, even at the cost of the party's traditional pro–civil rights stand.[33]

These changes in the parties' positions on race led to a slow reformation of their constituencies. Table 7.4 shows the changes between the 1950s and 2000 in the representation of various groups within the Democratic and Republican parties in the electorate. Look first at the dramatic changes with regard to race. Blacks were only 6 percent of the Democratic party in the electorate, on average, between 1952 and 1960; at this time, of course, very few southern blacks were permitted to vote. By the 1992–2000 period, blacks constituted almost 20 percent of all Democrats, and Latinos, Asian Americans, and Native Americans added another 10 percent. The change was especially profound in the South; exit polls in 2000 showed that blacks made up a majority (52 percent) of the Democratic voters in the Deep South states of Alabama, Georgia, Louisiana, Mississippi, and South Carolina.[34]

At the same time, southern whites, who were a quarter of the Democratic partisans in the 1950s, dropped to just 16 percent in the 1990s (and this is probably an exaggeration of Democratic strength in the South, because change in people's party ID often lags behind changes in their voting behavior). Surveys show that in 1956, 87 percent of white

TABLE 7.4   Change in the Parties' Coalitions, 1952–1960 to 1992–2000

	Democratic Voters		Republican Voters	
	1952–1960	1992–2000	1952–1960	1992–2000
Blacks	6%	19%	3%	2%
Latinos, Asian Americans, and Native Americans	1	10	0	7
Southern whites	24	16	8	26
Northern whites	69	55	89	66
Upper income	40	32	46	48
Middle income	30	34	26	32
Lower income	31	34	28	20
Protestant	61	53	83	66
Catholic	31	27	14	24
Jewish	6	4	2	1
Other, no religion	2	15	2	9
Married	82	47	79	66
Unmarried	18	53	21	34

Note: Entries are the proportion of all Democratic or Republican Party identifiers, among those who say they voted, who belong to the group named in the first column.

Source: American National Election Studies data calculated by Alan Abramowitz and excerpted with kind permission from Abramowitz, *Voice of the People* (New York: McGraw-Hill, 2004), p. 87.

southerners called themselves Democrats, but in 2000 only 24 percent did so.[35] The Democratic Party's loss was the Republican Party's gain; by the 1990s, southern whites had increased from a mere 8 percent to more than a quarter of the Republican party in the electorate, and northern whites had dropped from 89 percent to 66 percent of Republican partisans.

There have been other important changes in the parties' coalitions since Roosevelt's time. One has been an almost complete regional shift. The Northeast used to be a Republican stronghold, though dominated mainly by liberal and moderate Republicans. Now it is predominantly Democratic, as is the formerly Republican West Coast. The Mountain West used to be a Democratic region in the 1950s, but a relatively conservative one; now, like the South, it is strongly Republican. Another has been an even greater income difference between the two parties, as Table 7.4 shows. By 2000, upper-income people had become a smaller part of the Democratic coalition and lower-income people were even less prominent among Republicans. In addition, as we have seen, there are new fault lines that divide the parties now, involving religiosity, gender, sexual orientation, and marital status.

So the current Democratic party in the electorate differs from the New Deal coalition in several important ways. Although it continues to include big-city dwellers, lower-income and less-educated people, and a high concentration of minority races and religions, the Democrats have lost a portion of union members and Catholics and a majority of white southerners. On the other hand, as the box on page 133 shows, the party has gained a lot of support among liberals, Northeast and West Coast residents, unmarried people, gays, and those who don't consider themselves religious. In contrast, although the Republican coalition is still heavily white, higher-income, and Protestant, its Protestant base has shifted from the mainline denominations to the evangelical churches.

THE DEMOCRATIC COALITION IN 2004

Group (% of the Voting Population)	Percent Reporting a Vote for John Kerry
African American (11%)	88%
Liberal (21%)	85
Jewish (3%)	74
Family income under $15,000 (8%)	63
Family income under $50,000 (45%)	55
Have lost a job (17%)	63
Never attend church (15%)	62
Union household (24%)	59
Live in a big city (13%)	60
Not married (37%)	58
Live in Northeast (22%)	56
Postgraduate study (16%)	55
Age 18–29 (17%)	54
Latino (8%)	53
National economy is not good or poor (52%)	79
Same-sex couples should be able to marry legally (25%)	77
Abortion should always be legal (21%)	73
Government should do more to solve problems (46%)	66
Not a gun owner (59%)	57

Source: CNN exit poll, at http://www.cnn.com/ELECTION/2004/pages/results/states/US/P/00/epolls.0.html (accessed June 26, 2005).

Republicans have also gained more support from Catholics, southerners, people who live in suburban and rural areas, men, and those who define themselves as conservatives.

From Democratic Majority to Party Parity

The second major change has been the gradual wearing away of Democratic dominance in party identification. In the 1950s and early 1960s, many more Americans called themselves Democrats than Republicans or independents (see Figure 7.1). The Democratic edge began to erode after 1964, but Republicans were not immediately able to capitalize on the Democrats' losses. In fact, the proportion of Republican identifiers declined from 1964 through the 1970s, even when a Republican president, Richard Nixon, was elected in 1968 and reelected by a landslide in 1972. Democrats retained control of Congress, split-ticket voting was fairly common, the proportion of "pure independent" identifiers increased, and there was a steady stream of independent and third-party candidates.[36] These changes in partisanship struck many scholars as resembling a *dealignment,* or a decline in party loyalties.

Yet, even as both parties were losing adherents nationally, signs of the coming change were apparent in the South. The movement from Democratic to Republican partisanship in southern states began to speed up in the late 1960s and Republican

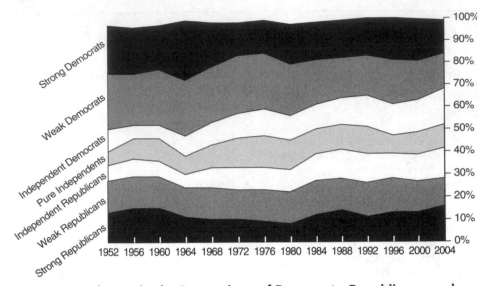

FIGURE 7.1 **Change in the Proportions of Democrats, Republicans, and Independents: 1952–2004**

Note: The data for this figure can be found in Table A.1 on page 324. The small percentage of "others" (apoliticals and third-party identifiers) is not included.

Source: American National Election Studies, University of Michigan; data made available through the Inter-University Consortium for Political and Social Research.

candidates reaped the fruits. In 1960, voters had no party choice in almost two-thirds of U.S. House districts in the South; there was no Republican candidate on the general election ballot. The only real competition was in the Democratic primary. But by 1968, the number of these one-party House races had been cut by half.[37]

The speed of partisan change increased again during the 1980s. Across the nation, for the first time in 50 years, young voters were more likely to call themselves Republicans than Democrats.[38] Two powerful reasons were President Ronald Reagan's popularity and the increased efforts of evangelical Christian groups to promote Republican affiliation. Republicans gained a majority in the U.S. Senate in 1980 that lasted six years, and in 1994 the GOP won control of both houses of Congress for the first time in 40 years. Republicans were now competing effectively with the Democrats in statewide races in the South, and in 1994, there was a Republican majority among the region's Congress members and governors for the first time since Reconstruction. In fact, in recent years, most Republican leaders in the U.S. House and Senate have been southerners.

How Can We Characterize These Changes: Realignment, Dealignment, or What?

A number of researchers have argued that these changes can best be called a party realignment—a term used to describe a significant and enduring change in the patterns of group support for the parties, usually (but not always) leading to a new majority party.

As a result, in this view, American politics has experienced two fundamental shifts: the New Deal Coalition is dead[39] and the Republican Party dominates the new party system.

Are these arguments convincing? It is not hard to show that there has been a significant and enduring change in the pattern of group support for the parties. The Republican coalition has become more southern, more evangelical, and more conservative, and a Democratic Party that used to draw much of its strength from the white South has lost the loyalty of most southern whites and now depends to a much greater extent on the votes of blacks, liberals, and secularists. These significant shifts have affected the parties' electoral prospects. After the 2004 election, in which President Bush carried almost 85 percent of southern counties, the Democratic Party chair of the sole southern white–majority county in Alabama won by Democrat John Kerry said, "We [Democrats] are out of business in the South."[40]

Even more important, these changes in the parties' coalitions affect their policy stands. A Democratic Party that draws a substantial minority of its followers from among blacks is likely to take different stands from a Democratic Party that depended heavily on conservative white southerners. And as southern whites slowly shed their traditional Democratic identification, they provided the critical mass for their new party, the Republicans, to adopt more socially conservative positions, not only on civil rights, affirmative action, and racial profiling, but also on welfare reform, abortion, women's rights, aid for inner cities, and support for public schools. Chapter 15 shows these changes in the two parties' platforms. Further, as the policy preferences of blacks, southern whites, and evangelical Christians have become more consistent with their partisanship, each party has become more homogeneous internally, and more distinct from the other party on issues, than had been the case in decades. The Democratic Party's identifiers in 2004 are much more consistently liberal than the Democratic party in the electorate in the 1970s, and Republican identifiers are even more homogeneously conservative. Liberal Republicans and conservative Democrats have become endangered species.

The second argument—that the Republicans are the new majority party—tends to focus on the successes of Republican presidential candidates since 1968, the growth of the GOP in the once one-party Democratic South and the Republican gains in Congress, leading to the current GOP majorities in both the House and the Senate.[41] But the close competition between the two national parties, as seen in President Bush's very narrow (51 percent) victory in 2004, weakens this claim. The Bush administration has worked diligently to create a Republican majority, for example, by trying to attract a larger proportion of the votes of Latinos, Catholics, and blacks, and by collaborating with evangelical preachers to increase the voter turnout of conservative Christians.[42] Although the proportion of "unchurched" Americans is growing faster than the percentage of those who attend church frequently, churches and other religious organizations are very effective "precincts" for political organizing, because they bring together in one place a lot of people who can influence one another's views and behavior.

Problems with the Idea of Realignment

Yet there are both practical and theoretical reasons why other scholars are reluctant to use the R word (realignment) to describe these changes. In practical terms, although Republican strength has steadily increased, Democrats still hold the edge among party identifiers. And in a theoretical sense, the idea of realignment is difficult to apply with any certainty. How much change has to occur in the parties' coalitions in order to call it a realignment? As political scientist David Mayhew points out, there are no clear standards for sorting elections into periods of realignment as opposed to nonrealigning periods.[43]

Changes in the partisanship of southern whites and blacks are highly significant. Yet in several ways the parties retain their New Deal character. The Democrats remain the party of the disadvantaged and of minority racial and religious groups, but the minorities have changed; as Catholics have entered the mainstream of economic and political life, they have divided more evenly between the two parties, but the Democrats still represent the majority of lower-income, black, Latino, and nonreligious people. And even if the movement of blacks and white southerners has been dramatic enough to propel the United States into a new party system, when did that system begin? Was it during the 1960s, when southern blacks regained the right to vote and the civil rights movement shook the South? Was it in the 1980s, when southern partisan change accelerated and Ronald Reagan attracted many new voters to the Republicans? Or was it in the early 1990s, when Congress finally came under Republican control? Or does it encompass all of these periods in a constantly evolving (so-called "secular") change?

The debate will rage on as to whether the concept of realignment is a valuable tool in understanding party system change. Perhaps a better approach is to recognize that there are many different kinds of party changes and that we have seen all of them to at least some degree in the last 50 years. The evidence for party organizational change, as presented in Chapters 3 and 4, is convincing. There is little doubt that the Democratic dominance of the New Deal party system has given way to a relative balance in national party strength. And whether we call it a realignment or not, there has been enough change in the two parties' coalitions to produce a palpable shift in campaign and congressional debate. When Democrats call for affirmative action and Republicans are opposed, and when Democrats support civil unions for gay couples, whereas Republicans agree with the pope on abortion, then we know that there is a broader agenda in national politics than simply the economic conflicts of the 1930s and 1940s.

So in the first decade of the 2000s, the American electorate is composed of three groups of roughly similar size. There is an expanding group of Republicans dominated by conservatives, southerners, and churchgoers, and a group of Democrats, including liberals, lower-income people, and minorities, whose size has shrunk a bit in recent years. And there is a third group that could truly be termed *dealigned,* in that it feels no lasting party loyalties and usually stays out of political activity.[44] Because the Democratic and Republican camps are so close in size, and because so many Americans consider themselves independent of party, it is also an electorate capable of producing mercurial election results within and across elections. This highly competitive party system could soon produce a Republican majority, or it could sustain the divided control of government that has characterized American politics for several decades. The trajectory of American politics, then, has the potential for rapid change.

Chapter 8

Who Votes—and Why It Matters

In the end, the 2000 presidential election came down to 537 votes in Florida. That was the margin by which George W. Bush beat his Democratic opponent, Al Gore, in the state. Under Florida's winner-take-all rules, Bush thus won all of its electoral votes— enough to give him a bare majority in the Electoral College and, as a result, the presidency. At the same time, about 2.6 *million* Floridians who were registered to vote did not go to the polls—almost 5,000 times the size of Bush's tiny margin of victory.

Does it matter who votes and who doesn't? Ask Al Gore. If just a few more African Americans or fewer conservatives had come out to vote in each Florida county, the nation might have had a different president. The question of who votes, then, is a central concern of party organizations and candidates, especially the thousands of candidates in close races each year. The question of how well these voters reflect the partisanship, opinions, and social characteristics of the larger adult population is a major issue for those interested in preserving democracy.

In a more basic sense, students of parties need to be concerned about who votes because the American parties have grown and changed in response to expansions of the *right* to vote. As the electorate was enlarged to include lower-status people and then women, minorities, and younger people, the parties were forced to change their organizations and appeals. Parties that failed to adjust to the new electorates—the early Federalists, for example—became extinct. Others, such as European socialist and labor parties, have gained strength by fighting to secure the vote for lower-status citizens and then using these voters' support to win power.

Now that most American adults have the right to vote, the Democrats and Republicans continue to adjust their organizations and appeals to changes in the types of people who choose to exercise that right. Because groups have different profiles of support for the parties, as Chapter 7 showed, parties and their candidates also try to expand (or reduce) access to the polls, and to mobilize some groups of voters and not others, in order to improve their odds of winning elections. The relatively low voter turnout in American elections heightens the impact of these group differences in party support.

THE LOW TURNOUT IN AMERICAN ELECTIONS

In 2004, many observers expected voter turnout to rise dramatically. In the recent past, only between 51 and 55 percent of voting-age Americans made it to the polls in the presidential elections between 1992 and 2000—low turnouts even by American standards.[1] But the political world was different in 2004. Feelings were still raw from the 2000 post-election battle, to the extent that in a 2004 *New York Times*/CBS poll, three-quarters of Democrats surveyed said that they didn't consider Bush to have been the legitimate winner in 2000.[2] These feelings led to a closely fought campaign in 2004, in which a variety of groups mounted feverish get-out-the-vote drives.

So how high did turnout rise in 2004? Around 60 percent of eligible voters went to the polls. That was not a trivial increase; in fact, it was the highest voting rate in the United States since the 1968 election (see Figure 8.1). Yet it was no higher than the voter turnout in the Iraqi election held two months later, when large numbers of Iraqi voters expected to dodge bullets on their way to the polls, and more than 50 were killed by bomb and mortar attacks during the voting.

The 60 percent American turnout hides even lower turnouts in many states. In 2004, for example, the Center for the Study of the American Electorate reported that only 48 percent of the voting-age citizen population cast a ballot in Hawaii and about 50 percent in Arkansas and Georgia. (At the high end, 76 percent voted in Minnesota and 74 percent in Wisconsin.) Even fewer people vote in off-year elections; in 2002, a mere 39 percent of those eligible cast a vote for the top office on the ballot. Turnout rates drop further in local elections and party primaries.

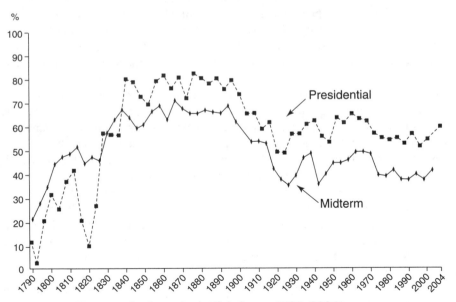

FIGURE 8.1   Turnout in American Elections: 1790–2004

Note: These are the percentages voting for president and for the office with the highest vote in midterm elections, calculated as described in note 1 to this chapter.

These low turnouts are a cause for concern. Some observers ask: How healthy can our democracy be when so many citizens don't bother to vote?[3] Others respond that the nation might be harmed by encouraging less interested, and presumably less informed, citizens to participate. Nevertheless, at other times and in other places, democracies have enjoyed much broader participation. Voting turnout in the United States was at its highest toward the end of the 1800s.[4] In more recent times, presidential turnout reached 63 percent in 1960 and turnout in off-year elections peaked at 48 percent in 1966. However, even these percentages are low compared with other countries. In almost no other industrialized democracy does such a small share of the voters take part in choosing the most important government officials.[5] In contrast, voters in nations such as Sweden and Denmark regularly turn out at rates of 80 percent or more.

What caused this drop in American voter participation? While the *right* to vote has greatly expanded, Americans have grown more reluctant to exercise that right. The major parties have played an important role in both these trends. Let us start with the expansion of voting rights.

THE EXPANDING RIGHT TO VOTE

The Constitution allows the states to decide who is eligible to vote. Since the Civil War, however, the national government has acted occasionally, most often through constitutional amendments, to keep states from imposing especially offensive restrictions on voting.

White male citizens were given the right to vote earlier in the United States than in any other democracy. In the early 1800s, the states gradually repealed the property, income, and taxpaying qualifications for voting by which they had so severely limited male suffrage.[6] By 1860, no states required property holding, and only four required substantial taxpaying as a condition for voting. About a century later, the Supreme Court, and then the Twenty-fourth Amendment, finally ended even the small poll tax as a requirement for voting.[7]

Women did not win the right to vote in all states until much later. By the mid-1870s, activists had begun to press state governments to let women vote; in 1890, when it was admitted to the Union, Wyoming became the first state to grant full voting rights to women. The push for women's suffrage then bogged down, especially in the eastern states, and women suffragists shifted their hopes to the U.S. Constitution. The Nineteenth Amendment, forbidding states to deny the vote on grounds of gender, was finally ratified in 1920.

Black Americans' right to vote has a more checkered history. Some New England states granted blacks suffrage before the Civil War. The Fifteenth Amendment, adopted after that war, declared that no state could abridge the right to vote on account of race. But the federal government soon turned its attention to other matters, and southern states worked effectively to keep blacks from voting by using devices such as poll taxes, outrageous "literacy tests," and outright intimidation. By the early 1900s, black turnout in the South had dropped to negligible levels. It remained that way in most southern states until the 1960s, when the federal government began to enforce the Fifteenth Amendment and new voting rights laws on the reluctant states.

The most recent change has been to lower the voting age to 18. In the 1960s, only a handful of states allowed people under the age of 21 to vote. In 1970, Congress lowered the minimum voting age to 18 in both state and federal elections. When the Supreme

Court decided that the act was unconstitutional for state and local elections,[8] Congress passed a constitutional amendment lowering the age to 18 for all elections; this was quickly ratified by the states in 1971.

The national government has taken other steps to expand the electorate. Congress banned literacy, understanding, and "character" tests for registration and waived residence requirements for voting in presidential elections. The so-called "Motor Voter" law, passed in 1993, required the states to let citizens register to vote at driver's license bureaus, by mail, and through agencies that give out federal benefits. Voter registration has surged in many areas as a result, although these increases have not been matched by greater voter turnout in most elections.[9]

LEGAL BARRIERS TO VOTING

In sum, the right to vote has been expanded enormously since the early 1800s through constitutional amendments, legislation, and supervision by the Supreme Court. But states continue to impose restrictions on those who would vote, including citizenship and residence requirements and the need to register before going to the polls.

Citizenship

Since the 1920s, all states have required that voters be United States citizens. As surprising as it may now seem, prior to 1894, at least 12 states permitted noncitizens to vote,[10] although some required the individual to have applied for American citizenship. The requirement of citizenship remains the biggest legal barrier to voting. There are millions of adults living in the United States, most of them concentrated in California, Florida, Texas, and New York, who are working and paying taxes but cannot vote until they are "naturalized" as citizens, a process that can take two or three years to complete.

Residence

For most of American history, states could require citizens to live in a state and locality for a certain period of time before being allowed to vote there. Most states had three-layer residence requirements: a minimum period of time in the state, a shorter time in the county, and an even shorter period in the local voting district. Southern states had the longest residence requirements (which kept migrant farm workers from voting), but other states also had long waits for eligibility.

A few states began to lower their residence requirements in the 1950s and 1960s as society became more mobile; many states set up even lower requirements for newcomers wishing to vote in presidential elections. In 1970, Congress limited states' residence requirements to a maximum of 30 days for voting in presidential elections. Since then, almost half of the states have dropped residence requirements altogether, and most of the rest have fixed them at one month or less.

Despite these changes, Americans' mobility is still a barrier to voting. The United States is a nation of movers. Those who have moved recently are much less likely to vote, in part because they must take the time and initiative to find out where and when they need to register (see following). Researchers estimate that with the impact of mobility removed, turnout would be about 9 percent higher.[11]

Registration

Another major obstacle to voting is the registration requirement—the rule in most states that citizens must register in advance in order to vote in an election. During most of the 1800s, voters needed only to show up on Election Day to cast a ballot, or to be listed on the government's voting roll—the same rules that most European democracies use today. Progressive reformers in the late 1800s urged states to require advance registration in order to limit illegal voting in the big cities. That increased the motivation needed to vote because it required a trip to the registration office well before many citizens had tuned in to the election. These registration requirements reduced the high turnout levels of that time.[12]

States have since relaxed these requirements to varying degrees. The relevant rules include the closing date for registration (which ranges from none to 30 days before the election), the frequency with which the registration rolls are purged of those who haven't voted recently, and the ease of registration.[13] North Dakota does not require its citizens to register at all, and six other states permit registering on Election Day; these states have higher turnouts.

These remaining requirements still raise the "costs" of voting. Studies estimate that turnout would be much higher if all states set regular as well as evening and Saturday hours for registering and did not purge for nonvoting. The greatest gains would be realized by allowing Election Day registration, which would let citizens cast a ballot even if they did not get interested enough to take part until the last, most engaging days of the campaign.[14]

THE SPECIAL CASE OF VOTING RIGHTS FOR AFRICAN AMERICANS

Legal barriers to voting were especially effective in denying the vote to southern blacks. The electoral system was manipulated in the South by a variety of laws, capricious election administration, and intimidation and violence when these subtler methods were not effective. The result was to keep blacks from the polls in the former Confederacy and some neighboring states for almost a century.

The Long Struggle for Voting Rights

For years after the end of Reconstruction, the states and the Supreme Court played a game of constitutional "hide and seek." States would devise a way to disenfranchise blacks, the Court would strike it down as unconstitutional, and the states would find another. One example was the "white primary." Faced with the threat of blacks voting in the Democratic primary, some states simply declared the party to be a private club open only to whites; therefore, blacks could not vote in the primary. The Republican Party barely existed in the South at this time, so the candidate who won the Democratic primary was assured of winning the general election. It took 21 years of lawsuits and five Supreme Court cases to end this practice.[15]

In addition, residence requirements were most strict in the South. Most states in that region required payment of a poll tax in order to vote—just one or two dollars, but often demanded well before an election, with the stipulation that the taxpayer keep a receipt

BARRIERS TO BLACK REGISTRATION IN THE SOUTH

In their account of the civil rights movement in the South, Pat Watters and Reese Cleghorn describe how blacks were prevented from registering by simple but effective administrative practices:

> Slowdowns were common. Separate tables would be assigned to whites and Negroes [the customary term for African Americans before the mid-1960s]. If a line of Negroes were waiting for the Negro table, a white might go ahead of them, use the empty white table, and leave. In Anniston, Alabama, a report said the white table was larger, and Negroes were not allowed in the room when a white was using it. Another variation was to seat four Negroes at a table, and make three wait until the slowest had finished, while others waited outside in line. These methods were particularly effective when coupled with the one or two day a month registration periods. . . . In one north Florida county, the registrar didn't bother with any of these refinements, and didn't close his office when Negro applicants appeared. He simply sat with his legs stretched out across the doorway. Negroes didn't break through them.

Source: Pat Watters and Reese Cleghorn, *Climbing Jacob's Ladder* (New York: Harcourt Brace Jovanovich, 1967), pp. 122–123.

and present it weeks later at the voting booth. Many states also required some prospective voters to pass a literacy test measuring reading ability and understanding. Local voting officials, who were usually hostile to blacks voting, had the power to decide who was "literate" enough to pass the test. These laws were intentionally directed at the poor and uneducated black population.

In addition, endless delays and other technicalities were designed to prevent blacks from registering to vote (see box on this page). Those who kept trying were often faced with economic reprisal (the loss of a job or a home) and physical violence. It is not surprising, in this relentlessly hostile environment, that only 5 percent of voting-age blacks were registered in the 11 southern states as late as 1940.[16]

Although courts finally struck down the white primary and the poll tax, they were not as effective against the more informal hurdles blacks faced. Reformers, then, turned to Congress and the executive branch. The federal Voting Rights Act of 1965, extended in 1982, authorized the U.S. Justice Department to seek injunctions against anyone who prevented blacks from voting. When the Justice Department could convince a federal court that a "pattern or practice" of discrimination existed in a district, the court could send federal registrars there to register voters. It could also supervise voting procedures in states and counties where less than 50 percent of potential voters had gone to the polls in the most recent presidential election.[17]

The Growth of Black Registration in the South

This unprecedented federal intervention in state elections, combined with the civil rights movement's efforts to mobilize black voters, enabled the black electorate to grow enor-

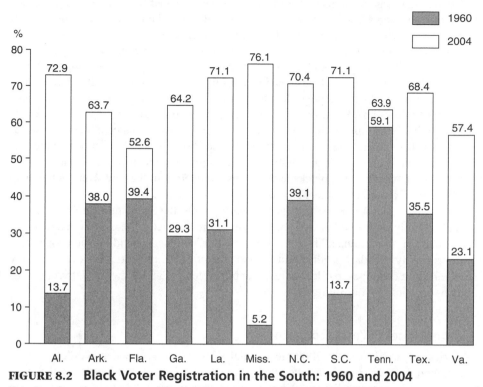

FIGURE 8.2 **Black Voter Registration in the South: 1960 and 2004**

Note: Bars show the percentage of blacks in the two years who were registered to vote.

Source: U.S. Census Bureau, http://www.census.gov/population/www/socdemo/voting/cps2004.html (accessed June 9, 2005).

mously in the South. Black registration increased from 5 percent of the black voting-age population in 1940 to 29 percent in 1960 and then to a level close to that of white southerners by the 1990s. White registration also increased slightly during this period. Yet black registration levels still vary among the southern states, depending on the size and socioeconomic characteristics of their black populations, states' political traditions, and the barriers they continue to raise to black participation (Figure 8.2).

From Voting Rights to Representation

Even though they are no longer systematically prevented from voting, African Americans still find it hard to gain an effective political voice in many areas of the South. In the debate over extending the Voting Rights Act in 1981 and 1982, the major issue was the effort by some states to dilute the impact of black votes. This was most commonly done by redrawing legislative district lines in order to divide black voters among several districts and by annexing white suburbs to offset black majorities in the cities.

After the 1990 census, the first Bush administration pressed southern states to redraw congressional district lines so as to create some districts with a majority of black or Latino voters, called *"majority-minority" districts.* It was assumed that these districts would be very likely to elect black legislators to Congress and thus improve the representation of

African Americans. A number of these districts were created by an interesting alliance of black and Latino Democrats with white Republicans. The result was an increase in the number of congressional seats held by black Americans.

Another effect of these majority-minority districts, however, was to elect more Republicans to Congress from the South—one reason why Republicans supported their creation. Because the districts are fashioned by packing as many (heavily Democratic) black voters into a district as possible, the neighboring districts are left with a higher proportion of whites and Republicans. So, according to one estimate, "for every overwhelmingly black Democratic district created, there is a good chance of creating two or more districts that are overwhelmingly white and Republican."[18] In turn, Democratic state legislatures try to pack the GOP vote into as few districts as possible and to draw other districts with enough blacks and Latinos, coupled with the few white voters who still support Democrats, to elect Democratic representatives.

In a series of close decisions since the early 1990s, the Supreme Court rejected the most flagrantly engineered of these majority-minority districts. The Court ruled that race cannot be the "predominant" factor in drawing district lines, overriding such considerations as county boundaries, compactness, and protecting incumbents. However, a closely divided Court continues to rule that race can be an element in redrawing district lines, as long as it is not the controlling factor.[19]

Getting Blacks' Votes Counted

Americans learned from the 2000 presidential election that even when people get to the polls, their votes are not always counted. Poorer and minority-dominated districts tend to have older and less reliable voting machines that are more likely to make errors in counting votes. The U.S. Commission on Civil Rights reported in 2001 that although it found no evidence of a systematic effort to disenfranchise blacks, they were ten times more likely than whites to have their ballots undercounted or rejected in the 2000 Florida vote because they lived in districts with less reliable voting systems.[20]

These frustrations are compounded by the fact that between 13 and 17 percent of black males have lost the right to vote because they have had felony convictions. Mandatory sentences for drug use appear to target drugs used more often by blacks, and almost all states deny felons the right to vote, at least while they are behind bars, and often for the rest of their lives. More generally, estimates are that more than 4 million Americans of all races have lost their right to vote because of a previous felony conviction.[21] Predicting from their SES and race, most of these people would probably vote Democratic. So, although black turnout rates are much higher now than they were in the mid-1900s, more subtle challenges to blacks' voting rights remain.

POLITICAL INFLUENCES ON TURNOUT

The *right* to vote, we have seen, is now almost universal in the United States. But people differ in their willingness to exercise that right. Among the forces that can affect turnout are various political factors, including the importance of the contest, the level of public interest it generates, the amount of competition between the parties, and the efforts of parties and other groups to bring voters to the polls.

The Excitement of the Election

American voters face more frequent elections than almost any other population in the world. Within four years, they will be called to the polls to select legislators, executives, and even judges at the national, state, and local levels, and in both general elections and primaries. In some areas voters will have to deal with initiatives, referenda, and recall elections. In 2003, Californians were asked to vote on whether to recall the governor they had elected just 11 months earlier. Americans pay dearly, in the currency of many and frequent voting decisions, for the right to keep government on a short electoral leash.

Voter participation varies a great deal depending on the type of election.[22] It is usually highest in presidential elections and lowest in local races. General elections normally attract far more voters than primaries. It is understandable why general election campaigns for the presidency and governorships entice more voters to participate. The personalities and issues involved are more highly publicized, the coverage is more intense, and people's party loyalties are aroused, in contrast with the situation of many nonpartisan local elections and party primaries.

Initiatives and referenda, the Progressives' devices for allowing voters to decide issues directly, bring out fewer voters than candidate elections; the issues are often complicated enough to confuse many would-be voters.[23] Yet under some conditions, even these Progressive reforms can provoke a large voter turnout. In the 2003 California recall election, though voters had to work their way through a ballot listing 135 candidates, the fact that they included movie star Arnold Schwarzenegger (the eventual winner), a porn actress, the publisher of *Hustler* magazine, a bounty hunter, a comedian, and a sumo wrestler generated enough interest, or perhaps entertainment, to mobilize voters.

Close Competition

Political competition brings voters to the polls. Voting participation increases in races that are hotly contested, regardless of the type of office, the nature of the electorate, and the district's historical voting trends.[24] Voter turnout rose in 2004, compared with 2000, by an average of 7.4 percent in the so-called "battleground" states, where a close vote was expected, compared with only 4.6 percent in other states.[25] In contrast, the 2004 Republican primaries, in which there was no competition, had the lowest turnout of any primary season on record. Closely fought races are exciting and give voters more assurance that their vote will make a difference.

Historically, changes in party competition have affected turnout levels. National politics was fiercely competitive in the two decades before 1900. In the late 1890s, however, the Populist movement was absorbed into the Democratic Party in the South and the Democrats' appeal declined in other areas. Participation in presidential elections then dropped markedly—from almost 80 percent of the voting-age population in 1876–1896 to about 65 percent in the early 1900s. It seems likely that the decline in party competition reduced the parties' incentive to work at mobilizing voters, and that produced a drop in turnout.[26] In more recent elections as well, the decisions of campaigns and parties to run ads only in the most competitive states can dampen turnout in such large states as California and New York, which are often considered safe for one party's presidential candidate.

The Representativeness of the Party System

Turnout tends to be much higher in European multiparty systems, and especially in those using systems of proportional representation,[27] where each sizable group in the society is often represented by its own party. The broad, coalitional nature of the two major American parties may make it more difficult for citizens to feel that a party gives voice to their individual needs. One price the United States may pay for its two-party system, then, is lower turnout.

The particular types of conflicts that shape the party system, whether social, economic, religious, or racial, can also affect voter involvement. Citizens who feel that they have a big stake in the prevailing political conflicts are more likely to see a reason to vote—for example, elderly Americans at a time when their Social Security and Medicare benefits, which depend so heavily on government decisions, are consistently an issue in national campaigns.

Organized Efforts to Mobilize Voters

One of the most important findings about voter turnout is that people go to the polls when somebody encourages them to do so. Person-to-person contact does a better job of increasing turnout than do mail or phone appeals.[28] Personal canvassing is especially effective in mobilizing first-time voters; in 2004, three-fifths of new voters said they came to the polls because "my family or friends encouraged me to vote," compared with only one-fifth of repeat voters.[29]

Face-to-face voter mobilization had become less common in the late 1900s. But during the past decade, a number of groups have developed programs to increase turnout among their supporters. Civil rights groups worked closely with the Democratic Party in the early 2000s to bring more blacks to the polls.[30] Organized labor mounted a major, and apparently effective, get-out-the-vote drive in 2000, built on union members' contacts with other members and their friends and neighbors. Sweeping voter registration drives were conducted in targeted areas in 2004 by both Democratic-related interest groups and Republicans. The Republican effort was particularly successful because it used local volunteers and targeted people whose lifestyles fit the profile of likely Republicans—for example, white small-town church-going Protestants and Catholics—but who had not been to the polls in recent years.[31]

Not all such efforts have been as effective. MTV's "Choose or Lose" campaign, aimed at teens and young adults, for example, has not made much of a dent in the low voting turnout of that age group. Because new campaign techniques allow campaigns to target the people most likely to vote, the existing racial and socioeconomic status (SES) differences between voters and nonvoters can be further entrenched. Once the mobilization has brought an individual to the polls, however, he or she is likely to return. Voting becomes a habit, which can help to explain the increasing tendency to vote as people age.[32]

TURNOUT: INDIVIDUAL DIFFERENCES

Differences among individuals also affect their likelihood of voting. We can think about the decision to vote in terms of its costs and benefits to the individual. Each of us pays some costs for the privilege of voting, not in cash but in time, energy, and attention. What we get in return may seem minimal; the influence of a single vote in most elections is likely to be small. From that perspective, it may be remarkable that anyone votes at all.[33] A variety of economic and social forces, from citizens' levels of education to their social connections, affect the ways in which individuals weigh the costs and benefits of going to the polls.

Socioeconomic Status

The biggest difference between voters and nonvoters is their SES; lower status Americans are much less likely to vote.[34] A careful study of voting argues that education level is the most powerful influence on turnout (see Figure 8.3, section A); the impact of income and occupational differences is minimal once education is taken into account. More education helps people understand the complexities of politics and shows them how to get the information they need to make political choices. People with more education are more likely to feel that they ought to vote, to gain satisfaction from voting,

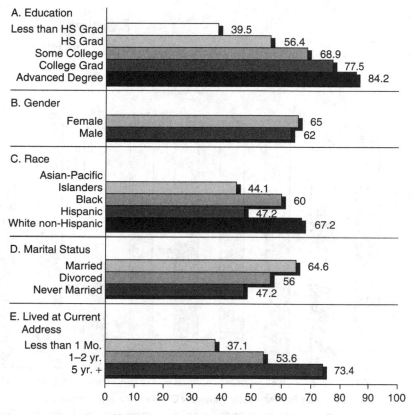

FIGURE 8.3 Group Differences in Voter Turnout: 2004

Note: Bars show the percentage of each group who reported having voted in the 2004 presidential election, based on the voting-age citizen population.

Source: U.S. Census Bureau, http://www.census.gov/population/www/socdemo/voting/cps2004.html (accessed June 9, 2005).

and to have the experience with meeting deadlines and filling out forms that will be necessary to register and vote.[35]

This relationship between SES and voting sounds so obvious that we would expect to see it everywhere. Yet the relationship is less strong in many other democracies. In these nations, labor parties and other groups work hard enough to bring less-educated and lower-income people to the polls that they compensate for the disadvantages of low SES that are so marked in American politics.[36]

Youth

After socioeconomic explanations, the next most powerful personal factor in accounting for differences between voters and nonvoters is youth. For a long time, younger Americans have been less likely to go to the polls than are older people, especially those over the age of 65 (see Figure 8.4). Much of the difference reflects the high "start-up" costs

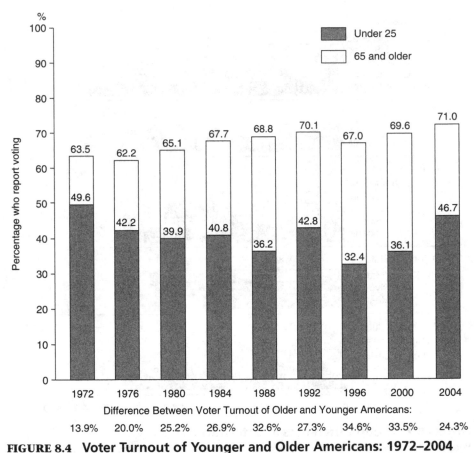

FIGURE 8.4   Voter Turnout of Younger and Older Americans: 1972–2004

Source: U.S. Census Bureau, http://www.census.gov/population/www/socdemo/voting/cps2004.html (accessed June 9, 2005).

younger people must pay when voting: the difficulties of settling into a community, registering for the first time, and establishing the habit of voting, all at a time when more personal interests dominate their lives. The lowering of the national voting age to 18 and the entry of the large "baby boom" generation into the electorate helped to depress voting rates more generally.

It was expected to be different in 2004. Surveys showed that young people were paying more attention to the election and more likely to consider it important than had been the case in 2000. And in fact, voter turnout among young voters increased; almost 5 million more people under the age of 30 showed up at the polls in 2004. But turnout increased among all other age groups as well, so the proportion of young people going to the polls rose only from 16.4 percent to 18.4 percent of the total.[37]

As a result, campaign agendas have become even more attuned to the concerns of older voters—Social Security, Medicare, prescription drugs—because they are much more likely to vote. Studies show that young adults hold attitudes different from those of their parents and grandparents. Younger people, on average, are more likely to accept the idea of privatizing public services (for instance, letting people invest some of their Social Security taxes in the stock market) than older people are, and also more tolerant of diversity, including women's rights, affirmative action, and gay marriage.[38] But the low turnout of young adults makes it less likely that these views will be heard.

Gender and Race

For many decades after getting the right to vote, women voted less often than men, but women's increasing education levels and changes in women's roles in society have largely eliminated this gender difference (see Figure 8.3, section B). The gap in voting rates between blacks and whites still persists, though it has gotten smaller (see Figure 8.3, section C). The remaining racial differences in voting are due almost entirely to differences in education and occupational status, on average, between whites and blacks.[39] Latinos and Asian Americans have the lowest voter turnout rates.

Social Connectedness

People who have a lot of social ties—those who belong to a variety of organizations and are closely connected with friends and family—are much more likely to participate in elections than others are. Members of organizations have much higher voting rates than nonmembers; this adds weight to the conclusion that organizations play an important role in mobilizing voters. Voting is also more common among people who are well integrated into the community through home ownership, long-time residence, church attendance, or a job outside the home. Even marriage or the loss of a spouse affects the likelihood that an individual will vote (see Figure 8.3, sections D and E).[40]

Political Attitudes

Attitudes toward politics affect individuals' motivation to vote. Those who find the current campaign more interesting and who have stronger party loyalties are more involved in elections. In addition, a cluster of "civic attitudes" predisposes individuals to vote. The

WHY DIDN'T YOU VOTE?

Here's why people said they didn't go to the polls in the 2004 election:

I was too busy	20%
Illness or disability	15
Just not interested	11
Didn't like the candidates	10
Out of town	9
I don't know why	8
Problems with registration*	7
I forgot	3
It was inconvenient	3
Transportation problems	2
The weather was bad	0.5
Other	11

* Only the answers of registered voters are reported here.

Source: U.S. Census Bureau, "Reasons for Not Voting," Table 12, at http://www
.census.gov/population/www/socdemo/voting/cps2004.html (accessed June 9, 2005).

most important of these are feelings that government is responsive to citizens (termed *external political efficacy*) and can be trusted to do what is right (*trust in government*), and a sense of responsibility to take part in elections (*citizen duty*).[41] Individuals' attitudes probably interact with the structure of the political system: Divided government and separated powers may depress turnout by making it harder for individuals to know who is responsible for what the government does.[42]

Personal Costs of Voting

Voting can be stressful for some people—for example, those who have a politically mixed environment, such as Democratic relatives and a Republican spouse.[43] Some people refuse to register because the registration rolls are used to choose citizens for jury duty, which they may want to avoid. There are even less pressing reasons to avoid voting (see box above).

WHY ISN'T VOTER TURNOUT EVEN HIGHER?

Despite all the efforts made by parties and interest groups to activate them, more than 78 million Americans who were eligible to vote in 2004 stayed home from the polls. The long recent decline in voter turnout, followed by a limited recovery in 2004, is puzzling to many observers because they have occurred at a time when a variety of events should have greatly increased Americans' likelihood of voting. Interestingly, there has been a marked recent decrease in British voter turnout as well.[44]

The Puzzle of Low Turnouts

There are many reasons why voting turnout ought to have risen dramatically since the mid-1900s. Americans' educational levels have increased substantially, and higher education is linked with higher voter turnout. It is easier to cast a ballot now, because of less strict registration, residence, and absentee voting rules; Oregon, for example, now votes entirely by mail. Canvassing and the Motor Voter law have led many more people to register. Yet the increase in actual voter turnout has simply returned the nation to the voting levels of the late 1960s.[45]

One main reason is that the American electorate has become more mobile since 1960. Americans are less inclined to attend religious services on a regular basis and less likely to be married. These declines in social "connectedness" weaken the ties that bind people to the social networks that stimulate participation. Personal canvassing by parties and interest groups also seemed to decline during the 1970s and 1980s, so citizens were less likely to be mobilized to go to the polls.

Another important factor is that the political attitudes that support participation, especially the belief that government is responsive to its citizens (external political efficacy), have declined since 1960. Alienation and cynicism have increased. When people don't feel connected to the political process, they don't vote. Among these nonvoters are some who are relatively well informed, better educated, younger, and with somewhat higher incomes than the average citizen but who have become disgusted with government or with particular candidates and who stay home from the polls as a form of protest. More education and easier access to the vote, then, do not tempt them to become more involved in politics.[46] And variations in the strength of people's partisanship are also connected with voter turnout; when party ID weakened in the 1970s, voter turnout declined.[47]

What Could Stimulate More Participation?

Yet there have been three elections since the late 1960s when voter participation went up. What can they tell us about the forces that increase voter turnout? In the 1992 and 1994 elections, although participation was still low by most standards, it reached its highest levels in a decade for midterm contests and in two decades for presidential contests.

Increased turnout in the 1992 race can easily be explained by the factors we have already discussed. It was the closest presidential race since 1976. The excitement of the campaign was heightened by a popular third-party candidate (Ross Perot) who entered the race, withdrew, and entered again, and spent a great deal of money in the process. Similarly, the political situation leading up to the 1994 congressional elections was dramatic enough to bring more people to the polls. The Republicans seemed to have their best chance to recapture control of Congress in four decades. Media attention focused on the "Contract with America," a statement of conservative principles signed by most Republican congressional candidates in an effort to nationalize the campaign. It proved to be an effective move; GOP House candidates drew almost 9 million more votes than they had in 1990 and Democrats lost nearly a million votes.

Three low-turnout races followed. But the aftermath of the 2000 presidential race generated passionate public reaction. The election was the closest in history; Al Gore won the popular vote, and George W. Bush won the electoral vote. Each side claimed victory, and the result was decided by the courts rather than in the voting booths. The consequence was an extremely intense and bitter race in 2004, in which the Republican vice president charged that terrorist attacks on the United States would increase if the Democratic candidate won and Democrats handed out bumper stickers saying "Re-Defeat Bush."

The lesson of the early 1990s and 2004, then, is that when an important race is up for grabs, when the candidates are entertaining and when elections turn on an identifiable set of divisive themes, political interest should increase and carry voter turnout along with it. Without the stimulation of an interesting contest, or the active mobilization of partisans, turnout in American elections is likely to remain low.

WHY DO THESE CHANGES IN TURNOUT MATTER?

This chapter has introduced two curiously related trends: The right to vote has been greatly expanded in the United States, but in recent years, with the important exception of 2004, Americans seem less and less willing to take advantage of that right. Both of these trends have important consequences for the parties.

Long-Range Effects

The addition of new groups to the electorate has reshaped the parties. When blacks began to vote in large numbers in the 1960s and 1970s, they voted overwhelmingly for Democratic candidates, and the events that led to their enfranchisement produced a countermovement of whites away from the Democrats, particularly in the South.[48] Chapter 7 discussed the impact of these changes on the two parties' stands on issues, ranging from civil rights to welfare reform.

Voting rights for 18- to 21-year-olds have had more mixed effects on the parties. Young voters were more likely to be Democrats than Republicans in the 1970s, but that trend reversed in the 1980s and re-reversed in the early 1990s. The youngest voters seem to pay more attention to the candidates and appeals of each particular election than to the parties' more fundamental differences.

The voting population has changed in other ways. The proportion of the electorate living in the South and West has increased; these are areas where Republicans have done especially well in elections. In addition, the aging of the population has enlarged the proportion of elderly voters in each successive presidential election. As these groups expand, the parties must pay greater attention to their distinctive interests when choosing candidates and taking positions on issues.

In the same sense, groups that shrink as a proportion of the electorate, either because they are becoming a smaller part of the population as a whole or because they are going to the polls in smaller numbers, will probably lose political influence. Elected officials and parties, understandably, think more about the needs of those who affect election results than those who don't. For example, recent studies show that members of Congress direct more federal spending to counties in their district with higher voter turnout than to those with lower turnout.[49]

The implications of this potential loss of influence are all the more serious because nonvoters are more likely than voters to come from disadvantaged groups. The average nonregistrant is younger than the average registered voter and is more likely to be black, Asian, or Latino. Although nonvoters do not differ much from voters in their views on particular issues, they do differ in the importance they attach to various issues. That is not surprising, because nonvoters tend to have fewer economic resources and greater need for government assistance.[50]

Effects on Particular Elections

Changes in turnout from election to election can affect the parties as well. The conventional wisdom is that large turnouts favor Democratic candidates. Most nonvoters come from groups usually inclined to vote Democratic. That is why proposals to make it easier to register and vote are often assumed to benefit the Democrats. It explains why organized labor spends so much money and effort on registration and get-out-the-vote campaigns. It is one reason why Republicans have lobbied to schedule gubernatorial elections in nonpresidential election years, because the smaller voter turnout would advantage Republican candidates. It even explains politicians' belief that rainy weather is Republican weather, in that Republicans will come to the polls anyway.

The conventional wisdom is not always correct, however. We have seen that people who are more interested and involved in politics are more likely to vote. So an increase in voter turnout in a particular election is likely to come from the segment of the electorate that is less politically interested. These less-involved people tend to vote only if they are motivated by a dramatic issue or a popular candidate, regardless of party. In fact, Republican presidential candidates have won most of the large-turnout elections in the past five decades.[51]

THE CHALLENGE TO THE PARTIES

This chapter began by citing one of the most striking facts about current American politics: that even in the most high-profile elections, four in ten potential voters stay home. The case for democracy often rests on the argument that the best decisions are made when the responsibility for decision making is most widely shared. Full participation in democratic self-governance, then, would seem to be a valuable ideal (see "Which Would You Choose?" on page 154). Yet American politics falls far short of that ideal, a finding that is all the more bitter when we see that voting turnouts are higher in most other democracies.

If widespread nonvoting is an insult to the democratic spirit, it also raises questions as to whether the major parties are doing an effective job of involving the whole electorate. The parties are the organizations that developed to mobilize citizens for political action. They have the great strength, compared with other kinds of organized interests, of being able to recruit large and diverse groups of people into politics. As instruments of mass democracy, it would seem that the parties ought to strive for the greatest possible citizen participation in elections.

However, the parties do not always seem to relish the challenge of attracting new voting groups, especially those of low SES. They have adjusted their strategies to the electorate as it now exists. They understandably work to increase turnout only among people who resemble their current supporters.

The fact that the active electorate in the United States is not as diverse as the nation's population probably reduces the amount of conflict in American politics and the range

WE NEED EVERY VOTE ...

Democracy is most vibrant when there is full debate among all viewpoints. When as many people as possible take part in elections, government is more likely to come up with the creative solutions needed to solve public problems.

Politicians pay more attention to the needs of those who vote than to those who don't. So the views and interests of the nonvoters, though real, may well go unrepresented.

The most committed voters tend to be older, more educated, have higher incomes, and are often more extreme in their viewpoints than other citizens are. These people will thus get more than their share of government benefits and attention from elected officials anxious to get their votes.

It is the more alienated and dissatisfied people who stay away from the polls. They can become ripe for extremist appeals. It's better to bring them into the political system where they can voice their concerns in more productive ways.

LET SLEEPING DOGS LIE ...

Those who are least likely to vote are also the least interested in government and the least well informed. Why, then, should we encourage them to have a voice in elections? If they don't care enough to vote, or don't know enough, shouldn't we be grateful that they don't show up at the polls?

If people have the right to vote and choose not to, maybe that means they are satisfied with things the way they are. If they really wanted change, they could use their votes to obtain it.

If we relax registration and residence requirements to encourage more people to vote, we're opening the floodgates to vote fraud: people voting more than once or voting under other people's direction.

American democracy has been vibrant enough to survive impeachments, financial scandals, and candidates who lose the presidency even though they won the popular vote. If it ain't broke, why fix it?

of political interests to which the parties must respond. That, in turn, makes it easier for the parties to be relatively moderate and pragmatic, compared with many parties in European democracies. On the other hand, the stability that results is purchased at the cost of the absence from the polls of large numbers of eligible Americans, who are on average less affluent, less educated, and younger than those who do take part in choosing the nation's leaders. Because the parties are most responsive to those who show up regularly at the polls, the low turnout rates and the underrepresentation of disadvantaged groups in the voting public should be real causes of concern.

PART FOUR

Parties, Nominations, and Elections

Elections are great political spectacles, full of crisis and resolution, comedy and tragedy.[1] They are also the main bridge that links the party organizations and identifiers, the first two parts of the American parties that we explored in Parts 2 and 3, with the party in government. During campaigns, party activists try to energize party identifiers and get them to the polls to support candidates who share the party label. The need to unite around the party's nominees and to work together in the general election are powerful reasons for the three parts of the parties to reconcile their differences—at least until the votes are counted. Elections also link the parties at different levels of government. The process of nominating and electing a presidential candidate binds the state and local parties into at least a brief coalition with the national party. Similarly, a statewide election focuses the energies of local party organizations and leaders within the state.

There is good reason why elections ought to encourage cooperation within the party. When candidates run more capable campaigns, they improve not only their own ability to attract money and other resources but also that of their party organization. When candidates win, their party's activists stand a better chance of getting action on their issue agenda. When a party's candidate wins the governorship or the local executive office in some areas, then party leaders may gain access to patronage jobs, which in turn can bring more activists into the party organization. In the effort to win, candidates and party activists have to mobilize as many of the party's identifiers as possible. Because victory holds so many attractions for all three parts of the party, it is a powerful lure for them to work together.

All this cooperative activity does not come easily. Almost every aspect of the electoral process, and especially the nominating process, can also pit the needs of one part of the party against those of another. Whenever primaries are used to select a party's candidates, there will be times when party voters choose a nominee regarded as a disaster by party leaders. Efforts by the party organization to raise money will compete with candidates' own fund-raising. Candidates get to choose which issues they will emphasize, which advisers they will hire and which strategies they will adopt, and these choices will affect the image of the party as a whole, even when the party's leaders, activists, and voters do not share these preferences. Once in office, the party's candidates may have reason to ignore or downplay some questions that are "hot button" issues to party activists.

In addition to the competition within each party, the parties also compete on the larger electoral stage with other political organizations. Groups such as single-issue organizations, labor unions, religious lobbies, reform groups, and corporations all get involved in campaigns in order to achieve their political goals. Some of these groups work very aggressively to help candidates get nominated, raise money, influence public opinion, and win the election. Democratic state party leaders, for example, will probably have to compete with environmental groups, women's rights groups, civil rights organizations, pro-choice activists, and unions representing teachers, trial lawyers, government employees, and a variety of other occupations to get the attention of a Democratic candidate for statewide office.

This competition and cooperation is guided by a set of rules, just as the cooperation and competition in a basketball game are. These rules range from laws to standard practices, and, as in basketball, they have a tremendous impact on the results. One of these "rules" is the widespread use of primary elections, which poses a major challenge to party organizations in their effort to control the nomination of candidates. Another "rule" is the set of voting systems used in communities across the nation, whose limitations became so painfully obvious in the 2000 and 2004 elections, and that can affect Democratic and Republican campaigns differently. Yet another is the set of rules that govern campaign fund-raising.

The first two chapters in this section focus on parties' involvement in nominating candidates. Chapter 9 explores the nomination process in general, and Chapter 10 considers the fascinating and peculiar practices through which the parties select their presidential candidates. In Chapter 11, we turn to the role of parties in general elections, and finally, Chapter 12 discusses money in politics. The constant search for dollars to run campaigns gave rise to extensive reform efforts in the 1970s and has prompted more recent debate about the effects of these reforms, leading to the passage of a new campaign finance reform law in 2002. This chapter traces the flow of money into campaigns and considers how it can both expand and contract the influence of parties on their candidates.

Chapter 9

How Parties Choose Candidates

In addition to public opinion polls, drive-through restaurants, and other means of democratizing life, Americans invented primary elections. In a primary (more formally known as a *direct primary*), the party electorate chooses which candidates will run for office under the party's label. Then, in a later *general election,* all voters can make the final choice between the two parties' nominees for each office. To American voters neck-deep in primaries during an election season, this may seem like the "normal" way for parties to nominate candidates. But in reality, although the idea of a primary election has spread recently, candidates in much of the rest of the democratic world are still selected by party leaders, activists, or elected officials, not by voters.[1]

These differences in nomination procedures explain a great deal about the contrasts between American party politics and those of other democracies. The shift to primaries has forced the American parties to develop a different set of strategies in making nominations, contesting elections, and trying to hold their candidates accountable after winning public office than we would find in nations that do not hold primaries.

The direct primary permeates every level of American politics. The great majority of states use it in all nominations, and the rest use it for most elective offices. It dominates the presidential nominating process (see Chapter 10). Even though it is just the first of two steps in electing public officials, it does the major screening of candidates by reducing the choices to two in most races. The selection of nominees in the primary can affect the party's chance for winning the general election. In areas where one party dominates, the voters' only real choice is made in the primary. What led to the use of this two-step election process? How does it work and how well does it serve the needs of voters, candidates, and parties?

HOW THE NOMINATION PROCESS EVOLVED

For the first 110 years of the American republic, candidates for office were nominated by party caucuses and, later, by party conventions. In both cases, it was the leaders and activists of the party organizations who chose the party's nominees, not the rest of the voting public.

Nominations by Caucus

In the early years, as the parties expanded from being coalitions in the Congress to establishing local and state organizations, they held local caucuses (meetings) to choose candidates for county offices. Caucuses of like-minded partisans in Congress continued to nominate presidential and vice-presidential candidates. Similar caucuses in state legislatures nominated candidates for governor and other statewide offices. These caucuses were informal; the participants were self-selected. There weren't even any procedures for ensuring that all the major figures of the party would take part.[2]

Nominations by Convention

As the push for popular democracy spread, these caucuses came to be seen as an aristocratic elite—"King Caucus"—that ignored public opinion. In 1831, a minor party called the anti-Masons held a national convention to nominate its presidential candidate, in the hope of getting enough press and public attention to gain major party status. The Jacksonian Democrats held their own convention in time for the 1832 election. From then on, through the rest of the century, conventions were the main means of nominating presidential candidates. These nominating conventions were composed of delegates chosen by state and local party leaders, often at their own lower level nominating conventions.

These large and chaotic conventions looked more broadly representative than the caucuses but often were not. Delegates were chosen and the conventions managed by the heavy hands of the party leaders. Reformers began to denounce the convention system as yet another form of boss rule. By the end of the 1800s, the Progressive movement led the drive against conventions. Sympathetic journalists, called "muckrakers," wrote stories about party leaders crushing any outbursts of democracy at national conventions.[3]

Nominations by Direct Primaries

The Progressives proposed a new way to nominate candidates. Instead of giving party leaders the power to choose, they suggested, let the voters select their party's candidates for each office directly. This direct primary (or first) election reflected the core belief of the Progressives: that the best way to cure a democracy's ills was to prescribe larger doses of democracy. Robert M. La Follette, a Progressive leader, argued that the caucus and convention served only to "give respectable form to political robbery." In a primary, in contrast, "the citizen may cast his vote directly to nominate the candidate of the party with which he affiliates. . . . The nomination of the party will not be the result of 'compromise' or impulse, or evil design . . . but the candidates of the majority, honestly and fairly nominated."[4]

Some southern states had adopted primaries at the local level in the years after the Civil War, often to legitimize the nominees and settle internal disputes in their one-party Democratic systems. In the first two decades of the twentieth century, all but four other states turned to primaries for at least some of their statewide nominations. This was a time when one party or the other dominated the politics of many states—the most pervasive one-party rule in American history. It might be possible to tolerate the poor choices made by conventions when voters have a real choice in the general election, but when the nominees of the dominant party have no serious competition, those shortcomings were harder to accept. So the Progressives, who fought economic monopoly with antitrust legislation, used the direct primary as their major weapon in battling political monopoly.

Although the primary was designed to democratize the nominating process, many of its supporters hoped that it would go further and cripple the political party itself. They felt that the best way to weaken the parties was to divest the party organization of its most important power—the nomination of candidates—and give it instead to party voters. In fact, some states, such as Wisconsin, adopted a definition of the party electorate so broad that it included any voters who chose to vote in the party's primary on Election Day.

Primaries were not the first cause of party weakness in the United States. If party leaders had been strong enough throughout the country when primaries were proposed, then they would have been able to keep these primary laws from passing. But primaries did undermine the party organizations' power even further. Elected officials who were nominated by the voters in primaries were unlikely to feel as much loyalty to the party organization as were officials who owed their nominations to party leaders. Largely because of the existence of primaries, party leaders in the United States have less control over who will receive the party nomination than in most other democratic political systems. In some states, the reforms required that the party organization's own leaders be chosen in primaries; the result was that the parties risked losing control even over their own internal affairs.

THE CURRENT MIX OF PRIMARIES AND CONVENTIONS

Although conventions are no longer common, they are still used to nominate candidates in a few states and, most conspicuously, in the contest for the presidency. Because states have the legal right to design their own nominating systems, the result is a mixture of primaries and conventions for choosing candidates for state offices.

All 50 states now use primaries to nominate at least some statewide officials, and 38 of them (plus the District of Columbia) use this method exclusively.[5] In four southern states, the party may choose to hold a convention instead of a primary, but only in Virginia has the convention option been used in recent years as a means of unifying the party behind a particular candidate.

The remaining states use some combination of convention and primary. Iowa requires a convention when no candidate wins at least 35 percent of the primary vote. Three states (Indiana, Michigan, and South Dakota) use primaries for the top statewide offices but choose other nominees in conventions. Seven (Colorado, Connecticut, New Mexico, New York, North Dakota, Rhode Island, and Utah) hold conventions to screen candidates for the primary ballot, though candidates in Connecticut can now bypass the convention by filing a petition signed by 2 percent of party members in the state or district.[6] This variety of choices reminds us that, in spite of the national parties' growing strength, the state and local parties still hold a great deal of independent power.

TYPES OF PRIMARIES

States also differ in the criteria they use to determine who can vote in their primaries. There are three basic forms, although each has many variations.[7] In the states with so-called closed primaries, only voters who have formally declared their affiliation with a party can participate. Voters in states with "open" primaries have more freedom to choose which party's primary they want to vote in. And there is still one state where Democratic and Republican candidates all run on the same primary ballot, so a voter can select some candidates of each party.

Closed Primaries

A slim majority of states hold *closed primaries,* in which there must be a permanent record of the voter's party affiliation before he or she can vote in that party's primary. In the 14 states with *fully closed* primaries, voters have to register as a Democrat or a Republican prior to the election.[8] Then they receive the primary ballot of only their own party when they enter the polling place on Election Day. If they want to vote in the other party's primary, they must formally change their party affiliation on the registration rolls well in advance of the primary. States with traditionally strong party organizations, such as New York and Pennsylvania, are among those that have been able to keep their primaries closed.

In the other 14 closed-primary states, often called *"semiclosed,"* voters can change their party registration at the polls, or they can simply declare their party preference at the polling place. They are then given their declared party's ballot and, in about half of these states, are considered to be enrolled in that party. The lack of preregistration makes it possible for independents and even the other party's identifiers to become "partisans for a day" and vote in a party's primary. From the point of view of the voter, these semiclosed primaries are not very different from an open primary. The difference is important from the party's perspective, however, because in many semiclosed primaries there is a written record of party registration that can then be used by party organizations to target direct mail and other appeals to the people who claim to support them.

Open Primaries

Citizens of 21 states can vote in the primary of their choice without ever having to make a public declaration as to which party they favor.[9] There are different types of *open primaries.* In *"semiopen"* primaries, used by 11 states (most of them in the South), voters can pick whichever party's ballot they choose but will need to ask for a particular party's ballot at the polls. (They often do not need to say that they favor that party but simply that they want to vote in its primary.) The other ten states hold *fully open* primaries, in which voters receive either a consolidated ballot or ballots for every party and they select the party of their choice in the privacy of the voting booth. They cannot, however, vote in more than one party's primary in a given election. Many of these states have histories of Progressive strength.

Blanket Primaries

The state of Washington adopted the *blanket primary* in 1935. It gives voters even greater freedom. The names of candidates from all parties appear on a single ballot in the primary, just as they do in the general election, so that a voter can choose a Democrat for one office and a Republican for another. In short, just as in an open primary, voters who are not affiliated with a party are permitted to help choose that party's candidates. Alaska later adopted the blanket primary as well.

California voters approved an initiative in 1996 to hold a blanket primary. Proponents said it would boost voter participation in the primary, which it did, and encourage the choice of more moderate candidates. Party leaders saw it differently. They claimed that the plan prevented the party's loyal supporters from choosing the candidates who best represented their views. That, they said, would keep the party from offering a clear and consistent message to the voters. They argued that the result was to violate the First Amendment's guarantee of freedom of association. In 2000, the U.S. Supreme Court sided with the parties and gave the right to decide who votes in a primary, at least in California, back to the party organization.[10] California then moved to a semiclosed primary. The Alaska Republican Party followed, but as of late 2005, Alaska's Democrats and some minor parties plan to continue using the blanket primary. Washington has moved to an open primary system, but the courts, as always, will have the final say.

Louisiana still uses a type of blanket primary, sometimes called a "unitary" or "nonpartisan" primary, in which any candidate who wins more than 50 percent of the votes in the primary is elected to the office immediately. If no candidate wins an outright majority, then the general election serves as a runoff between the top two vote getters, even if they are of the same party.

WHY DOES THE TYPE OF PRIMARY MATTER?

These varieties of primaries represent different answers to a long-standing debate: Is democracy better served by competition between strong and disciplined parties or by a system in which the parties have relatively little power? The closed primary reflects the belief that citizens benefit from having clear choices in elections, which can best be provided by unified, strong parties; therefore, it makes sense for a party's candidates to be selected by that party's loyal followers. In contrast, open and blanket primaries are consistent with the view that rigid party loyalties are harmful to a democracy, so candidates should be chosen by all voters, regardless of party.

Most party organizations prefer the closed primary in which voters must register by party before the primary. It pays greater respect to the party's right to select its candidates. Prior party registration also gives the parties a bonus—published lists of their partisans. Further, the closed primary limits the greatest dangers of open and blanket primaries, at least from the perspective of party leaders: crossing over and raiding. Both terms refer to people who vote in the primary of a party that they do not generally support. They differ in the voter's intent. Voters *cross over* in order to take part in a more exciting race or to vote for a more appealing candidate in the other party. *Raiding* is a conscious effort to weaken the other party by voting for its least attractive candidates.

Studies of primary contests in Wisconsin and other states show that crossing over is common in open primaries. Partisans rarely cross over in gubernatorial primaries because that would keep them from having a voice in other party contests. But because only one office is at stake in a presidential primary, both independents and partisans often cross over. In the 2000 presidential race, for example, more Democrats and independents voted in some Republican primaries than Republicans did. Candidates running in open primaries often encourage cross overs by discussing issues that appeal to the other party's voters.[11]

Organized raiding would be a bigger problem. It is a party leader's nightmare that opponents will make mischief by voting in the party's primary for the least appealing candidate. Studies of open primaries have found little evidence of raiding, however. Voters usually cross over to vote their real preferences rather than to weaken the party in whose primary they are participating.[12]

HOW CANDIDATES QUALIFY

States also vary in the ease with which candidates can get their names on the primary ballot and in the support required to win the nomination.

How Do Candidates Get on the Ballot?

In most states, a candidate can get on the primary ballot by filing a petition. State election laws specify how many signatures the petition has to contain—either a specific number or a percentage of the vote for the office in the past election.[13] States vary a lot in the difficulty of this step. New York, with its complicated law that favored party insiders, long had the strictest requirements for filing (see box on page 163) but liberalized them in 2003 for the Republican presidential primary. In some other states, a candidate needs only to appear before the clerk of elections and pay a small fee. A few states, including California, even put presidential candidates on the ballot if they are "generally recognized" to be running.

These simple rules have consequences for the parties. The easier it is for candidates to get on the ballot, the more likely it becomes that dissident, or even crackpot, candidates will enter a race and engage the party's preferred candidates in costly primary battles. Sometimes such candidates even win. In states with easy ballot access, citizens can be treated to grudge campaigns, in which people file to oppose the sheriff who arrested them, for instance, or who simply enjoy the thought of wreaking havoc in a primary.

Runoffs: When Too Many Candidates Get on the Ballot

What if the leading candidate in a primary gets less than a majority of the votes? In most states' primaries, a plurality is enough. Almost all the southern and border states, however, hold a runoff between the top two candidates if one candidate does not win at least 50 percent. This southern institution was developed in the long period of one-party Democratic rule of the South. Democratic factionalism often produced three, four, or five serious candidates for a single office in a primary. The runoff was used to ensure a majority winner in order to present a unified face to the electorate and to ward off any challenges from blacks and other Republicans.

In recent years, the southern runoff primary has become very controversial. Citing instances in which black candidates who received a plurality in the first primary in the South have lost to whites in the runoff, some have charged that runoffs discriminate against minority groups and are in violation of the Constitution and the federal Voting Rights Acts. Others have countered that it is the voters, not the runoff, who produce this result and that, in fact, the runoff helps to force southern parties to build biracial coalitions. This debate is far from being resolved.[14]

JUMP HOW HIGH? GETTING ON THE BALLOT IN NEW YORK

Five weeks before the New York primary in the 2000 presidential race, a state judge threw Senator John McCain off the primary ballot in much of the state. McCain was one of the two leading contenders for the Republican nomination. The state's Republican establishment, which supported Texas Governor George W. Bush for the nomination, had initiated the action, reportedly in order to help the governor of New York, who hoped to become Bush's running mate.

Under New York's ballot access rules, passed by the state legislature at the request of the state party, candidates had to circulate petitions in each of the state's congressional districts under very restrictive rules. This system, described as "tortuous," was the toughest in the nation. It was especially hostile to candidates who did not have the state party's support; those who did could rely on party volunteers to conduct the separate petition drives in each district. A McCain lawyer commented, "It demonstrates the absurdity of the election law when a candidate such as John McCain, who is a leading candidate in the race, can't get on the ballot in more than a third of the election districts."

McCain's campaign made good use of the controversy in portraying himself as an outsider running against a corrupt political system. He was later added to the ballot after a successful appeal to a federal judge. Imagine battling to get on the primary ballot in New York despite these hurdles and then dealing with the varying ballot access rules of 49 other states as well! As a result of the controversy, the state legislature modified its rules in 2003 for the Republican presidential primary; now a candidate gets on the ballot if he or she is discussed in the media, qualifies for federal matching funds, or submits 5,000 signatures. But tough qualifying rules remain in effect for the Democratic presidential primary.

Sources: New York Times stories by Clifford J. Levy: "McCain Off Ballot in Much of Upstate New York," January 28, 2000, p. A1; "McCain on Ballot Across New York as Pataki Gives In," February 4, 2000, p. A1; and "Judge Adds McCain to New York Ballot and Rejects Rules," February 5, 2000, p. A1.

WHAT PARTIES DON'T LIKE ABOUT PRIMARIES

The Progressives designed the direct primary to break the party organization's monopoly control of nominations, and, in important respects, it did. In the process, it compromised parties' effectiveness in elections more generally, in several ways.

Difficulties in Recruiting Candidates

Candidate recruitment has never been an easy job, especially for the minority party. The direct primary makes the challenge even more difficult. If an ambitious candidate has the opportunity to challenge the party favorite in the dominant party's primary, he or she is less likely to consider running for office under the minority party's label. So, some argue, the minority party will find it even harder to recruit good candidates for races that it is not likely to win, and the office goes to the other party's nominee by default. Little by little, the majority party becomes the only viable means of exerting political influence and the minority party atrophies.[15]

This argument should not be taken too far. One-party politics declined after primaries became more common. The proportion of noncompetitive races is increasing again, from Congress to state legislative and other elections,[16] but even in areas dominated by one party, the internal competition promoted by primaries can keep officeholders responsive to their constituents.[17] Nevertheless, the fact that party organizations cannot guarantee the outcome of their own primaries means that they have less to offer the candidates they are trying to recruit.

The Risk of Unattractive Nominees

Normally, only about half as many voters turn out for a primary as for a general election.[18] If this smaller group of primary voters is not representative of those who will vote later, then it may select a weak candidate—one who, because of his or her issue stands or background, may not appeal to the broader turnout in the general election. In particular, party leaders fear that primary voters could choose a candidate who is more extreme than the party's electorate as a whole. Imagine the discomfort of Republican party leaders, for instance, when the controversial right winger Oliver North, who had been convicted on three felony counts for his role in a Reagan White House scandal, won the 1994 GOP nomination for senator in Virginia over a far more electable conservative. North went on to lose the general election. In another classic case, some Democratic Party leaders in southern California even felt the need to disown their own candidate when a former official of the Ku Klux Klan captured the Democratic nomination for Congress in a multicandidate primary race.

Another reason why primary voters might choose a weak candidate is that in a race in which all the candidates are of the same party, voters cannot use their party identification to select candidates, and many voters may not have any other relevant information available. They may choose a candidate because his or her name is familiar or may simply vote for the first name listed on the ballot (see "We Nominated . . . WHO?" on page 165). If the nominations were made by a party convention, it is often argued, convention delegates would know the prospective candidates better, so they would not be prone to these misjudgments.

Divisive Primaries

Primaries can create conflict that may reopen old party wounds or create new ones. As one observer described it, "a genuine primary is a fight within the family of the party and, like any family fight, is apt to be more bitter and leave more enduring wounds than battles with the November enemy."[19] A divisive primary election can have a number of effects on the party in the short term. Activists who campaigned for the losing candidate in the primary may sit out the general election rather than work for their party's nominee, although the excitement of the primary may bring in new activists to take their places.[20] Because this is a public fight, the wounds the candidates inflict on one another and on their followers can take a long time to heal.[21] The charges raised by a candidate's primary opponent are often reused by the opposition in the general election, a source of free campaign

WE NOMINATED . . . WHO?

When voters choose a party's candidates in a primary election, sometimes the results are surprising. Voters in the 2002 Missouri primary, for example, selected Allen D. Hanson as the Republican candidate for state auditor, the office responsible for rooting out waste and abuse in the state budget. Hanson, it turns out, had spent nine months in a Minnesota jail for felony theft and swindling. He defeated Jay Kanzler, the general counsel of highly respected Washington University in St. Louis, who had been endorsed by several Missouri Republican leaders. Kanzler had raised $107,000 for his primary campaign. Hanson raised less than $500, but won about 65 percent of the vote. What was the secret of Hanson's success? Neither candidate was well known to the voters, and Hanson's name was listed first on the ballot. After the primary election, state Republican leaders urged Republican voters not to support this Republican candidate.

A columnist for the *St. Louis Post-Dispatch* warned that this lapse was not the only problem with Missouri elections. Two years earlier, the state had elected its former governor to the U.S. Senate a few weeks after he had died, and earlier in 2002, the state's other senator brought his 13-year-old springer spaniel onto the Senate floor to display the dog's voter registration card as proof that there was vote fraud in St. Louis. The columnist concluded, "They say that people get the kind of government they deserve. This is not a happy thought."

Sources: Kevin Horrigan, "Missouri Elections: 'Show Me' the Madness," *St. Louis Post-Dispatch,* August 11, 2002, p. B3; and Juliet Eilperin, "Mo. GOP: Felon's Win Is a Fluke," *Washington Post,* August 12, 2002, p. A4.

help to the other party (see "The Illinois Senate Candidate from Maryland," on page 166). Finally, if a bitter primary is expensive, it may eat up much of the money the primary winner would need to run an effective campaign in the general election.

These risks have increased recently. After the redistricting that followed the 2000 U.S. Census created so many U.S. House districts that were considered "safe" for one party, many ambitious candidates saw primary elections as the best and least expensive way to win a House seat. That attracted the attention, and the lavish spending, of dozens of national interest groups who wanted to change the ideological orientation of Congress. In 2002, there were more than 100 significant primary contests in House races, resulting in some bruising battles.

The Democratic Party is famous for its internal disputes, but we can see just as much evidence of the effects of divisive primaries in the Republican Party, such as when candidates linked to the Christian Right challenge Republicans who are more moderate on social issues.[22] Other groups have also entered Republican primaries to try to unseat moderate incumbent Republicans. In 2003, the antitax group Club for Growth angered the White House and congressional Republican leaders by announcing that it would finance several intraparty fights. It wanted to warn Republicans that if they didn't take the strictest possible antitax position, they would face primary opposition.[23] "If you want to influence politics and policy, you really have to play in the primary game," said the Club president.[24]

THE ILLINOIS SENATE CANDIDATE FROM MARYLAND

Illinois Republican Senator Peter Fitzgerald was in obvious electoral trouble. His approval ratings in the state were low and falling, and he announced that he would not seek reelection in 2004. The primary race to replace him was highly contested. In addition to a retired general, a state senator, and a dairy owner, the eight candidates included Jack Ryan, a millionaire investment banker who had left his Wall Street brokerage firm four years earlier to teach at an all-black boys' private school. Ryan, a telegenic candidate, spent $3 million of his own money on the campaign and soon became the front-runner.

Just before the primary election, a staff member of a rival Republican candidate charged that according to sealed divorce records, Ryan had allegedly pressured his then-wife, *Boston Public* TV star Jeri Ryan, into visiting what she called bizarre sex clubs (he called them "romantic getaways") and having sex with her husband in the presence of others. A media firestorm erupted. Because the divorce records were sealed, the reports could not be confirmed. Turnout in the primary was low. Ryan won with 36 percent of the vote. He managed to ride out the storm for a full three months, even hosting Vice President Dick Cheney at a fund-raiser in early June.

Then the Ryans' divorce records were unsealed by the court, confirming his primary opponent's charges. Ryan withdrew from the race in late June, saying that he wanted to avoid a "brutal, scorched-earth campaign." U.S. House Speaker Dennis Hastert quickly announced that Ryan had "made the right decision. I know it must have been a difficult one."

That led to an equally tough decision for his party. Under Illinois law, the Republican State Central Committee had the right to choose a replacement candidate. Mike Ditka, the fiery coach of the Chicago Bears, pondered the opportunity very publicly for a week before saying no. Party leaders concluded that they should try to counter the remarkable appeal of the Democratic nominee, Barack Obama, whose father was black, with another African-American candidate. So they offered the nomination in August to Alan Keyes, a very conservative former ambassador and Republican presidential candidate. The offer was complicated a bit by the fact that Keyes was a resident of Maryland, but he moved to Illinois long enough to lose the November election to Obama by a landslide.

Sources: "Ryan Drops Out of Senate Race in Illinois," CNN.com Inside Politics, June 25, 2004, on the Internet at http://www.cnn.com/2004/ALLPOLITICS/06/25/il.ryan/ (accessed July 22, 2005); and Rick Pearson and Liam Ford, "GOP Leaders Say They Felt Misled on Ryan File," *Chicago Tribune*, June 23, 2004, p. 1.

Problems in Holding Candidates Accountable

When candidates are chosen in primaries rather than by party leaders, the party loses a powerful means of holding its candidates and officeholders accountable for their actions. In England, for example, if an elected official breaks with the party on an important issue, party leaders can usually keep him or her from being renominated. However, if the party cannot control or prevent the renomination of a maverick officeholder, then it has no way of enforcing loyalty. That, of course, is just what the Progressives had hoped. Thus, primaries have the following disadvantages:

- Primaries permit the nomination of candidates hostile to the party organization and leadership, opposed to the party's platform, or out of step with the public image that party leaders want to project.

- Primaries create the real possibility that the party's candidates in the general election will be an unbalanced ticket if primary voters select all or most of the candidates from a particular group or region.

- Primaries greatly increase campaign spending. The cost of a contested primary is almost always higher than that of a convention.

- Primaries extend political campaigns, already longer in the United States than in other democracies, to a length that can try many voters' patience.

THE PARTY ORGANIZATION FIGHTS BACK

Parties are clearly aware of the threats posed by primary elections, but they are just as aware that a direct attempt to abolish primaries would be futile. So party organizations have developed a range of strategies for trying to limit the damage primaries can cause. The success of these strategies varies; some local parties have neither the will nor the strength to try to affect primary election results, but others have been able to dominate the primaries effectively.

Persuading Candidates to Run (or Not to Run)

The surest way to control a primary is to make sure that the candidate the party favors has no opponent. Some party organizations try to mediate among prospective candidates or coax an attractive but unwilling candidate to run. If they have a strong organization, they may be able to convince less desirable candidates to stay out of the race by offering them a chance to run in the future, or they may threaten to block a candidate's access to campaign money. Even if they have little to offer or withhold, many party leaders have the opportunity to try to influence prospective candidates' decisions; researchers have found that almost 70 percent of nonincumbent state legislative candidates discussed their plans to run with local party leaders before announcing their candidacy.[25]

Endorsing Candidates

Some of the stronger state parties, such as those in Massachusetts and Minnesota, go beyond this informal influence on candidate selection and offer some form of preprimary endorsement to the candidates whom they prefer. Recall that in seven states, at least one of the parties holds a convention to formally endorse candidates for state office. Usually, a candidate who gets a certain percentage of the convention's vote automatically gets his or her name on the primary ballot, though candidates who are not endorsed by the party can still be listed on the ballot in several of these states by filing a petition. These endorsements are sometimes accompanied by campaign money and organizational help. In some other states, including Illinois, Ohio, and Michigan, party leaders meet informally to endorse some candidates.

How much influence do these endorsements have on the voters? The record is mixed. Formal endorsements can often discourage other candidates from challenging the party's choice in the primary and can keep some interest groups from flooding a race with outside money in support of a nonendorsed candidate. Besides, the process of winning a formal endorsement usually involves the candidate in so many face-to-face meetings with party activists that the resulting visibility, and the resources that the endorsing party can provide, can give the endorsed candidate at least some vote-getting benefits.[26]

On the other hand, since 1980, when there has been competition in the primary, the endorsed candidate has won only about half the time—a big drop compared with the success rate of endorsed candidates in the 1960s and 1970s.[27] Some states have legal requirements that make the endorsement less valuable; the parties in Utah, for example, are required by state law to endorse two candidates for each office. Other states have passed laws to prevent parties from endorsing candidates in advance of the primary.

When the parties are restricted to offering informal endorsements before the primary, their effectiveness is even more limited. These informal endorsements are not listed on the ballot. As a result, only the most politically attentive voters are likely to know that the party is supporting a particular candidate and they are the ones least in need of the guidance provided by a party endorsement.[28]

Providing Tangible Support

If the party is not able to prevent a challenge to its preferred candidates, then it must fall back on more conventional approaches. It may urge party activists to help the favored candidates circulate their nominating petitions and leave the other candidates to their own devices (as John McCain learned in the 2000 New York primary). It may make party money and expertise available to the chosen candidates. It may publish ads announcing the party's endorsements or print reminder cards that voters can take right into the polling booth. On the day of the primary, the party organization may help to get party voters to the polls.

Although state and local parties vary in their efforts to influence primary elections, recruiting candidates is probably the most frequent form of activity. Trying to clear the field for a favored candidate is less common. The parties' efforts are complicated by the fact that, in most parts of the country, parties are only one of a number of groups seeking out and supporting men and women to run for office. Local business, professional, farm, and labor groups; civic associations; ethnic, racial, and religious organizations; and other interest groups and officeholders may also be working to recruit candidates. The party organizations that seem best able to control candidate recruitment are generally the parties that endorse and support candidates in the primary itself.

CANDIDATES AND VOTERS IN THE PRIMARIES

Two facts help make the primaries more manageable for the parties: often only one candidate files for each office in a primary and the majority of voters do not vote in them. The party may be responsible for one or both of these situations. There may be no competition in a primary, for example, because of the party's skill in persuading and dissuading potential candidates. No matter why they occur, however, the result is that nomination politics can be more easily controlled by aggressive party organization.

Many Candidates Run Without Competition

All over the United States, large numbers of primary candidates win nominations without a contest. Probably the most important determinant of the competitiveness of a primary is the party's prospects for victory in the general election; as mentioned earlier, candidates rarely fight for the right to face almost certain defeat. Primaries also tend to be less competitive when an incumbent is running (unless the incumbent is already thought to be vulnerable), when parties have made preprimary endorsements, and when the state's rules make it harder to get on the ballot.[29]

The power of incumbency to discourage competition is one of the many ironies of the primary. In an election in which voters cannot rely on the party label to guide their choices, name recognition and media coverage are important influences. Incumbents, of course, are more likely to have these resources than are challengers. To dislodge an incumbent, a challenger will often need large amounts of campaign money, but few challengers can raise large campaign budgets. By weakening party control of nominations through the direct primary, then, Progressive reformers may have unintentionally made it harder to defeat incumbents.

. . . And Voters Are in Short Supply

If competition is scarce in the primaries, so are voters. One important fact about primaries is that most people don't take part in them. One reason for the low turnout is that there is no competition in many primary races. Turnout tends to be lower in the minority party's primary, in primaries held separately from the state's presidential primary, and in elections in which independents and the other party's identifiers are not allowed to vote.[30] In addition, the fact that no one is elected in a primary probably depresses turnout; a race for the nomination lacks the drama inherent in a general election that is followed by victorious candidates taking office. (There are some notable exceptions, however; see "A Day in the Life" on page 170).

Because it is such a small sample of the eligible voters, the primary electorate is distinctive in several ways. Many primary voters are strong party identifiers and activists, which makes them more responsive to party endorsements of certain candidates. As would be expected, people who vote in primaries have higher levels of education and political interest than nonvoters do. They are often assumed to hold more extreme ideological positions than those of other party voters. Although early studies of Wisconsin's open primary found little support for that assumption, other research suggests that it is accurate.[31] Even if the ideological positions of primary voters turn out not to be distinctive, the intensity of their ideological commitment may be.

Primary voters often make unexpected choices. Primary campaigns tend to get little media coverage, so the candidates are often not well known, and the issues, if any, may be unclear. Thus, the voter's choice in a primary is not as well structured or predictable as that in a general election. Many voting decisions are made right in the polling

MORE THAN JUST "THE LESBIAN CANDIDATE FOR CONGRESS"

Soon after finishing law school, Tammy Baldwin won a seat on the county board of supervisors. At age 30, she moved on to the Wisconsin state legislature, where she was the youngest woman and the first openly gay person to serve in that body. Six years later, when the Republican U.S. Representative in her district announced his intention to retire, she entered the Democratic primary to replace him.

It was a long shot. The district's previous Democratic incumbent had endorsed another of the four candidates for the nomination. Even many Democrats considered Baldwin to be too liberal to win. She was forthright about her approach to politics, arguing that, as a woman, she would take on issues that most congressmen would not. In particular, she called for tougher environmental regulations, publicly financed day care, and long-term care for the elderly.

It was inevitable that Baldwin's sexual orientation would be an undercurrent in the campaign. By 1998, there were gay members of Congress, but all had gone public about their homosexuality *after* having been first elected to the House. Tammy Baldwin did not make an issue of her sexual orientation, but neither did she try to hide it. In fact, it offered one political advantage: She was able to raise a large campaign budget through her appeals to gay and women supporters. Antigay rhetoric was not common in the primary race, but stereotyping was. It took more than a month for her campaign manager to persuade newspapers to stop referring to the candidate as "Tammy Baldwin, the lesbian candidate for Congress."

Was she expecting to win? "Well, you know, throughout my political career," she says, "I've always been dealing with the skeptics and the cynics, who say, 'This isn't going to be our best candidate to win the primary.' And, you know, 'She's too progressive, she's too young, she's a woman, she's lesbian. . . .' Hey, folks, this is a democracy, and in a democracy the cynics don't decide who's elected to office unless you let them—unless they're the only ones who vote. We decide. And that's a message that pervaded the entire campaign—stop listening to those people who say, 'You can't, you shouldn't, it won't work,' and start deciding that we can do it." And she did; after narrowly winning the Democratic primary, Baldwin won the general election and went to Congress in 1999. She was reelected in 2000 by a narrow margin and then won comfortable victories in 2002 and 2004, when she served as a vice-chair of the 2004 Democratic National Convention. When Baldwin first ran for office, there were about a dozen openly gay and lesbian elected officials across the nation. Now there are more than 200.

Sources: Ruth Conniff, "Tammy Baldwin," *The Progressive,* http://www.progressive .org/baldwin9901.htm (accessed August 15, 2003). See also David T. Canon and Paul S. Herrnson, "Professionalism, Progressivism, and People Power," in Michael A. Bailey, Ronald A. Faucheux, Paul S. Herrnson, and Clyde Wilcox, eds., *Campaigns & Elections* (Washington, DC: CQ Press, 2000), pp. 83–92.

booth. It is small wonder that parties are rarely confident about primary results and poll-sters find it hard to predict them accurately.

Southern primaries in earlier years were the one great exception to the rule that turnouts are low in primaries. Because winning the Democratic nomination in a one-party area was tantamount to winning the office itself, competition existed only in the Democratic primary, so turnout in the primaries was relatively high. When the Republican Party became stronger and more competitive in the South, however, the Democratic primaries lost their special standing. The result is that participation has declined in southern primaries. Republican primaries are attracting more voters now because their candidates' prospects in the general election have greatly improved, but the GOP increase has not been large enough to compensate for the decrease in Democratic turnout. So turnout in southern primaries has become less and less distinctive.[32]

THE IMPACT OF THE DIRECT PRIMARY

Americans have had a century of experience with the direct primary. On balance, how has it affected us? Has the primary democratized nominations by taking them out of the hands of party leaders and giving them to voters? Has it weakened the party organizations overall? In short, have the Progressives' hopes been realized?

Has It Made Elections More Democratic?

It is true that more people take part in primaries than take part in conventions or cau-cuses. In that sense, the process has been made more democratic. But the democratic promise of primaries is cut short by the number of unopposed candidates and the low levels of voter turnout. If voters are to have meaningful alternatives, then there must be more than one candidate for an office. If the results are to be meaningful, people must go to the polls.

By its very nature, however, the primary tends to reduce participation. Would-be candidates are discouraged by the cost of an additional race, the difficulty of getting on the primary ballot, and the need to differentiate themselves from other candidates of the same party. The large number of primaries and the frequent lack of party cues reduce the quantity and quality of voter participation. If widespread competition for office and extensive public participation in the nominating process were goals of the primary's architects, then their hopes have not been realized.

The direct primary has not fully replaced party leaders in making nominations. Cau-cuses and conventions are still used, most visibly in presidential nominations, although they are more open than they used to be. And as we have seen, parties can influence the competition in primaries. If only 25 or 30 percent of registered voters go to the polls, then 15 percent will be enough to nominate a candidate. Parties count on the fact that a large part of that group will probably be party loyalists who care about the party leaders' recommendations. Thus, strong party organizations—those able to muster the needed voters, money, activists, and organization—can still have a big influence on the results.

Even so, trying to influence primary elections is very costly and time-consuming, even for strong parties. The Jacksonian tradition of electing every public official from senator to surveyor means that party organizations need to deal with large numbers of contests. The time and expense force many parties to be selective in trying to affect primaries. Parties sometimes stand aside because picking a favorite in the primary might heat up old resentments or open new wounds. Of course, the greatest fear of party leaders is that if they support one candidate in a primary and the other candidate wins, they could lose all influence over the winning officeholder.

In some ways, then, the primary has been a democratizing force. In competitive districts, especially when no incumbent is running, voters have the opportunity for choice envisioned by the reformers. In all districts, the primaries place real limits on the power of party leaders. Parties, even strong ones, can no longer whisk just any warm body through the nomination process. The primary gives dissenters a chance to take their case to the party's voters, so it offers them a potential veto over the party leaders' preferences (as "A Day in the Life" shows). And the tendency for primary voters to be more extreme in their views, and thus less representative of general election voters, can be moderated by using open rather than closed primaries.[33]

How Badly Has It Harmed the Parties?

On the other hand, is it possible to say that the direct primary has strengthened democracy in the United States if it weakens the political parties? From the risk of divisive primary races to the added campaign funding and voter mobilization that they require, primaries strain party resources and create headaches for party leaders and activists. Although we have seen the methods used by some state party organizations to maintain some control over their primaries by making preprimary endorsements or holding conventions to nominate some candidates, the bottom line is this: When a party organization cannot choose who will carry the party label into the general election, the party has been deprived of one of its key resources.

The direct primary has redistributed power within the parties. The Progressives' goal was to shift the power to nominate candidates from the party organization to the party in the electorate, but a funny thing happened along the way. Because candidates (especially incumbents) can win the party's nomination even when they defy the party organization, the idea of party "discipline" loses its credibility. Just as the direct primary undercuts the ability of the party organization to recruit candidates who share its goals and accept its discipline, it prevents the organization from disciplining partisans who already are in office. The primary, then, empowers the party's candidates and the party in government at the expense of the party organization. This sets the United States apart from many other democracies, in which the party organization has real power over the party in government.

Primaries also contribute to the decentralization of power in the American parties. As long as the candidates can appeal successfully to a majority of local primary voters, they are free from the control of a state or national party and its leaders. In all these ways, the direct primary has influenced more than the nominating process; it has helped to reshape the American parties.

Is the Primary Worth the Cost?

How party candidates should be nominated has been a controversial matter since political parties first appeared in the United States. It raises the fundamental question of what a political party is. Are parties only alliances of officeholders—the party in government?

That seemed to be the prevailing definition in the early years when public officials selected their prospective colleagues in party caucuses. Should the definition be expanded to include the party's activists and leaders? The change from a caucus to a convention system of nominations, in which the party organization played its greatest role, reflects this change in the definition of party.

Should we extend the idea of party well beyond the limits accepted by most other democracies and include the party's supporters in the electorate? If so, which supporters should be included—only those willing to register formally as party loyalists or anyone who wants to vote for a party candidate in a primary election? The answer has evolved over the years toward the most inclusive definition of party. Even though the Supreme Court insists that the parties' freedom of association is vital, the "party," especially in states with an open or blanket primary and, in practice, in semiclosed primary states, has become so permeable that its boundaries are hard to define.

The methods that we use to nominate candidates have a far-reaching impact. The Jacksonians promoted the convention system in order to gain control of the party from congressional party leaders. Progressives used their preference for the direct primary as a weapon with which to wrest control of the party and, ultimately, the government from the party organization regulars. Because of the importance of nominations in the political process, those who control the nominations have great influence on the political agenda and, in turn, over who gets what in the political system. The stakes in this debate, as a result, are extremely high.

Chapter 10

Choosing the Presidential Nominees

The system that Americans use to nominate a president is unique. It takes almost a year, costs hundreds of millions of dollars, and differs from the way in which every other democratic nation chooses its chief executive. In fact, it differs from the process by which candidates for every other major office are selected in the United States. Understanding this process helps us understand the relationship between the parties and the presidency itself.

In a formal sense, each of the two major parties nominates its candidate for president at the party's national convention, held every four years. In reality, the convention delegates simply ratify the choices that have actually been made months before the convention's opening gavel, by voters in their states' delegate selection events (see the box on page 175). Most states use primary elections, the benefits and drawbacks of which were explored in the last chapter, for that purpose.

THE MOVE TO PRESIDENTIAL PRIMARIES

It took decades for primaries to become established in the presidential nominating process. Florida adopted the first presidential primary in 1904, and many other states quickly followed. Within a decade, a majority of states were using this method of nomination. The use of primaries soon faded, however. Advocates may have lost faith in the effectiveness of primaries; opponents probably worked hard to get rid of them and restore party leaders' control over nominations. By 1936, only 14 states were still holding primaries to choose their delegates to the national conventions that select the parties' presidential candidates. That number had hardly changed by 1968.[1]

In most states, then, the state parties regained the power to choose the delegates to the national conventions. Party leaders dominated the process and often even hand-picked the state's delegates. The selection was usually done in a series of party-controlled caucuses, or meetings, beginning at the local level and culminating in statewide party conventions. Even in many states that held primaries, voters could take part in only a "beauty contest" to express their preferences about presidential candidates; the delegates who went to the national convention and chose the candidates were selected elsewhere. A

HOW A PRESIDENTIAL CANDIDATE IS CHOSEN

Step 1: *Assessing Their Chances.* Many people who think they might have public support—governors, senators, House members, people well known in another field—consider running for president. They take private polls to see how much backing they would have and how they are viewed by the public. They contact consultants, fund-raisers, and potential donors to assess their chances of getting the resources they'd need and to get well-respected consultants to commit to their candidacy. They campaign for congressional candidates in order to win their loyalty.

Timing: At least a year, and usually several years, before the presidential election.

Step 2: *Entering the Race.* Those who feel they have a good chance—and some who don't—formally declare their candidacy and work to get on every state ballot. They set up political action committees or foundations to raise money. They travel often to states with early primaries and caucuses and where large fund-raising events can be held.

Timing: Typically during the year prior to the election year.

Step 3: *Primaries and Caucuses.* Voters cast a ballot in their states for the candidate they want their party to nominate for president. Most states hold primary elections for this purpose; the rest use participatory caucuses and state conventions. Delegates are chosen to represent each state and to vote in the party's national convention for the candidates selected by the voters.

Timing: Between mid-January and early June of each presidential election year.

Step 4: *National Nominating Conventions.* The delegates vote in the two major parties' conventions to ratify the choice of presidential candidate made by the voters in the nominating season (Step 3) and the candidate's choice of a vice-presidential nominee and to adopt a party platform.

Timing: By tradition, the party that does not currently hold the presidency has its convention first, usually in July; the other party's convention is held in August or early September.

Step 5: *General Election.* The two major parties' candidates run against one another.

Timing: From the conventions until the first Tuesday after the first Monday in November.

fascinating story began to unfold in 1968, however, in which the national Democratic Party took control of the delegate-selection process away from the state parties and gave new life to the movement toward presidential primaries.

Turbulence in the Democratic Party

The 1968 Democratic convention was a riotous event. Struggling with the painful issues of civil rights and American involvement in the Vietnam War, the convention nominated the party leaders' choice, Vice President Hubert Humphrey, as the Democratic presidential candidate, even though he hadn't run in a single state primary. Insurgent forces within the party protested that Humphrey's nomination violated the wishes of many Democratic activists. To try to make peace with their critics, the national party leaders agreed that the next convention's delegates would be selected in a more open and democratic manner.

A commission chaired by Senator George McGovern of South Dakota (and later by Representative Donald Fraser of Minnesota) recommended, and the Democratic National Committee and the next Democratic convention approved, major changes for the 1972 nominating process. One of the striking elements of this story is the remarkable ease with which state Democratic Party leaders accepted rule changes that greatly reduced their influence on the awarding of the party's greatest prize, the presidential nomination.[2]

In trying to comply with the complicated new rules imposed by the national Democratic Party, many states stopped using caucus-convention systems and reinstituted primaries.[3] The few caucuses that remained were guided by strict party rules requiring delegates to be selected in open and well-publicized meetings. Techniques formerly used by state party organizations to control the caucuses were outlawed. In the process, not only were the delegate selection procedures radically changed, but also the principle was established that the national parties, not the states or the state parties, make the rules for nominating presidential candidates.

Once the reform genie was let out of the bottle, it was hard to contain. The Democrats tinkered with their presidential nomination process prior to almost every election for the next 20 years. First, they used national party leverage to make the process more open and more representative of women, blacks, and young people. Then, the Democrats "fine-tuned" the rules so that voter support for candidates was more faithfully represented in delegate counts. Ever since 1992, candidates who win at least 15 percent of the vote in primaries or caucuses are guaranteed a share of the state's delegates proportional to their vote total. Later, to bring party leaders (and their "peer review" of candidates) back into the process, many elected and party officials were guaranteed a vote at the convention as uncommitted "superdelegates" (to be discussed later).

The result has been a stunning transformation of the process by which the Democrats select their presidential nominees. Many state legislatures responded to the new Democratic requirements by changing state election laws for both parties. When states decided to run a primary for one party, for example, they typically did it for both. Thus, the Republicans became the unwilling beneficiaries of the Democratic reforms. Republicans have preserved their tradition of giving state parties wide latitude in developing their own rules, however, which has kept the national party out of much of the rules debate. So even while being swept up in the movement toward primaries, state Republican Parties have tended to stay away from proportional representation; instead, they have retained statewide winner-take-all primaries. In addition, the Republicans have not followed the Democrats' lead in reserving delegate seats for party and public officials or in developing affirmative action programs for women or minorities.

Presidential Primaries Today

Presidential primaries are now used in more than two-thirds of the states, including most of the largest (see Figure 10.1). Because the decision to use primaries or caucuses is made by states and state parties, these numbers change from one presidential election

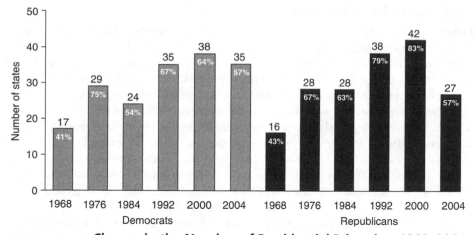

FIGURE 10.1   Change in the Number of Presidential Primaries: 1968–2004

Note: The number above each bar is the number of states that held primaries to select delegates (not primaries that were purely advisory) in that year; inside the bar is the percentage of convention delegates elected in those primaries. All 50 states plus Washington, DC, are included, but not the territories (American Samoa, Guam, Puerto Rico, Virgin Islands) or Democrats Abroad. Delegate percentages include Democratic superdelegates.

Sources: For 1968–1996, Michael G. Hagen and William G. Mayer, "The Modern Politics of Presidential Selection," in William G. Mayer, ed., *In Pursuit of the White House 2000* (New York: Chatham House, 2000), pp. 11 and 43–44. Figures for 2000 were kindly provided by Mayer, and figures for 2004 were calculated by the author.

to the next. In 2004, for instance, a number of primaries were canceled or replaced by party caucuses: eight state legislatures decided to reduce state spending by eliminating both parties' presidential primaries, and the parties held caucuses or conventions instead. (The state pays for the costs of a primary election, but the parties foot the bill for caucuses.)

In the primaries, the popular vote determines how the state's delegates are apportioned among the presidential candidates. In earlier years, primary voters in some states were permitted to select only the convention delegates themselves, without any assurance as to which presidential candidates these delegates supported. Now, however, the names of the presidential candidates appear on the ballots, and the candidates or their agents usually approve the members of their own delegate slates. This all but guarantees that the popular vote for candidates will be faithfully translated into delegates committed to the respective candidates at the national convention, even though there are no laws requiring delegates to support the popular vote winner in their state.[4]

Most party leaders prefer some form of closed primary (see Chapter 9). Democratic Party reform commissions tried several times to ban open primaries, which allow non-Democrats to have a voice in selecting party candidates. The open primary has survived these assaults, however. After a long struggle, the national party allowed Wisconsin to return to its cherished open primary in 1988, and the other states that hold open primaries need no longer fear a veto by the national party.[5]

Some States Use Party Caucuses

Other states use a longer delegate selection process that begins with precinct caucuses. Participants in a caucus do not just stop at a polling place quickly to cast a ballot. They gather in local schools and other public areas, often for at least an hour or two, to debate which candidates for president will best represent their party and the issues they believe in. Then they choose delegates to communicate their presidential preference to caucuses at higher levels, typically at the county, congressional district, and then the state level. The state's final delegate slate for the national convention is determined at the higher-level conventions. The first-in-the-nation Iowa caucuses, for example, began with precinct meetings in January 2004, but Iowa's national convention delegates were not chosen until the district and state conventions in April and June. State and local party leaders' preferences and candidates' organizational skills generally have a greater impact on turnout and voters' choices in a caucus than in a primary.

The selection of delegates in the caucus states attracted little media coverage until 1976, when a little-known Democratic governor, Jimmy Carter, made himself a serious presidential candidate by campaigning intensively in Iowa and winning an unexpectedly large number of delegates. Since that time, the Iowa caucuses have joined the New Hampshire primary as the first and most significant delegate selection events. An estimated half to three-quarters of the media attention devoted to the nomination race focuses on these two states' events.[6]

THE RACE TO WIN DELEGATE VOTES

Every presidential nomination in both parties since 1956 has been won on the convention's first ballot, and since 1968, that first-ballot nominee has always been the winner of the most delegates in the primaries and caucuses. How does a candidate get to that coveted spot?

The "Invisible Primary"

It takes years to prepare for a presidential race. Almost all serious candidates begin several years before the election to take polls, raise money, identify active supporters in the states with early primaries, and compete for the services of respected consultants. Their aim is to win a place for themselves in the group of candidates who are described by the media as "front-runners."

In the year before the first convention delegates are selected, at a time when the coming presidential race is not yet even on the radar screen for most Americans, journalists try to get the scoop on who will eventually win the nomination. Because money and organization are so crucial to a candidate's chances, media people tend to pick a likely winner by tracking the various candidates' fund-raising success and polls in the year before the election. This process has become so important to the eventual result that it has come to be called the *invisible primary* or the "money primary."[7]

By the end of 2003, for example, several Democrats—former Vermont Governor Howard Dean, Massachusetts Senator John F. Kerry, and General Wesley Clark—had been called front-runners by virtue of having raised a great deal of money for the 2004 nomination race (with Dean on top at $41 million), and President Bush, who was unopposed for the Republican nomination, had collected over $132 million. Prospective candidates who don't raise as much money as prominent observers expect them to, or who perform poorly in public opinion polls, are likely to be winnowed out of the nomination race well before Iowa and New Hampshire voters choose their convention delegates. "Every time I think it can't begin earlier," wrote *Newsweek* reporter Howard Fineman about the speeding up of the nomination race, "it does."[8]

Candidates' Strategic Choices

Those who are still considered serious candidates near the close of the "invisible primary" must make endless strategic choices in preparing for the early delegate selection events. They need to decide how much effort and money to put into each state and which of their many issue stands and personal qualities to emphasize. As the dynamics of the race change, they will probably reconsider these choices many times.

The most important factor to be weighed in making these choices is the candidate's standing relative to the opposition. Someone who comes into the nominating season as a front-runner, for example, normally has to demonstrate overwhelming support in the early delegate selection events. Otherwise, his or her supporters' and contributors' confidence may be so badly undermined that the candidate's hopes for the nomination fade. A classic instance was Howard Dean's campaign for the Democratic nomination in 2004. In early January of 2004, Dean was the front-runner in both fund-raising and media coverage, polling around 26 percent among Democrats nationally, and Kerry was at around 9 percent. Hardly more than a week later, Kerry began a dramatic turnaround that ended in a victory in the Iowa caucuses. Within days, Kerry's poll numbers had shot up to 30 percent nationally, and then to 49 percent after he won the New Hampshire primary the following week. Dean dropped to about 12 percent in the polls.[9] Dean's candidacy never rebounded from the shock of that loss, and media coverage of his response to the Iowa caucuses doomed any hopes of a recovery (see box on page 180).

The nominating process is structured by a number of rules that affect campaigns' strategic choices. One is that campaign finance reforms, including caps on individual contributions, keep candidates from raising large amounts of money quickly from a few sources. Instead, presidential candidates have the option of receiving federal dollars to match the small ($250 or less) contributions they attract during the nomination race (see Chapter 12). To qualify for matching funds, a candidate must bring in a lot of small contributions in at least 20 states well before the first primary. The public funding comes with a number of conditions, however. Candidates who accept it are limited in how much they can spend in each state and in the nomination race as a whole. So these candidates will not be able to spend massively in the crucial early primaries and caucuses. Even worse, the eventual nominee will probably reach the overall spending cap by March or April and will have to survive for months without advertising until federal funding for the general election kicks in after the party conventions. The logic of declining the matching funds became clear when George W. Bush did so in 2000, raised an unprecedented sum for the nomination race, and was able to continue spending after the campaign of his Democratic rival Al Gore, who had accepted the matching funds and spending ceilings, ran out of money in April. As a result, Bush, Dean, and Kerry all declined the matching funds in 2004, as any serious candidate is likely to do in 2008.

MEDIA AND PRIMARIES: HOWARD DEAN'S "I HAVE A SCREAM" SPEECH

The seeds of Howard Dean's demise as a candidate for the Democratic presidential nomination were present even while reporters were calling him the party's front-runner. His campaign made the decision during the summer of 2003 to expand into most states rather than to focus on the lead-off Iowa caucuses and New Hampshire primary. The expansion was only loosely controlled by Dean's headquarters, so it took on a life of its own, as when collections of liberal college students descended on conservative small towns to knock on the doors of startled residents and explain why they ought to support Dean. Key staff members feuded with one another. Dean's own relationships with staffers were often strained. As a long-time Vermont aide put it, "You don't manage Howard Dean," but that didn't stop people from trying. Dean's testy exchanges with media people led many reporters to suspect that the candidate's emotions were not very well controlled. References to Dean's anger and combativeness became more frequent in news reports.

Dean led the other Democratic candidates in the polls throughout the fall of 2003, though the proportion of Democrats who supported him never rose much above 30 percent. Although his poll numbers began to drop just before the Iowa caucuses, Dean had run one of the most expensive caucus campaigns in the state's history, and he still had hopes of coming in first. But the polls proved prophetic on caucus night and both John Kerry and John Edwards surpassed Dean's vote totals.

Dean had not prepared a concession speech. A ballroom full of thousands of supporters awaited him, raucous and desperate for a pep talk. Advisers urged him to stride confidently into the ballroom, strip off his suit jacket and roll up his sleeves, and make it plain to the crowd that he was still going to win in the upcoming state events. Dean yelled over the din, "Not only are we going to New Hampshire . . . we're going to South Carolina and Oklahoma and Arizona and North Dakota and New Mexico, and we're going to California and Texas and New York! And we're going to South Dakota and Oregon and Washington and Michigan! And then we're going to Washington, D.C., to take back the White House!" Red-faced, he then punched the air with an emphatic "Yeaaaahr!"

It was just too tempting for media people to ignore: Howard Dean, demonstrating so vividly why reporters had described him as passionate to the point of weirdness. The fist-pumping "Yeaaahr!," in what was quickly dubbed the "I Have a Scream" speech, was remixed, set to music, and replayed literally thousands of times on the Internet, talk radio, cable TV, and late-night comedy shows for days. (*Tonight Show* host Jay Leno commented, "It's always a bad sign when at the end of your speech, your aide is shooting you with a tranquilizer gun.") Some media outlets, including CNN, later apologized for overplaying the incident. Candidates can survive attacks by their opponents, but the overwhelming media response to these few seconds of Dean's campaign was much harder to overcome.

Sources: Jodi Wilgoren and Jim Rutenberg, "Missteps Pulled a Surging Dean Back to Earth," *New York Times,* February 1, 2004, p. 1; and CNN's "Inside Politics," "Dean: We Have Just Begun to Fight," http://www.cnn.com/2004/ALLPOLITICS/01/20/elec04.prez.dean.tran/ (accessed August 2, 2005).

Another informal rule is that a candidate who expects to do especially well among independents will need to concentrate resources in states with open primaries, in which independents and other partisans can vote, as John McCain did in 2000. These rules of the game differ from party to party. Because Democrats require a "fair reflection" of candidate strength in the selection of delegates, a candidate with significant support will not be shut out in any state. The Republican Party permits winner-take-all primaries, however, and most state Republican Parties hold them, so it is still possible for a Republican candidate to win 49 percent of the votes in a state and come away without a single delegate.[10] The winner-take-all rule gives the leading candidate an even greater advantage.

Win Early or Die

The strongest imperative is the need to win early. Victories early in the nominating process create momentum; they bring the resources and support that make later victories more likely. Early successes attract more media coverage for the candidate and, in turn, more name recognition among voters. The candidate looks more and more unstoppable, so it is easier to raise money. The other candidates fall further and further behind.

The early front-runners have gotten even more of a boost in recent elections because the nomination process has become highly *"front-loaded."* Many states have moved their primaries forward in the election calendar in order to benefit from the attention attracted by these early delegate selection events, not to mention the campaign spending that comes with it. The nominating calendar was even more front-loaded in 2004 as a result of a rules change by the national Democratic Party. Then-DNC Chair Terry McAuliffe thought that Democrats would have a better chance of winning the general election if they were to agree on their candidate as soon as possible. The stampede among states to occupy an early position in the 2004 election calendar was so intense that both the Democratic and Republican nominations were wrapped up in the first seven weeks of a five-month nominating season. Almost a quarter of the Democratic delegates were selected in the first five weeks after Iowa, and 80 percent of the Democratic delegates were chosen by the end of March (see box on page 182).[11]

What Is the Party's Role?

The party organizations' interests in this process are not necessarily the same as those of the aspiring presidential candidates. State and local parties want a nominee who will bring voters to the polls to support the party's candidates for state and local offices; a weak presidential candidate may hurt their chances. Party leaders also generally prefer early agreement on a presidential candidate. A hotly contested race often heightens conflict within local and state parties, which can weaken the party in the general election.

Historically, the state parties protected their interests by selecting delegates uncommitted to any candidate and then casting the state's delegate votes as a bloc for a particular nominee or platform plank. The ability to swing a bloc of delegates to a candidate could increase the state party's influence at the convention. But the current nominating system prevents the state parties from sending an uncommitted delegation. In most primary states, it is the candidates who set up their delegate slates, so the delegates' first

FRONT-LOADING THE NOMINATION PROCESS

The New Hampshire primary in 1972, the first event of that year's nominating season, took place during the first week in March. In that week in 2004, George W. Bush and John F. Kerry wrapped up their parties' nominations by winning a majority of delegate votes. The nominating process in 2004 had begun on January 19 with the Iowa caucuses. So, although the primaries and caucuses extended till early June, the real work of choosing the nominees was completed within seven weeks after opening day.

The nomination race, in short, has become more and more "front-loaded." During the past two decades, more and more states have wanted to position their delegate-selection events close to the beginning of the process, when they would get more media coverage, bring in more money from campaign advertising, and give the state's voters more of a chance to influence the choice of their parties' nominees. Some states moved up the date of their primary or caucus by as much as a month in time for the 2004 contest. And the movement is continuing; the DNC appointed a committee in 2005 to debate whether other states should be allowed to hold their delegate selection events between the traditional lead-off Iowa caucuses and the New Hampshire primary.

Front-loading has had several important effects on the nominating process. It forces presidential candidates to raise money early; if the nomination will be wrapped up within weeks after the first state caucus, a candidate has to begin raising serious money at least a year before the season starts. George W. Bush, for example, had raised more than $132 million by the time of the first caucuses in 2004 even though he had no Republican opponent!

Front-loading gives an extra advantage to the candidates who were front-runners during the "invisible primary." When there are only a few days or weeks between the earliest primaries and the rest, there is not enough time for a long-shot candidate to get enough of a boost from an early primary win to raise the money needed to compete in California or New York, and the cost of a strategic mistake in these early events could be very high. This "rush to judgment," as two political scientists call it, makes the nominating system "less deliberative, less rational, less flexible and more chaotic."

Sources: Andrew E. Busch and William G. Mayer, "The Front-Loading Problem," in William G. Mayer, ed., *The Making of the Presidential Candidates 2004* (Lanham, MD: Rowman & Littlefield, 2004), pp. 1–43 (quotation at p. 15); and James W. Ceaser and Andrew E. Busch, *Red Over Blue* (Lanham, MD: Rowman & Littlefield, 2005), p. 75.

loyalty is to the candidate. In caucus states, delegates committed to a candidate simply have greater appeal to caucus participants than do uncommitted delegates.

Party leaders, then, have a harder time protecting the party's interests in a nominating process that is dominated by the candidates and their supporters. The Democrats tried to enhance the party's role in 1984 by setting aside delegate seats at the national convention for elected and party officials. These *superdelegates*—all Democratic governors and members of Congress, current and former presidents and vice presidents, and all members of the Democratic National Committee—were meant to be a large, uncommitted bloc totaling almost 20 percent of all delegates, with the party's interests in mind.

But because the nomination race has concluded so quickly in recent years, superdelegates have not been able to play an independent role in the nominating process.[12] Presidential candidates, then, owe their nomination largely to their own core supporters, rather than to the party organization. That limits the party organization's influence on the president, once he or she has been elected.

VOTERS' CHOICES IN PRESIDENTIAL NOMINATIONS

The move to primaries has greatly increased citizen participation in the process of nominating a president. What determines the level of voter participation and guides the voters' choices in these contests?

Who Votes?

Turnout varies a great deal from state to state and across different years in any one state. The Iowa caucuses and the New Hampshire primary usually bring out a lot of voters because of the high media attention to those early contests. More generally, turnout tends to be higher in states with a better-educated citizenry and a tradition of two-party competition—the same states where there is higher turnout in the general election. The nature of the contest matters, too. Voters are most likely to participate in early races that are closely fought, in which the candidates spend more money and the excitement is high, all of which increase voter interest in the election.[13]

Are Primary Voters Typical?

However, turnout is lower in primary than in general elections, especially after the parties' nominations have been largely wrapped up. Are the people who turn out to vote in the primaries, and who therefore choose the nominees for the rest of the public, typical of other citizens? Critics of the reforms have charged that they are not and, thus, that candidates are now being selected by an unrepresentative group of citizens. In particular, critics have argued that the first two delegate selection events in Iowa and New Hampshire are even less representative than other states' events. Both states are relatively small and largely white, but they play so disproportionate a role in selecting the parties' nominees that, as one senator suggested, "Candidates visit them probably 50 times more than any other state."[14]

We can explore this question in several ways. When we compare primary voters with nonvoters, we find that those who vote in primaries are, in fact, better educated, wealthier, and older, but then, so are general election voters. A more appropriate comparison is with party identifiers because primaries are the means by which the party electorate chooses its nominees. Using this comparison, there are not many important differences. Just as is the case with primary voters more generally, voters in presidential primaries tend to be slightly older, better educated, more affluent, better integrated into their communities, and less likely to be black or Hispanic, but their positions on key policy issues are similar to those of other party identifiers.[15] So there is not much support for the argument that presidential primary voters are less representative of the party than are other groups of voters.

Do Voters Make Informed Choices?

Another criticism of the primaries is that voters do not make very well-informed decisions. Compared with voters in the general election, primary voters have been found to pay less attention to the campaign and to have less knowledge about the candidates. An Annenberg poll in January 2004 of Democrats who intended to vote in their state's caucus or primary found that four-fifths said they didn't know enough about the candidates to make an informed choice.[16] Especially in the early contests, voters are influenced by candidate momentum, as bandwagons form for candidates who have won by a large margin, or even just exceeded reporters' expectations. Candidates' personal characteristics influence voters in the primaries, but issues often have only a minor impact. The result, so this argument goes, is a series of contests decided mainly on the basis of short-run, superficial considerations.[17]

Most analysts think that this is too strong an indictment. They feel that voters respond with some rationality to the challenge of having to choose among several candidates in a short campaign without the powerful guidance provided by party labels. Primary voters make decisions based on candidates' chances of winning, personal and demographic characteristics, and whatever inferences can be drawn about their policy positions.[18]

Is it rational for voters to be drawn to a presidential candidate who is gathering momentum in the primaries? Some would say yes: that party voters do not always see many big differences among their party's candidates and just want to pick the candidate who has the best chance of winning the nomination and the presidency. Momentum seems to matter especially when voters are being asked to sort through a pack of candidates about whom they know little[19] and when there is no well-known front-runner.[20] Even then, the candidates who move to the head of the pack are usually subjected to more searching evaluations, which give voters more reasons to support or oppose them. Momentum probably matters the least in the campaigns of incumbent presidents and vice presidents; because they are better known, their candidacies are less likely to be affected by the ups and downs of the polls, unless their chances of winning decrease substantially.

In short, even though primary voters often base their decisions on less information than do general election voters, their choices are not necessarily irrational. In contests that pit a party's candidates against one another, issue differences among candidates are likely to be minor. It should not be surprising, then, that other factors, including candidates' characteristics and issue priorities, as opposed to issue positions, would become important. The basis for voters' decisions in primaries may not differ very much from those in caucuses or general elections.[21] Besides, the questions raised about the quality of voter decision making in primaries could be raised just as easily about the judgment of the party leaders who selected candidates under the earlier caucus-convention system.

Do Primaries Produce Good Candidates?

Both the current primary-dominated system and the earlier caucus-convention system have attractive and unattractive qualities. Talented and engaging candidates have been nominated by both and so have less distinguished candidates. The earlier nominating system tended to favor mainstream politicians, those who were more acceptable to the party's leaders and activists, including some candidates who had earned their nomination through party loyalty rather than through either their personal appeal or their skills at governing. Primaries are more likely to give an advantage to candidates whose names are well known to the public and those who have the support of issue activists and ideological extremists.[22]

Compared with the earlier, party-dominated nominating process, primaries give presidential candidates a better chance to demonstrate their public support, raise more campaign money, and test their stamina. Candidates' performance in the primaries may not be a good indicator of their likely competence in the White House, but they do give voters at least some measure of the candidates' ability to cope with pressure. The openness of the primary system means that candidates cannot cut deals with state party leaders in order to gain delegate support. On the other hand, the momentum of the front-loaded nominating system increases the risk that party voters will choose a nominee too hastily and later experience buyer's remorse.

ON TO THE NATIONAL CONVENTIONS

Once the states have chosen their delegates in primaries and caucuses, the Democrats and Republicans assemble as national parties in conventions. These mass meetings bring together the party organization and activists and the party in government, but the main purpose of the convention—to select the party's presidential nominee—has already been accomplished in those primaries and caucuses. Aside from formally approving the candidates who have won the most delegates, what is left for the convention to do?

Roots of the Conventions

The national party convention is an old and respected institution, but it began, at least in part, as a power grab. In 1832, the nomination of Andrew Jackson as the Democratic-Republican candidate for president was a foregone conclusion, but state political leaders wanted to keep Henry Clay, the favorite of the congressional caucus, from being nominated as vice president; they preferred Martin Van Buren. So these leaders pushed for a national convention to make the nominations. In doing so, they wrested control of the presidential selection process from congressional leaders. By the time the Republican Party emerged in 1854, the convention had become the accepted means through which major parties chose their candidates for president and vice president. The GOP held its first convention in 1856. Ever since then, the two major parties have held national conventions every four years.

What Conventions Do

Months before the convention, its major committees begin their work (see box on page 186). What these committees decide can be overruled by the convention itself, which acts as the ultimate arbiter of its own structure and procedures. Some of the most famous battles on the floor of the convention have involved disputes over committee recommendations. The convention warms up with the keynote address by a party "star," tries to maintain momentum and suspense as it considers the platform, and reaches a dramatic peak in the nomination of the presidential and vice-presidential candidates. This general format has remained basically the same for decades.

KEY COMMITTEES OF THE NATIONAL PARTY CONVENTIONS

The national conventions have four important committees:

Credentials deals with the qualifications of delegates and alternates. In earlier years, fierce battles sometimes took place over the seating of delegations—for example, in the 1964 Democratic convention, when the all-white Mississippi delegation was challenged as being unrepresentative of all Mississippi Democrats. Now, the state procedures are regularized, so this committee is no longer as crucial.

Permanent Organization selects the officials of the convention, including the chair, secretary, and sergeant at arms.

Rules sets the rules of the convention, including the length and number of nomination speeches. The committee may also argue over the procedures to be followed at future conventions.

Platform (or Resolutions) drafts the party's platform for action by the convention. Because internal party battles focus increasingly on issues, this committee takes on special importance.

Approving the Platform   In addition to nominating candidates, the convention's main job is to approve the party's *platform*—its statement of party positions on a wide range of issues. The platform committee may begin public hearings long before the convention opens, though in 2004 the Republican platform was written in the White House and the platform committee met only briefly at the convention. The finished platform is then presented to the convention for its approval.

Party platforms don't always get much respect. Even party leaders sometimes ignore them; the 1996 Republican presidential nominee, Senator Bob Dole, admitted that he had not read his party's platform. Because they are approved in nominating conventions whose main purpose is to choose a presidential candidate, platforms have usually reflected the candidate's views—or the bargains that the candidate has been willing to make to win support or preserve party harmony.[23] So a platform usually includes a laundry list of the preferences of various groups in the party's (and the candidate's) supporting coalition. Platforms are also campaign documents, intended to help the party's candidates win their races.

Yet platforms are much more than just a laundry list of promises. They often define the major differences between the parties, as the leading scholar of party platforms shows.[24] As a result, they can provoke some spirited debates in the convention because many delegates care deeply about this single statement of the party's beliefs. The completed Democratic and Republican platforms have presented voters with clearly differing sets of stands on a number of issues, most notably abortion, taxes, gun control, racial policy, the environment, and American involvement in the world (see Chapter 15).

Formalizing the Presidential Nomination   The vote on the party's candidate for president begins with nominations made by delegates, shorter seconding speeches, and brief but passionate demonstrations by the candidate's supporters. These events are low key compared with the rambunctious conventions of earlier years. The presence of media coverage encourages party leaders to aim for a carefully crafted picture of the party's strength and vision. This tends to deprive conventions of much of the carnival and drama that were central to their tradition.

Once the nominee has been presented, the secretary calls the roll of the states (and other voting units), asking each delegation to report its vote. The result in recent times has taken only one ballot—far from the days when, in 1924, the Democrats plodded through 103 ballots in muggy New York's Madison Square Garden, before John W. Davis won the majority needed for the nomination. In the past, when a convention had more than one candidate for the nomination and the first ballot did not produce a majority, intense negotiations would follow. The leading candidates would need to protect their image as likely winners by keeping other candidates from chipping away their supporters and by negotiating for the votes of delegates who had come committed to minor candidates. It is hard to imagine how these negotiations could work in conventions today because the delegates are tied to candidates rather than to state party leaders.

Approving the Vice-Presidential Nominee   The day after the presidential nominee is chosen, delegates vote again to select the vice-presidential candidate. This process, too, is ceremonial; presidential nominees choose their own running mates and conventions ratify their choice.[25] This method of selecting vice-presidential candidates has drawn criticism—not so much because they are handpicked by the presidential nominee as because the decision is often made by a tired candidate and then sprung, at the last minute, on convention delegates. George H. W. Bush's nomination of Senator Dan Quayle in 1988 was attacked on these grounds. But without any viable procedure to replace it, this choice will remain in the hands of the party's presidential nominee.

Launching the Presidential Campaign   The final business of the conventions is to present their party's presidential choice to the American voters. The nominating speeches and the candidates' own acceptance speeches are the opening shots of the fall campaign. Most nominees generally get a boost in public support (a "convention bounce") from this campaign kickoff, though John Kerry was an exception in 2004. For the winning candidates, then, the most important role of the convention is as a campaign event.

Many other events take place at the conventions as well. Lobbyists host hundreds of events for delegates. Since the banning of "soft money" contributions to the national parties in 2002 (see Chapter 12), paying for lavish dinners, receptions, and cruises at national conventions has become a means for lobbyists to curry favor with elected officials. Protesters have been drawn to some conventions, especially in times of war and social ferment; there were more than 100,000 demonstrators at the 2004 Republican convention in New York representing causes from AIDS to Iraq.

WHO ARE THE DELEGATES?

Convention delegates are among the most visible of the party's activists. They help to shape the public's image of the two parties. Who are these delegates?

Apportioning Delegates Among the States

It is the parties that determine how many delegates each state can send to the convention. The two parties make these choices differently. The Republicans allocate delegates more equally among the states; the Democrats weigh more heavily the size of the state's population and its record of support for Democratic candidates. These formulas affect the voting strength of various groups within the party coalitions, as they do in the two national committees (see Chapter 4). The GOP's decision to represent the small states more equally with the large states has been an advantage to its conservative wing. In contrast, by giving relatively more weight to the larger states with stronger Democratic voting traditions, the Democrats have favored the more liberal interests in their party.

How Representative Are the Delegates?

The delegates to the Democratic and Republican conventions have never been a cross section of American citizens or even of their party's voters. White males, the well educated, and the affluent have traditionally been overrepresented in conventions. Reflecting their different coalitional bases, since the 1930s, Democratic delegations have had more labor union members and African Americans, and Republican conventions have drawn more Protestants and business entrepreneurs.

Demographics   Since the nomination reforms, the delegates of both parties, but especially the Democrats, have become at least somewhat more representative of other citizens. The Democrats used affirmative action plans after 1968 to increase the presence of women, blacks, and, for a brief time, young people. At the 2004 Democratic convention, a full 40 percent of the delegates were people of color, and since 1980, the DNC has required that half of the delegates be women. The percentage of female delegates at Republican conventions has gone up somewhat during this period as well, but without party mandates. The Democratic National Committee has urged its state organizations to recruit more low- and moderate-income delegates, but the lower political involvement levels of these groups and the high price of attending a convention stand in the way. So conventions remain meetings of the wealthy and well educated (see Table 10.1). In 2004, for instance, 27 percent of Republican delegates and 14 percent of Democrats said they were millionaires, a larger proportion than in 2000 or 1996.[26]

Political Experience   We might assume that delegates would be recidivists, making return appearances at convention after convention. But that was not the case even before the reforms; even then, a comfortable majority of delegates at each convention were first timers. With the move to primaries, the percentage of newcomers jumped to about 80 percent before declining to about 55 percent in 2004. The decline became more

TABLE 10.1   How Representative Were the 2004 Democratic and Republican Convention Delegates?

	Dem. Delegates (%)	Dem. Voters (%)	All Voters (%)	Rep. Voters (%)	Rep. Delegates (%)
Gender					
Female	50	57	51	47	43
Race					
Black	18	28	14	2	6
White	68	61	78	94	85
Latino	12	15	11	12	7
Education					
HS graduate or less	5	44	37	34	6
Some college	18	27	32	33	20
College grad	24	15	19	23	29
Postgraduate	53	13	11	9	44
Household income					
Under $50,000	15	57	45	37	8
Over $75,000	61	22	29	35	58
Religion					
Protestant	43	55	57	68	65
Evangelical or Born-again*	13	27	34	48	33
Catholic	32	24	25	25	26
Jewish	8	3	2	0	2

*Asked in a separate question, so percentages for "religion" do not add up to 100 percent.

Source: Data on convention delegates are from *New York Times*/CBS News polls taken during June 16–July 17, 2004 of Democratic National Convention delegates and August 3–23 for Republican delegates. "Voters" are all registered voters in nationwide polls taken by the same polling organization during July 11–15 and August 15–18.

marked when the Democrats granted convention seats to politically experienced superdelegates.

Even if many delegates are new to conventions, however, the great majority are long-time party activists. In 2004, most of a random sample of delegates reported that they had been active in their party for at least 20 years, and a majority said they currently hold party office. In spite of the high turnover, then, these national party meetings still bring together the activists of the state and local party organizations and the leaders of the party in government.

Issues   Convention delegates are also more extreme in their views and more aware of issues than is the average party voter. Democratic delegates are more liberal than Democratic voters (41 percent compared with 34 percent) and much more liberal than the average voter (20 percent); Republican delegates are about as conservative as GOP voters

TABLE 10.2   Views on Issues: Comparing Delegates and Voters in 2004

	Dem. Delegates (%)	Dem. Voters (%)	All Voters (%)	Rep. Voters (%)	Rep. Delegates (%)
Government should do more to solve national problems	79	48	42	35	7
Abortion should be permitted in all cases	64	37	26	13	8
Favor death penalty for murder	19	39	50	65	57
Government should do more to promote traditional values	15	26	40	61	55
All or most of the tax cuts Congress has passed since 2000 should be made permanent	7	33	49	68	95
U.S. did the right thing in taking military action against Iraq	7	21	46	78	96
Federal government should do more to regulate businesses' safety and environmental practices	85	71	59	45	15
Gay couples should be allowed to legally marry	44	36	26	11	3
Presidential candidates should discuss the role of religion in their lives	33	32	48	68	81

Note: Figures are the percentage of each group who agreed with the statement.
Source: Same as Table 10.1.

(63 percent compared with 61 percent) but much more conservative than voters generally (36 percent).

The distance between delegates and their party's voters varies from issue to issue. As Table 10.2 shows, Democratic delegates in 2004 came closest to the views of Democratic voters (and all voters) in believing that the United States should have stayed out of Iraq, in wanting government to regulate businesses' environmental and safety practices, and in feeling that the role of religion in the candidates' lives should not be a part of the presidential campaign. But these Democratic delegates were substantially more liberal than most voters on several other key issues. Republican delegates were closer to the views of Republican voters, as well as the average voter, in their views on abortion, the death penalty, and the belief that government should promote traditional values, but scored well to the right on other questions. The Democratic and Republican delegates differed most from one another on the war in Iraq and the continuance of the Bush tax cuts.

The degree to which delegates hold more extreme views than party voters bears on a long-standing debate about the nominating process. Democrats who promoted the 1970s reforms were motivated in part by the argument that the old caucus-convention system, dominated by party leaders, did not represent the views of grassroots party supporters. In turn, the critics of the reforms contend that the delegates selected under the new rules are even more out of step with the beliefs of party voters and the electorate in general.

The reality is that the reforms have not made the conventions more representative of the *views* of party identifiers. Prior to 1972, it was the Republican conventions whose delegates appeared to be more out of step with party voters and even more compared with the general voting public.[27] The Democratic reforms first seemed to reverse that pattern. Democratic delegates in 1972 were more ideologically distant from their party identifiers than Republican delegates were and even farther away from the public, and some charged that the reforms were at fault.[28] These disparities on issues seem to have been reduced a little in later Democratic conventions.[29]

The real effect of the reforms has been to link the selection of delegates more closely to candidate preferences. As a result, when an issue-oriented candidate does well in the primaries and caucuses, more issue-oriented activists become convention delegates. At those times, conventions may be less representative of the party in the electorate. However, they may offer clearer choices to voters.

Amateurs or Professionals?   The reforms were also expected to result in delegates with a different approach to politics. Using the terms described in Chapter 5, some convention delegates can be described as amateurs, others as professionals. Amateurs are more attracted by issues, more insistent on internal party democracy, less willing to compromise and less committed to the prime importance of winning elections. Professionals, in contrast, are more likely to have a long-term commitment to the party and to be more willing to compromise on issues in the interest of winning the general election.

There is some evidence that the Democratic Party's reforms had, as intended, reduced the presence of party professionals between the 1968 and the 1972 conventions.[30] As we have seen, however, the party later moved to reverse this trend, particularly by adding superdelegates. Research shows that even after the reforms, delegates have remained strongly committed to the parties and their goals.[31] It may be that for both professionals and amateurs, involvement in this highly public party pageant strengthens delegates' commitment to the party's aims.

Who Controls the Delegates?   It would not matter how representative delegates are if they act as pawns of powerful party leaders. In fact, for most of the history of party conventions, that is exactly how the state delegations behaved. State party leaders and big-city mayors had a commanding presence, especially at Democratic conventions.

Now, however, strong party leaders no longer control the convention by dominating their state delegations. When the Democrats eliminated their long-standing unit rule in 1968, through which a majority of a state delegation could throw all the delegation's votes to one candidate, they removed a powerful instrument of leadership control. Perhaps the most powerful force preventing state party leaders from controlling the conventions is the fact that the delegates in both parties now come to the conventions already committed to a candidate. That makes them unavailable for "delivery" by party leaders. If anyone controls the modern conventions, then, it is the party's prospective nominee for president, not leaders of the state parties.

HOW MEDIA COVER CONVENTIONS

In addition to all these changes in the convention's delegates and power centers, media coverage of conventions has changed significantly. On one hand, conventions have been reshaped and rescheduled to meet the media's needs.[32] On the other hand, ironically, media attention to the conventions has declined sharply in recent years.

Beginning with the first televised national party conventions in 1948, TV journalists and politicians found ways to serve one another's needs. In the early days of television before the convenience of videotape, networks were desperate for content with which to fill broadcast time. So they covered the party conventions live, from gavel to gavel. For television news, the convention became a major story, like the Olympics, through which it could demonstrate its skill and provide a public service. Reporters swarmed through the convention halls, covering the strategic moves of major candidates, the actions of powerful figures in the party, and the reactions of individual delegates. Even the formerly secret work of the platform committee came to be done in the public eye.

For party leaders, television coverage offered a priceless opportunity to reach voters and to launch the presidential campaign with maximum impact. So they reshaped the convention into a performance intended as much for the national television audience as for the delegates. Party officials gave key speaking roles to telegenic candidates, speeded up the proceedings, and moved the most dramatic convention business into prime-time hours. More and more, the aim of the convention shifted from the conduct of party business to the wooing of voters.

These two sets of goals, however—the networks' interest in a good story and the parties' interest in attracting supporters—increasingly began to conflict. Once the nomination reforms took effect, the choice of the parties' presidential candidates was settled before the convention started. That took most of the drama and suspense out of the conventions. To keep their audience, media people searched the conventions for new sources of excitement, such as potential conflicts. But party leaders had no interest in making their disputes public; that would interfere with the positive message they were trying to convey. As the conventions' audience appeal continued to decline, the major networks reduced their coverage to broadcast only the most significant events. Although convention "junkies" still can turn to C-SPAN, MSNBC, or other cable sources for comprehensive coverage, the number of hours of coverage on ABC, CBS, and NBC decreased from about 60 per convention in 1952 to a grand total of 3 hours in 2004.[33]

Media coverage, of course, is not always a boon for the parties. Television's capacity to dramatize and personalize can make a convention come to life for its audience, as it did in covering the struggles in the Democratic convention hall and streets of Chicago in 1968, which led to the nomination reforms. However, the sight of bloody demonstrators and angry delegates did not help the Democratic Party to attract voter support for its candidates that year. Television cameras can encourage some participants to use the convention as a podium to advance their own causes even if they risk undermining the party's interests. For better or worse, the televised conventions of 2004 had become a shadow of their former selves, in which a shrinking audience watched snippets of roll-call votes, shots of people wearing funny hats, and intense discussions among media commentators.

DO CONVENTIONS STILL HAVE A PURPOSE?

Since the nomination reforms, then, conventions have greatly changed. They are no longer the occasions when the major parties actually select their presidential nominees. That happens in the primaries and caucuses; the conventions simply ratify the results. The national conventions have lost much of their deliberative character and independence.

In another way, however, the conventions have become more significant. Because candidates must mobilize groups of activists and voters in order to win primaries and caucuses and because many of these groups are concerned with particular policies, the nomination reforms have made issues all the more important in convention politics. Many delegates arrive at the convention committed not only to a candidate but also to a cause. The pressures exerted by Christian conservatives at recent Republican conventions on behalf of such causes as school prayer and opposition to abortion and homosexuality are a good illustration.

In spite of all these changes—or perhaps because of them—the national conventions are living symbols of the national parties. They provide a unique occasion for rediscovering common interests and for celebrating the party's heroes and achievements. Conventions motivate state and local party candidates, energize party workers, and launch presidential campaigns. They give new party candidates some time in the media spotlight. They may not win Emmy awards for compelling viewing, but they frequently remind party activists and identifiers why the party matters to them.

SHOULD WE REFORM THE REFORMS?

The increasing use of primaries in the presidential nominating system was part of a time-honored pattern in American politics: efforts by reformers to break up concentrations of party power. As we have seen, however, the reforms have had many unintended effects as well. Primaries can create internal divisions in state party organizations that may not heal in time for the general election. The low turnouts in primaries and caucuses may increase the influence of well-organized groups on the ideological extremes: the right wing of the Republican Party and the left wing of the Democrats. The results of a few early contests in states not very representative of the nation have a disproportionate effect on the national outcome.[34] By the time most voters know enough about the prospective nominees to make an informed choice, the nominations have already been decided. And candidates must invest such an enormous amount of time, energy, and money in the nomination process that the ultimate winner can arrive at the party convention personally and financially exhausted.

But there is no going back to the old system. As the reformers charged, it was controlled by state and local party leaders who were often out of touch with the electorate. It kept many party voters and even party activists out of the crucial first step in picking a president. It violated the desire for a more open, democratic politics, and it did not help presidential candidates learn how to prepare for the most powerful leadership job in the world.[35]

What Could Be Done?

Could the reforms' drawbacks be fixed by more reforms? One possibility is to create regional nominating events, in which the states in a given region would all schedule their primaries on the same day. That might bring more coherence to the welter of state contests by limiting the number of dates on which they could be held and reducing the enormous strain on the candidates.

For a time in the late 1980s and 1990s, one regional primary existed; most southern states chose to hold their primaries early in March on a date referred to as Super Tuesday. The aim of these states was to draw greater attention to southern concerns and to encourage the nomination of moderate candidates acceptable to the South. By 1996, New England states also scheduled their primaries on this date. In 2000, six southern and southwestern states attempted another southern primary, but the front-loading of other states' events reduced its impact.

Regional primaries, however, have drawbacks, too. Which region would go first? Even if the order were rotated from one election to the next, the first region to vote, with its peculiarities and specific concerns, would have a disproportionate effect on the nominations. Regional primaries could still produce all the complaints just listed, from internal party divisions to low turnouts. Given the fact that the only major war fought on American soil was a regional dispute—the Civil War—some might ask whether it is wise to encourage regional divisions.

Another option might be to hold a national primary in which all the states' delegate selection events took place on the same day. But this would serve the interests of neither the parties nor the states. States would lose their chance of becoming key players in the nomination race. The parties would lose even more control over presidential selection, throwing the contest for the presidency wide open to any candidate who could mobilize a national constituency (and a great deal of money). A national primary could be accomplished only by ending the long tradition of state and party control over the presidential nomination process—and even after all the reforms that we have seen in recent decades, there is little chance that will happen.

Chapter 11

The General Election

Imagine a meeting of the media consultants for two presidential candidates in 2008—let's say Hillary Clinton and John McCain—and consultants in the 1948 presidential campaign of Harry Truman and the 1896 campaign of William McKinley. What would they talk about? McKinley's adviser might describe the remarkable sight of thousands of people traveling by train to McKinley's home town of Canton, Ohio, where McKinley would emerge every day to give a speech to the crowds. Truman's consultant would speak of his candidate addressing the nation on radio and reporters filing their stories by telegraph. And both would listen in awe as Clinton and McCain staffers explained computerized database targeting and fund-raising on the Internet.

Technological change has profoundly altered the nature of American campaigning, and the pace of change is accelerating. Now, if you plan to run for statewide or national office (or even local offices in many areas), you would expect to hire a long list of professional political consultants ranging from pollsters to media specialists, direct mail experts, web page designers, fund-raisers, accountants, and others. They will do the work—for a fee, of course—that would have been done for free (or at least for no monetary payment) in the days when state and local party leaders were the main planners and managers of campaigns.

It would be easy to assume, as a result, that these independent consultants and their powerful campaign techniques have completely replaced the party organizations as influences on campaigns. But the parties are highly adaptable. Throughout their history, the Democratic and Republican Parties have adjusted to changing circumstances; their adaptability helps account for their long lives. Instead of relegating the parties to the sidelines, then, we need to examine their current role in campaigns.

Earlier chapters have discussed important parts of the campaign environment: the parties' organizational strength, political activists, party loyalties, voter turnout, and the rules governing party nominations. We will begin this chapter by looking at the "rules" by which elections are run. Then we will examine the decisions that candidates can make to take advantage of those rules.

ELECTIONS: THE RULES AFFECT THE RESULTS

The rules in politics, as well as everything else, are never neutral. Each rule of the electoral process—for example, how votes must be cast or when elections must be held—not only limits a campaign's choices, but also affects different parties and candidates differently. For example, if polling places close at 6:00 P.M. (as they do in Indiana and Kentucky), so factory and office workers find it hard to get to the polls on time, then the Democratic Party may lose a disproportionate number of votes. If the state makes it easy to vote by mail, then any local party organized enough to distribute mail-in ballots to its supporters will benefit. Over the years, reformers have changed the rules in order to weaken the parties, and party leaders have tinkered with the rules to gain strength. The reformers have won these rules battles more often than the parties have. Here are some prominent examples.

The Secret Ballot

American elections did not always use secret ballots. In the early 1800s, in many areas, voters simply told the election officials which candidates they preferred. Gradually, this "oral vote" was replaced by the use of ballots printed by the parties or candidates. The voter brought the ballot of a particular candidate or party to the polling place and put it in the ballot box. The ballots of different parties differed in color and appearance, so observers could tell how an individual had voted. That was not accidental; if party leaders had done a favor for a voter in exchange for a vote, they wanted to be sure they had gotten their money's worth.

To discourage vote buying, a new ballot system came into widespread use in the 1890s. Called the Australian ballot after the country where it originated, these ballots were printed by the government and marked by the voter in secret. By the early twentieth century, its success was virtually complete; only South Carolina waited until 1950 to adopt it. Because the ballot is administered and paid for by the government, this reform involved the government in running elections, which opened the door to government regulation of the parties. It also enabled voters to split their tickets—to vote for the candidates of more than one party on the same ballot.[1]

The Format of the Ballot

The *format* of this secret ballot varies from state to state, however, which makes a difference in the role of the parties.

The Order of Candidates' Names   It is a curious fact that some voters are more likely to select the first name on a list of candidates than they are to select a name listed later.[2] So some states randomly assign the order in which candidates' names appear on the ballot or rotate the order among groups of ballots; in other states, incumbents' names or the candidates of the majority party appear first. The decision to list incumbents first increases their already substantial electoral advantages. The order of the candidates' names probably matters most in primaries and nonpartisan contests, when voters can find no information about the candidates on the ballot itself.

The Long Ballot   Another important "rule" is that American voters are asked to elect large numbers of state and local officials who would be appointed in other democracies. In many areas, voters also cast ballots on issues. In 2002, for example, San Francisco voters faced 19 ballot questions on everything from parental leave to whether the city should grow its own marijuana. Voters also received a 300-page booklet of citizens' and groups' opinions about these ballot measures plus a 112-page guide to other ballot questions and candidates for state office.

Citizens would need to process a lot of information (and have a lot of patience) to cast a meaningful vote in such an election. Many people consider this an invitation to stay away from the polls. Those who do vote may cast ballots for some offices but not others. This partial voting, called roll-off, is most often seen on minor offices and referenda in which as many as 20 or 30 percent of the voters abstain.[3] The voter fatigue caused by the long ballot leads people to use various shortcuts to make their choices; party identification, of course, is one.

Voting Systems

Most of us assume that, even if a ballot is long, it is easy enough to understand: You choose a candidate, push a button or pull a lever, and that candidate gets your vote. At least, we *would* have made that assumption until the aftermath of the 2000 presidential race. Recounts prompted by the closeness of the vote showed that on 1.5 to 2 million ballots (about 2 percent of all those cast), the counting machines found no presidential vote or votes for more than one candidate; these voters' ballots, then, were not counted. Some of these "undervotes" or "overvotes" could have been intentional, but studies showing that these problems occurred much more frequently in some types of voting machines (such as punch card systems) suggest that the voting system itself may have been the culprit (see box on page 199).[4]

In other cases, analysts charged that confusing ballot layout, such as the so-called "butterfly ballot" used in Palm Beach County, Florida, led many voters to cast their ballot for a different candidate than they had intended (see Figure 11.1). This was an especially worrisome issue in Florida, which decided the election for Bush by a margin of only 537 votes. There were other problems as well, such as voters turned away from polling places, malfunctioning voting machines, and outright fraud.

Why does this happen? There are about 193,000 voting precincts in the United States. They contain about 700,000 voting machines tended by almost 1.5 million poll workers who are typically poorly paid, lightly trained partisan volunteers.[5] Simple human error is as likely to occur in running elections and counting votes as it is in any other large-scale activity. Because elections are decentralized, voters in one state, even in one county, may be treated differently from voters in another. In particular, counties differ in their ability to pay for the most reliable (and costly) voting systems. The result is that error-prone systems are more likely to be found in poorer counties, which tend to vote Democratic.

In the wake of these revelations, Congress passed the 2002 Help America Vote Act (HAVA) to set minimum federal standards and provide $3 billion to help cash-starved states upgrade their procedures. Many counties rushed to install electronic voting systems; in 2004, these touch-screen machines were used by almost 30 percent of voters.

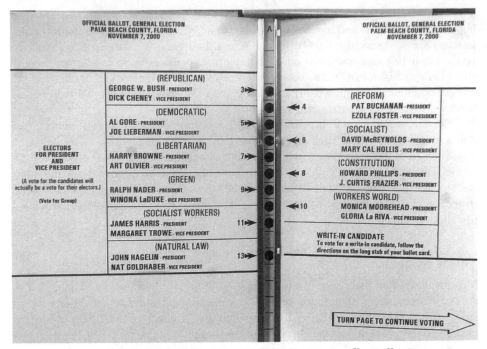

FIGURE 11.1   The Famous Palm Beach, Florida "Butterfly Ballot"
This ballot format was designed by a Democratic official in Palm Beach County to make it easier for visually challenged older voters to read. As illustrated in this graphic by Daniel Niblock of the South Florida *Sun-Sentinel* (showing the angle at which most voters would have seen the ballot), the problem was that the punch card holes did not always line up with the candidates' names, so in order to vote for Al Gore, whose name was second on the list of candidates, voters had to punch the *third* hole. Source: Robert Duyos/South Florida *Sun-Sentinel*. Reprinted by permission of the South Florida *Sun-Sentinel*. Photograph by Susan Stocker.

Thirty-two states allowed some form of early voting in person or by mail, a big increase over 2000, which enabled election officials to identify and fix some problems before Election Day. And the fact that the presidential outcome wasn't as close in 2004 helped to reduce the controversy over voting procedures.

New problems still arose, however. HAVA provided that anyone whose eligibility to vote was challenged by an election official had the right to cast a "provisional" ballot. But Congress set no uniform national standards as to which of these provisional ballots should be counted, so concerns remained about partisan and unequal treatment. And the newly purchased e-voting systems raised issues that were familiar to anyone who has used a college computer lab: technological glitches and programming errors, ranging from the simple (candidates for the U.S. Senate didn't appear on the screen in some Maryland precincts) to the complex, including computer crashes and the possibility of hacking and rigged machines. Most e-voting systems leave no paper record of the votes cast (because systems with a paper trail are more costly), so there is nothing tangible to recount. One Florida newspaper found that voters in counties using touch-screen machines were six

DEMOCRACY ON THE CHEAP: WHY CAN'T WE COUNT VOTES ACCURATELY?

Even after widespread publicity about the problems with voting systems used in the 2000 election, things weren't much better in 2004:

- In a nation where the latest handheld computer is considered a staple of many professions, 19 percent of all voting in the United States (72 percent in Ohio) is done on punch-card machines, where voters must punch out a perforated rectangle (called a "chad") next to the candidate's name. Sometimes, however, the chad doesn't fall out or is pushed back in as the voter moves down the ballot. When that happens, the voter's choice can't be read by the voting machine.

- In one precinct in suburban Columbus, Ohio, George W. Bush got 4,258 votes—out of a total of 638 votes cast. (It was a computer error, which was later corrected; Bush's total was actually 365). In Youngstown, 25 electronic machines accidentally transferred an unknown number of votes from Kerry to Bush. And throughout Ohio, between 5,000 and 15,000 would-be voters went home without voting because waits at the polls, caused by too few voting machines, sometimes ranged from four to ten hours.

- Most Louisiana and New York precincts use pull-a-lever voting machines so old that they aren't made anymore, and breakdowns are common. The machines can be rigged using pliers, a screwdriver, a cigarette lighter, and a Q-tip. The late Louisiana Senator Earl Long used to say that he wanted to be buried in Louisiana so he could keep voting.

- Indiana's voting registration lists include hundreds of thousands of people who are ineligible to vote because they are dead, felons, or have registered more than once. Alaska has more registered voters than people of voting age.

- There was a big increase in mail-in ballots in 2004. Anticorruption laws prevent party workers from "helping" voters mark their ballots at the polls, but there is no guarantee that mailed-in ballots will be free from such influence.

As one expert put it, "We'd never tolerate this level of errors with an ATM. The problem is that we continue to do democracy on the cheap."

Sources: Paul Farhi, "3 Days Late, Bush Is Awarded Iowa," *Washington Post,* November 6, 2004, p. A7; Robin Toner, "For Those Behind the Scenes, It's Old News That Elections Are Not an Exact Science," *New York Times,* November 17, 2000, p. A23; and quotation from Michael Powell and Peter Slevin, "Several Factors Contributed to 'Lost' Voters in Ohio," *Washington Post,* December 15, 2004, p. A1.

times more likely to have their vote go unrecorded as were voters in counties using optical-scan devices, like those often used to grade multiple-choice exams.[6]

Legislative Redistricting

Yet another rule of the electoral process is that some types of candidates—legislative incumbents—have the unique opportunity to change the nature of the districts they represent in order to improve their chances of reelection. Every ten years, after the

U.S. Census, state legislatures must redraw the boundaries of congressional and state legislative districts in order to take into account changes in population size and distribution. How these opportunities have been turned to political advantage is a continuing story of the creativity and resourcefulness of American politicians.

Two methods have traditionally been used to turn redistricting opportunities into political gains. The first and most obvious was simply to ignore population changes. Many states used this tactic for most of the 1900s by refusing to shift legislative districts and thus political power from the shrinking rural and small-town populations to the growing cities. By the 1960s, many state legislatures and the U.S. House of Representatives better represented the largely rural America of 1900 than the urban nation it had become. Such *malapportionment* worked to the disadvantage of Republicans in the South and Democrats elsewhere and of the needs of cities everywhere. In a series of decisions in the 1960s, the Supreme Court ended these inequities by requiring that legislative districts be of equal population size and by applying this "one person, one vote" rule to all types of legislatures.[7]

It is still very common, however, to *gerrymander*—to draw district lines in a way that maximizes one party's strength and disadvantages the other party. That can be done by dividing pockets of the other party's strength among several districts to prevent it from winning office. Alternatively, if the other party's strength is too great to be diluted, then a gerrymander can be created by consolidating that party's voters into a few districts and forcing it to win elections by large, wasteful majorities.

The party in power when it is time to redistrict is probably always tempted to gerrymander. Its ability to do so has been enhanced by computer programs that can draw districts to maximize a party's chances of success, and by the increasing party polarization, which has given state legislators the will to try. After the 2000 U.S. Census, the redrawing of House districts within each state offered ample opportunities for partisan gain. For instance, Republicans controlled the redistricting process in Florida, Michigan, and Pennsylvania in 2001, and the GOP won six more seats in those states in the 2002 elections than they had in 2000.[8]

In states where power is split between the two parties, they often agree on a gerrymander that protects incumbents of both parties by making their seats safer. A California gerrymander after the 2000 census, for example, was so effective that only three of the state's 173 state and national legislative districts changed parties in 2002, and none at all in 2004. The number of competitive House races dwindles as a result. There were almost as many competitive House districts in Iowa, where a nonpartisan agency did the redistricting, as in California, New York, Illinois, and Ohio combined. Not all gerrymanders work as planned, however. In 2002, two of four open House districts in Georgia, drawn carefully by the state legislature's Democratic majority in order to elect Democrats, went Republican instead.[9]

After the 2000 redistricting had been completed, Republicans won newfound majorities in several states in the 2002 elections. U.S. House Majority Leader Tom DeLay urged Republicans in these states, including DeLay's home state of Texas, to conduct an unprecedented second round of redrawing district lines in order to improve their prospects for the 2004 elections. The Texas saga, in which minority Democratic legislators fled the state to keep the redistricting from passing, made headlines all over the world (see box on page 201).

THE TALE OF THE TEXAS 62

First, 51 Democratic state representatives from Texas slipped quietly across the border to Oklahoma under cover of darkness. The Republican governor dispatched state police to arrest them and bring them back. The U.S. Department of Homeland Security went looking for them. Republican legislators pasted the faces of the missing Democrats on milk cartons. The Democrats, hunkered down at a Holiday Inn in Ardmore, finally returned. Two months later, 11 Senate Democrats decamped for Albuquerque.

What was going on here? In 2003, Republicans took control of both houses of the Texas state legislature for the first time in 130 years. In a session that was termed "extraordinarily venomous" and partisan, the new Republican majority proposed to redraw the lines of the state's U.S. House districts. Texas's congressional district lines had already been redrawn following the 2000 U.S. Census. However, Republicans saw the chance, in a rare second redistricting, to bring the partisan composition of the state's House delegation more in line with what they perceived to be citizens' current party preferences. The proposal, drawn up by U.S. House Majority Leader Tom DeLay, was expected to result in big Republican gains.

Democratic legislators called the proposal a "power grab." Outnumbered, most of the Democrats decided to fight it by leaving town, thus depriving the legislature of a quorum (the minimum number of legislators who must be present to do business). The state Republican chair called the Democrats "cowards" and "betrayers of the people of Texas." Democratic lawmakers agreed to come home when Republican leaders, who could not pass any other legislation (including the state budget) without a quorum, promised to drop the redistricting proposal.

But the Republican governor then called a special legislative session, in which the state House passed the pro-Republican plan. Now it was the Senate Democrats who left town. When one Democrat broke ranks and came back, however, the battle was over. The redistricting plan passed the state legislature and was signed into law by the governor and upheld by a three-judge panel. Texas Republicans did defeat four Democratic incumbents in the 2004 elections; that provided the wins necessary to give the Republican Party a net gain of three U.S. House seats nationwide.

Sources: Lee Hockstader, "Democrats Take Flight to Fight Tex. Redistricting," *Washington Post,* May 13, 2003, p. A1; and Lee Hockstader, "Texas Democrats Trying Fight, Not Flight, Over Districts," *Washington Post,* July 1, 2003, p. A4.

CAMPAIGN STRATEGY

Taking account of all these "rules" and challenges, candidates and their consultants have to plan how to win their race.[10] Campaigners must consider a number of important variables in designing a strategy: the nature of the district and its voters (as created by redistricting), the ballot format and voting system, the type of office being sought, the candidate's skills and background and those of the opponent, the availability of money and other resources, the party organizations and other organized groups in the constituency. Once they have identified their campaign's likely strengths and weaknesses, they must choose how to spend their scarce time and money.

The most important factors affecting the campaign's decisions are incumbency and the competitiveness of the race. Incumbents have impressive advantages in running for reelection.[11] They are greatly advantaged by having put together a successful campaign for that office at least once before. Part of that campaign organization is likely to remain in place between elections, some of it perhaps employed as members of the incumbent's office staff. Incumbents normally have greater name recognition, more success in attracting media coverage, and greater appeal to campaign contributors than do most of their potential opponents.

In painful contrast, most challengers, especially if they have not won any political office before, do not start with an experienced organization, proven fund-raising skills, or the other incumbent advantages.[12] In the days when party organizations dominated campaigns, this might not have been a problem. Now it is. One obvious answer might be to purchase an experienced campaign organization by hiring political consultants, but most challengers do not have the money to do that. Thus, the predictable cycle begins: The challenger lacks an existing organization and enough money to attract the interest of well-known consultants and buy media time, so he or she cannot reach many voters, and without these vital resources, a challenger will not raise enough money to be able to afford either one.

Candidates for open seats (those where no incumbent is running) are more likely to run competitive races. Those who choose to run for the most visible offices—the presidency, governorships, the U.S. Senate, major city offices—typically start with considerable name recognition, which increases because of the attention given to the race. They can raise enough money for extensive media campaigns. Their major challenge will be to spend their money effectively and to succeed in defining themselves to the voters before their opponents get the opportunity to define them.

The George W. Bush campaign provided a textbook example of preemptively defining an opponent in 2004. Right after John F. Kerry wrapped up the Democratic presidential nomination in March, the Bush campaign ran a six-week, nearly $50 million ad campaign attacking Kerry as a "flip-flopper." The term stuck, in part because Kerry's campaign treasury had been depleted by the nomination race and couldn't counter the Bush ads and in part because of Kerry's own description of his votes on a measure that would allocate $87 billion to American troops in Iraq and Afghanistan: "I actually did vote for the $87 billion before I voted against it."

HOW CAMPAIGNING HAS CHANGED

Within less than a generation, American political campaigning has been revolutionized. Campaigns have found effective ways to apply advances in polling, media use, and computer technology. They have done so with the help of a burgeoning industry of professional campaign consultants whose services are available to candidates who can afford the price.

Professional Consultants

Political consultants deliver a variety of services to campaigns.[13] Some are general consultants, similar to the general contractors who oversee the construction of a home; others concentrate on the details of mailing lists or web page design. Some are experts in the development of media messages and others in how and where to place media ads. Some provide organizational skills; they can organize rallies, coffee parties, and phone banks. Others provide lawyers and accountants to steer the campaign away from legal shoals and to handle the reporting of campaign finances to state and federal regulators. Some are publicists who write speeches and press releases; some sample public opinion, and others are skilled in raising money.

Professional consultants typically work for several different campaigns at a time. Although they work independently of the party organizations, they almost always work with clients from only one party—some consultants restrict themselves even further to one wing, or ideological grouping, within the party—and they normally maintain a cooperative relationship with that party's leaders. In fact, national party committees often play a matchmaking role in bringing together consultants and candidates.

American consultants have also exported their campaign expertise to the rest of the democratic world. Pollster Stan Greenberg, for instance, worked for former President Bill Clinton in 1996. Then he was hired by campaigns for prime minister in England in 1997, Germany in 1998, and Israel in 1999 before signing on to Al Gore's presidential campaign in 2000. In 2005 he was advising Britain's Labour Party in the May national election, along with another former Clinton pollster, Mark Penn, and two former consultants to Howard Dean, Karen Hicks and Joe Trippi.

Sources of Information

Computers   Experienced candidates develop a picture of their constituency in their minds. As the result of years of contact with constituents, they know what kinds of people support them and how they believe they can trigger that support again. In past years, this "theory" of the campaign would have guided the candidate's strategy, even if the beliefs were inaccurate or the constituency had changed.

Computer technology now provides a much more sophisticated check on the candidate's beliefs. Computerized records produce faster and more accurate answers to questions about voter behavior than even the most experienced party workers are able to do. By entering canvassers' information into databases, party organizations can aim specific appeals to people likely to be sympathetic to those appeals. Fund-raisers can merge mailing lists from groups and publications whose members may be predisposed to favor their candidate and then produce targeted mailings within hours. Using computerized records, "oppo" researchers can locate statements made by the opponent on any conceivable issue.

Polls   No campaign technology has been more fully exploited than the public opinion poll.[14] Candidates poll before deciding whether to run for an office in order to assess voters' views and to probe for weaknesses in the opposition. When the campaign begins, polls are used to determine what issues are uppermost in voters' minds and how the candidate's first steps are affecting his or her "negatives" and "positives." Poll data can help the campaign decide whether its ads should emphasize party loyalties or ties with other party candidates. Close to the end of the race, *tracking polls* can follow the reactions of small samples of voters each day to measure immediate responses to a campaign event or a new ad.

Methods of Persuasion: The Air War

Because of the large size of most state and federal election districts, the main means of persuasion are the broadcast media: television, radio, newspapers, and the Internet. Even older-style communications are pursued with the media in mind: A candidate takes the time to address a rally largely in the hope that it will be covered by local television news.

Television   Television often consumes most of the campaign's money. In the early and inexpensive days of television, candidates bought large chunks of time for entire speeches that were carried nation- or statewide. Now, however, because of television's increased cost and voters' decreased attention spans, campaign messages are compressed into 30-second spot ads that can be run frequently in competitive areas. Between March and late September of 2004, for example, residents of Toledo were exposed to more than 14,000 ads about the presidential race on the city's four leading TV stations.[15] Placement of these spot ads is a major concern of media specialists. In 2004, the Bush campaign aimed at Republican men by running ads on crime shows, whereas the Kerry campaign hoped to attract single and middle-aged women with ads on *Judge Judy* and *Oprah*.[16]

Because of the high cost of network television, candidates and consultants also look for alternatives. The cost of advertising on cable TV is often lower than on the networks and may be more efficient for local campaigns, whose constituencies are too small to warrant buying time in major media markets. Most cable stations, such as BET (Black Entertainment Television) and radio stations aimed at Spanish-speaking listeners, have more specialized "niche" audiences than do the big networks. This permits campaigns to target their messages (called *narrowcasting*).

In addition, campaigns try to maximize their exposure in the *free media* (sometimes called *earned media*) of television and newspaper coverage. When newscasts and print reporters cover a candidate, the information may seem more credible and "objective" than if it is conveyed through the campaign's own spot ads. Some candidates do a masterful job of attracting free media coverage that transmits the images they want voters to see. John McCain, for example, who began a run for the Republican presidential nomination in 2000 in relative obscurity, gained flattering media coverage by remaining almost constantly available to reporters aboard his "Straight-Talk Express" campaign bus. Unaccustomed to such a refreshing degree of candor, television and print reporters transmitted positive images of McCain's personal history and political stances that helped make him the chief alternative to the frontrunner, George W. Bush.

To get free media coverage, campaigns need to provide material that meets the media's definition of "news."[17] If "news" is that which is dramatic, controversial, and immediate, then a candidate is not likely to earn media coverage with yet another rendition of a standard stump speech. Dave Barry offers this illustration: "Let's consider two headlines. FIRST HEADLINE: 'Federal Reserve Board Ponders Reversal of Postponement of Deferral of Policy Reconsideration.' SECOND HEADLINE: 'Federal Reserve Board Caught in Motel with Underage Sheep.' Be honest, now. Which of these two stories would you read?"[18] Candidates who depend on free media need to stage campaign events that make for good television, using the tamer, political equivalent of the underage sheep: dramatic confrontations, visually exciting settings, or meetings with well-known or telegenic people.

The Internet   The newest means of campaign persuasion is the Internet, first used by candidates and consultants in 1996. By now, every major campaign has a website, as do many local races.[19] By using the Internet, campaigns can reach their supporters directly, without having to deal with the gatekeepers of the broadcast media. Campaigners can even load their spot ads online and distribute them nationally without paying for costly TV time. Many websites ask visitors to register, which allows the campaign to contact them later via e-mail. Because not all voters have ready access to the Internet, online campaigning is more likely to benefit candidates who seek the voters most likely to be "wired": young, highly educated, more affluent people. But its use is growing fast; almost one-third of the voting-age population looked for political information online in 2004, an 83 percent increase over 2000.[20]

New uses of the Internet develop with each election. In the 2004 Democratic nomination race, the big innovator was former Vermont Governor Howard Dean. His campaign used the website Meetup.com to organize meetings in hundreds of local communities during 2003. Dean raised most of his funds—tens of millions of dollars—through his website, expanding the pioneering use of the web for that purpose by John McCain in 2000.

The Ground War: "Under the Radar"

The broadcast media are an efficient way to reach large numbers of citizens. Their greatest strength, however, the breadth of their reach, is also one of their greatest weaknesses. (The other is their high cost.) If you were running for office, you would want to target different messages to different kinds of people so that you could speak to each individual about the issue that concerns him or her the most. A pro-life activist would be especially interested in your views on abortion, whereas someone concerned mainly about terrorism might find a TV ad about your position on abortion to be irrelevant or, worse, evidence that you didn't view homeland security as a priority.

The value of broadcast advertising in campaigns has been reduced by other trends as well. The major networks have lost viewers; more and more TVs are tuned to cable, DVDs, and videogames. In many election districts, television stations are swamped with political ads during a campaign, and viewers now have the technology—from the "mute" button to TiVo—to screen out candidates' commercials.

Increasingly, then, candidates are turning to more carefully targeted appeals than the broadcast media can offer. These are known collectively as the ***ground war:*** nonbroadcast activities such as house-to-house canvassing, computer-targeted mailings, and mass phone calls that permit communication with selected groups of people. These ground-war techniques, some of them time-tested but constantly updated, were used with particular sophistication in Republican campaigns in 2004.

Direct Mail   By merging mailing lists of people who are of special interest to a campaign, consultants can direct personalized letters to millions of people who might be inclined to respond to a particular appeal. A candidate who wants to appeal to pro-gun voters, for example, could send computer-generated letters to people on mailing lists of the National Rifle Association (NRA), donors to other pro-gun candidates, and subscribers to hunting magazines. Because these messages are designed to be read by sympathetic individuals in the privacy of their homes, direct mail appeals can be highly emotional and even inflammatory, appeals that would not work well in the "cool" medium of television.

As the advantages of targeted communication become clearer, huge amounts of direct mail are aimed at especially competitive races. Consider the 2002 South Dakota Senate race, an extremely close and hard-fought campaign. Some voters reported receiving six to ten pieces of campaign mail *a day,* at times containing harsh personal attacks that would not have withstood the broad exposure that TV provides.[21]

E-mail   Like direct mail, e-mail can be targeted precisely. Beginning in the 2000 elections, for example, the Republican National Committee developed a computerized version of a phone tree, in which a core group of Republican supporters each created an e-mail distribution list (called a "virtual precinct") to send campaign information to other supporters, who in turn spread the information more widely. E-mail has the great advantage that it is cheaper than regular mail; fund-raising appeals using direct (regular) mail cost about 40 cents for each dollar raised, compared with about one penny per dollar raised on the Internet.[22]

Canvassing and Phone Banks   The big increase in canvassing was one of the major stories of the 2004 election. In recent years, organized labor has reminded the parties of a lesson from their past: the effectiveness of personal contact to identify and mobilize supporters on Election Day. For decades, labor unions have used their large memberships to phone or visit the homes of people who might support union-backed candidates. Recently, that effort has become much more sophisticated. Using phone banks, it is possible for volunteers or computers to dial thousands of phone numbers (at least those who do not have Caller ID) and convey a campaign appeal.

Like direct mail, these appeals can be carefully targeted to people who have been identified as concerned with a specific issue. In the 2002 South Dakota race, many South Dakotans opposed to gun control received tape-recorded phone messages, called "robocalls," from Charlton Heston, then president of the NRA, urging them to support the Republican candidate for Senate, John Thune. In fact, some phone bank efforts are programmed to play only when an answering machine picks up, giving the impression that the political "star" has called them personally. Canvassers for the Democratic candidate in that race carried nine different scripts, each with a particular issue message, so the canvasser could choose the appropriate script for the demographic characteristics of the occupants of each house. In the state's 2004 Senate race between Thune and incumbent Tom Daschle, the state's Republican Party took this approach further by assigning callers who matched the characteristics of the targeted voter: having veterans speak to veterans and pro-lifers call other pro-lifers.[23]

Increased opportunities for early voting in 2004 gave state and local parties another reason to expand their canvassing. By checking to see who voted early, a practice permitted in most states, party workers could then contact partisans who had requested early ballots but not yet sent them in. Locking up those early votes gained parties more time on Election Day to target undecided voters. Both parties are stepping up their use of these techniques; 45 percent of respondents to a national poll reported that they had been contacted by a political party in 2004, the largest percentage by far in more than 50 years, and about 25 percent said that they had been contacted by the Kerry or the Bush campaign.[24]

Negative Campaigning

All these techniques can be used to deliver negative as well as positive messages. It has become a staple of political consulting that, when a candidate is falling behind in the polls, one of the surest ways to recover is to "go negative" and attack the opponent. Negative campaigning is nothing new; politicians since the earliest days of the Republic have been the focus of vicious attacks. Concern about negative campaigns has increased recently, however, because they can be spread much more quickly and widely now. Rumors about a candidate's personal life that were once circulated mainly within political circles can now be accessed on the Internet in Honolulu and Fairbanks.

Negative ads are also more likely to become the focus of news coverage, which spreads their message to even more people. Information about the savage ads of the "Swift Boat Veterans for Truth" in the 2004 campaign, making the unsubstantiated claim that John Kerry had not deserved the medals he was awarded for heroism in the Vietnam War, reached between half and three-quarters of the respondents in national surveys even though the ads were broadcast in only seven small media markets, such as Green Bay and Wausau, Wisconsin. Outside funders (interest groups and party organizations) are more likely than the candidates themselves to use negative themes in their ads and direct mail.[25]

Does negative campaigning work? Given that 75 percent of Bush ads were classified as negative in 2004 compared with only 40 percent of Kerry's, some might assume that negative advertising is effective.[26] The research findings are mixed, however. Some researchers find that negative ads are particularly memorable and that a negative campaign drives down turnout because it increases voter cynicism. Others suggest that the emotionally engaging aspects of negative ads actually increase turnout.[27] One of the biggest challenges in tracing the impact of negative ads is the difficulty of defining "negative"; what one person considers an attack ad is helpful, "comparative" information to another. However, there are appeals, such as the mailing sent by the Republican National Committee (RNC) to religious voters in Arkansas and West Virginia claiming that Democrats plan to ban the Bible, which most people would probably characterize as negative.

The 2002 and 2004 Campaigns

These campaign techniques were used widely in 2002 and 2004, but they were increasingly limited to the most competitive races. In past elections, parties had spread their efforts widely, providing money and other resources even to secure incumbents. Because the two parties were so evenly matched in the U.S. House and Senate in 2002 and 2004, and because the overwhelming majority of House incumbents were expected to coast to easy wins, both parties and many interest groups ignored most congressional races and focused their resources on two or three dozen competitive seats as well as the presidential race. In the 2004 presidential contest, the air wars were limited to between 12 and 20 states at any given time. Voters in eight of the ten biggest media markets—New York, Los Angeles, Chicago, Washington, San Francisco, Boston, Dallas, and Houston—saw no sustained advertising for Bush or Kerry because their states were regarded as locked up for one candidate.[28]

In contrast, the residents of the targeted states and districts were exposed to a virtual hurricane of campaign advertising. In addition to a huge volume of broadcast ads, an unprecedented amount of money and effort went into the ground war. In 1998 and

2000, Democrats had mounted major get-out-the-vote drives, especially among blacks, that had helped reelect several U.S. House members and governors. So the national Republican Party started early in the 2002 election cycle to try to neutralize the anticipated canvassing drives by organized labor and the Democrats.

After a series of experiments to find out how best to reach voters, the GOP developed programs to flood precincts in competitive states with Republican volunteers and paid staffers. These campaigners would use door-to-door canvassing and phone calls to reach known Republican supporters and urge them to go to the polls. One, the "72-Hour Project," focused its efforts on the closing 72 hours of the campaign. At $200 million, it was an expensive effort, but observers felt that it increased Republican turnout by about 3 percent in 2002 compared with the last midterm election in 1998, and Republicans won most of the close contests, maintained control of the House, and narrowly regained control of the Senate.[29]

As so often happens in campaigns, party officials and consultants drew the lesson from Republican successes in 2002 that they needed to follow the Republican model in 2004. A full year before the 2004 election, the Bush campaign had put together plans for a massive ground war campaign and was already training thousands of volunteers to recruit canvassers for the last few days before the election. Because the president had no opponent for the Republican nomination, the full force of his enormous campaign budget, which finally totaled $356 million, could be focused on the general election.

The result was a massive ground game on both sides in 2004, but especially by the Republicans. Party strategists had determined that few Republican sympathizers live in heavily Republican precincts, so the party would have to identify these sympathizers individually instead, using commercial databases. The party put together data on people's viewing habits, magazine subscriptions, and purchasing preferences. They learned that people who watch Fox News or the Golf Channel, drive BMWs and Porsches, go to exercise clubs after work, drink Coors beer, watch college football, and have Caller ID are inclined to support Republicans. They also confirmed that a lot of potential Bush voters don't trust the mainstream media and are more likely to view talk shows, religious programming, and country stations.

Using this research, the Bush-Cheney campaign and the RNC worked to cherry-pick likely Republican voters. In particular, they decided to target Republican sympathizers who had not voted regularly in the past: 7 million infrequent Republican voters and 10 million conservative-leaning independents. By merging the demographic information with public opinion data, they identified which issues were the most likely to anger each of a series of types of voters. One voter type could be approached with a mailing or a phone call about gay marriage; another might receive an appeal about the threat of terrorism. "They were much more sophisticated in their message delivery," said Democratic National Committee (DNC) chair Terry McAuliffe.[30]

In the crucial swing state of Ohio, for instance, the Republican grassroots campaign was led by 150 field staff members who recruited 85,000 volunteers. In the 72 hours before Election Day, they made an estimated 1.8 million phone calls and three-quarters of a million personal visits. The ground war in Ohio was so well coordinated that thousands of residents received a recorded phone call from President Bush encouraging them to vote absentee on the same day that they received a mailing containing an absentee ballot application.[31]

Another of the Bush campaign's innovations in 2004 was to enlist conservative Christian churches to spread the Bush message. Churches' political involvement is limited by law; they cannot use church resources to support a political candidate without risking their tax-exempt status. But the Bush campaign urged churches to send the campaign their directories, hold voter registration drives, and distribute voter guides in church, which were regarded as legally permissible activities. In all these ways, the Republicans mobilized to surpass the traditional Democratic advantage in personal canvassing.

The Kerry campaign and the national Democrats put a lot of emphasis on the ground war as well. Canvassing, phoning, and other forms of voter contact were organized by the Democrats on a massive scale. The DNC's voter contact list, known as "Demzilla," contained 150 million names, though it was not as sophisticated as the RNC's list. Much of Kerry's canvassing and almost 40 percent of his TV advertising was done by independent groups, however, who raised money in order to help the Democratic ticket compete under the constraints of the 2002 campaign finance reforms (see Chapter 12). By law, these independent groups were not allowed to consult with the Kerry campaign in planning or conducting their activities, nor could they ask people directly to vote for Kerry, so their messages and efforts were not always closely integrated with those of the campaign.

In the end, the Bush volunteers had an easier sell. A large majority of Bush voters were enthusiastic about their candidate, whereas a large minority of Kerry voters were motivated primarily by their dislike of Bush. The Kerry campaign and the Democrats increased their presidential vote by about 8 million votes compared with 2000, while Bush increased his by about 11 million. As one analyst wrote, "Kerry did well. Bush did better."[32] Though the presidential race was close, Bush eked out a narrow victory, and his party kept control of the House and slightly increased its Senate majority.

DO CAMPAIGNS MAKE A DIFFERENCE?

Because so much attention is drawn to the drama of a campaign and so much money and effort is invested in it, many people naturally assume that campaign events are responsible for the election's outcome. Successful campaign managers usually do nothing to discourage the impression that it was their brilliant strategy that led to their candidate's election. Yet careful statistical analysis shows that election results can normally be predicted fairly well from conditions that existed before the campaign began, such as the incumbent's previous poll ratings, economic conditions, and the distribution of party loyalties in the district. In fact, Bush's percentage of the vote in 2004 was almost the same as his net approval rating in June 2004, before much of the Republicans' high-tech voter targeting had been put to practical use. That doesn't leave much room for the events of a campaign to determine the outcome. Instead, it seems to suggest that, at most, campaigns simply remind voters of these longer lasting conditions and, in this way, help them move toward a largely preordained outcome.[33]

Does this mean that the relative strengths of the Democratic and Republican strategies made no difference? Would voters' fears of terrorism have narrowly re-elected the president whether the Democratic nominee was John Kerry or Howard Dean? Observers' answers often vary depending on the observer's own agenda (see box on page 210). Researchers have used a variety of methods to measure campaign impact, and, not surprisingly, they have come up with a variety of conclusions.

WHY DID GEORGE W. BUSH WIN?

Many Republicans argued: Bush got a mandate for his assertive response to terrorism and his strong stand for moral values. Voters, then, want strong and consistent leadership.

   Conservative Republicans argued: Voters rejected Democrat John Kerry as a liberal and felt that Kerry and his supporters disdained American values. Voters, then, want *conservative* leadership.

   To moderate Democrats: Incumbent presidents usually win, especially when their party has held the White House for only one term. Kerry was not a strong candidate because he was aloof, complicated, and had a rather unusual wife. Voters didn't reject Democrats; Democrats just didn't organize well enough.

   To liberal Democrats: The Bush campaign used fear tactics to drum up bigotry against gays and to claim that Democrats weren't for family values, and Democrats didn't counter those tactics effectively. Voters were manipulated; Democrats need to stand up for liberal values.

Sources: Charles Krauthammer, "Using All of a Mandate . . . ," *Washington Post,* November 5, 2004, p. A25; George F. Will, "America's Shifting Reality," *Washington Post,* November 4, 2004, p. A25; and David S. Broder, "An Old-Fashioned Win," *Washington Post,* November 4, 2004, p. A25.

The Argument That Campaigns Matter

A long line of evidence suggests that one form of campaigning, party canvassing, has a small but meaningful effect on both turnout and voters' choices,[34] as the parties believed in 2002 and 2004. Canvassing probably has more influence in local elections than in presidential races because there are fewer alternative sources of information in local contests. Researchers find that personal contacts activate voters more than mailings do, and door-to-door canvassing has more influence than telephone calls.[35] With regard to voters' other decision—their choice of candidates—we find that where a party is active, its vote share can increase by at least a few percentage points, which could be the critical margin in a close race.[36]

   Television news and advertising—and the money that pays for it—may have an even greater influence on voters' decisions. Since the early 1960s, television has been citizens' most important and most trusted source of political news.[37] The source of this news has changed over time. A poll in 2000, for instance, found that almost one-half of 18- to 29-year-olds said that they got information about the presidential campaign from late-night talk shows, and more than one-fourth from comedy shows such as *Saturday Night Live.*[38] Despite (or perhaps because of) these changes, TV has supplanted the parties in providing campaign information. Even with the big increase in voter contacts by the party organizations, many more people see the campaign on TV.

   This widespread exposure to TV news and ads can make a difference, especially when they give viewers new information about a candidate.[39] Campaign debates, to which most voters are exposed only through television, have been found to affect election results under some circumstances.[40] All these sources of campaign information, taken together, seem to improve citizens' knowledge and increase voter turnout.[41] Different kinds of campaign events—debates, conventions, TV ads—affect some voters differently than others, depending on the voter's party identification, level of interest in politics, and feelings about the current president. Independents, undecided and uninformed voters, and people who are leaning toward a candidate of the opposite party are most likely to be affected by these campaign events.[42]

The Argument That They Don't

There are several reasons why campaigning may have only a limited effect, however. First, television news, ads, and ground war activities offer viewers a wide range of conflicting messages about candidates—positive, negative, and neutral information and opinions, all mixed together. The inconsistency of these messages makes it harder for a campaign to change viewers' minds about candidates.[43] We know that voters pay selective attention to media and other campaign communications, just as they do to most other experiences. They tend to surround themselves with friends, information, and even personal experiences that support their beliefs and loyalties.[44]

So even though most voters are exposed to campaigns on TV, they may pick and choose among the differing messages and ignore those that conflict with their existing beliefs and opinions. Most campaign communications, then, probably have the effect of activating and reinforcing the voter's existing political inclinations, as they always have. That can explain why so much campaign effort is directed at getting people out to vote— to act on whatever opinions they already hold—rather than at trying to change their voting decision.[45]

News coverage of campaigns can have a more subtle influence, however. By the kinds of issues and events that they emphasize, the media affect what people come to consider important in a campaign; this process is known as *agenda-setting.* In directing viewers' attention in this way, media coverage "primes" viewers to look for some qualities in candidates rather than others.[46] News coverage of the 2000 presidential race, for example, focused intently on Al Gore's boasts and exaggerations rather than on those of George W. Bush and on Bush's slips of the tongue rather than those of Gore.[47] Because of time constraints, coverage must inevitably simplify its presentation of a campaign. So rather than reflect a nuanced portrayal of each candidate, coverage usually pays attention to a limited number of themes or "frames," which then come to drive later coverage.[48] This kind of media influence is indirect and thus hard to measure, but its effects on election results could be profound.

Some Tentative Answers

There is much left to learn about the effects of campaigns on voters. It seems clear that canvassing and media coverage have some impact on voter turnout and voters' decisions. As a rule, campaign communications are most effective in bringing weak partisans back into the fold when they have had doubts about their party's candidate.[49] In the information-rich environment of current campaigns and among the large numbers of independents, the potential for campaigns to shape voters' perceptions may be higher than it has ever been. There are times when dramatic events during a campaign may actually decide the outcome and when even well-established candidate images can be revised (see box on page 214). The impact of campaigns, however, will continue to be limited by the same forces that have always constrained it: voters' tendency to pay attention to the messages with which they already agree and their ability to tune out most political messages altogether.

CANDIDATE-CENTERED OR PARTY-CENTERED CAMPAIGNS?

The new campaign techniques that we have explored in this chapter have affected the balance of power in campaigns between parties and candidates. Until about the middle of the 1900s, party organizations provided much of the money and volunteers for campaigns, just as they do now in most other democracies. Since then, American campaigning has become more *candidate centered*, focusing on the actions and strategies of the candidates rather than on the parties.

It is the candidates and their advisers, not the parties, who make the strategic decisions in most campaigns. Candidates have their own headquarters and staffers rather than using the party's facilities. Candidates communicate directly with voters rather than having to rely on the party organization as an intermediary; voters often see candidates as being more moderate on issues than they see the candidate's party.[50] Interest groups and other political organizations can work directly with candidates to support their campaigns. Campaign finance laws (see Chapter 12) have put limits on party spending comparable with the limits on nonparty groups. Party organizations, rather than running campaigns, work instead to enhance the appeal of individual candidates, and they compete with consultants, interest groups, and others for the chance to do so.

Many of the nation's electoral rules make it easier for campaigns to be candidate centered. The American electoral process has few institutions, such as parliamentary-cabinet government or proportional representation, which would encourage voters to see elections as contests between parties for control of government. Instead, rules ranging from campaign finance regulations to the separate scheduling of national and state elections encourage candidates to run as individuals, not as members of a party ticket, and even make it hard for parties to coordinate the campaigns of several candidates. Progressive reforms strengthened this tendency: The direct primary, for example, allows candidates to run without the party organization's approval.[51]

Campaign technologies can also help candidates to resist party influence. Broadcast media, in their quest to get and keep an audience, tend to focus on individual personalities rather than institutions such as parties. Because tools such as direct mail and TV advertising are available to any candidate who can pay for them, these technologies let candidates communicate with voters without the party's help. If the American parties had been as strong organizationally as those in many other nations when these technologies developed, then they might have been able to monopolize the use of TV and other media for campaign purposes. In fact, as we have seen, the American parties have always struggled to maintain their power in a political culture hostile to their functioning.

Party Influence in Competitive Campaigns

The parties, however, are fighting back. The large sums of money that have flowed into the national parties in the past two decades have helped them to assist individual campaigns with money and other services.[52] As Chapter 4 noted, soft money enabled the party organizations to pour millions of dollars into campaign ads in a few battleground states in 2002, such as the Senate races in Iowa, Missouri, and South Dakota. And as we have seen above, massive party fund-raising and voter contact drives increased the party presence in the 2004 elections.

As a result, the national parties have become more visible, especially in highly competitive races. Although party-funded ads generally follow the lead of the candidate's own advertising, sometimes they do not. Consider the comment of then–National Republican Congressional Committee Chair Tom Davis about party-run ads in the House campaign of Republican Melissa Hart in Pennsylvania: Hart "doesn't have any say about what we do in the race. . . . We have to protect our candidate whether she likes it or not."[53] Clearly, in these few highly competitive races, the parties have a shot at taking control of the campaign away from the candidate. But in most races, the level of competition is low, and the party role is not nearly as noticeable.

The Continuing Struggle Between Candidates and Party Organizations

An expanded party role in campaigns can make economic sense. Party organizations can distribute appeals for a number of candidates at the same time and mount voter registration drives to help the entire ticket. Parties can buy media advertising and consultants' services for use by several candidates at cost-effective prices. Party organizations can coordinate Election Day activities for all the party's candidates, providing poll-watchers to guard against voting irregularities, sending cars to get people to the polls, and checking voter lists to mobilize nonvoters late in the day.

This efficiency, however, is inevitably bought at the cost of limiting each candidate's independence. In the competitive races that were the targets of party spending in 2002 and 2004, party-funded ads and those funded by interest groups sometimes stressed messages different from those that the campaign itself wanted to emphasize, and, frequently, more negative messages than the campaign's own advertising.[54] Because voters rarely pay attention to the source of any particular message, candidates got blamed for negativity and claims that they had not made.

Party organizations and candidates do not always have the same goals. The party wants to maximize the number of races it wins, so it strives to put its scarce resources into the most competitive campaigns and to spend as little as possible on the races it considers hopeless. Each candidate, in contrast, is committed above all to his or her own victory and to gaining the resources needed to achieve it, no matter how unlikely that victory may be. The party, in its drive to win every competitive race, is likely to do whatever it takes, whether through negative or positive campaigning. The candidate, in contrast, has to face the voters; to do so by means of a constant barrage of attack ads may be personally uncomfortable.

The result is a continuing struggle between party organizations and candidates—the party in government—for control of campaigns. If they are going to have a role in

THE REINVENTION OF HILLARY CLINTON

Put yourself in Hillary Clinton's place. In 1999, you are the butt of jokes on TV talk shows. Your husband has had an affair with a young White House intern, and virtually everybody in the country can recite the gory details.

Six years later, you are a United States Senator from New York and, in many opinion polls, the front-runner for the 2008 Democratic presidential nomination.

How did Hillary Clinton change her political image? During Bill Clinton's presidency, many saw her as a dyed-in-the-wool liberal, a strident feminist, and the author of a national health care proposal that gave much of the business community fits. A lot of conservatives had become Hillary Haters, who disliked her intensely no matter what she did. She was pilloried in the tabloids as cold and calculating.

In 2000 she won a close, big-spending contest for New York's open Senate seat. When she returned to Washington, Senator Clinton's actions surprised many of these observers. She asked for a seat on the Armed Services Committee. She took a stand in favor of the death penalty. She made frequent visits to conservative areas of her new state and worked closely with Republican members of the New York delegation to bring more federal money to those localities. She collaborated with a number of conservative Republicans in the Senate, including some who had fought hard to impeach and convict her husband, and became well liked among her Republican colleagues.

After the 2004 election, Senator Clinton continued taking steps to show that she was a more centrist Democrat than media reports had portrayed. As she had done for many years, she referred in her speeches to prayer and faith and encouraged those on both sides of such divisive issues as abortion to find common ground. These moves, combined with her assiduous cultivation of New York voters, seem to have made a difference. Her job approval rating among New Yorkers jumped to 69 percent in mid-2005, and, even more significantly, her high negative ratings were dropping, even among Republicans.

Her high level of name recognition—her name had long been used effectively to raise money for *both* enthusiastic Democrats and outraged Republicans—made her a leader in the polls for the Democratic presidential nomination in 2008. South Carolina Republican Senator Lindsey Graham said, "Some people would work morning, noon, and night to beat her, and some people would sell their firstborn for her to win. There are Republicans who are saying, 'Bring her on.' But my counsel to them is, *Watch what you wish for*."

It isn't easy for someone with such a lengthy political history and such a polarizing image to reinvent herself successfully. But as a writer for *New York Magazine* put it, "No two people are more adept at writing their own story than the Clintons."

Sources: Raymond Hernandez, "Clinton's Popularity Up in State, Even Among Republicans," *New York Times,* February 22, 2005, p. 1; and Jennifer Senior, "The Once and Future President Clinton," *New York Magazine,* February 21, 2005, on the Internet at http://newyorkmetro.com/nymetro/news/politics/national/features/11082 (accessed September 9, 2005).

campaigns now, party organizations have to earn it. In most elections, the candidates are winning the fight. Even if the parties have more to offer candidates than they did just a few years ago, party organizations still contribute only a fairly small percentage of candidates' overall campaign spending in all but the most competitive races. In contrast, European parties often provide more than half the funding used by most candidates.

This central role of the candidates and their staff members and consultants in most American campaigns has an important effect on governing. When they control their own campaigns, winning candidates can develop ties with their constituents that are free of party loyalty and party organizational control. They are free to form alliances with political action committees, independent groups, and other nonparty organizations, which enhance the ability of these groups to influence public policy. In short, candidate-centered campaigning underscores the power of the party in government relative to that of the party organization. It also poses an important question: If strong party organizations can help to hold elected officials accountable for their actions, then how much accountability do voters get from a candidate-centered politics? The increasing party presence in competitive races may help voters gain more responsible government.

Chapter 12

Financing the
Campaigns

The average member of the U.S. Senate running for reelection in 2004 spent $6.6 million on his or her campaign.[1] If you were that senator, and even if you started raising money the very day after your last election, you would still need to collect more than $21,000 *every week of your six-year term,* on average, to raise that sum. If you went a week without asking for money, then you'd need to raise $42,000 the following week. The need to raise campaign money is inescapable in American politics, and it's nothing new. When George Washington ran for the Virginia House of Burgesses in 1757:

> He provided his friends with the "customary means of winning votes": namely 28 gallons of rum, 50 gallons of rum punch, 34 gallons of wine, 46 gallons of beer, and 2 gallons of cider royal. Even in those days this was considered a large campaign expenditure, because there were only 391 voters in his district for an average outlay of more than a quart and a half per person.[2]

Washington was, by all accounts, a very well-qualified candidate, yet he still felt that he needed to spend freely in order to win. Today, campaign finance plays a much larger role in American elections. As candidates have come to depend on paid professionals, television, and computers, money has become key to mobilizing the resources needed for a viable campaign. So candidates, especially for statewide and national office, are not likely to be taken seriously unless they start with a big campaign budget or a proven talent for fund-raising.

Until the campaign finance reforms of the 1970s, much of the money used in campaigns was collected and spent in secret. Candidates were not required to disclose how they raised funds, and contributors were often reluctant to make their names public. The few laws governing campaign contributions were full of loopholes.

As a result of the 1970s reforms, we now have a flood of data about campaign spending and contributions. The regulation is mind-boggling in its complexity. It is constantly under assault by candidates and contributors who are adept at finding loopholes through which they can pursue their aims. Despite all this change, the basic questions remain the same. How much money is spent to elect candidates to office, and who spends it? Who contributes the money? What is the party's role in funding campaigns? What has government done to control the power of money in politics, and how well has it worked?

HOW MUCH MONEY IS SPENT ON CAMPAIGNS?

Election fund-raising and spending has increased enormously during the past 40 years, to a total of about $5 *billion* for candidates at all levels of office in the United States in 2004. Inflation has reduced the purchasing power of the dollar during this period, so the real, inflation-adjusted increase is not nearly as dramatic. But the growth in real spending since 1996, which has coincided with the increasing polarization of the major parties, is notable by any standard.

Presidential Campaigns

The reelection race of President George W. Bush dominated the 2004 elections to an even greater extent than presidential races usually dominate American politics. The result was the most expensive political campaign in American history (see Figure 12.1). The Kerry-Edwards and Bush-Cheney campaigns themselves spent a total of $674.5 million in the primaries and the general election campaign, more than twice what the candidates had spent in 2000. In all, the campaigns and the parties and groups supporting them raised and spent a total of about $2 billion (see Table 12.1), with the Bush campaign holding a slight edge on the Kerry campaign. That, too, was remarkable; although the Republican presidential campaign set records in fund-raising and spending, the Democrats came closer to matching the Republican totals than had been the case since the 1970s. Because he chose to decline public matching funds in his race for the Democratic nomination, John F. Kerry was able to raise about five times as much money as any previous Democratic presidential candidate during the nominating season.

This unprecedented pursuit of campaign money began during the invisible primary of 2003. It was fueled by a level of passion on both sides that went well beyond the norm for American campaigns and by campaign organizations more capable of reaching willing givers than ever before. Candidates for their party's presidential nomination (as you'll see later in the chapter) can receive grants from the federal government to match the small ($250 or less) contributions they receive. If they accept these matching funds, then they must agree to spending limits in each state's primary or caucus and in the nominating season as a whole. George W. Bush had refused the matching funds in 2000, thus freeing himself from the spending limits, and he announced in 2003 that he would do so again. By December 31 of that year, he had raised $132.7 million, though he was unopposed for renomination.

The ten Democrats contending for their party's nomination had collected a total of $139.6 million in 2003. John F. Kerry had brought in only $25.3 million of that amount and had spent almost all of it. His only chance, he felt, was to follow the lead of the Democratic front-runner, Howard Dean, and Bush in declining the matching funds and raising every dollar he could. Once Kerry shot to the top of the Democratic pack in the early primaries and caucuses, his campaign's bottom line began to improve markedly. His advisers set a goal of raising $80 million before the Democratic convention. Even they, however, were amazed by the depth of the anti-Bush feeling among

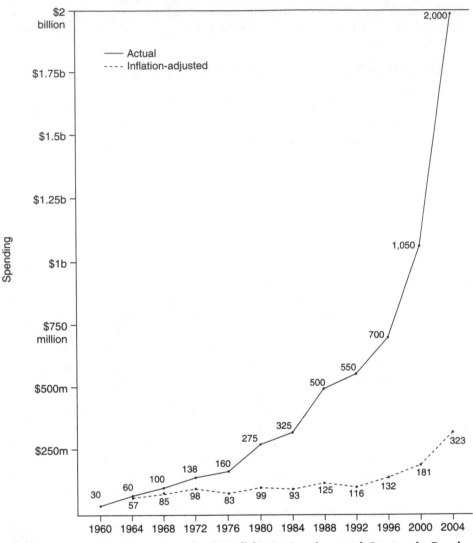

FIGURE 12.1   Total Spending by Candidates, Parties, and Groups in Presidential Elections, 1960–2004

Note: Estimates are for two-year cycles ending in the presidential election years. Inflation-adjusted figures are computed by deflating the actual expenditures using the Consumer Price Index (with 1960 as the base year). *Sources:* John C. Green, ed., *Financing the 1996 Election* (Armonk, NY: M. E. Sharpe, 1999), p. 19; For 2000: Candice J. Nelson, "Spending in the 2000 Elections," in David B. Magleby, ed., *Financing the 2000 Election* (Washington, DC: Brookings, 2002), Table 2-1 (for candidates' spending); David B. Magleby, "Conclusions and Implications for Future Elections," in David B. Magleby, ed., *The Other Campaign* (Lanham, MD: Rowman & Littlefield, 2003), p. 229 (for interest groups); and Anthony Corrado, Sarah Barclay, and Heitor Gouvea, "The Parties Take the Lead," in John C. Green and Rick Farmer, *The State of the Parties,* 4th ed. (Lanham, MD: Rowman & Littlefield, 2003), p. 107 (for parties). For 2004: Michael J. Malbin, ed., *The Election after Reform* (Lanham, MD: Rowman & Littlefield, 2006). Consumer Price Index deflator is based on Table 697 in the U.S. Census Bureau, *Statistical Abstract of the United States: 2004–2005* (Washington, DC: U.S. Government Printing Office, 2005), p. 461.

Democratic loyalists. Once Kerry became the presumptive Democratic nominee in March 2004, he raised $38 million that month alone. Kerry outraised Bush for several months in the spring and summer, when the Bush campaign was steering contributions to the Republican Party instead of to the campaign. In all, the Kerry campaign pulled in a total of $207 million between Super Tuesday on March 2 and the Democratic convention in late July.

Once each party has held its national convention, the candidate it nominates can choose to receive public funding for the general election campaign, and every major party candidate since 1976 has done so. To get the public money, candidates must agree to raise no other funds (except the money needed to pay lawyers and accountants to deal with federal campaign finance laws, called "compliance costs"). Thus, in 2004, the Bush and Kerry general election campaigns were able to spend $74.6 million each, plus the compliance costs (see part III in Table 12.1). In all, the Bush campaign raised $356.4 million during 2003–2004, and Kerry's campaign amassed $318.1 million.

The campaigns' own spending in presidential races is overshadowed by that of other groups. In most other democracies, party organizations rather than candidates do most of the campaign spending, and in American elections, the parties have become increasingly important as fund-raisers. A variety of other groups and individuals also pay for advertising and voter mobilization. The fact that these groups' messages play a major role in American campaigns has important implications. As we saw in Chapter 11, their advertising may be more negative than the candidate would prefer, may emphasize issues that the candidate would like to avoid, or simply divert voters' attention from the campaign's own agenda. Much of these groups' spending, by law, cannot even be coordinated with the candidates' campaigns (as will be discussed later in the chapter).

Party organizations can put money into presidential races in four different ways, as Table 12.1 shows. They can use *coordinated spending:* money spent by party organizations *in coordination with* a candidate's campaign to purchase services such as media advertising or polling for the campaign. The parties, as well as individuals and other political groups, can also spend as much as they choose independently, to expressly support or oppose a candidate, as long as they do so *without consulting with their candidate*. This is known as *independent spending,* and there was more of it in 2004 than ever before. Because the Democratic convention took place five weeks earlier than the Republican convention, and each candidate was limited to spending the $74.6 million in public funds as soon as the party's convention is over, Kerry had to make his public funds last much longer than Bush did. So the Democratic National Committee (DNC) spent $120.3 million independently to supplement the Kerry campaign's advertising. Parties are also allowed to spend money in combination with the candidate's campaign on generic ads that mention both the presidential candidate and other party candidates and to mobilize voters through grassroots efforts.

"Internal communication costs" in Table 12.1 are the funds spent by groups to urge their members to vote for a particular candidate; labor unions and corporations account for most of this money. Unions, corporations, and membership associations also spent millions on "nonpartisan" voter mobilization—mainly in programs to register voters and get them to the polls on Election Day. (Spending by PACs and 527 groups will be discussed later.)

TABLE 12.1   What It Cost to Nominate and Elect a President: 2004

	Amount (in Millions)	
I. Prenomination Receipts and Spending	Raised	Spent
Republicans	$269.6	$268.9
Bush	$269.6	$268.9
Democrats	$401.8	$389.7
Kerry	$234.6	$224.8
Dean	51.1	50.2
All others	116.1	114.8
II. Conventions		
Public funding for party conventions		$29.8
Private funding		142.5
III. General Election		
Candidate Funds		
Public funding for major party candidates		$149.2
Third-party candidates (including Nader, Badnarik)		6.8
Compliance costs		21.1
Party Funds (nomination and general)		
Parties' coordinated expenditures		$32.1
Parties' independent expenditures		138.5
Parties' contributions to generic ("hybrid") ads financed jointly with candidates		69.6
Parties' voter mobilization (field operations) efforts		205.0
Group Funds (nomination and general)		
PAC independent spending		$42.8
Spending by 527 groups	405.1*	398.5*
Internal communication costs		24.3

* Although most of this spending went into the presidential race, an unspecified portion was spent on House and Senate campaigns. The figures represent groups that raised $200,000 or more by the end of November 2004.

Source: Based on Federal Election Commission data as of August 15, 2005. PAC data on April 13, 2005. Data on group funds from Steve Weissman and Ruth Hassan, "BCRA and the 527 Groups," in Michael J. Malbin, ed., The Election after Reform (Lanham, MD: Rowman & Littlefield, 2006), Chapter 5, p. 2 and Table 5.4. Data on parties in part from Anthony Corrado, "Party Finance in the Wake of BCRA," in Malbin, ed., The Election after Reform, Chapter 2, pp. 11–14 and Table 2.2. Data on 527 groups from the Campaign Finance Institute. I am grateful to Anthony Corrado and Michael Malbin for their help.

Congressional Campaigns

In contrast to presidential races, it is the candidates who are the biggest spenders in most congressional campaigns. Like the presidential races, however, spending in the 2004 congressional races was unprecedented, even after adjusting for inflation (see Figures 12.2 and 12.3). Although the number of competitive races was very small, especially in the House of Representatives, candidate spending reached $1.2 billion in the nomination and general election campaigns.

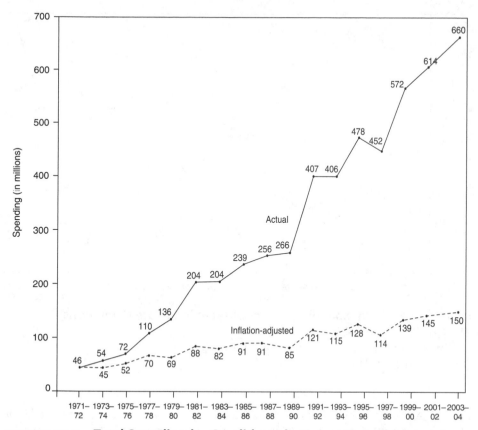

FIGURE 12.2   Total Spending by Candidates in House Campaigns, 1971–1972 to 2003–2004

Note: Inflation-adjusted figures are computed by deflating the actual expenditures by changes in the price level as measured by the Consumer Price Index (yearly averages) using 1972 as the base year.

Source: FEC data from John C. Green, ed., *Financing the 1996 Election* (Armonk, NY: M. E. Sharpe, 1999), Table 2.7, p. 23 for actual spending through 1995–1996; FEC press release dated June 18, 2003, for 1997–2002, and "Congressional Candidates Spend $1.6 Billion During 2003–2004," FEC press release dated June 9, 2005, on the Internet at http://www.fec.gov/press/press2005/20050609candidate/ 20050609candidate.html (accessed August 17, 2005) for 2003–2004. CPI deflator is the same as that listed for Table 12.1.

The Senate was considered more "in play" than the House in 2004, in that control of the Senate had switched parties three times since 2000 and there were several contested Republican primaries in 2004. Residents of South Dakota were subjected to the most expensive Senate race in 2004 (and probably in American history) in per capita spending. The two candidates, Senate Minority Leader Tom Daschle and former Republican Representative John Thune, combined to spend $34 million, or $87 per voter. When we look at median spending, to keep the results from being skewed by these high-dollar races, we find that the median winning Senate candidate spent more than $6 million in 2004; that surpassed the 2002 figure by $1.5 million, and was $2.5 million greater than

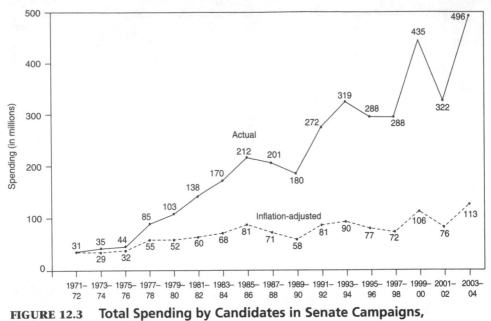

FIGURE 12.3   Total Spending by Candidates in Senate Campaigns, 1971–1972 to 2003–2004

Note: Inflation-adjusted figures are computed as in Figure 12.1.

Source: Same as Figure 12.2.

in 2000. And even though most observers did not expect to see a change in party control of the House in 2004, or even much change in personnel, spending in House races broke all records.

Incumbents greatly outraise and outspend their challengers in every election year, and their financial advantage grew in 2004. The average House incumbent raised about $1.1 million for his or her campaign and spent $1 million, compared with about $273,000 and $269,000 for the average major-party challenger.[3] The few winning challengers each spent more than $1.5 million to overcome the incumbent's advantages.[4] Again looking at the medians (the level at which half the campaigns spent more and half spent less), we find that the median incumbent spent $810,000 and the median challenger only $54,000—hardly enough even to be noticed in the noise of a presidential year. In Senate races, incumbents raised and spent an average of $6.6 million compared with about $2.5 million for challengers. Out of each dollar raised and spent in a House race between an incumbent and a challenger, then, the average challenger accounted for about 20 cents, and in a Senate race, the average challenger spent a little over a quarter. Candidates for open seats—those where no incumbent is running—spent even more than incumbents did.

The fund-raising advantage has gone to Republicans during much of the past decade. Until 1994, most congressional incumbents in most election years were Democrats, so Democratic candidates were normally able to outspend Republicans. However, in 1994, the Republican Party won majorities in both the House and Senate for the first time in 40 years. Their status as the majority party gave the Republicans an increasing financial advantage going into the next two congressional elections. In 2000 and 2002, when the two parties' prospects looked more equal, the Republican edge decreased or disappeared. But it returned in the 2004 House races; Republican candidates, on average, raised $144,000 more than Democrats did. In contrast, Democratic Senate candidates outraised and outspent their Republican rivals in 2004, mainly because of Democratic fund-raising dominance in a few races, including those in California, Illinois, and New York.

State and Local Campaigns

Much less is known about spending practices in the thousands of campaigns for state and local office, mainly because there is no central reporting agency comparable to the national Federal Election Commission (FEC). The range in these races is enormous. Many local candidates win after spending a few hundred dollars. On the other end of the scale are some top-dollar mayoral races. In 2001, Michael Bloomberg spent $69 million of his own money to become mayor of New York, about $68.7 million more than the job's annual salary.[5] In 2005 Bloomberg beat his own record by giving $78 million to his reelection campaign, or more than $100 for each vote he received.

Campaigns for governor in large states often cost as much as, or more than, races for the U.S. Senate; California typically sets the records. The major candidates in the bizarre 2003 election to recall California Governor Gray Davis managed to spend a total of $83 million in only 77 days. Winning a state legislative race in a large state is an increasingly expensive proposition as well. In 2003, for example, some legislative campaigns in New Jersey cost more than $1 million each, largely because their "local" media originate in the expensive markets of New York and Philadelphia.[6] Even state supreme court elections have become big-spending contests. The average candidate for a state supreme court seat in 2000 raised almost half a million dollars, much of it from trial lawyers who have a big stake in the judges' rulings.[7]

These figures must be kept in perspective. Even with these big increases, the total cost of all American campaigns still doesn't match the amounts some large corporations spend each year to advertise soap and cigarettes (see box on page 224). Although few would dispute the benefits of soap, our futures are affected more profoundly by the choices made in state and federal elections. So, to the extent that campaigns give us the chance to learn about the strengths and weaknesses of the people who would govern us, the amounts spent on campaign advertising could be considered a real bargain.[8] The motivations of contributors and the disparities among candidates, however, remain a source of concern.

WHAT IS THE IMPACT OF CAMPAIGN SPENDING?

Money does not buy victory—but it certainly doesn't hurt either. In the general election for president, both sides have enough money to reach voters with their messages, so the candidate with the largest war chest does not gain an overwhelming advantage. Money matters more in the nomination race for president, especially in buying the early visibility that is so vital to an underdog. The availability of federal matching funds was critical in giving several Democratic candidates a shot at competing with John Kerry and Howard Dean for the nomination in 2004.

CAMPAIGN SPENDING: TOO MUCH OR TOO LITTLE?

What will $5 billion buy in the United States?

- About 40 percent of the cigarette advertising and promotion run in 2002
- Less than a year's advertising (in 2004) for Procter & Gamble plus General Motors
- 7 percent of the amount spent in the United States in 2003 on all forms of gambling
- One Nimitz-class aircraft carrier (not counting operating costs)
- All the political campaigns run at all levels of government by and for all candidates in 2004

Sources: http://www.lungusa.org/site/pp.asp?c=dvLUK9O0E&b=44462 (on cigarette advertising); http://www.centerformediaresearch.com/cfmr_brief.cfm?fnl=050318 (on GM and Procter & Gamble); http://grossannualwager.com (on gambling); and http://en.wikipedia.org/wiki/Aircraft_carrier (on aircraft carriers; all accessed August 18, 2005).

There are times when an unusual candidate can win office in spite of, or sometimes even because of, relatively little spending. Recall the case of Jesse Ventura, a former professional wrestler, who ran as the Reform Party candidate for governor of Minnesota in 1998. Ventura won the three-way race after spending only $400,000 on his campaign, while his Democratic and Republican rivals spent more than $4 million between them. Among other factors, Ventura's forceful personality and the novelty of his campaign brought free media attention that helped to make up for a small campaign budget.

In congressional elections, however, where we have the most evidence of the impact of campaign spending, most researchers find that money does make a real difference. The more challengers can spend when they run against incumbents, the better their chances are of victory. The same is not always true for incumbents. Gary Jacobson found that the more incumbents spend, the worse they do in the race.[9] It is not that incumbent spending turns voters off, but rather that incumbents tend to spend a lot when they face serious competition. A big budget for an incumbent, then, signals that he or she has (or worries about) an unusually strong challenger.

Other researchers disagree and report that when incumbents spend more, they do get a return in terms of votes. The dispute turns on thorny questions about the proper way to estimate the impact of spending, but there is general agreement on three points. First, House incumbents rarely face a serious challenge for reelection. Second, challengers need a lot of money to have a chance of beating an incumbent. Third, when they do have a strong opponent, incumbents may not be able to survive the challenge by pouring more money into their reelection effort.[10] For political scientists, measuring the effects of particular types of campaign spending is a challenging task. For candidates, the answer is simpler: More is better.

WHERE DOES THE MONEY COME FROM?

Candidates raise their campaign funds from five main sources: individuals, political action committees (PACs), political parties (including the party in government), the candidates' own resources, and public (tax) funds. There are no other sources from which candidates can raise large amounts of money. Campaign finance reform, then, cannot do much more than mandate a different mix among these five or try to eliminate one or more of these sources altogether.

Individual Contributors

Most of the money contributed directly to candidates comes from individuals, not parties or PACs (see Table 12.2). Although public funding has reduced the role of the individual donor in presidential general elections, individuals still provide the largest portion of the money for nomination races, both by their contributions and through the federal matching funds that they generate. Individuals also donate the largest portion of congressional campaign funds. In the 2004 elections, individuals accounted for 56 percent of the contributions to House candidates and 65 percent of the money given to Senate candidates. Data on state elections are harder to obtain, but individual givers probably provide the majority of funds here as well.[11]

The nature of the individual contributor has changed, however. Before the 1970s campaign finance reforms, congressional and presidential candidates were allowed to take unlimited sums of money from individuals. For example, insurance magnate W. Clement Stone and multimillionaire Richard Mellon Scaife donated a total of $3 million to President Nixon's reelection campaign in 1972. Well-supported fears that these "fat cats" were getting something in return for their money—preferential treatment ranging from tax breaks to ambassadorships—led Congress to pass the *Federal Election Campaign Act (FECA)* amendments of 1974, which limited an individual's donation to any federal candidate to $1,000.

For the next two decades, these limits seemed to work. Because of the reforms, congressional campaigns were financed not by a handful of big givers but by a large number of people making small (under $1,000) donations. That was also true of the nomination phase of presidential campaigns. Even so, this expanded group of small donors remains a very small percentage of the population, and they tend to be older, more likely to be male, more involved in politics, more conservative, more Republican, and wealthier than the average American voter.[12] But they resemble the typical American much more closely than the Stones and the Scaifes did.

The $1,000 limit meant that campaigns had to learn new ways to separate prospective donors from their money. When "fat cats" were the preferred funding source, they were wooed by star-studded dinners and personal visits and phone calls with the candidate. The small contributors are usually solicited by mail and e-mail. In the 2004 nomination race, Howard Dean got a majority of his individual donations in contributions of less than $200 over the Internet. Dean's innovative fundraisers tied their Internet fundraising to current news events. In July 2003, when Vice President Dick Cheney planned an appearance at a $2,000-a-plate Republican luncheon, the Dean campaign responded with "The Cheney Challenge." Accompanied by a video of Dean eating a turkey sandwich, his website asked supporters to contribute more money on the Internet than the luncheon would raise for Cheney. The luncheon produced $250,000 from 125 attendees;

TABLE 12.2   Sources of Campaign Funds for Presidential and Congressional Candidates (in Millions)

| | Presidential, 2003–2004 | | | | | |
| | Democrats | | Republicans | | Total | |
	Nomination	General	Nomination	General	Nomination	General
Individuals	$351.0	$0	$258.9	$0	$611.4	$2.9
Candidates	> 0.1	0	0	0	0.1	0
PACs	1.0	0	2.6	0	3.5	0
Party coordinated*	0	16.0	0	16.1	0	32.1
Party independent*	35	120.3	0	18.2	35	138.5
Public funds	27.2	74.6	0	74.6	28.4	149.2
Legal, accounting	0	8.9	0	12.2	0	21.1
Other	22.6		8.1	10.8	30.5	10.8
Total	$401.8	$83.5	$269.6	$97.6	$673.9	$184.0

| | Congressional, 2003–2004 | | | | | | |
| | Democrats | | Republicans | | Total | | Grand |
	House	Senate	House	Senate	House	Senate	Total
Individuals	$178.3	$169.0	$217.4	$154.6	$396.7	$324.1	$720.8
Candidates							
Contributions	3.4	23.7	4.0	14.3	7.8	38.2	46.0
Loans	14.2	16.6	33.0	23.1	47.4	39.8	87.2
PACs	98.6	28.4	126.6	35.3	225.4	63.7	289.1
Party	0.9	0.9	1.3	1.2	2.2	2.1	4.3
Party coordinated*	3.1	10.2	3.5	9.3	6.7	19.4	26.1
Party independent*	36.9	18.7	47.3	19.4	84.2	38.1	122.3
Other receipts	12.0	12.0	16.9	17.6	29.0	29.7	58.7
Total	$307.4	$250.6	$399.2	$246.1	$708.5	$497.6	$1,206.1

*Party coordinated and independent expenditures are spent on behalf of the candidate rather than given to the campaign, so they are not included in the totals at the bottom of the table.

Note: Candidate loans are personal loans by the candidate to her or his campaign. The figures for Democrats and Republicans often do not add up to the sums in the "total" columns because the latter include funds for minor party candidates as well.

Source: For President, based on Federal Election Commission data as of August 15, 2005; for Congress, "Congressional Candidates Spend $1.16 Billion During 2003–2004," press release June 9, 2005, on the Internet at http://www.fec.gov/press/press2005/20050609candidate/20050609candidate.html (accessed August 17, 2005).

Dean's challenge raised $500,000 from 9,700 donors, as well as a lot of media coverage.[13] Kerry's campaign learned from Dean's efforts and raised a record $82 million over the Internet.

Political Action Committees

PACs are political groups, other than party organizations, whose purpose is to raise and spend money to influence elections. Most PACs have been created by corporations, labor unions, or trade associations; these "parent" groups can support a PAC as it begins its work of raising money. Others have no sponsoring organizations; these so-called *nonconnected PACs* are most likely to be ideological groups of the right or the left. PACs can give money directly to candidates and party organizations and can also use it on independent expenditures or issue ads (see following).

The number of PACs grew markedly in the 1970s and 1980s; there were about 4,200 by the beginning of 2005. In particular, corporate and nonconnected PACs have proliferated; the proportion of corporate PACs increased from 15 percent of the 1974 total to 39 percent by 2005, and nonconnected PACs grew from 0 to 29 percent. Recently, there have also been large increases in "leadership PACs"—those set up by incumbents to distribute money to other candidates. Members of Congress contribute to other candidates to gain their support in elections for party leadership positions in Congress or because their Hill committee has insisted that they "share the wealth."[14] Corporate committees are the biggest PAC givers overall; together with trade association PACs (most of which are business related), they provided almost two-thirds of the PAC contributions to federal candidates in 2004. Labor union PACs gave only a quarter as much. But because labor unions give almost all their PAC money to Democrats, they help to compensate for the Republican edge in corporate and trade association contributions (see Table 12.3).

One main reason for the growth of PACs was the campaign finance reforms of the post-Watergate years, which permitted PACs to donate up to $5,000 per candidate, whereas individuals could give only a maximum of $1,000. The reforms also explicitly permitted corporations doing business with government to have PACs. Federal court decisions and the FEC confirmed the legality of PACs and the right of sponsoring organizations to pay their overhead expenses as long as the PAC's political funds are collected and kept in a separate fund. The sponsoring organization cannot use its regular assets and revenues to make political contributions. Once their legality was clarified and their fundraising advantages became obvious, their numbers exploded.

PACs are not generally a major source of funds for presidential candidates. In the 2004 campaign, PACs gave a total of just $3.5 million to candidates seeking their party's presidential nomination and spent a larger sum ($42.8 million) on independent spending for and against presidential candidates, though this was a huge increase over 2000. Instead, they put the bulk of their money into congressional races. PACs gave a total of $289.1 million to House and Senate candidates in 2003–2004 (Table 12.2), an 18 percent increase over 2000. They also made $57.3 million in independent expenditures. Because House candidates are less well funded overall than Senate candidates, PAC money accounts for a higher proportion of House campaign budgets. Overall, PACs provide about a quarter of the revenue for congressional campaigns.

Candidates and parties work hard to get PAC money. Both parties' congressional campaign committees connect their candidates with PACs likely to be sympathetic to their causes. Campaigners also seek PAC help directly, assisted by directories that list PACs by their issue positions, the size of their resources, and their previous contributions. Incumbent Congress members invite PACs or the lobbyists of their parent organizations to fund-raising parties in Washington. PACs take the initiative as well. Unlike most individual donors, they are in the business of making political contributions, and they don't necessarily wait to be asked.[15]

What do PACs buy with their donations to congressional campaigns? Most PAC money is intended to gain access for the giver: the assurance that the legislator's door will be open when the group needs to plead its case on legislation. The result is that most PAC contributions go to incumbents—in 2004, more than $10 for every $1 donated to a challenger. There is little advantage, after all, in getting access to a likely loser. PAC money, like individual donations, therefore flows to the party with the most incumbents, and since the 1994 elections, that has been the Republicans. Party competition in the 2004 House and Senate races was close enough, however, that only a small majority (about 56 percent) of PAC money at the federal level went to Republican candidates.

It seems likely that PAC contributions help them get access to lawmakers. What elected officials will slam the door shut on representatives of interests that donated money to their campaigns? It is harder to determine, however, how intently they listen and whether the PAC's concerns will influence their legislative behavior. There is not much evidence that PAC contributions affect the recipients' roll call votes,[16] although legislators who receive PAC money do seem to be more active on congressional committees on behalf of issues that interest their PAC donors.[17]

There are many reasons why PAC money rarely "buys" votes. Because most PACs give much less than the $5,000 maximum per candidate, many PACs could be considered small donors. PACs give most of their money to incumbents, who normally have an easy time raising other campaign funds. PACs generally support legislators who have shown that they already favor the PAC's interests. That limits the opportunity for PAC money to change legislators' votes. In some cases, their limited success may be due to their structure as organizations. Many large PACs are set up as federations. Their local members, who provide most of these PACs' money, may want to support local incumbents even when those incumbents are not helpful to the national PAC.[18] PAC influence is also limited because they have so much competition—from party leaders, constituents, and other PACs—for the ear and the vote of a legislator. Their influence tends to be greatest when they represent powerful interests in the legislator's district, when they are not in conflict with his or her party's position, and when the benefit that they want is of little concern to anyone else (such as a small change in the tax laws that gives a big break to a particular corporation).

Parties

At the time of the 1970s reforms, the party organizations' role in campaign finance could easily have been overlooked. However, party money, or, more accurately, money raised by the party organizations from individuals, elected officials, PACs, and other interests, now plays an increasingly important role in campaigns. The two parties raised a whopping $1 billion in the 2000 election cycle and almost matched that amount in 2002, even with no presidential candidates on the ballot. In 2004 party fund-raising increased to $1.2 billion.

In congressional races, parties are allowed to make small contributions directly to candidates' campaigns. In the 2004 races, for example, Republican committees gave a total of $2.5 million directly to House and Senate candidates and Democrats contributed $1.8 million. More substantial are the two parties' coordinated spending—the funds that they spend on behalf of their candidates and in coordination with the candidate's campaign, typically for services such as television and radio ads and polling. Federal law limits the parties' coordinated expenditures in each race: In the 2004 House campaigns, each party was permitted to spend $37,310 per election, except in states with only one House district, where the limit was $74,620. The state party can spend the same amount or transfer its spending authority in an "agency agreement" to the national party. In

Senate campaigns, the limit varied with the size of the state's voting-age population: from $74,620 in Delaware to almost $2 million in California.

Counting direct contributions by the party's national committee, the relevant congressional campaign committee, and the state party, plus the national and state shares of coordinated spending, each party could put over $100,000 in direct and coordinated spending into a House race and much more into a Senate race. Coordinated spending is useful to the party because party committees have more control over how the money is spent than they do in making direct contributions to candidates. Parties' coordinated expenditures have greatly increased, but they still amounted to only about 4 percent of Senate candidates' total spending in 2004, and less in House races.

Parties are also allowed to do independent spending in federal candidates' campaigns; they use the money to fund TV ads, polls, and direct mail. This independent spending was heavily concentrated on a few competitive races in 2004. The two parties put $84 million into independent spending in 30 House races and $38 million into 12 Senate campaigns—an average of around $3 million per race. In seven Democratic and ten Republican House campaigns, counting coordinated and independent spending, the party actually outspent the candidate.[19]

As Chapter 4 showed, members of the party in government have become increasingly important campaign contributors in the last two congressional elections. Party leaders in the House and Senate are now expected to make major contributions to the congressional campaign committees from their personal campaign accounts and by raising money for the party and its endangered candidates. Members who hope for leadership positions have an incentive to raise these funds as well. The new money coming from House and Senate incumbents is evidence of the value they place on strong congressional parties in the effort to reach their policy and political goals.

The Candidates Themselves

Candidates, as they always have, continue to spend their personal wealth in trying to win political office. In 2004, 1 percent (a total of $8 million) of House candidates' campaign funds came from their own pockets, plus another 7 percent in loans, and Senate candidates donated $38 million (8 percent) of their campaign budgets and loaned their campaigns another 8 percent (Table 12.2). Twenty-two first-time candidates each spent more than $1 million of their own money on House and Senate races, for a total of more than $40 million. Being willing to fund one's own campaign does not guarantee victory; two-thirds of these self-funders lost their primaries, and only one of them won the general election. But self-funding can help a candidate to be taken seriously. When John Kerry's campaign for the Democratic nomination was almost out of money, in debt, and all but dead in November 2003, Kerry mortgaged his Boston home for $6.4 million and invested it in his campaign. The infusion of cash saved his candidacy by permitting him to campaign in the Iowa caucuses, which he later won.

Public Funding

In federal elections, public funding is available only for presidential campaigns. Congress voted in the early 1970s to let taxpayers designate a dollar (now $3) of their tax payments to match small contributions to candidates for their party's presidential

TABLE 12.3   The Top Ten (Plus Two) List of the Biggest PACs (in Contributions to Federal Candidates, 2003–2004)

		Contributions to Federal Candidates		
Rank	PAC	Total (in millions)	% to Democrats	% to Republicans
1	National Association of Realtors	$3.8	47%	52%
2	Laborers Union*	2.7	86	14
3	National Auto Dealers Association	2.6	27	73
4	Electrical Workers*	2.4	96	4
5	National Beer Wholesalers	2.3	24	76
6	National Association of Home Builders	2.2	33	67
7	Association of Trial Lawyers	2.2	93	6
8	United Parcel Service (UPS)	2.1	28	72
9	American Medical Association	2.1	21	79
10	United Auto Workers*	2.1	98	1
11	Carpenters & Joiners*	2.1	74	26
12	Credit Union National Association	2.1	42	58

*Labor union PACs. Totals do not always add up to 100 percent due to rounding error.

Source: FEC data on the Internet at http://www.opensecrets.org/pacs/topacs.asp?txt=A&Cycle=2004 (accessed August 10, 2005).

nomination and to foot most of the bill for the major-party nominees in the general election. The intent was to reduce corruption by limiting the role of private funds. In 2004, public matching funds in the nomination and general election campaigns totaled $177.2 million—less than in 2000, because Bush, Kerry, and Dean all declined matching funds in the 2004 nomination race. The number of tax filers agreeing to contribute to the Presidential Election Campaign Fund is dropping, however, from 29 percent in 1978 to only about 11 percent now. Congress has chosen not to extend public funding to its own races.

MONEY IN STATE AND LOCAL CAMPAIGNS

State campaigns generally follow a pattern similar to those at the national level. Individual donors are the most important source of candidates' campaign funds, followed by PAC contributions, and then, at greater distance, by party and candidates' personal funds. There are exceptions, of course. In an increasing number of states, parties' legislative leaders and caucuses are donating to state legislative candidates. Individual donors are even more important in local campaigns because parties and PACs play a lesser (although expanding) role at this level.

REFORM OF THE CAMPAIGN FINANCE RULES

For years, American campaign finance laws were a flimsy structure of halfhearted and not very well-integrated federal and state statutes. Reformers tried periodically to strengthen legal controls over the raising and spending of campaign money. A new episode of reform was under way in the early 1970s when the Watergate scandals broke. The revulsion caused by these fund-raising scandals produced the most extensive federal law on the subject in U.S. history: the *Federal Election Campaign Act (FECA)*

TABLE 12.4 Limits on Campaign Contributions Under Federal Law

		Limit on Contributions	
	Individual	Political Action Committee	State or National Party Committee
To candidate or candidate committee per election	$2,000	$5,000*	$5,000†
To all candidates combined, per 2-year cycle	37,500	No limit	No limit
To a national party committee per year (An individual's total contribution to all national party committees and PACs per 2-year election cycle is limited to $57,500.)	25,000	15,000	—
To a state or local party committee per year	10,000	5,000	No limit
Total per 2-year election cycle	95,000	No limit	No limit

*If the political action committee qualifies as a "multicandidate committee" under federal law by making contributions to five or more federal candidates, the limit is $5,000. Otherwise the committee is treated as an individual with a limit of $2,000.

†The limit is $5,000 for contributions to presidential and House candidates. National and Senate (campaign) party committees can contribute a joint total of $35,000 to each U.S. Senate candidate per election.

Note: These are the limits on so-called hard-money contributions for the 2004 elections. Individual limits are indexed for inflation; PAC limits (and individual limits to PACs and state parties) are not.

Source: The Campaign Finance Institute.

amendments. The Supreme Court invalidated some of these reforms in 1976. Congress then revised the law and did so again in the late 1970s. The resulting legislation put limits on federal campaign contributions and spending and set up a system of public funding for presidential campaigns.

Contribution Limits

The law limited the amounts of money an individual, a PAC, and a party organization can give directly to a candidate in each election (primary or general) in a given year in order to eliminate the big contributors. Legislation passed in 2002 raised the limits for the first time in almost 30 years (see Table 12.4). These limits apply only to federal campaigns—those for the president and Congress. Corporations and labor unions are not allowed to contribute directly, but they may set up PACs and pay their overhead and administrative costs. The money contributed under these regulations is called **hard money**—contributions that fall under the "hard limits of the federal law."

Spending Limits

FECA also limited spending by presidential candidates. Those who accept federal money in the race for their party's nomination must also accept spending limits in each of the 50 states and in the nomination race as a whole. In the general election, presidential candidates who accept federal subsidies can spend no more than the law permits.

Congress tried to limit spending in House and Senate campaigns as well, but the Supreme Court would not agree. The Court's majority accepted the arguments of a group of strange bedfellows, including conservative New York Senator James Buckley, liberal Democratic Senator Eugene McCarthy, and the New York Civil Liberties Union that the law's restrictions on campaign spending infringed on the right to free speech. Therefore, in *Buckley v. Valeo*,[20] the Court ruled that Congress could limit campaign spending only for candidates who accepted public funding. Congress could apply spending limits to its own campaigns, then, only as part of a plan for subsidizing them. That would mean subsidizing their challengers' campaigns as well. For congressional incumbents, who are normally quite capable of outspending their challengers, this was not an appealing idea.

Public Disclosure

A vital part of the FECA reform was the requirement that campaigns had to publicly disclose their spending and the sources of their contributions. Reformers assumed that providing information about the sources of candidates' cash would enable voters to punish greedy or corrupt campaigners with their ballots. All donations to a federal candidate must now go through and be accounted for by a single campaign committee; before the reforms, candidates could avoid full public disclosure by using a complex array of committees. Each candidate must file monthly or quarterly reports on his or her finances during the campaign, through December 31 after the election. All contributors of $200 or more must be identified by name, address, occupation, and name of employer.

Earlier legislation had tried and failed to achieve this goal. The new legislation improved the quality of reporting by creating the FEC to collect the data and make them available. Some members of Congress still try to undercut the FEC's powers by threatening to reduce its funding, but the commission's public files, available on the Internet (at http://www.fec.gov), have provided a wealth of campaign finance information for journalists and scholars.

Public Funding of Presidential Campaigns

As another means of removing "interested money" from elections, Congress passed laws in 1971 and 1976 to provide public (tax) funding for presidential candidates. To get the money, a candidate for a party's presidential nomination must first raise $5,000 in contributions of $250 or less in each of 20 states, as a way of demonstrating broad public support. After that, public funds match every individual contribution up to $250. In return, the candidate was allowed to spend no more than about $45 million in the 2004 nomination race.[21] In addition, the two major parties each received $14.6 million in public funds to help pay for their 2004 national conventions. Finally, each major party's candidate gets public money to pay for his or her general election campaign. The amount, which rises with increases in the Consumer Price Index, reached $74.6 million in 2004.

Minor parties fare less well. They receive only a fraction of that total and then only after the election if they have received at least 5 percent of the vote. Once they have reached that milestone, however, they qualify to receive their payment before the next presidential election. Because Ross Perot won 8 percent of the vote as the Reform Party's presidential candidate in 1996, the party's candidate in 2000 was guaranteed to receive $12.6 million in advance of that campaign. That clearly enhanced the attractiveness of the Reform Party's nomination. No other minor party has ever qualified for public funding. Because of the need to pay cash for many campaign expenses, this provision of FECA adds to the difficulty of financing even a modest third-party campaign.

THE LOOPHOLES THAT ATE THE REFORMS

This set of reforms was far-reaching. Yet, not long after the legislation was passed, those affected by it began to find and exploit loopholes in its provisions. The FECA amendments of 1979 and action by the FEC and the Supreme Court steadily chipped away at the framework of the FECA reforms.

Independent Spending

If an interest group or individual runs a campaign ad to support a candidate and works with the campaign in doing so, then the law treats that ad as a campaign contribution. But as long as the individual or group does not coordinate its advertising with a candidate's campaign, it is regarded by the Supreme Court as *independent spending,* and the group is permitted to spend unlimited amounts of money on it. The Court majority's reasoning in *Buckley v. Valeo* was that free speech is fundamental to democracy, and since "free" speech normally costs money to disseminate through radio, television, and other media, Congress cannot limit the amount that groups or individuals can spend on campaign ads that are run independent of a candidate's campaign. In 1996, the Supreme Court said that political parties could spend independently on campaigns as well, and the Court applied this ruling in 2003 to publicly-financed presidential campaigns.[22]

The advantage of independent spending, for a party, is that the communication can call expressly for the election or defeat of a candidate without breaking the legal limits on the party's *direct* contribution to that candidate. So in 2004 the parties greatly increased their independent expenditures. In addition to the $120.3 million spent by the DNC, the Republican National Committee (RNC) paid for $18.2 million worth of presidential campaign ads, and the Democratic and Republican Hill committees invested $56 million and $67 million, respectively, into independent expenditures in congressional races. The disadvantage of this spending is that, by law, it cannot be coordinated with the candidate's campaign. So the parties had to segregate the staffers involved with independent spending from those who worked with the candidates. Their only legal way to alert a candidate to the party's efforts was to hope for media coverage describing the extent and content of the party's planned advertising.

Independent spending poses many challenges. For one, it can encourage irresponsible campaign attacks. If a *candidate* launches an outrageous attack, voters can protest by voting for his or her opponent. However, if a party, interest group, or individual runs an outrageous ad as an independent spender, who can be held responsible? The independent spender can't be punished at the polls; he or she isn't running for anything. And because independent spenders, by definition, are not supposed to be coordinating their efforts with a candidate, is it fair to punish the candidate for the offensive ad? Therefore, independent spenders are free to say whatever they wish and the candidate whom they favor can't be held accountable.

Soft Money

As a means of strengthening state and local party organizations, Congress amended FECA in 1979 to exempt from federal regulation any money raised and spent by state and local parties for party building, voter registration, and get-out-the-vote activities. This came to be called *soft money,* or, because it was exempt from federal law, *nonfederal money.*

The law was interpreted to allow unlimited contributions not only to be donated to state and local parties but also to pass through national party committees on their way to the state parties. So, although FECA permitted individuals to give no more than $1,000 each to a federal candidate per election, citizens could also give unlimited amounts of money to party organizations as soft money. These funds could not be spent directly on federal campaigns, but they could pay for any nonfederal portion of a campaign effort, and they had a tendency to migrate wherever they were needed.

In effect, then, soft money became a way for individuals and PACs to launder large contributions through a party organization. The parties pushed hard to get the money. In a letter made famous by a Supreme Court case, for example, then-RNC Chair Jim Nicholson sent a draft of the party's health care legislation to the drug company Bristol-Myers Squibb and asked for any suggested changes—and a $250,000 contribution to the RNC.[23] Fat cats, in short, had reentered the building. It was not the law's stated intention for soft money to become an end run around the limits on hard money, but the difficulty of monitoring the uses of these funds made it so. In most states, soft money could be raised not only from individuals and PACs but from corporations' profits and labor union dues as well—funds that could not be donated directly to federal candidates under FECA.[24]

Tremendous sums flowed through the soft-money conduit from the early 1990s until 2002, when it was banned at the federal level. In the 2002 election cycle, the national parties' last-ditch drive to beat the deadline for soft money resulted in an intake of $496.1 million, an unprecedented take in a midterm election. Soft money had become so attractive a source of funding, especially for the Democrats, who did not have as many hard-money donors, that in 2002, it comprised more than half of the Democratic Party's receipts and more than one-third of those of the Republicans (see Figure 12.4).

Issue Advocacy Ads

Soft money has been used to fund a number of different campaign efforts—for example, to pay some of the party organization's overhead expenses and for registration and get-out-the-vote drives or to be transferred to state and local parties for their use. Most soft money, however, has been used to fund *issue advocacy ads.* These are campaign ads that do not include the terms "elect," "vote for," "support," or "oppose." As long as an ad does not use these "magic words" or ones like it, the courts defined it as "issue advocacy" instead of election advertising (or "express advocacy"). Therefore, it falls under the First Amendment's right to freedom of expression and cannot be regulated by FECA. The DNC was the first to exploit this loophole to support President Clinton's reelection in 1996.[25]

Here are two examples of ads that met the definition of "issue advocacy" in 2004. Thus, they could be funded with unlimited amounts of soft money, in this case by interest groups, and fully coordinated with the candidate's campaign:

> (Video shows pictures of terrorist attacks and terrorist leaders such as Osama bin Laden. The announcer intones:) "These people want to kill us. . . . Would you trust Kerry against these fanatic killers? President Bush didn't start this war, but he will finish it." (Sponsored by Progress for America)[26]
>
> "Prescription drug costs are climbing, yet President Bush sided with the drug companies, blocking Medicare from negotiating lower prices and banning Americans from importing low-cost drugs from Canada." (Sponsored by The Media Fund)[27]

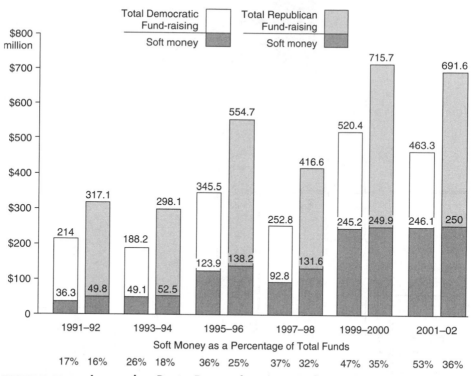

Soft Money as a Percentage of Total Funds

17%	16%	26%	18%	36%	25%	37%	32%	47%	35%	53%	36%

FIGURE 12.4   Increasing Party Dependence on Soft Money: 1991–2002

Note: Bars represent total party fund-raising and the portion of it received in the form of soft money for each election cycle.

Source: FEC data, issued by press release on March 20, 2003.

These certainly sound like campaign ads. But because they don't use the "magic words," they give these groups, as well as corporations, unions, and big individual donors, a perfectly legal way around the spending limits imposed by FECA (see Figure 12.5). Why does this make sense? The Supreme Court has ruled that the right of individuals and groups to express their ideas freely carries more weight than concerns about campaign corruption. The result is that in some recent campaigns the volume of issue ads funded by interest groups threatened to drown out the voices of the candidates.

From the candidate's perspective, that can be a mixed blessing. Just as is the case with independent spenders, the issue ads run by outside groups may convey different messages than the campaign would prefer. In a close House race in Colorado in 2002, for instance, a TV ad run by the national party showed a grainy image of the opponent, with a narrator asking, "What kind of person works for a group that wants to force people to pay rent in a nursing home up to 90 days after they die?" The ad concluded by asking viewers to call the opponent and ask, "What kind of person are you?" The candidate's campaign manager conceded that many of these ads were "pure, harsh hate."[28] There have been other cases where candidates' poll numbers have declined after being "helped" by a group running intense issue advocacy ads.[29]

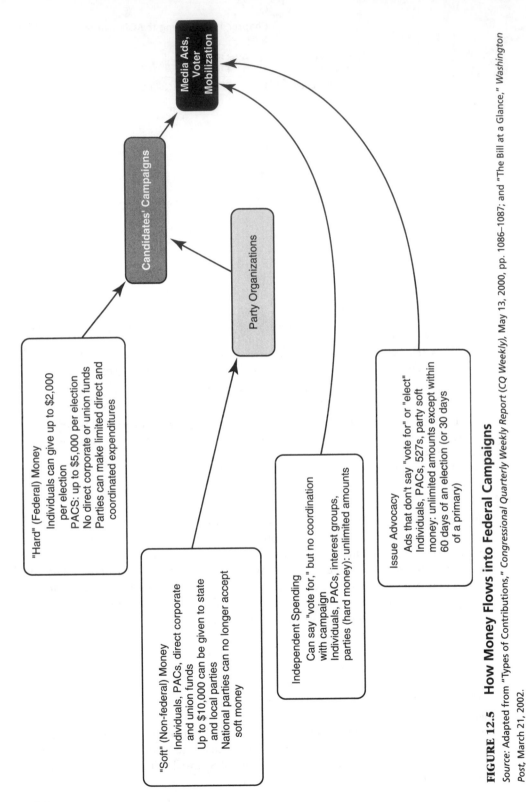

FIGURE 12.5   How Money Flows into Federal Campaigns

Source: Adapted from "Types of Contributions," *Congressional Quarterly Weekly Report (CQ Weekly),* May 13, 2000, pp. 1086–1087; and "The Bill at a Glance," *Washington Post,* March 21, 2002.

"527" Advocacy Groups

One major news feature in the 2004 campaign was the increase in partisan political groups called "527s." This odd name refers to the provision of the U.S. tax code that allows certain tax-exempt groups to raise and spend unlimited sums on campaigns as long as they do not expressly call for the election or defeat of specific candidates and do not coordinate their activities with federal candidates or parties. These groups could register voters, run get-out-the-vote drives, broadcast ads, send direct mail, and distribute voter guides, among other activities.

When Congress voted in 2002 to stop the national parties from accepting soft-money contributions, Democrats worried that their party, which had depended heavily on soft money, would be greatly outspent. In particular, if the 2004 Democratic presidential nominee accepted matching funds in the primaries, and thus hit the spending ceiling in the early spring, the campaign would be overwhelmed by the huge hard-money treasury of the Bush campaign. So with seed money from a few wealthy individuals, Democratic activists created a series of 527 groups in 2003 that could spend soft money to support the Democratic nominee when his or her funds ran low. The biggest of these Democratic 527s were Americans Coming Together (ACT), created to do ground war voter mobilization; The Media Fund; and MoveOn.org Voter Fund. These three groups spent a total of over $150 million to supplement the Kerry campaign's efforts (see box on page 238).

At first, Republicans found it difficult to build their own network of 527s. Publicity about corporate scandals made business leaders uneasy about contributing to these controversial groups. The RNC instead sought an FEC ruling preventing 527s from giving to campaigns. When the FEC declined to rule, Republican groups such as Swift Boat Veterans for Truth and Progress for America geared up quickly during the summer of 2004, raised tens of millions of dollars, and began putting up ads, though they were still outspent four to one by Democratic 527s. All federal 527s combined raked in a total of $405 million through November 2004, which replaced part but not all of the soft money the national parties had received in 2002.[30]

The engine powering all this spending was a relatively small group of wealthy partisans with strong ideological commitments. More than a quarter of the funds raised by all 527 groups combined came from only 15 individuals, who together gave a total of $125 million. The two biggest donors, financier George Soros and insurance magnate Peter Lewis, each contributed $23 million to Democratic 527s. Ninety percent of the money raised by Republican 527s came in amounts of $250,000 or more, as did 80 percent of donations to Democratic 527s. The notorious Swift Boat Veterans and POWs for Truth (see Chapter 11) got most of their funds from just four people, who gave a total of $12.7 million combined.[31] In all, 63 percent of the money received by 527s came from individuals and another 28 percent from labor unions.[32] The 527s, in short, were the major new avenue for soft-money contributions.

These groups posed major challenges for campaign finance reformers in 2004 and 2006. As partisan (and often extremist) groups, the 527s clearly intended to boost specific candidates, even if their issue advocacy ads could not say so explicitly. They were able to use individual donations to broadcast issue ads right up to Election Day, many of which were among the most vicious attack ads of the presidential campaign. And although they were not permitted to coordinate their activities with candidates' campaigns, there is little doubt that they did so in 2004. The coordination was much more

THE TOP GIVERS AMONG 527 GROUPS

These were the biggest-spending 527 groups (and their partisan leanings) during the 2003–2004 election cycle:

Americans Coming Together (Democratic)	$78 million
The Media Fund (Democratic)	$54 million
Service Employees International Union (Democratic)	$40 million
Progress for America (Republican)	$36 million
Swift Boat Vets and POWs for Truth (Republican)	$23 million
AFSCME (State and local government workers union; Democratic)	$22 million
MoveOn.org (Democratic)	$21 million
College Republican National Committee (Republican)	$17 million
New Democrat Network (Democratic)	$13 million
Citizens for a Strong Senate (Democratic)	$10 million
Club for Growth (Republican)	$9 million

Source: FEC data from the Center for Responsive Politics, on the Internet at http://www.opensecrets.org/527s/527cmtes.asp?level=C&format=&cycle=2004 (accessed August 8, 2005).

effective on the Republican side, however; Democratic 527s didn't always follow the Kerry campaign's lead in their advertising.

Congress voted in 2000 to require 527s to disclose their contributors and expenses. Soon after, some of these groups reorganized themselves as for-profit organizations or nonprofits under different provisions of the tax code to avoid the need for disclosure. Organizations called 501(c) groups, again after the provision of the tax code that permits them, are also tax-exempt and do not need to report their donors, even though some of these groups are allowed to register voters and others can be involved in elections as long as this spending is less than half of their budget. These 501(c) groups were estimated to have spent between $70 and $100 million in the 2004 election.[33]

Each of these types of groups has advantages for certain kinds of fund-raising and spending. So some organizations find it useful to set up several different types of groups: a 501(c) to do voter mobilization with money that the givers do not want to be disclosed, a 527 for issue advocacy with soft money, and a PAC to provide direct financial contributions to candidates in limited amounts. The effort to regulate these groups continues; beginning in 2005, for example, at least half of the cost of 527 groups' voter registration drives has to be financed with hard money as long as they refer to both federal and non-federal races. But the 501(c) groups can still accept unlimited soft money and keep their donors' names secret, so they can be expected to become even bigger players in campaign finance in the 2008 elections.

WHAT DID THE 1970S REFORMS ACCOMPLISH?

With loopholes this size, there was reason to wonder, by the end of the 2000 campaign, if the federal regulation actually regulated anything. Public funding and money raised under the limits of FECA had been swamped by massive quantities of issue advertising, paid for largely by unregulated soft money. As one expert noted, "In the world we live in today, practically speaking, there are no limits on what you can give to a campaign."[34] So—did the reforms accomplish anything?

Intended and Unintended Effects

At first, the FECA reforms seemed to achieve *most* of their goals. They slowed the growth of campaign spending in presidential races, at least in spending by the candidates' own campaigns. Between 1960 and 1972, presidential campaign expenditures had tripled. From 1972 to 2000, however, real spending increased more slowly, and in three of the eight elections, spending actually declined. In the early days of the reforms, the contribution limits made small donations more valuable than ever to candidates, which broadened the base of campaign funding. The reforms also opened much of the campaign finance process to public scrutiny.

Like all reforms, however, the campaign finance laws of the 1970s had some worrisome, unintended effects. One of the largest was the imbalance between hard money contributions to candidates, which are limited, and the unlimited spending that soft money, issue advocacy ads, and independent expenditures made possible. The cap of $1,000 on hard-money contributions was not raised until 2002, although inflation had greatly eroded its value during that time. These relatively low ceilings on individual contributions made soft money and independent spending all the more attractive to parties and interest groups. Both these forms of spending raise real questions of accountability and bring back the types of money—big money from individuals and corporate and union treasuries—that the sponsors of FECA had hoped to clean out of federal campaigns.

In the long run, then, the reformers' efforts failed to meet one of their major goals: reducing the influence of "interested money." Currently, probably no more than 1 percent of Americans give money to any federal candidate,[35] and only about one-fourth of 1 percent give $200 or more.[36] The other givers are groups—corporations, labor unions, and other organized interests—that want something specific from lawmakers. On a single evening in the spring of 2002, for instance, one Republican dinner raised a record-breaking $33 million. Some of the biggest givers, including drug and telecommunications companies, had a major interest in pending legislation, and Democrats were working hard to do the same.[37]

Effects on the Parties

For the first two decades after FECA was passed, the prevailing view was that the reforms had harmed the party organizations. By limiting parties' direct contributions to presidential and congressional candidates, FECA treated the parties as no more privileged in the campaign process than were PACs or other groups. In addition, the public funding of presidential campaigns goes to the candidates themselves, not to the parties, as it does in most other democracies. That creates more distance between the party organization and the presidential campaign.

Since 1996, however, the loopholes in the reforms, including independent spending, soft money, and issue advocacy, gave the national parties the means to raise and spend much more money than ever before. Large amounts of party money went into TV and radio advertising and the beefed-up voter mobilization programs so prominent at the conclusion of the 2000 and 2002 campaigns. State and local parties, energized by money received from the national parties and by their own fund-raising success, became more involved in campaigns as well. Some put major effort into the labor-intensive grassroots work that was the staple of party organizations in an earlier era. Soft money allowed the parties to play more of a role in the most competitive races than had been the case in more than half a century. Party organizations invested some of these new riches in long-term state and local party building.[38] Very few of the party-funded issue advocacy ads even mentioned the party labels, however, so it probably did not help in any other way to strengthen the parties' ties with voters.[39]

Another Try: The Bipartisan Campaign Reform Act (BCRA)

The unintended effects of the 1970s reforms—and some of the intended effects as well—created pressures for new reforms. They also led to cynicism about the chance for genuine change. When respondents were asked in a Fox News poll in 1997 whether they were more likely to see Elvis or to see real campaign finance reform, Elvis won, 48 percent to 31 percent.[40]

Nevertheless, in 2002, thanks to the dogged determination of Senators John McCain (R-AZ) and Russ Feingold (D-WI) and another set of fund-raising scandals, Congress passed *the Bipartisan Campaign Reform Act* (known as *BCRA,* pronounced BICK-ra).[41] In order to cut off the soft-money "end run" around federal contribution limits, this act banned soft-money contributions to national parties. State and local parties can still accept soft money from corporations and labor unions in amounts up to $10,000 per donor per year, called Levin funds (after the sponsor of this exception). They can spend this money in combination with hard money to run generic voter registration and turnout drives, though state organizations made very little use of this provision in 2004, and can still collect unlimited soft-money donations for use in state elections. Beyond that, state parties can now spend only hard money on federal election activities. To help them raise this money, the limit on individual donations to these parties was raised from $5,000 to $10,000.

BCRA also limited the use of issue advocacy ads. Broadcast ads that mention a federal candidate but don't use the "magic words" of express advocacy (such as "vote for," "elect," and "defeat") are now to be termed "electioneering" communications. Such ads cannot be aired within 60 days of a general election or 30 days of a primary unless they are funded entirely by federally regulated hard money or by soft money contributed only by individuals. Ads funded by corporations or unions cannot be run during this "window," though they can still be aired at any other time. Because the new rule applies only to broadcast media ads, advocacy groups can continue to use soft money for direct mail, phone banks, and voter registration during this time, and in fact many groups did move their soft money into these activities.[42]

BCRA also increased the individual contribution limit to $2,000 for federal campaigns, increased the overall limit on individual contributions to candidates, parties, and other political committees combined, and provided that some of these limits would now rise with inflation. A complicated ruling by federal district court judges struck down the soft-money ban for a time in 2003, but a sharply divided Supreme Court reinstated it and other key parts of BCRA later that year in *McConnell v. the Federal Election Commission*. The Court ruled that even the appearance of corruption justified the restrictions.

Although most congressional Democrats voted for the bill, Democratic leaders worried that their party's fund-raising would be seriously undercut once BCRA took effect. For decades, Republicans have been much more successful than Democrats in raising hard money; many more of the individuals able to contribute $2,000 to a campaign are Republicans. In recent elections, Democrats were able to narrow the fund-raising gap somewhat by raising soft money from big donors such as labor unions and some wealthy individuals. A ban on soft money, they thought, would increase the Republican advantage. In fact, the RNC, with its extensive hard-money donor base, had three times as much cash on hand at the beginning of 2004 as did the DNC.

The ink on the legislation was barely dry, however, when new loopholes had been opened. As we have seen, unlimited amounts of soft money could still be donated to groups such as 527s and 501(c)s, which can then spend money on campaigns. BCRA also exempted the host committees for the parties' national conventions from the ban on soft money. As a result, wealthy individuals, corporations, and labor unions were still able to contribute unlimited amounts to the national parties to help pay for the 2004 conventions. Donors gave a total of $142.5 million to the parties' host committees in 2004; one of the checks was for $5 million. And the RNC, in particular, contended that it could share some of the cost of a presidential candidate's campaign ads as long as the ads contained a generic party message. This "hybrid" spending expanded the party's role in the presidential campaign beyond its direct contributions, coordinated spending, and independent spending.

The new law also had the effect of encouraging increased use of an older practice known as **bundling.** Although individual contributions to a campaign are limited to $2,000, an individual or interest group can solicit large numbers of these individual donors, combine ("bundle") their contributions, and deliver them to a campaign in order to take credit for a much more substantial donation without breaking the law. Groups such as the pro-choice EMILY's List and the conservative Club for Growth have delivered donations totaling hundreds of thousands of dollars to a single candidate. Because these are hard-money donations, they can be used for almost any purpose in campaigns. Although bundling is a clear end run around the effort to limit contributions, it has not been ruled illegal.

The 2004 Bush reelection campaign took bundling to new heights. In a program Bush fund-raisers first developed in 1998, supporters who solicited donations that added up to at least $100,000 were rewarded with the title "Pioneers"; those who raised more than $200,000 were termed "Rangers," after the Texas Rangers, the baseball team once owned by Bush; and those who topped $300,000 in bundled donations to the Republican Party became "Super Rangers." By Election Day, there were 425 Pioneers, 221 Rangers, and 104 Super Rangers. Most of the Rangers were corporate CEOs and lawyers, lobbyists, and doctors who, like other big donors, have interests in the policies being set by the federal government.[43] Democrats lagged far behind in bundling; 17 "Trustees" raised at least $250,000 for the DNC in 2004, the 266 people who collected at least $100,000 for the Kerry campaign were invited to call themselves "vice chairs" of the campaign, and 298 "co-chairs" raised $50,000 or more.

In short, BCRA's doubling of the individual contribution limit offered a golden opportunity to the presidential campaigns. Almost half of Bush's individual contributors gave the maximum of $2,000, and more than three-quarters of the individual donors to both the

Kerry and Bush campaigns contributed at least $1,000. These big contributions enabled the campaigns to expand and refine their canvassing and get-out-the-vote drives as well as their broadcast advertising. At the same time, the number of small contributors (of under $200) quadrupled over 2000. The Democratic Party increased its direct mail list from 1 million to 100 million names and its Internet contacts from 70,000 to 1 million,[44] and expanded its small contributor base tenfold—no mean feat for a party that had depended on big soft-money donors through 2002. Some of this increase in small donors probably reflected the parties' efforts to make up for the loss of soft money, but some of it was due also to the intense competition and interest in the presidential contest.

The loss of federal soft money did not seem to seriously damage the parties, then, perhaps because much of the soft money in recent years had simply moved through the parties on its way to campaigns. But some party organizations, such as the congressional campaign committees, were not as successful in compensating for the loss of soft money as the DNC and RNC were. State and local parties' fund-raising also declined somewhat due to the lack of soft-money transfers from their national organizations. Democratic state and local parties were hit especially hard because the soft-money transfers had accounted for a substantial amount of their budgets in recent elections. These losses caused the state parties to reduce their broadcast advertising, direct mail, and phone bank activity (see Chapter 4). In particular, state parties' broadcast ads for federal candidates, on which these parties spent $236 million in 2000, nearly disappeared in 2004. Many state parties helped to make up for these losses by increasing their own fund-raising efforts. But most found it challenging to comply with the complicated provisions of BCRA.[45]

Some observers had hoped that the ban on federal soft money would help make congressional campaigns more competitive. When the national parties could put unlimited soft money into the most competitive races, and the close balance in Congress made these competitive races vital to party control, party funding drained away from the slightly less competitive challengers. Without soft money, party coordinated spending and direct contributions to candidates did increase, and some not-so-competitive candidates reaped some benefit. But the benefits were limited because both national parties put a substantial amount of their increased funding into independent spending.[46]

In sum, BCRA forced the parties to change the ways in which they raised and spent money. They adapted successfully through a big increase in hard-money fund-raising and more intensive programs to reach small donors. But these changes inevitably led to new reform proposals—for example, to prevent 527s from spending soft money, to let a candidate whose opponent opts out of matching funds raise an equal amount of money, to increase the amount of the tax check-off to pump up the Presidential Election Campaign Fund, and to raise the size of the match for smaller contributions in the nominating season and increase the overall spending ceiling. Unless the current system is reformed to keep up with the increase in campaign costs, no presidential candidate can realistically expect to compete for his or her party's nomination in 2008 by accepting public funding in the primaries.

State Regulation and Financing

Even more complicated than this tangled federal reform are the 50 different sets of state regulations. The Watergate scandals triggered a reform movement in many states during the 1970s, focusing mainly on requiring public disclosure. The movement has broadened since then. When the federal government pushed a number of conflict-filled issues (abortion policy, for example) back to the states, interest group activity and PAC formation at the state level increased as a result, and so did efforts to regulate it. As of 2005, 37 states limited campaign contributions by individuals—a right upheld by the Supreme Court in 2000. About the same number either prohibited or limited PAC donations and regulated labor union contributions, and almost all regulated corporate contributions.[47] Some states have even limited contributions from the candidates themselves—a step that the Supreme Court would not let Congress take in federal elections. More than half of the states limit party contributions to campaigns.

A growing number of states, now nearly half, have ventured into public funding for state elections. Several states (Maine, Arizona, Vermont, New Mexico, and North Carolina) and even some cities (such as Portland, Oregon) now provide full public funding for at least some types of candidates. The amount of the funding provided is not large, however, and is not typically accompanied by limits on campaign spending.[48] In most states, as at the federal level, the agencies designed to enforce these rules are small and poorly funded. Public support for these programs, as seen by taxpayers' willingness to direct their tax money to these funds, has declined sharply.[49]

MONEY IN AMERICAN POLITICS

Both before and after these reforms, money has played a bigger role in American elections than in those of most other democracies. The sheer size of many constituencies in the United States tempts candidates to buy expensive mass media. The large number of elected officials combined with frequent primary and general elections has produced a year-round election industry. Fund-raising occupies a great deal of the candidates' time even after they are elected, which raises public suspicions of corruption (see box on page 244).

Campaign finance in Britain works very differently. British election campaigns run for only about 30 days, and candidates and parties cannot buy TV and radio time for ads during this period. Instead, British parties get free time on the government-run BBC network. They can each run five TV ads of two and a half minutes in length, each shown only once. British campaigns are organized around their national party leaders, but there is considerable integration between the local parliamentary candidate and the leader rather than the largely separate campaigns of American congressional and presidential candidates. Campaign spending is pocket change by American standards; the parties are permitted to spend no more than about $38 million a year. On the other hand, interested Britons have the opportunity to watch daily, and often contentious, news conferences by the parties' leaders.

The American system of campaign finance has its consequences. The fact that candidates dominate the fund-raising in American campaigns gives them greater independence from their party organizations once they take office. The parties are working hard to increase their role in the raising and spending of campaign money. Their ingenuity was sorely tested by FECA and now by BCRA, but both parties have shown a lot of resilience in adapting to these reforms. Their need to adapt will continue; in the area of political money, reform is always a work in progress.

A FORMER CONGRESSMAN VIEWS
THE MONEY CHASE

When I first ran for the House in 1964, my total campaign budget was $30,000; my final campaign, in 1996, cost $1 million. The current system of financing congressional elections is a problem, and a serious one, for a variety of reasons.

Members of Congress must spend an enormous amount of time fund-raising. The money chase distorts the political process, crowding out other activities like writing laws, thinking about public policy, or meeting with ordinary voters. Incumbents know that the way to scare off competition is to raise a lot of money, and it has become a chief campaign tactic.

Many who contribute money are concerned about a "shakedown" atmosphere. They often feel they cannot get their views across unless they contribute generously to politicians they may dislike. The rising flood of money that flows into campaigns also undermines general public trust in the political system.

Changing the campaign finance system is terribly difficult. The blunt fact is that most members of Congress and both political parties prefer the system under which they were elected. . . . It is a system they know how to work for their advantage, and under which they have risen to the top. Moreover, it is very difficult to devise a system that will reduce the disproportionate influence of money in politics and still not trample on constitutional rights to express political views.

Source: Excerpted from Lee Hamilton, "Comments on Congress," Center on Congress, Indiana University, September 26, 2002. Used with permission.

PART FIVE

The Party in Government

In the spring of 2003, President George W. Bush had an advantage that few other recent presidents have enjoyed: His party was in the majority in both houses of Congress. With unified party control of both the White House and the legislative branch, it should have been a slam dunk for Bush to get his legislative proposals through the House of Representatives and the Senate. Yet when Bush asked his House Republican colleagues to soften the image of his proposed tax cuts by providing a larger child tax credit to low-income families, House Republican Majority Leader Tom DeLay had a concise response: "Ain't going to happen."[1]

Bush and DeLay are both important members of the Republican *party in government.* As you recall from Chapter 1, the party in government includes *any elected or appointed public officials* who see themselves as belonging to that party. They are vitally important to the party as a whole because it is the members of the party in government who pass and enforce laws. They, rather than the party organization or the party electorate, are the people who can legislate the party's proposals on college student loans, pornography, gun control, and child tax credits.

So if Bush and DeLay are part of the same party in government, why did they disagree on this bill? The Republican Party in government, like its Democratic counterpart, is a diverse group. In addition to the party in Congress, which consists of everyone elected to the House or the Senate as a Republican, and the Republican president, the Republican Party in government includes Republicans who work for federal, state, and local administrative agencies; Republican governors and state legislators; Republicans who serve in local elective and appointive office; and even judges (and Supreme Court Justices) who see themselves as Republicans. The 23-year-old Republican city council member in a small Michigan town may have a different perspective on some issues from the Republican U.S. secretary of state.

The design of the American political system works against a unified party in government. Because members of Congress are elected separately from the president, they do not need to act as a single Democratic or Republican "team." State and local officeholders, too, have been elected as individuals. They are not chosen to run by their party organization; rather, they become the party's candidates by winning voter support in primary elections. They deal with different constituencies and different pressures, so they may have different ideas from one another as to what their party in government should be doing. Federalism and the separation of powers, then, are formidable obstacles to the development of a united party that works at all levels of government to achieve a single, coherent set of policy objectives.

For decades, reformers have dreamed of an alternative. One of the most discussed is the idea of *party government,* or *responsible parties.* Its proponents suggest that American democracy would be improved if the parties were to offer clearer and fuller statements of their proposed policies, nominate candidates pledged to support those policies, and then see to it that their winning candidates enact those programs.[2] The parties would then let voters choose not only between candidates but, more importantly, between alternative sets of policies and be assured that the winning set would be put into effect. That would greatly strengthen the parties' role in American politics. Local, state, and national parties would work together as the main link between citizens and the uses of government power. Voters, the argument goes, would be better able to hold their government accountable.

Several European parties do behave more like responsible parties. In Britain, for example, the parliamentary system encourages the kind of legislative party unity that the advocates of responsible parties have in mind. The House of Commons selects the government's chief executive, the prime minister, from its own ranks; he or she must keep a legislative majority in order to stay in office. To do so, the parliamentary party is also likely to consult with the local party organizations that nominate candidates. This creates a powerful incentive for responsible parties. The party in government then tries to carry out a program that was adopted with the help of party leaders, activists, and members at party conferences.

Could this work in the United States? Probably not. The design of the American system is not likely to change. Because of the separation of powers, Republicans can hold a majority in Congress while a Democrat sits in the White House, or one party can dominate the House while the other controls the Senate. In fact, in the past half-century, divided control of government has been the norm at the national level and in most states. That makes it difficult for a party to implement all its preferred policies; instead, legislation is likely to involve compromise. Even at times when one party controls both Congress and the presidency, the legislative party might not always be in perfect agreement with its colleague in the White House, as the story of Bush and DeLay shows. The party organization can't guarantee that all the party's candidates, selected in primary elections in differing constituencies across the nation, will run on the party's platform. And the party electorate is still only loosely connected with the party organization.

However, the Democrats and the Republicans have been acting more like responsible parties in recent years. Congress and state legislatures now divide more along party lines than they have in decades. Partisanship has a major influence on the staffing of top executive offices and the appointment of judges. As more citizens are being attracted to party work because of particular issues that concern them, the pressure builds for greater party responsibility.

As a result, government policies change depending on the makeup of the party in government because the party winning the presidency is usually able to carry out much of its platform. Even after Republicans won majorities in both the House and Senate in 1994, for instance, an Associated Press analysis showed that there was a movement of federal spending from some areas of the nation to others, reflecting the priorities of the newly dominant Republicans. Cuts in public housing grants, food stamps, and child care programs took money away from poor rural and urban areas. On the other hand, increases in business loans and farm subsidies gave more federal spending to suburbs and farm areas. These are real, tangible indicators of a shift in priorities associated with the change in congressional party control, even though the presidency remained in Democratic hands.[3] It would be too strong to call the result an American twin of British party government, but we are probably safe in describing it as a distant cousin.

Why have these changes occurred? What does this party polarization mean for American politics? The chapters in Part Five address these questions of party influence in government. Chapters 13 and 14 examine the roles of the parties in the organization and operation of the legislature, the executive branch, and the courts. Chapter 15 looks at the degree to which party government can be said to exist in American politics.

Chapter 13

Parties in Congress and State Legislatures

Robin Hayes, a Republican, represents a North Carolina district where local textile companies have lost thousands of jobs. Hayes voted against a trade agreement backed by President Bush and the House Republican leadership, worried that it would further damage those textile companies. His party leaders in the House wouldn't take "no" for an answer, however; they kept the voting open for almost an hour, pressuring and pleading with a handful of rebellious Republican members to change their votes. In the end, Hayes reluctantly gave in after winning concessions for his district, and the measure passed by a two-vote margin. Party leaders warned another Republican that his district's sugar growers would be targeted for future legislative cuts if he didn't vote yes on the bill. "It was difficult, a gut-wrenching night," he said.[1]

The pressure on Robin Hayes is one of many examples of legislative party leaders "cracking down on wayward members . . . centralizing power and demanding discipline."[2] Party is even more central to the workings of Congress and most state legislatures today than it was for most of the 1900s. Congress and almost all state legislatures are organized by party. Each of the four congressional parties—the House Democrats, House Republicans, Senate Democrats, and Senate Republicans—is more unified internally, and legislative voting is more intensely partisan now than it has been for decades. There are sharp differences on important issues between the congressional Republicans and their Democratic colleagues. Yet there are still party "mavericks," legislators who vote against their party's position, sometimes even on big issues, who continue to be reelected by their constituents and who manage to live with their party leaders' disapproval.

The parties' recent increase in strength has not come easily. To be effective, they must fight an uphill battle against the system's design. One of the most basic rules of American politics, the separation of powers, undermines efforts at party unity. In a political system without a separation of powers—a parliamentary regime, such as that of Great Britain—the party that wins (or can put together a coalition of parties to win) a majority of seats in the legislature becomes the governing party and its leader becomes the prime minister. If the governing party is not able to muster a majority in parliament on a major issue, then either the governing cabinet must be reshuffled or the legislature must be dissolved and its members sent home to campaign for their jobs again. So there is little incentive for a legislator to vote for a bill sponsored by the opposition party. This creates powerful pressures for the legislative party to remain united.

American legislators do not face these pressures. They can reject the proposals of a president, a governor, or a legislative leader of their own party without bringing down the government and having to face a new election. Their constituents probably will not punish them for doing so. Yet in Congress and many state legislatures in the early 2000s, several forces are encouraging members of each legislative party to hang together.

How is this happening, even though the institutional rules don't require it? To some analysts, these increasing levels of party unity don't reflect the power of *party* in legislative life at all. Rather, they suggest, legislators rely on their own preferences on issues when they vote, and it happens that legislators from the same party tend to agree on their policy preferences.[3] However, there is ample evidence that party leadership, organizational reforms, and changes in the parties outside of Congress have expanded the roles of the legislative parties, and that parties structure the action in most state legislatures as well.[4] Let us begin with changes in the legislative leadership.

HOW THE PARTIES ARE ORGANIZED IN CONGRESS

When a new congressional session begins, the members of each party come together in both houses of Congress. These party meetings (called *caucuses* by the Democrats and *conferences* by the Republicans) select the leadership of the party (the leaders, whips, and committee chairs; see box on page 250). They also structure the chamber itself by nominating candidates for its presiding officer (the Speaker of the House of Representatives or president pro tempore of the Senate) and setting up procedures for appointing party members to congressional committees. In this way, the organization of the two parties is closely interwoven with the organization of the House and Senate as a whole.

The majority party dominates the organization of both houses. In the House, the majority party's elected leader, the Speaker, has extensive power over the working of the House. In the Senate, the majority leader manages floor action, to the degree that floor action can be managed in that highly individualistic institution. The majority party chooses the chairs of all the committees in both houses. It hires and fires the staff of these committees and of the chambers. Most of each committee's members come from the majority party, by a margin that is usually larger than the majority's margin in the chamber.

Especially in the House, then, the majority party controls the action in the committees and on the floor. From the early 1950s until 1994, the Democrats held this position in the House; since then and for much of the period since 1980 in the Senate, the Republicans have been in charge. This system was sorely tested in 2001 when, in what was justifiably called "uncharted territory," the Senate split 50–50 between the two parties. After a few months' experience with power sharing under a Republican "majority" (because Republican Vice President Dick Cheney had the power to break any tie votes), one Republican senator renounced his party ties and became an independent. That gave control to the Democrats—the first time in American history that party control of a house of Congress switched in the middle of a legislative session. Republicans regained the majority in 2002.

PARTY LEADERSHIP POSITIONS IN THE HOUSE AND SENATE

Each party creates its own leadership structure in each house of Congress; the individual leaders are elected by the entire party membership of the chamber. At the top of the hierarchy is the party leader (called the *majority* or *minority leader,* depending on whether the party controls the chamber). In the House of Representatives, the *Speaker* ranks above the majority leader as the true leader of the majority party. These party leaders have assistants called *whips* and *assistant whips* who tell members the party's position on bills, try to convince them to vote the way the party leadership wants, and keep a head count of each bill's supporters and opponents.

Each congressional party also has several specialized leadership positions. There is a *caucus* or (among Republicans) *conference chair* to head the meeting of all party members. Other chairs are selected for the *Steering Committee,* which assigns party members to committees; the *Policy Committee,* which identifies the party's position on proposed legislation and issue priorities; the *Campaign Committee,* which provides campaign support to the party's congressional candidates; and any other committees the legislative party may create. Variations do occur; House Democrats, for example, have a single Steering and Policy Committee.

Changes in the Power of House Party Leaders

The power of congressional party leaders has varied a lot over time. Much of the change reflects differences in the degree to which a party's members in Congress are willing to accept strong leadership. Because party leaders in Congress are chosen by the votes of all members of their legislative party, their power is, in effect, delegated to them by their party caucus (or conference) and they serve subject to its approval.[5] In addition, party leaders have differed in their styles of exercising power.

The Revolt Against "Czar" Cannon   Years ago, power in the House of Representatives was highly centralized in the hands of the Speaker. In the first decade of the 1900s, powerful Speaker Joe Cannon chaired the Rules Committee, the "traffic cop" through which he could control the flow of legislation to the floor. He appointed all standing committees and their chairs, putting his chief supporters in key positions, and generally had the resources and sanctions needed to enforce party discipline.[6] In 1910, however, dissidents within his own party combined with the minority Democrats to revolt against "Czar" Cannon. For decades after that, Speakers were not able to muster the kind of power that Cannon commanded. Instead, they had to operate in a much more decentralized House in which party discipline could be maintained only through skillful bargaining and strong personal loyalties. Successful Speakers during this era, such as Sam Rayburn and Tip O'Neill, were skilled negotiators rather than commanders.[7]

Growing Party Coordination   Party coordination has increased more recently, however, particularly in the House. The Republicans took a small step in this direction in the late 1960s, by giving rank-and-file party legislators more opportunity to influence policy through the party conference. In the 1970s, the Democrats, under the prodding of the reform-minded Democratic Study Group and the wave of liberals elected in the wake of the Watergate scandals, took more serious steps toward the same goal by strengthening both the party caucus and the party leadership.

Until that time, chairs of the standing committees that dealt with proposed legislation were selected using the *seniority rule:* the longest-serving member of the majority party on a committee automatically became its chair. Because of this rule, members of the majority party could win a chairmanship simply by being reelected to Congress many times, even if they did not support their party leadership's position on issues—in fact, even if they voted with the *other* party more often than with their own. That gave experienced party members a base of power in Congress independent of the party leaders. Committee chairs could, and often did, use that power in an autocratic manner.

To enhance its own power and to give rank-and-file Democrats more rights on their committees, the Democratic caucus revised the seniority rule in the mid-1970s. The caucus gave itself the power to challenge and even oust committee chairs by secret ballot. Soon after, some chairs were, in fact, challenged in the caucus and a few were defeated and replaced by the caucus's choice, who was not always the second most senior party member.[8] By reducing the power of the committee chairs, this reform expanded the power of their main competitors, the party leaders. That fundamentally changed the structure of authority within the Democrat-run House.

The power to assign members to committees was vested in the new Steering and Policy Committee chaired by the Speaker. The Speaker was also allowed to choose, with the caucus's approval, the chair and other Democratic members of the Rules Committee, whose independence had formerly been a real thorn in the side of the party leadership. Thus, the Speaker gained more power over the careers of other party legislators and over the fate of the bills that they wanted to pass. The whip system, a set of deputies responsible for informing their party colleagues about the party's stands and for finding out how many members are supporting those stands, was enlarged and made more responsive to party leaders.[9]

Policy Leadership   These reforms gave the legislative party in the House, with its strengthened leadership, the ability to use its new power to promote certain policy goals. Individual party members in the House were becoming more willing to use the party caucus to achieve these goals. One main reason is that both parties in the House became more ideologically homogeneous during the 1970s and 1980s.[10] Southern voters were leaving the Democratic Party in increasing numbers, and fewer conservative southern Democrats were being elected to Congress. Democratic House members, then, were more cohesively liberal than had been the case in many years. Because of the committee reforms, the remaining conservative southerners were losing their strongholds of committee power. Congressional Republicans had become more ideologically unified as well and were energized by the conservative policy leadership coming from the White House under Ronald Reagan in the 1980s.

When a party is ideologically cohesive, it is easier for the party caucus to agree on a unified position on legislation. The members of each of these ideologically cohesive parties could better trust that their leaders would share their policy concerns and protect their reelection interests. In addition, at this time, the two congressional parties were more at odds with one another on issues than they had been for some time. So the legislators of each party became more willing to grant power to their legislative party leaders, including the power to pressure straggling legislators to fall in line, in order to pass the party's legislation.[11]

Even with these changes, some party leaders were more willing than others to make use of the new opportunities for power. Speaker Jim Wright, during his brief tenure as party leader in the late 1980s, did take advantage of the changes to become one of the most assertive Democratic leaders in decades. His successor, Thomas Foley, was not as inclined to aggressive partisanship, and returned to a more collegial style before being defeated for reelection in the Republican surge of 1994.

The Gingrich Revolution

Ironically, given that the Democrats in the House had been the agent of stronger legislative party leadership during the 1970s and 1980s, it was a Republican who brought party leadership to its recent position of strength. The Republican minority had had no input into the Democratic procedural reforms of the 1970s and 1980s, but the 1994 election produced landmark changes. Republicans won a majority of House seats that year, after a campaign centered on their "Contract with America," a set of comprehensive, conservative policy pledges made most visible by the party's leader in the House, Representative Newt Gingrich.

The election of a number of new conservative members made the House Republicans even more cohesive. Most of these newcomers had gotten campaign help from Gingrich, and, together with their more senior colleagues, credited him with engineering their party's takeover of the House—the first Republican House majority in 40 years. However, the Republicans had only a slender majority in the House, and they faced a Democrat, Bill Clinton, in the White House. In order to fight for the goals of the Contract, GOP members were willing to accept strong party leadership and discipline.[12] They elected Gingrich Speaker and gave him unprecedented authority to push the Republican agenda.

One of the most important tools given to the leadership by the House Republican conference was the power to depart even more fully from the seniority rule. The leadership could now pick all the committee chairs on the basis of their commitment to bringing the party's desired bills to the floor, and each committee chair was limited to a six-year term. Gingrich was very willing to exercise that power. Why did the committee chairs, the chief losers in this extraordinary usurpation of committee power, agree to it? The new Republican majority was so uniformly conservative that the change may well have reflected their dedication to the party's policy agenda, the chairs' personal loyalty to Gingrich, or perhaps even fear for their political careers if they resisted. It was a giant step in the expansion of party power in the House, and Gingrich became the strongest Speaker in modern times.[13]

The result, at least initially, was a level of party discipline with which "Czar" Cannon probably would have felt comfortable. When the ten sections of the Contract with America came to a vote in the House, out of a possible 2,300 Republican voting decisions (ten provisions times 230 Republican House members), there were a grand total of only 111 "no" votes; 95 percent of the Republican votes supported the party leadership's position. To a greater extent than had been seen in almost a century, the party discipline was directed toward achieving the congressional party's policy goals.

. . . and Its Aftermath

Later in 1995, Gingrich's aura of invincibility started to crumble. When a standoff on the national budget between President Clinton and House Republicans led to a shutdown of the government, Gingrich and his colleagues got the blame. The Speaker was dogged by charges of ethics violations and declining popularity ratings. House Republicans were frustrated by his uneven leadership style. An aborted effort to oust him from the Speakership in 1997 had quiet help from some other Republican leaders. Then, when the GOP lost a net of five House seats in the 1998 election, there were widespread demands among House Republicans for new leadership. Gingrich resigned three days later; many wondered whether he had been better suited to lead a contentious minority than to manage the day-to-day demands of a majority.

Gingrich's successor, Dennis Hastert, did not begin by demanding unshakable party discipline, and his party colleagues, in 1999, were not as inclined to give it. Committee chairs were allowed to take the lead on most legislation, though the Republican Party leadership maintained control over the chairs' selection. Those who hoped to head committees after the first term-limited chairs had to step down in 2001 were in the unusual position of having to submit to interviews by Hastert and other party leaders as well as to the judgment of the party's backbenchers before the appointments were made.

After the Republicans made gains in the 2002 elections, the leadership, most of whom were conservative southerners, took the party leaders' power to a new level; as a Democratic strategist stated, the new Majority Leader, Tom DeLay, "exerts the kind of discipline that hasn't been seen in decades."[14] The term limit on the Speaker was eliminated, seniority rules were undercut even more in order to move loyal leadership allies into powerful subcommittee chairs, and party leaders cracked down on Republican colleagues who refused to follow the party's lead. Electoral gains in 2004 emboldened the leaders to force out two committee chairs for failing to toe the party line.[15] Democrats complained that they were being shut out of conference committees and other deliberations. Even though it commanded a relatively slim majority, the Republican leadership had become legendary at pushing legislation through the House.

The legend tarnished a bit in 2005. DeLay, nicknamed "The Hammer" for his relentless use of power, was forced to step down from his post after being indicted for campaign finance violations. A drop in President Bush's public approval ratings made it more difficult for his successor, John Boehner, to deliver Republican votes. The party's vaunted string of legislative successes began to fray. Legislative party cohesion, then, depends not only on broad policy agreement but also on the approach and skills of the party leaders and the party's standing in the wider political environment.

Parties in the "Individualist" Senate

Clearly, the job of a House party leader is challenging. But the work of the Senate's party leaders is more like herding cats. By the mid-1970s, Barbara Sinclair explains,[16] the U.S. Senate had moved from an institution governed by elaborate "rules" of reciprocity, specialization, and apprenticeship, in which powerful committees dominated the legislative work, to a much more individualistic body. Increasingly, and with avid media attention, members of the Senate established themselves as national spokespersons on various policy questions. Once they had become political "stars," these senators expected to participate more fully in the Senate's work, on their way, many hoped, to greater glory and higher office.

By the late 1980s, that individualism had led to a big increase in use (or the threat) of the unique Senate institution of the filibuster—the right of extended debate, used to talk a bill or a nomination to death if the votes were not available to defeat it in any other way. Senators are also able to use nongermane amendments (those with different subject matter from that of the bill) as a means of stalling it or getting other favored bills through. By the same time, changes in southern politics had led to greater party polarization in the Senate, just as they had in the House. Because it takes 60 votes to stop a filibuster, even a united majority party would not normally have enough votes to pass controversial bills without the help of at least some members of the minority party.

The combination of these rules with the increasing party polarization was potentially explosive. Issues reaching both houses of Congress were often contentious. Add to this a more partisan Senate and a set of rules that permitted any member to tie up the work of the institution for an indefinite period, and the result is a desperate need for a legislative traffic cop. Increasingly, it has been the party leadership in the Senate that has tried to direct the traffic. The Senate's rules do not allow the centralization of power in the party leadership that has been seen in the House since the 1990s, however.[17] So the Senate's majority and minority party leaders consult extensively with their party colleagues, rather than command them, to build the unanimous consent agreements that allow bills to be brought to a vote without risking a filibuster by an unhappy senator.

That has been an extremely difficult job. Small, organized groups of partisans intent on blocking a bill have become the main obstacles to these unanimous consent agreements. In fact, a central element in the minority party's strategy since the 1990s has been its ability to use the Senate's elaborate rules to take control of the legislative agenda from the majority party. In this polarized atmosphere, individual senators have come to depend on their party leaders to promote the legislative party's interests, both inside and outside the Senate chamber.

Even though the Republican Senate majority leader still defers to committee chairs to a greater extent than his House counterpart (the Speaker) does, the powers of party leaders in the Senate have been increased. Term limits were placed on committee chairs in 1995, and in 2005 Senate Majority Leader Bill Frist got the right to name half the membership of the most valued Senate committees. Frist did not need to follow seniority in awarding these seats. Because of the Senate's more individualistic rules, and the greater proportion of moderates in the Senate than in the House, this consolidation of power has taken time. Slowly, however, the Republican Revolution in the House is moving into the Senate.[18]

Parties in the State Legislatures

As in Congress, the legislative parties organize the legislatures in almost every state.[19] They structure everything from the legislative leadership to its committees. The power of the legislative parties varies, however, depending in part on the legislature's rules and on the personal skills and resources of the party leaders. In a few state legislatures, daily caucuses and strong party leadership make for a party every bit as potent as the Republicans in the post-1994 U.S. House. In others, especially the traditionally one-party states, party organization is weaker than it was in Congress before the reforms of the 1970s. There are states, for example, in which a majority party's caucus has split, either because of ideological differences or personal rivalries.

Most state legislative party leaders have a lot of power over the day-to-day workings of the legislature. They do not usually have to defer to powerful steering or policy committee chairs. The party leaders can appoint the members as well as the chairs of these committees, often without having to consider the members' seniority. Party leaders, then, can choose committee chairs and members on the basis of their support for the party leader personally or for their views on issues that the committee will consider. Even so, party leaders increasingly feel the need to consult with other legislators as they exercise their power. Members of state legislatures have become less tolerant of autocratic leadership, so the job of party leader is now "more complex and more challenging than in the past."[20]

Party leaders exercise their influence, in part, through the party caucus. Caucuses can be used for a number of purposes. In many states with strong two-party systems, party leaders call meetings to give members information about upcoming bills, learn whether their membership is united or divided on an issue, and encourage legislators to support the party's position. Leaders in a few of these states even try, occasionally, to get the caucus to hold a "binding" vote that calls on all members to support the party's position on an important issue. Where the state parties are not as strong, it is more common for the party caucus simply to offer information or allow leaders to hear members' opinions but not to try to build consensus.[21]

In sum, although the parties' legislative organizations look similar across the states—their party leadership positions are fairly uniform—they differ in their behavior. Party leaders' power can vary even between the two houses of the same state legislature, as do the influence and effectiveness of the party caucus.[22]

METHODS OF PARTY INFLUENCE

How do legislative parties and their leaders exercise their power? What resources can they use to influence their members' behavior?

Carrots and Sticks

Congressional party leaders have a variety of tools available to try to shape the behavior of their party colleagues. They tend to rely more on incentives than on punishments because the most effective punishments are limited in their use and occasionally have been known to backfire. The most powerful punishment would be to remove a maverick legislator from his or her seat in the House or Senate. Except in rare cases, however, such as that of Ohio Democrat James Traficant, who was in jail when the House expelled him in 2002, party leaders do not have that power. Only the legislator's constituents can do that, and they are not likely to serve as the agents of the congressional party leadership. So representatives and senators can normally vote against their party's leadership, or against major bills proposed by their party's president, without fear of losing their jobs.

Even the in-your-face disloyalty of supporting the other party's presidential candidate in the general election has not been punished consistently in Congress. In 1965, the

House Democratic caucus stripped committee seniority from two southern Democrats who had supported the Republican presidential candidate, Barry Goldwater, the year before. In 2000, however, a conservative Texas Democrat, Representative Ralph Hall, endorsed Republican George W. Bush for president and faced no sanctions from his party. (Hall switched parties in 2004.)

Perhaps the most famous example of the weakness of party penalties is the story of Phil Gramm, elected as a Democratic representative from Texas. The House Democratic leadership gave Gramm, a conservative, a seat on the prestigious House Budget Committee in return for his promise to cooperate with party leaders. But in 1983, members of the Democratic caucus were outraged to learn that Gramm had leaked the details of secret Democratic Party meetings on the Reagan budget to Republican House members. The caucus took away Gramm's seat on the Budget Committee.

Gramm did not accept his fate quietly. He resigned from the House and then ran—as a Republican—in the special election held to replace him. His constituents reelected him to the House and later to the Senate as a Republican. In fact, he was soon back on the House Budget Committee, courtesy of the Republican leadership! As long as legislative party leaders cannot keep a party maverick from being renominated and reelected and in districts where voters are not impressed by a legislator's party loyalty, party influence will be limited. So this step is taken only rarely. Several of Gramm's southern Democratic colleagues had voted for the Republican budget in 1983 but were not disciplined in any way. In fact, in 2004 President George W. Bush agreed to campaign in the Pennsylvania Republican primary for moderate Sen. Arlen Specter, who had voted against many of Bush's proposals, because the White House feared that Specter's conservative opponent, if he were to win the party's nomination, might lose the general election and thus endanger the GOP's Senate majority.

In sum, the House and Senate party leaders have a fairly short list of punishments at their command when trying to unify their parties, and using these punishments might do more harm than good. There is always the risk, especially when the two parties are closely matched in numbers, that punishing a legislator will cause him or her to defect or lose his or her seat to the other party or will give the party leadership a bad public image.

So the party organizations in Congress are more likely to rely on incentives to gain their members' loyalty. Party leaders can offer or withhold desirable committee assignments to cultivate party support. By using their control of floor activities, party leaders can set the agenda so as to maximize party unity on important matters.[23] They can help in passing a member's bills, promote pork barrel projects in the member's district, or help to protect local industries, as the example of Robin Hayes (see page 248) showed. They can give members useful information about the status of a bill on the legislative schedule. Some researchers find that junior members of Congress are more likely to vote with their party than are more senior members, perhaps because the newer legislators have greater need for the information or other resources that party leaders can provide.[24]

Party leaders have other persuasive resources as well. They can give speeches and raise money for a member's reelection effort. The parties' congressional campaign committees, with their newfound riches and services, have been a major factor in promoting party cohesion in Congress.[25] Some party leaders have enlisted the help of Washington lobbyists to help convince a member to vote with the party; business lobbyists have served this function for the House Republican leadership recently. Leaders can use their personal relationships with party colleagues to cajole them through careful listening and dialogue or through more hard-edged persuasion. On a recent House vote on school vouchers, for example, a *Washington Post* reporter described House Republican leaders surrounding a Kentucky Republican who had opposed the leadership on this bill the week before. A senior Democrat, "Representative David R. Obey (D-WI) took to the microphone. 'Is anyone from the office of the attending physician present?' he deadpanned. 'I understand someone's arm is being broken.'" The Republican did decide to vote for the bill.[26]

PARTY INFLUENCE ON LEGISLATIVE VOTING

How effective is this party influence? In voting on a bill, a member of Congress could be affected by any of several forces: not only party, but also his or her socioeconomic status, rural or urban roots, beliefs about the proper size of government, pressures from the president and campaign contributors, or regional concerns. Yet researchers have found that throughout American history, with only occasional exceptions, congressional votes have lined up along one primary dimension: that of liberalism versus conservatism. It is the parties in Congress that help to structure these voting patterns, whether through the direct impact of party leaders' persuasion or because of the ability of a member's partisanship to structure issues and create loyalties within his or her own mind.[27]

How Unified Is Each Legislative Party?

Several measures can be used to determine the impact of party on roll call votes. The first, *party voting,* is the proportion of roll calls on which most Democrats vote one way on a bill and most Republicans vote the other way. The second, *party unity scores* (or *party support*)*,* is the degree to which legislators vote with their party's majority on these party votes.

Party Voting   One way to measure party voting is to use the toughest test: any legislative roll call in which at least 90 percent of one party's members vote yes and 90 percent or more of the other party vote no. By such a strict test, party discipline appears regularly in the British House of Commons and the German Bundestag, but not as often in American legislatures. Under Czar Cannon, about a third of all roll calls in the House met this standard of party discipline. From 1921 through 1948, that dropped to only 17 percent,[28] and it declined steadily to about 2 to 8 percent in the 1950s and 1960s. During approximately the same period in the British House of Commons, this striking party division occurred on almost every roll call.

Since the 1990s, however, there has been a notable increase in "90 percent votes" in Congress. In 2005, for example, both houses were almost perfectly divided by party on a number of President Bush's proposals (see Figure 13.1), including the war in Iraq, funding for education and other social services, environmental issues, and taxes. Generally, Republicans were more likely to reach this 90 percent level than were Democrats. Consider Case 4 in Figure 13.1, which shows the party division in the Senate on legislation that would have held gun manufacturers responsible for gun violence.

Two years earlier, House members surpassed even this high level of party voting. During the first three months of 2003, House Republicans voted *unanimously* 44 percent

Case 1: Should the U.S. get out of Iraq as soon as possible by transferring responsibility for Iraq's security to the Iraqi people?

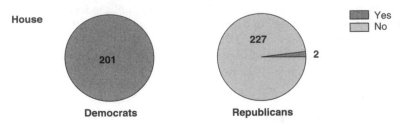

Case 2: Should some (faith-based) job training programs be able to use religion as a factor in their hiring decisions?

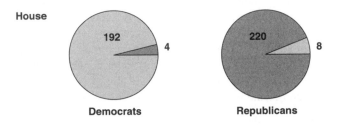

Case 3: Restore education funding that had been cut by the Bush administration?

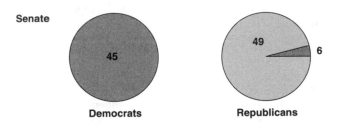

Case 4: Should cities and individuals be able to sue gun manufacturers in order to hold them responsible for gun violence?

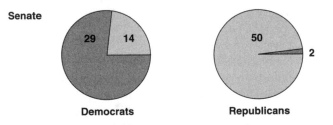

FIGURE 13.1   Congressional Party Unity and Disunity: 2005

Note: The figure shows the numbers of Democrats and Republicans in the Senate and House casting "yes" and "no" votes on the bills named. Representative Bernard Sanders (I-VT) and Senator James Jeffords (I-VT) are counted as Democrats because they caucus with the Democrats.

Source: CQ Weekly, March 21, 2005, p. 739 (restoring cuts in education funding); August 8, 2005, p. 2195 (civil lawsuits against gun manufacturers); July 25, 2005, p. 2062 (Iraq); and March 7, 2005, p. 586 (job training).

of the time, and their Democratic counterparts did so on almost one-fourth of all roll calls. The number of unanimous roll call votes was higher in all of 2003 than it had been in more than 40 years.[29] These levels dropped in 2004 as the congressional elections approached. Yet in a system of separated powers, this is a remarkable demonstration of party solidarity.[30]

The 90 percent standard is too strict, however, for a look at the American legislative experience over time. So researchers have focused on a less demanding measure: the *party vote,* or the percentage of roll calls in which the *majority* of one party opposed a majority of the other. By this measure, the 1990s produced the highest levels of congressional party voting in many years.

Let us start where senators think we should—with the Senate. During the late 1960s and early 1970s, a majority of Democrats opposed a majority of Republicans in only about one-third of all Senate roll-call votes.[31] By 1995, the figure was up to 69 percent, the highest recorded in the Senate since the 1950s. That dropped to an average of 54 percent beginning in 2000, but not because the two parties were less unified. Rather, the Senate was so closely divided that party leaders avoided bringing highly partisan issues to a vote unless they felt confident of winning. When these issues *did* come to a vote and a majority of Republicans opposed a majority of Democrats, the former voted with their party's position 90 percent of the time in 2004, compared with 83 percent for the Democrats.

Party voting has been even more prevalent in the House at times. In the 1800s, congressional party voting was substantial (although still far below that of the British Parliament). This was a time when the parties were competitive in most congressional districts, party leaders wielded considerable legislative authority, and Congress was a much less professionalized institution. After 1900, following a decline in the party-based link among candidates for different offices and the development of a more professionalized Congress,[32] party voting decreased markedly. The start of the New Deal party system in the 1930s increased the frequency of party votes for a time, before it fell again to twentieth-century lows in 1970 and 1972 (27 percent).

Beginning in the mid-1980s, for reasons we will discuss shortly, party voting in the House reached levels not seen since the partisanship of the New Deal; a 50-year high of 73 percent was recorded in the rancorous 1995 session (see Figure 13.2).[33] These levels could not be sustained after 1995; the figure remained in the 45 percent range from 2000 until 2004. However, as was the case in the Senate, on votes in which a majority of Republicans did oppose a majority of Democrats, a full 88 percent of Republicans voted with their party in 2004, as did 86 percent of Democrats.

In state legislatures, there is a lot of variation in levels of party voting, both across the states and within a given state from one political generation to the next. We are most likely to see party voting in states where the two parties are closely balanced in strength in the legislature, so both parties feel they have a chance to get their bills passed. It is also more common where the two parties represent distinctive groups of voters—for example, in urban, industrialized states where Democratic strength is concentrated among union members and blacks in the big cities, and Republican state legislators tend to represent suburban and rural districts that are largely white and conservative. As is the case in Congress, state legislative parties are more likely to accept strong party leadership when the parties are highly polarized. Party voting in southern states, then, such as Texas and Florida, has been increasing in the 1990s.[34]

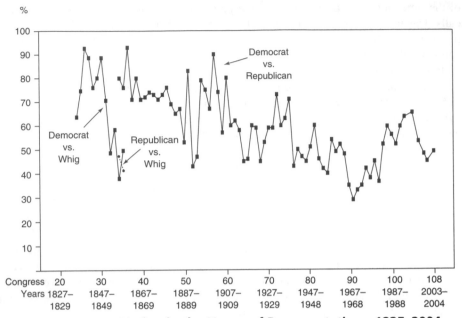

FIGURE 13.2   Party Voting in the House of Representatives: 1835–2004

Note: Entries are the percentage of roll-call votes on which a majority of one party opposed a majority of the other party. Because party voting tends to decrease in the even-numbered years, as an election approaches, the data are averaged across the two sessions of each Congress.

Source: For 24th through 36th Congresses, Thomas B. Alexander, *Sectional Stress and Party Strength* (Nashville, TN: Vanderbilt University Press, 1967). For 37th through 93rd Congresses, Jerome B. Chubb and Santa A. Traugott, "Partisan Cleavage and Cohesion in the House of Representatives, 1861–1974," *Journal of Interdisciplinary History* 7 (1977), 382–383. More recent data are from *CQ Weekly,* reported in December or early January issues.

Party Support   To what extent do legislators support their party on party votes? From the 1940s into the 1960s, conservative southern Democrats often crossed the aisle to vote with Republicans in the House and Senate, and their defections were tolerated by the decentralized party leadership of that time. This cross-party alliance, known as the *conservative coalition,* came together to oppose civil rights bills and Democratic labor and education proposals, and lowered party support scores, especially among the Democrats.

The reshaping of the Democratic Party's supporting coalition in the South seriously undercut the conservative coalition in the 1960s and 1970s, however. As we have seen, when the Voting Rights Act brought southern blacks into the electorate, some of the conservative southern Democrats in Congress switched to the Republican Party, and others were defeated by more moderate and liberal Democrats. Thus the dwindling ranks of southern Democrats were dominated by more liberal representatives. That meant fewer policy disagreements between northern and southern Democrats. The organizational reforms discussed earlier in the chapter, which reduced the power of committee chairs and strengthened the power of party leaders, also made it easier for the

THE DARK SIDE OF PARTISANSHIP: A LACK OF CIVILITY

With partisanship at a recent high in both the House and the Senate, it would not be surprising if the elaborate rituals of respect that characterized Congress decades ago had begun to fade. After some glimmers of bipartisan cooperation in 2001, particularly after the terrorist attacks of September 11, one observer had this to say about the events of one week in February 2002: "Capitol Hill is breaking down into fierce, partisan encampments. . . . All thought of a bipartisan, working relationship in Congress has been wiped aside by bitter, incendiary language and incriminating gestures of contempt and disparagement.

"In short, it's back to business as usual."

Then things got worse. In July 2003, the House Ways and Means Committee met to discuss a bill to revise the pension system. Democratic committee members objected to Republican chair Bill Thomas's effort to substitute his own version of the bill for the bipartisan draft under consideration. After some taunting remarks by the chair, outraged Democrats left the room and gathered in a nearby library. Thomas demanded that the Capitol Police remove the migrating Democrats. A police commander, reluctant to arrest House members for milling around in a library, declined to handcuff or evict them. Thomas later apologized on the House floor.

This was one in a long series of incidents showing the heavy-handed use of majority power that has characterized the Congress in recent years, under both Republican and Democratic majorities. In a sign of the times, in 2004 the usual bipartisan "civility retreat" for House members was canceled for lack of interest. "Some people don't want to get along with members of the other party," said a Republican leader. "They view them as the enemy."

Sources: John Cochran, "Disorder in the House—And No End in Sight," *CQ Weekly,* April 3, 2004, p. 790; and Juliet Eilperin and Albert B. Crenshaw, "The House That Roared," *Washington Post,* July 19, 2003, p. A1.

Democratic leadership to unify its party and fend off Republican appeals to more conservative Democrats.[35] By the 1990s, then, the Democratic Party in both House and Senate was more unified than it had been in decades.[36] The new Republicans elected from the South contributed to the growing conservatism of congressional Republicans in the 1970s and early 1980s, and since that time, non-southern Republicans have become more conservative as well.[37]

For these reasons, party support scores continued to rise, especially among the Republicans once they took control of Congress in 1995 (see Figure 13.3). As a result, there are very clear—and often bitter—differences on issues between the House Democrats and the House Republicans (see box on this page). Consider this example: When the Americans for Democratic Action (ADA), a liberal group, examined how often legislators voted with the ADA's position on 20 key votes, the median score for Democratic senators in 1999 was 100 percent and that of the Republicans was zero. The House pattern was almost as stark.[38]

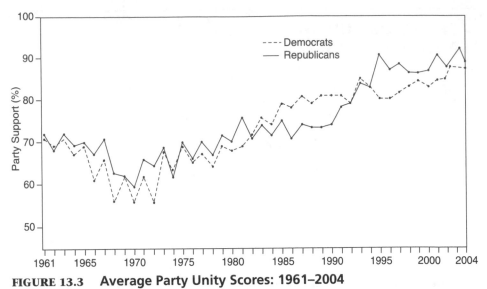

FIGURE 13.3 **Average Party Unity Scores: 1961–2004**

Note: Entries are the average percentages of members voting in agreement with a majority of their party on party unity votes—those in which a majority of one party voted against a majority of the other party. Figures for the House and Senate are combined.

Source: CQ Weekly, December 11, 2004, p. 2952.

Greater Polarization of the Congressional Parties

This increase in party voting and party support, then, has accompanied an increasing polarization of the two parties in the House and Senate (see Figure 13.4). The Democratic parties have become more liberal and the Republican parties more conservative than had been the case in 50 years, and the party leadership has become more polarized and partisan as well. Although the major cause of this polarization has been the change in southern party coalitions, anticipated and encouraged by southern candidates and party leaders, the declining competitiveness of House elections has had an impact as well. If their district has been drawn to favor a candidate of their party, then the only competition candidates need fear is from another candidate of their party, in the primary election. In a primary, a Republican incumbent is most likely to be challenged from the right; for a Democratic incumbent, challenges tend to come from the left. That encourages House members to move toward the extreme of their party rather than toward the center. This pressure is substantial; one study finds that a credible primary challenge moves a typical candidate for Congress fully 10 points along a 100-point conservative-to-liberal scale.[39] Thus, safer House seats, at least in the current political environment, may well discourage moderation or compromise across party lines.

When Are the Parties Most Unified?

Students of Congress and state legislatures find that three types of issues are most likely to prompt high levels of party voting and party support: those touching the interests of the legislative party as a group, those involving support of or opposition to an executive program, and those concerning the issues that clearly divide the party voters.

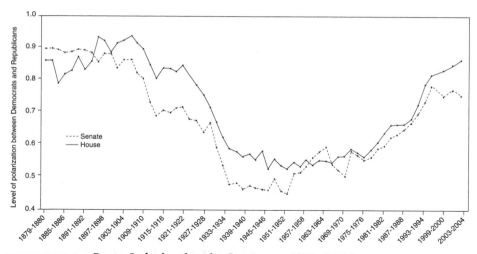

FIGURE 13.4 **Party Polarization in Congress: 1879–2004**

Note: Entries are the difference in mean DW-NOMINATE scores between the Democratic and Republican Parties in each house for each Congress. These scores estimate the position of each legislator on a liberal-conservative dimension by using the scaling of roll call votes; higher values (closer to 1.0) mean greater difference between the parties.

Source: Keith T. Poole, http://pooleandrosenthal.com/Polarized_America.htm (accessed September 24, 2005). See Keith T. Poole, Howard Rosenthal, and Nolan McCarthy, *Polarized America* (Cambridge, MA: MIT Press, 2006).

Issues That Touch the Interests of the Legislative Parties produce the greatest party unity. Among the best examples are the basic votes to organize the legislative chamber. In Congress, for instance, it is safe to predict 100 percent party unity on the vote to elect the Speaker of the House. In 2005, when the 109th Congress began, Republican Dennis Hastert got every Republican member's vote for Speaker and lost every Democratic vote. (Hastert did get one Democratic vote for Speaker in 2001, from the eccentric Representative Traficant, prior to his move to a federal prison.)

The parties also tend to be highly unified on issues affecting their numerical strength. In a 1985 vote on whether to award a congressional seat to Democrat Frank McCloskey or Republican Richard McIntyre after a disputed Indiana election, for instance, House Democrats voted 236 to 10 to seat McCloskey and Republicans voted 180 to 0 for McIntyre. Party discipline runs high in state legislatures over issues such as laws regulating parties, elections, and campaigning; the seating of challenged members of the legislature; and the creation or alteration of legislative districts, all issues that touch the basic interests of the party as a political organization.

The Executive's Proposals Legislators often rally around their party's executive or unite against the executive of the other party. This partisanship has been mounting. Figure 13.5 traces the support that each legislative party has given to the president on issues that he clearly designated a part of his program. In the late 1960s, on average, members of a president's party in Congress voted for his program about 60 percent of the time; by the early 2000s, it was almost 90 percent. In 2003, the recent high point in these scores,

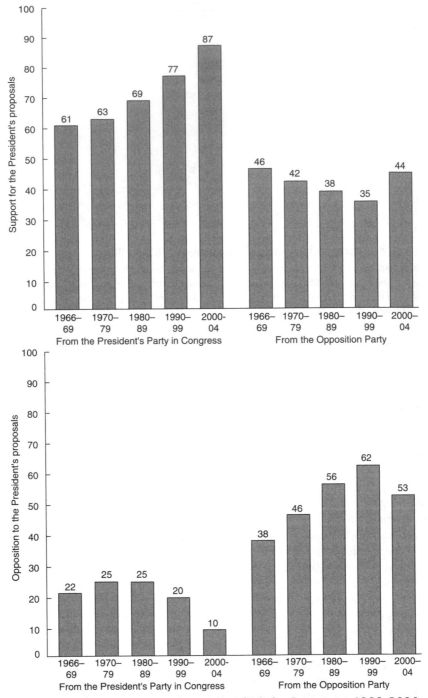

FIGURE 13.5   Party Support of the President in Congress: 1966–2004

Note: Entries are the percentages of the time, averaged by decade, that members of each party supported the announced position of the president.

Source: CQ Weekly, December 11, 2004, p. 2946.

Republican senators supported President Bush's position 94 percent of the time and Republican House members did so on 89 percent of these votes.

Conversely, the opposition party's support for a president's program has decreased steadily,[40] at least until the terrorist attacks of 2001 interrupted the downward trend. During the 1990s, the opposition supported the president's proposals only about one-third of the time, on average. The Clinton presidency is an excellent example of this party polarization. In the early years of Clinton's first term, Democrats' support for their president was higher than it had been since the mid-1960s, and Republicans' support was relatively low. The president became an even more powerful partisan trigger in 1998, when Clinton was impeached by the House for lying about his sexual relationship with a White House intern. Sparked by strongly antagonistic congressional party leaders on both sides of the aisle, the House vote to impeach and the Senate vote to acquit Clinton were close to being party-line votes. As an expert observer puts it, "On what everyone claimed was a conscience vote, 98 percent of Republican consciences dictated a vote to impeach the president, while 98 percent of Democratic consciences dictated the opposite."[41] In 2000, Clinton's last year as president, there was a difference of almost 50 percentage points between Republicans' and Democrats' support of the president's position.

When the president's party in Congress marches in lock-step with the president's proposals, then it is important to ask whether Congress continues to play an independent role in the business of governing. It is the White House now where the main debates over budget priorities take place. The minority party's united opposition can be a potential check on the executive, of course. But especially in the House, where even a slim majority can exercise a great deal of control, there is reason to ask whether Congress has given up some of its own powers to the president.

Policies Central to the Party System   Legislative parties are especially unified on issues that fundamentally divide the parties in the electorate—the "label-defining" issues.[42] At the time of the Civil War, the questions of slavery and Reconstruction generated the greatest party conflict and internal party cohesion. These issues were displaced by conflicts between agrarian and industrial interests in the 1890s. Now the parties are most cohesive on the role of government in the economy and in people's personal lives, including taxes, the regulation of business, abortion, and gay marriage.

In many state legislatures, for instance, an attempt to change the rules governing the hiring of teenagers by local businesses will pit one unified party against another, with the legislators' pro-labor or pro-management stands reinforced by their roots in their home districts and by their own values. Other such issues include Social Security, welfare, environmental issues, the rights of women and minority groups, and aid to agriculture. In Congress, a similar set of issues—social welfare, government management of the economy, and agricultural aid—has produced the most cohesive partisan voting over the years.[43]

Party divisions on issues are especially sharp in the early years of a new party system, when the coalitional bases of the parties have undergone substantial change.[44] The trend line in Figure 13.2 confirms that party voting in the House has generally peaked during these times. These changes can focus attention on national rather than local issues, so they overcome the inherent localism of Congress. They promote party unity and encourage party discipline on the issues most central to the new party system.

Does Party Competition Promote Party Unity?

The amount of competition between the two parties has an interesting relationship with party voting. At the level of the individual legislator, those from marginal districts, where the two parties have relatively equal shares of the electorate, are less likely to vote with their legislative party than are those from safer districts. Two characteristics of marginal districts encourage a legislator to be highly sensitive to the constituency at times when constituency opinion conflicts with the party's position on an issue. In many marginal districts, the groups that support Democrats or Republicans differ from those more typically associated with the party. When party voters in a district hold different views from the national or state party on a big issue, a representative will usually need to bend to constituency wishes in order to get reelected, even if that means opposing his or her legislative party's position. Party leaders may not insist on the member's party loyalty in such situations; they would rather have a legislator who will at least vote for the party's candidate for Speaker than a totally loyal legislator who is defeated for reelection because his or her constituents do not want what the national party is selling. And both parties in marginal districts often have strong organizations and appealing candidates. Where constituency and party point in different directions, most legislators remember that their constituents, not their party leadership, gave them their job.

In the current Congress, small groups within both parties resist the influence of their legislative party leaders and cling to more moderate positions "because they are convinced that is what their constituents want."[45] Within the Democratic Party, a group of about 35 "Blue Dogs"—many of them southerners—sometimes votes with the Republicans on tax and social issues. In contrast with the earlier conservative coalition, however, the "Blue Dog Democrats" have largely been frozen out by the Republican leadership. So, although the Blue Dogs' party support scores are about 10 percent lower than the average Democrat, these scores are higher than they were in 1995.

Even the highly unified Republicans struggle to deal with a small group of moderates within their ranks. About two dozen moderates in the House and a handful in the Senate, mainly from the Northeast, continue to break with their party on environmental, fiscal, and social issues because their constituencies are unlike those of most of their GOP colleagues. During Senate debate over President Bush's tax cut proposals, for example, less than a handful of moderate Republicans, just enough to swing the close vote, succeeded in reducing the cuts and offsetting some of them with savings in other areas. A few Republican senators balked at the president's request that Congress slow the growth of Medicaid spending in 2006, because their home states' governors worried about the impact on state budgets. Many more Republicans declined the opportunity to support Bush's plan to revise Social Security, in the face of mounting public disapproval. As long as the American parties cannot protect legislators from constituency pressures, and as long as what it means to be a Republican in New York differs from what it means to be a Republican in Texas, then party cohesion will suffer.

At the level of the legislature as a whole, however, close party competition can increase party voting. When there are clear differences between the parties on issues, closely competitive parties feel the need to hold on to every legislative vote. In contrast, when a party wins a comfortable majority, it can become flabby and vulnerable to squabbles among regional or personal cliques. That was true of many legislative parties in the South during the period of one-party Democratic rule. It is true today in state legislatures in which one party has a lopsided majority, such as the Republicans in the Idaho and Kansas state legislatures.[46]

COMPARING PARTY POWER IN CONGRESS AND STATE LEGISLATURES

In sum, based on what we know about the role of parties in the U.S. House and Senate and the state legislatures, we can draw some conclusions about the conditions most likely to produce strong legislative parties and the places where they are likely to appear.

Party Polarization and Cohesion   Legislators are more likely to accept strong party leadership if there are clear differences between the parties: if the two parties represent different sets of interests in the state or nation. So legislative party strength has long flourished in northeastern states, such as Connecticut, New York, and New Jersey, where the two parties have quite different bases of support. The increasing party polarization at the national level has been associated with an increase in party strength in Congress as well, especially in the House, whose rules, as we have seen, permit greater control by the leadership. When the constituencies represented by a party are similar across districts, then the party's legislators are more likely to be cohesive in their interests. This also encourages them to accept strong party leadership in order to translate those interests into policy.

Greater Interparty Competition   When the two parties in a legislature are relatively evenly balanced numerically, "the majority party must stick together to get legislation passed, and the minority party has some realistic chance of winning if it can remain cohesive."[47] Close party competition gives both parties an incentive to remain unified, as do situations in which a governor has been elected from the minority party, which sees the opportunity to pass the governor's program if it stays together. Party cohesion in the U.S. House and Senate has increased during recent years in which the two houses have been closely divided by party.

No Competing Centers of Power   A legislature's standing committees may serve as sources of power rivaling those of the party leaders, as was the case in Congress when seniority was the only criterion for becoming a committee chair. When committee chairs are chosen on the basis of some criterion other than party loyalty, then chairs owe less to their party leadership. As we have seen, this is no longer the case in either the Senate or the House, and seniority is not often used in state legislatures as a basis for appointing members to powerful positions. Other centers of power in some states—powerful business groups, labor unions, ideological groups or other big contributors—are often closely allied with one party's leaders.

Other Needed Resources   Where the party organizations have more to offer a legislator, he or she will be more inclined to follow the organization's lead in legislative voting. In many state legislatures as well as Congress, party leaders can use their power over the legislative agenda to help a member get a desired bill passed. Pork barrel projects in the member's home district can be moved up or down on the agenda by legislative party leaders to help to maintain the loyalty of their party colleagues, as happens in Congress and in at least some parliamentary democracies.[48] In some states, these material rewards, which also include patronage and other forms of governmental preference, are more abundant than in the national government.

The party organizations outside the legislature can also influence legislative voting if they control important resources. Just as in Washington, the leaders of many state parties have become more active in recruiting candidates for the legislature, and some may be able to convince local activists and voters to oppose the renomination of candidates disloyal to the party (although that ability can always be undermined by primary elections). Further, it is not as rare in the states, as it is in Washington, where serving in Congress is a full-time job, for state and local party leaders to *be* legislative leaders as well.

State and local parties are also important to state legislative candidates because of the campaign money that they can provide. Many states place no ceilings on party contributions to campaigns, so parties can make substantial investments, if they wish. The parties' legislative campaign committees help out in most states, and legislative party leaders' personal political action committees help in some.[49] Given the shortage of campaign funds at this level, many candidates look beyond the legislative campaign committees to the state parties themselves for campaign money and services. The state parties are better prepared to respond now than they have been in the past.

Lesser Legislative Professionalism   Congress has evolved into a highly professional legislative body. Each member controls a sizable and well-paid personal staff and a considerable budget, which are used to meet the member's legislative and reelection needs. The office has become a full-time job with high pay and good benefits. Although state legislatures have become more professional as well, very few provide ordinary members with levels of support that even approach those in the Congress. Staff and budget resources are usually minimal. Most state legislators are lucky to have as much as a private office and a personal secretary. Many state legislatures meet for only part of the year and pay so little that most members must hold other jobs and live only temporarily in the capital. With such limited personal resources, legislators in most states welcome additional help in performing the tasks of legislative life. Party leaders can often provide such help. When a state legislator depends on the party leadership for needed resources, he or she has a greater incentive to listen when a leader calls for party discipline.

Styles of Individual Leaders   Just as party leaders in the U.S. House and Senate have varied in their leadership styles and in their willingness to take up the tools of strong leadership, so do legislative party leaders in the states. Their experiences and abilities interact with the situation of their party, whether it is a powerful majority, a competitive minority, or a weakened minority, to determine whether they function effectively in uniting their party members and getting their bills passed.

THE POWER OF LEGISLATIVE PARTIES

The story that this chapter tells is complex. On the one hand, parties are at the very center of the legislative process. Some even view them as "legislative leviathans" that dominate the business of Congress in order to benefit their individual members.[50] Party affiliation does more to explain the legislative behavior of state legislators and Congress

---

WHICH WOULD YOU CHOOSE?

SHOULD YOUR REPRESENTATIVE LISTEN MORE CLOSELY TO THE PARTY OR TO THE CONSTITUENTS?

To the constituents: This sounds like a no-brainer. If we elect members of Congress, they ought to represent the interests of their constituents, right? We have a single-member district system with candidate-centered campaigns; that encourages us to focus on the qualities of individual candidates rather than on the party's platform or plans. We vote for a candidate, and he or she goes to Washington and is then supposed to do whatever we ask. Why should the legislator listen to the party leadership?

To their party: This constituent-centered approach sounds good, but it isn't realistic. How are members of Congress supposed to know what each of their 675,000 constituents wants? Isn't it better for the two major parties to offer competing answers on issues, press their legislative party members to pass these policies, and then let voters decide whether they like the results? That asks less of us as voters and probably corresponds more closely to the (minimal) time that we are willing to spend on politics. Besides, by taking a longer view, the parties can look beyond local concerns to a broader national interest.

To both: As we have seen, when the various constituencies that a party's legislators represent become more similar in views and more different from the constituencies of the other party, then most legislators don't have to choose between constituents and party. At these times, members can vote with their party colleagues and also speak for the interests and the voters who, in their view, sent them to the legislature. So party and constituency are not necessarily in conflict.

---

members than does any other single factor in their environment. There has been an increase in party unity and polarization in recent years in both the U.S. House and Senate.

Yet even now, most American legislative parties are not as unified as those of most other democracies. Although the legislative parties in Congress and the states have been strengthened, the primary relationship in American legislatures is between representatives and their constituents rather than between legislators and their party leaders or party organizations (see "Which Would You Choose?"). The increasing polarization of constituents, however, has made the choice less difficult for most members of Congress.

This is another instance in which the fragmenting institutions of American government have left their mark. Because of the separation of powers, there is no institutional need for a party to remain internally unified, as there is in parliamentary systems.[51] Under certain conditions, such as when the party's legislative constituencies are more alike in their preferences and more different from those of the other party, the legislative parties will be more unified and party voting will be common. That has been strikingly true in the U.S. Congress and many state legislatures in recent years. However, at other times, when greater localism and sectionalism have existed, the legislative parties have been weak and fractured.[52] In legislatures in the U.S., party leaders cannot take their power for granted.

Chapter 14

The Party in
the Executive
and the Courts

Although more than a hundred million Americans went to the polls in 2000, the final decision as to who would be president was made by 16 judges. First, the Florida Supreme Court, all of whose members had been appointed by Democratic governors, ruled in favor of Democratic candidate Al Gore, who had argued that a hand recount of ballots in Florida should be allowed to continue. Then the U.S. Supreme Court decided that the recount should be shut down, thus handing the presidency to George W. Bush. All five of the Supreme Court justices who voted to support Bush, a Republican, had been appointed by Republican presidents.[1]

This looks suspiciously like partisan behavior—but how could that be, in high courts that most Americans prefer to see as nonpartisan? Could it have been a remarkable coincidence? Or is it time to set aside the notion that the courts are "above party politics"?

In fact, as we see in this chapter, American executives and judges have been in the thick of party politics since the nation began. Many presidents and governors behave like party leaders, and even though the writers of the Constitution designed an independent federal court system with lifetime appointments, hoping that it would be protected from the bruising battles of partisanship, it has never been possible to design judges who are free of party identification. The heated partisan confrontations over the nomination of Supreme Court judges show very clearly that judicial appointments are matters of great partisan concern.

In many ways, partisanship has penetrated more deeply into the executive and judicial branches in the United States than it has in other Western democracies. As Chapter 2 showed, the push for popular democracy led to the election of public officials who would be appointed to their jobs in most other nations, such as state school superintendents and local judges. When judges and administrators are elected, the door is open to party influence in their elections. Even when these officials are appointed, one legacy of the long tradition of patronage in American politics is that party affiliation is a common criterion in the appointment process.

If partisanship affects their selection, does it also influence the ways in which judges and administrators use their powers? Do Democratic voter registration officials make different decisions from their Republican brethren? If you go to court as a criminal defendant, will you get a different ruling from a Democratic judge than you would from a Republican? If so, does this reflect party organizations' efforts to influence the behavior of executives and judges? Or is it simply that people who consider themselves Democrats tend to share similar attitudes toward political issues, whether they are voters, county surveyors, or Supreme Court justices, and the same is true of those who identify as Republicans?

PRESIDENTS AND GOVERNORS AS PARTY LEADERS

American presidents were not always the dominant figures that they are today. In the 1920s, it was possible for President Calvin Coolidge to sleep for ten or eleven hours every night, followed by a three-hour afternoon nap; government and politics went on without him. But as the United States' role as a world power grew and Franklin D. Roosevelt expanded the federal government to bring the nation out of the Great Depression, presidents were pulled into the public spotlight.

The spread of television and radio into almost every American home further elevated the presidency. These media naturally focus on individual personalities such as presidents and governors; it is harder for the media to tell an interesting story about faceless institutions such as Congress. Presidents, in particular, have become leading public figures, capable of arousing the most passionate loyalties and hatreds. This increase in personal leadership can be seen even in nations with parliamentary systems, whose election campaigns increasingly center on the potential prime ministers.[2]

As the most visible members of the party in government, presidents often come to personify their party at the national level, just as many governors do within their states. In the words of a congressional aide, "The president becomes the face of your party."[3] To the extent that presidents and governors are central to their party's public image, then their successes and failures can affect their party's fortunes in elections.

Presidents don't normally serve as formal party leaders, although they do choose the leadership and shape the functioning of their party's national committee. In recent years, however, several presidents have involved themselves extensively in party organizational efforts by helping to recruit party candidates, campaigning with them, and raising money for the party. These efforts have helped to strengthen the bond between presidents and the party colleagues in Congress for whom they campaign. Especially in the current polarized atmosphere in Washington and in many state capitals and when the party division in the legislature is close, executives have good reason to nurture their ties with their party's legislators in order to get the votes needed to pass their policies.

The President as Campaigner-in-Chief

Recent presidents have invested a lot of energy in their party's campaign activities. One especially welcome form of help involves raising money; presidents are normally a big draw on the fund-raising circuit. George W. Bush, who has broken all campaign finance records in his own races, has been an unparalleled fund-raiser for Republican congressional and statewide candidates as well.

Presidents can do a great deal more for their party organizations. They are, for example, persuasive recruiters of candidates. The state or national party organization often finds itself in the difficult position of trying to convince an attractive but reluctant prospect to run for a governorship or to give up a safe House seat in order to challenge a potentially vulnerable opposition senator. When the unwilling target of the party's affections is invited to dinner at the White House to hear how personally important the race is to the president of the United States, the party's job gets easier.

Take the example of the South Dakota Senate race in 2002. To have a chance of regaining control of the U.S. Senate, the national Republican Party needed a highly effective candidate to run against Democrat Tim Johnson. Party leaders set their sights on Republican John Thune, a popular House member. Thune had planned to run for governor that year, a race he was expected to win easily. After repeated conversations with Bush and top Republican strategists, Thune gave up the "easy" governor's race and ran against Johnson instead.[4]

White House leverage is also useful in clearing a path for the party's preferred nominee. In 2001, for instance, Vice President Dick Cheney persuaded a Minnesota Republican to give up a bid for the state's 2002 Senate nomination—just 90 minutes prior to the scheduled press conference at which he was to announce his candidacy—to clear the way for a candidate the party regarded as stronger. "I was de-cruited," explained the suddenly retired candidate.[5] Fund-raisers featuring President Bush have been scheduled in states and congressional districts more than a year before the election, to give the Republican favored by the White House an early fund-raising lead and thus to scare off potential opponents.

In the 2002 campaigns, with party control of the Senate on the line, the president took frequent trips to states where Republican House and Senate candidates were in close races and where the president was popular. During the week before the election, he visited up to five states a day to increase Republican turnout. One was Georgia, where Representative Saxby Chambliss was running behind incumbent Democratic Senator Max Cleland in the polls. Chambliss, who had been recruited to run by the White House, asked for Bush's help; "There's only one guy who can juice" potential Republican voters, said Chambliss' aide.[6] Three days later, Chambliss upset Cleland.

The President as the "Top of the Ticket"

Even when the president doesn't actively campaign for other candidates, presidents' public images and successes or failures in office, and those of governors as well, can affect the electoral fates of other candidates of their party. For example, Ronald Reagan's victory in 1980 and landslide reelection in 1984 were accompanied by higher than normal levels of success for other Republican candidates. Republicans gained control of the Senate in 1980 for the first time since the 1952 election, and Republican House candidates won a higher percentage of the votes cast in 1980 and 1984 than in the preceding and following midterm elections, when Reagan was not on the ballot.

Coattail Effects   This link between presidential success and party victories is traditionally explained by the metaphor of *coattails.* Presidents ran "at the top of the ticket," the explanation goes, and the rest of the party ticket came into office clinging to their sturdy coattails. (Nineteenth-century dress coats did have tails.) This coattail effect was very common in the 1800s when the parties printed their own ballots, so a voter was limited to casting a ballot for an entire party ticket.

Coattail effects declined from the end of World War II through the 1980s.[7] Members of Congress became extremely good at cultivating their constituency by attending closely to its interests and providing services to individual constituents; this helped to insulate them from outside electoral forces, including presidential popularity.[8] Incumbents gained impressive advantages over their challengers in fund-raising and other campaign resources, especially in House races.

The relationship between presidential and congressional election results has become visible again since the early 1990s, as the parties have become more polarized.[9] For instance, during this time, people who defected from the presidential candidate of their party were also much more likely to vote for the other party's candidate for the House or Senate.[10] Coattail effects can reach even into nonfederal races; from 1944 through 1984, when a president ran strongly in a state, the president's party typically did better in state legislative contests on the same ballot.[11] Thus, many states moved their state legislative and governor elections to years when the presidency was not on the ballot, to insulate state elections from presidential politics.

Coattails Even Without the Coat   Presidential leadership seems to be able to influence election results even when the president is not on the ballot. During the period leading up to a midterm congressional election and in the elections themselves, voters' approval of the president's job performance is usually closely related to their support for candidates of the president's party.[12] A Gallup Poll just before the 2002 midterm election found that a majority of the respondents were voting "in order to send a message that [they] support [or oppose] George W. Bush," and when New Jersey voters elected a governor in 2005, 27 percent said they thought of their vote for governor as a vote against Bush, and 11 percent saw it as a vote in support of the president.[13]

Most often presidents' public approval has dropped by the midpoint of their terms and analysts find that the president's party has almost always suffered a decline in its share of House seats in the next midterm election.[14] For example, drops in President Clinton's approval rating at the time of the 1994 midterm election coincided with big Democratic losses in the House and Senate. It may be that the president's declining popularity has dragged down congressional candidates of his party or discouraged attractive candidates of his party from running. Citizens who disapprove of the president's performance seem to vote in larger numbers in midterm elections than those who approve, and their disapproval can lead them to vote for the other party's candidates.[15] It may be that voters have learned more since the presidential election about the capabilities or policies of the president's party.[16] Or it may suggest that, just as a popular presidential candidate can boost the chances of his party's candidates in the presidential year, his absence from the ticket may deprive them of this advantage at midterm.

This pattern of midterm losses by the president's party didn't hold in the 1998 and 2002 elections. The Democrats gained seats in 1998 during President Clinton's second term, and Republicans expanded their House majority and won a slim Senate majority in 2002. In both cases, voters' approval of the president was either holding steady or increasing. Clinton's public approval was on the upswing in time for the 1998 elections, and although President Bush had begun his first term with fairly low approval ratings, his popularity soared to almost 90 percent after the September 11 terrorist attacks. His approval ratings remained consistently above 60 percent as the 2002 election approached. Observers reported that his 90 percent approval among Republicans, in particular, made a difference in close campaigns.[17]

Presidents' Impact   In sum, presidents' popularity and campaign choices can affect the electoral fates of other candidates of their party.[18] Presidential coattails vary in strength, but at least some voters seem to be influenced by the president's performance when they cast ballots for other offices. This happens especially if the candidates emphasize their connection with the president in their advertising and if the president campaigns actively for them, as was the case in 2002 and 2004.

Not all presidents are inclined to nurture this link with other candidates of their party. Jimmy Carter, for example, ran for president in 1976 as a political and party outsider, at a time when voters' partisanship was weakening; when he won, he was repaid by a marked lack of cooperation from Democrats in Congress. Nevertheless, there are many ways in which presidents can dominate their party in government, just as most governors do in their state parties.[19] An especially attractive president can add luster to a party's public image for years by making a big positive impression on young adults who are just entering the electorate, as Ronald Reagan seems to have done for the Republican Party. It is difficult for any other leader to compete with a president or a governor in representing the party to the public or in enjoying as much legitimacy as the center of party leadership. What, then, do presidents do with their leadership of the party in government?

PARTY LEADERSHIP AND LEGISLATIVE RELATIONS

Presidents aim to get their programs passed by Congress. To do so, they draw on the capital they can generate as leader of the party in government: their command of the media, the coattails that they may have provided, and whatever public approval they may have at the time. They appeal to their shared party ties with members of their party in the House and Senate. They refer to whatever lingering patronage or preferments they can command (a judicial appointment here, a government project there). Members of the president's party know that if they make him look bad, they might also make themselves and their party look bad. That can encourage them to rally around the president on important votes, even if they would prefer to vote differently.

Legislative Support for Executives

Popular support is a valuable resource for the chief executive in getting Congress to go along with his programs. Bush's rise in public popularity after September 11 helped him to gain considerable success on the Hill. Clearly, it helps as well when a president's party controls both houses of Congress; these periods of time, as indicated by the dotted lines in Figure 14.1, are typically the president's greatest opportunities for success on legislation.

Unified party control of Congress does not *guarantee* success, however. President Carter had only about a 75 percent success rate with a Democratic Congress and President Clinton scored about 10 percent higher during his first two years in office, when the

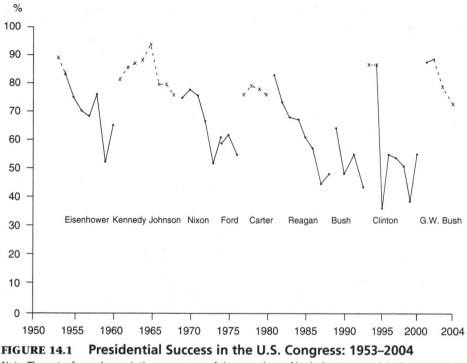

FIGURE 14.1   Presidential Success in the U.S. Congress: 1953–2004

Note: The entry for each year is the percentage of time members of both the House and the Senate voted in support of the announced position of the president. Years in which the president's party controlled both houses of Congress are indicated by an "x" and connected by dotted lines. Years in which the opposition party controlled at least one house of Congress are indicated by a "." and connected by solid lines.

Source: Congressional Quarterly Weekly Report, December 31, 1994, 3654, and, for 1995–2004, other December *CQ Weekly* issues.

Democrats held majorities in both the House and Senate. President Bush's legislative success rate actually dropped when his party regained control of Congress. The bipartisan response to the terrorist attacks had faded by the time Republicans regained a Senate majority in 2002, and because Republicans had only a slim majority, even a few defections could scuttle legislation proposed by the White House. Those defections soon appeared. Some congressional Republicans made it clear that they didn't like the big increase in the federal budget deficit accepted by the Bush administration in its efforts to cut taxes, and many Republicans were nervous about the president's intention to restructure Social Security, a vital concern of senior citizens.

Divided Control of Government   Presidents generally get much less support, of course, when Congress is in the hands of the opposing party. Unhappily for modern presidents, divided government has been the rule, not the exception, in the past five decades. During the same period, almost all of the states have also experienced divided party control of the legislature and the governorship. (The next chapter has more to say about divided government.)

In times of divided government, it can be risky for presidents and governors to rely heavily on partisan appeals. Because of the close party division in many legislatures and the unreliability of some legislators of their own party, executives must also curry favor with some legislators in the opposing party. That requires them to walk a fine line, using partisan appeals to legislators of their own party and nonpartisan, or bipartisan, appeals to those in the opposition. There are times when especially effective presidential leadership can get even a Congress controlled by the other party to go along with what he wants. Bill Clinton deftly used the veto and threats of the veto to get the Republican Congress to accept many of his initiatives after 1995.[20] However, American presidents have never been able to gain as much support in Congress as prime ministers naturally enjoy in parliamentary systems.

Governors, on the other hand, can often exercise greater party organizational power over the legislators of their party. In the many state legislatures that do not use seniority rules, governors can take an active part in selecting committee chairs and party floor leaders when the legislative session begins. A few governors lead powerful state party organizations; legislators who cross them may risk undermining their legislative career as well as their ambitions for higher office. In short, the average governor has greater control over party rewards and incentives than a president does. On the other hand, governors are not as visible as presidents are, so their coattails and prestige are normally less influential than those of presidents.

PARTY INFLUENCE IN EXECUTIVE AGENCIES

The president is the tip of an iceberg. Below the surface, huge and powerful, lies the rest of the executive branch. The bureaucrats who work there in cabinet-level departments such as Defense and Transportation and in other agencies such as the Environmental Protection Agency (EPA) are charged by the Constitution with carrying out the laws Congress passes. In spite of a burst of deregulation in the 1980s and 1990s, these executive agencies still regulate vast areas of the economy—food safety, prescription drugs, and pollution, for example—under congressional mandates that require a lot of interpretation. The bureaucrats who implement these laws, therefore, must make important decisions on public policy; they shape policy by applying it. It is they, for example, who determine whether morning-after contraception will be available over the counter rather than by prescription only. Because of their power, we need to ask whether presidents and governors are able to hold these administrators responsible for implementing a party program—or any program at all.

Bureaucrats Have Constituents Too

Perhaps the biggest problem executives face in enforcing party discipline on their subordinates is the same problem faced by legislative party leaders: constituency pressure. Just as individual legislators try to meet the needs of their constituents, administrators deal with demands from a variety of groups. Top-level administrators know that their best political protection is the support of their client groups. The EPA, for instance, works very closely with the industries it regulates as well as with a variety of professional and citizen groups. If its rulings in applying the Clean Air Act enrage automobile manufacturers and oil companies or if they outrage big environmental groups, the EPA will be in the political hot seat. Party loyalties do not compete very well with the power of these constituencies; in the executive as well as the legislative branch, the party has less to give and less to take away than the constituency does.[21]

Many other factors limit an executive's ability to unify an administration and hold it accountable for achieving a party's policy goals. Several of these limits were put in place by Progressive reforms aimed at crippling party power:

- Legislatures can protect top-level bureaucrats from presidential influence (and, through the president, party influence) by giving them terms of office longer than that of the president, by limiting the president's (or governor's) power to remove them, or by requiring that they be chosen through a merit system, rather than a political appointment process.

- Legislatures can prevent party control of an administrative agency by requiring that its leadership include members of both parties. The Federal Election Commission board, for example, must be composed of three Democrats and three Republicans— and at least *four* board members must agree to investigate any suspected campaign finance abuse. (This, of course, is as much a guarantee of gridlock as it is of bipartisanship.)

- Top administrators in many states are elected. So voters may choose, say, a Republican for governor and a Democrat for state treasurer to work together in an uneasy alliance. Even if both officials are of the same party, their offices are often politically and constitutionally independent.

- Most American executives are term-limited; presidents can run for only two terms, and most governors can serve only one or two consecutive terms. As the end of their term approaches, their authority over other officeholders lessens.

Holding Bureaucrats Accountable

Some high-level administrators are easier to hold responsible for promoting a party program than others. The people appointed to head cabinet departments—the biggest and best-known parts of the executive branch, such as Health and Human Services, Agriculture, and Commerce—have often had a long history of party activity, so they are likely to feel some degree of commitment to the party's goals and programs. All but one of President Bush's cabinet appointees in 2001 had been active in Republican Party politics: a Republican state party chair, the wife of a Republican House member, a former director of the National Republican Senatorial Committee, two Republican governors, two other Republican elected officials, four political appointees in previous Republican administrations—and, as the lone exception, a Democratic House member.

So party remains a source of talent for modern administrations. Presidents are no longer as explicitly partisan as they once were in making cabinet appointments; they no longer use these positions as rewards for loyal *party* service. Instead, they look for loyalty to the president's *own* aims. Nevertheless, most presidential appointees have been active partisans whose values and political careers have been shaped to a significant degree by their party.

Just below this top level, officeholders are less likely to have party experience. These officials are most often chosen for their administrative skills and only secondarily for their political credentials. The party organization's role in their selection may extend only to verifying that they are politically acceptable (that is, not offensive) in their home states. Yet they continue to come largely from the party of the president, and the party link can produce a commitment to a common outlook.

Modern presidents can make only about 3,000 political appointments, however— fewer appointive positions than some governors have—to try to gain control of an executive branch employing several million civilian employees. Many of these appointees are novices with little time to "learn the ropes" and little hope of gaining the necessary support of career bureaucrats. As Hugh Heclo has shown, together they comprise "a government of strangers": a set of executives whose limited familiarity and interaction with one another keep them from acting as an effective team and who are therefore likely to be overwhelmed by a huge, fragmented and more or less permanent bureaucracy.[22]

It is a difficult task, then, to establish political control over the executive bureaucracy, especially at the national level.[23] In response, recent presidents, and especially Republican presidents, have relied more and more on their immediate White House staff and the Office of Management and Budget when they try to mobilize the executive branch to achieve their policy goals.[24] Party can help in organizing an administration, serving as a recruitment channel for executive talent and a common bond between the executive and top bureaucrats, but it does not have the power to hold the executive branch responsible for carrying out a party program.

Changing Political Outlooks in the Federal Bureaucracy

Even though the executive's party is not able to enforce party discipline, the federal bureaucracy (and many state bureaucracies) does show some responsiveness to partisan forces over the long run. As the federal government expanded in the 1930s, President Roosevelt drew people into the career bureaucracy who were committed to his programs. They then became a bulwark against later efforts to weaken these programs, especially as these dedicated New Dealers came to be promoted to more and more senior positions in their agencies.

This pro-Democratic slant could still be seen in the federal bureaucracy decades later. By 1970, Joel Aberbach and Bert Rockman found that nearly a majority of these career bureaucrats said they normally voted Democratic and only 17 percent usually voted Republican. In federal social service agencies, even the administrators who were not Democrats said that they favored liberal policies. So Republican President Richard Nixon, in office at that time, faced a federal bureaucracy that had little sympathy for his conservative agenda. His administration spent a lot of time trying to control the bureaucracy by appointing Nixon loyalists to top bureaucratic positions.[25]

By 1992, however, the bureaucratic environment had changed. In the intervening two decades, Republicans had held the White House for all but four years. When Aberbach and Rockman returned to interview career administrators in comparable positions to those they interviewed in 1970, they now found slight Republican pluralities, although the career executives were still much more Democratic and liberal than the Reagan and Bush political appointees. As older civil servants retired, a new generation, less committed to New Deal and Great Society programs, had been recruited into senior executive positions. Changes in civil service laws further allowed positions formerly reserved for career employees to be filled by political appointees who could be carefully screened by the White House. The bureaucracy was no longer as unsympathetic to Republican initiatives.[26] The Reagan and George W. Bush administrations also made serious efforts to put their own stamp on the federal bureaucracy's administration of the laws. Yet the difficulties of controlling dissent in even a sympathetic agency remained; in the words of one observer, "nobody has come close to succeeding."[27]

In sum, although there is party influence in the executive branch, most presidents and governors use their party leadership role to promote their own programs and their own reelection, not the programs of their party. To the extent that the executive's goals are similar to those of his or her party, of course, the party's program benefits. Many governors do use some patronage appointments purely to boost their state party and presidents may use some cabinet appointments to recognize various groups within their party. For most American executives, however, the goals and interests of their party organization are secondary to their own policy goals and political careers.

TRACES OF PARTY IN THE COURTS

Courts and judges are affected by party politics as well. Most American judges—even most justices of the U.S. Supreme Court—are political men and women who took office after careers that involved them in some aspect of partisan politics (see box on page 280). Although reformers have tried to insulate the judicial system from party politics, the selection of judges continues to be shaped by partisanship in elections and through appointments. Because of the nature of the judiciary, however, the influence can be subtle.

Judicial Voting Along Party Lines

Hints of party influence appear when we examine the voting in American appellate courts. Several studies show that judges split into partisan blocs on several types of cases. Judges appointed by Democratic presidents tend to be more liberal than those appointed by Republican presidents on issues such as civil liberties, labor issues, and regulation.[28] In a study of state and federal courts, in comparison with Republican judges, Democratic judges were found to decide more often in favor of the defendant in criminal cases, for the government in tax cases, for the regulatory agency in cases involving the regulation of business, and for the claimants in workers' compensation, unemployment compensation, and auto accident cases.[29] An environmental research group found that in 2001–2003, federal judges appointed by Democratic presidents were several times more likely to rule in favor of environmentalists than Republican-appointed judges were.[30] These are the kinds of differences that we might expect to find when comparing the views of Democrats and Republicans outside the courtroom.

Similarly, in recent redistricting cases, U.S. District Court judges have tended to uphold plans enacted by their party more than those enacted by the opposing party.[31] That was often the case in 2001 when state legislatures deadlocked over redistricting plans, which were then kicked to the courts. Judges show much less party cohesion than members of legislatures do, and it appears only in certain types of cases. Yet it does

THE PARTISAN BACKGROUNDS OF U.S. SUPREME COURT JUSTICES

Justices Appointed by Republican Presidents

John Roberts (chief justice; appointed by G. W. Bush) served as an aide to the attorney general and the White House counsel in the Republican Reagan administration and was the principal deputy solicitor general in the Republican G. H. W. Bush administration.

John Paul Stevens (Ford) is a registered Republican, though he was never active in Republican Party politics.

Antonin Scalia (Reagan) was named general counsel for the Office of Telecommunications Policy in the Republican Nixon administration and then assistant attorney general under Republican Gerald Ford.

Anthony Kennedy (Reagan) was a Republican activist and campaign donor in California and then became a legal adviser to Reagan as governor.

David H. Souter (G. H. W. Bush) was never active in party politics but was appointed deputy attorney general and then attorney general in New Hampshire, in both cases by Republican governors.

Clarence Thomas (G. H. W. Bush) served on the staff of Missouri's Republican attorney general and as assistant secretary for Civil Rights and director of the Equal Employment Opportunity Commission in the Republican Reagan administration. Thomas's wife was a senior aide to House Republican Majority Leader Dick Armey.

Samuel A. Alito, Jr. (G. W. Bush) was assistant to the solicitor general and deputy assistant to the attorney general in the Republican Reagan administration. Republican G. H. W. Bush appointed Alito to the U.S. Court of Appeals.

Justices Appointed by a Democratic President

Ruth Bader Ginsburg (Clinton) had no formal party positions or appointments prior to her nomination to the Court.

Stephen G. Breyer (Clinton) was a special assistant to the assistant attorney general under Democratic President Lyndon Johnson, assistant special prosecutor in the Watergate investigation, and special counsel and then chief counsel to the Democratic-led Senate Judiciary Committee.

appear; Democratic judges rule differently under some circumstances than their Republican colleagues.

What Causes Partisan Behavior on the Courts?

Very little of this apparent partisanship is due to active efforts by Democratic and Republican Party leaders to influence court decisions. It does happen occasionally, for example, in the case of a local judge who continues to be deeply involved in party politics even after being appointed to the bench. A judge who is closely tied to the local party may provide some patronage for the party organization through guardianships, receiverships in bankruptcy, and clerkships that can be given to party loyalists who are attorneys. In most areas, however, openly partisan activity by a judge or pressure by a party leader to decide a case in a certain way would now be seen as violating the norms of the judicial system.

A much better explanation for the impact of party on judges' behavior is simply that judges, like most other well-educated people, hold party identifications and can bring these partisan frames of reference to their work on the court. Just as the two parties reflect different sets of values, so do their identifiers, including those who become judges. Two judges might vote together on the regulation of business because of values they share about the proper role of government in the economy. Those values may have led them to join the same party years earlier or were developed out of experience in that party. In other words, it is not usually the external pressure from a party leader but rather the party *in* the judge that can lead judges with similar partisan backgrounds to make similar decisions. (See "A Day in the Life" on page 282.)

Those who appoint judges to their positions are well aware of the importance of judges' value systems. They know that judges have discretion in deciding some cases and that the choices they make may reflect, at least in part, their own experiences and beliefs. So the selection of judges, especially for the higher courts that receive the most challenging cases, has traditionally taken into account the values and attitudes of the possible nominees.

Party and Judicial Appointments

Parties can affect the selection of judges in several ways. In many states, party leaders may advise on the nominations of prospective judges. That gives them a means to advance party goals by encouraging the appointment or election of judges who believe in the party's values. It also permits them to further the careers of lawyers who have served the party loyally. Even when party organizations don't have that opportunity, the nomination of judges by a governor or a president permits the influence of the party in government on judicial appointments.

Federal Judges   Presidents nominate candidates for federal judgeships; the Senate has the right to confirm or deny them. Because prospective judges' party and ideology are important indicators of their attitudes and, thus, can affect their decisions in some kinds of cases, every American president for the past century has made at least 80 percent of his judicial appointments from within his own party; the average is higher than 90 percent.

The Reagan and first Bush administrations took special care to screen candidates for their dedication to conservative principles. In fact, since 1980 the Republican platform has pledged to nominate (or, in 2004, to "support") only prospective judges who believe in the sanctity of human life—in other words, those who oppose abortion. These administrations modified the tradition of allowing the presidential party's senators to select candidates for district and appellate judgeships. Senators were asked to submit three names for consideration, and the administration made the final choice.[32]

As a result, Reagan and Bush appointees were even more ideologically distinctive (as well as more likely to have been active in party politics) than average among recent presidents. By contrast, the Clinton administration gave a larger role to Democratic senators and other party leaders in suggesting judicial nominees and was less concerned with ideological screening. Clinton also appointed a somewhat lower percentage of federal

A WOMAN'S PLACE IS IN THE COURTHOUSE

Accompanying their parents to a trial, two young girls happened to glance through the windows of the courtroom next door. "Ooh, look at that!" said one, gazing up at the bench. "She's a judge and she's a girl! I didn't know girls could be judges!"

Circuit Court Judge Mary Ellen Diekhoff, the "girl" on the bench, may have felt the same way when she was growing up. The daughter of a single mother who worked as a secretary in a steel mill, Diekhoff had never met a lawyer. But "in seventh grade, a very brave teacher decided to take us to the Statehouse in Indianapolis and told us that this is where the laws were made. And I realized that I *loved* the Statehouse." When she got home, she announced to her astonished mother, "I'm going to be a lawyer."

Years later, after law school and a private practice, she became a prosecutor. For 17 years she got a thorough grounding in the highs and the lows of the justice system by preparing and trying criminal cases. Then, when the only two local women judges retired, she was approached by several people who suggested that she run. Circuit Court judges in Indiana are chosen in partisan elections. She filed as a Democratic candidate and was both surprised and relieved that no one filed to run against her in either the primary or the general election.

With no opponent, there was no real need to campaign. "But I was ready to campaign," she said. "I guess I have a litigator's personality: You prepare, prepare, and prepare. I kept it up even till the day of the election. Really, I think if you're running for office, you should be out there talking to the voters. Besides, I thought that not campaigning was like tempting the universe: that at the last minute, somehow, somebody would find a loophole and I'd be opposed after all!" In fact, she was the third-highest vote-getter in the county.

"I don't think of myself as a partisan when doing my job," she says. "But we are all the product of our life experiences. If you have a civil case where a credit card company is suing a credit card holder, for instance, I could imagine moments where different judges might see the principles in the case differently. It's not honest to say that as a judge, you don't have opinions. A good judge has to say that he or she does have opinions, acknowledge them, and then look through them to apply the law, even in cases where you have to sign some orders that you don't like personally."

Would she prefer not to run in a partisan election? "I can see both sides. It would be better if a judge could run without a party label. It's good that a judge can't say in a campaign, 'I'm in favor of the death penalty,' but if you run for office under a party's flag, people make assumptions about your stands on issues that may not be true. On the other hand, if you're appointed for a lifetime term, that's not always a good idea either. As a judge, you get a lot of respect. As a prosecutor, lots of people would argue with me. But when you become a judge, you walk into the courtroom and everybody stands up. Nobody criticizes you—at least not to your face. If you became a judge fairly young, I could imagine that over time you'd begin to believe that you were invincible. That's dangerous in a democratic society.

"Historically, though, I think that Supreme Court justices and other judges have been able to get past their appointments by partisan officials and think like judges, even if they disappoint the president who appointed them. And that's important; it's the judiciary that will guard the Constitution, and I'm proud to be a part of it."

judges from his own party than most of his predecessors did and was less inclined to choose judges with records of party activity.[33] George W. Bush's judicial selections returned to the pattern of Reagan and Bush's father.

Senate action on the president's nominations to federal judgeships has become increasingly partisan during the last two decades. Early shots were fired in the 1980s and early 1990s, when Senate Democrats and their allies waged major battles over the confirmation of two conservative nominees to the Supreme Court: Robert Bork and Clarence Thomas. (In fact, the former case gave rise to a new verb. When an intense, usually partisan campaign has been mustered against a nominee, he or she is said to have been "Borked.") By the end of the Clinton administration, the level of partisan animosity over judicial appointments was so high that Republican Senate leaders were refusing to schedule debate on some of the president's nominees.

Examples of bare-knuckles partisanship continued in 2001, when the situation was reversed and the Senate's Democratic leaders sat on the judicial nominations of the Republican president.[34] The atmosphere surrounding judicial appointments became more and more acrimonious as the parties came to see the battles over the nomination of federal and Supreme Court judges as a way to mobilize their core support in the electorate. President Bush was forced to withdraw some nominations of federal judges when Senate Democrats filibustered; it took an extraordinary bipartisan agreement of 14 senators to get some of Bush's nominees confirmed (see box on page 284).

State Court Judges   State court judges are selected in a very different manner; in fact, the selection process can vary even within a single state. In 13 states, candidates for at least some types of judgeships must run in partisan elections. At times, however, both parties will endorse the same candidate, who is often the choice of the state bar association. Twenty states try to take partisanship out of the selection process by electing at least some of their judges on a nonpartisan ballot. (In some of these states, it is common for each party to endorse its own slate of candidates publicly, so the "nonpartisanship" is a sham.) In 29 states, at least some judges are appointed to their posts. Most of these—24 states—use a "merit appointment" system in which nominating commissions screen prospective judges, who must usually run in a retention election within 4 to 12 years of their appointment. In the remaining five of these states, the governor or state legislature appoints judges without the advice of a nominating commission.[35]

Many of these alternatives leave room for partisan influence. Even in cases where judges are appointed at the recommendation of independent commissions, judicial terms tend to be long, often as long as ten years. The security of a long term and the high probability of reelection (thanks to incumbency) can free judges from any explicit party pressures, or even pressures from the governor or president. But partisanship is so often already internalized in the judge's values and preferences that a long-term judgeship merely allows them to flourish.[36]

Many European countries have different selection procedures. Someone prepares to be a judge through study, apprenticeship, and then by scoring well on a special exam. In the United States, in contrast, there is no special training process for judges—no exam to take, no advanced degree in "judgeship." Any lawyer can be a judge if he or she can win election or appointment to the job. But although the specialized training process

FALLOUT FROM THE "NUCLEAR OPTION"

Partisan battles over presidents' judicial nominations reached new heights (or new lows) during the Clinton and Bush administrations. The increasing role of courts in a variety of high-octane social issues from abortion to gay marriage, and the fact that federal judges serve lifetime appointments, made control of the courts a very tempting goal for presidents and their supporters.

Senate Republicans had bottled up many of President Bill Clinton's liberal judicial nominees in committee. In turn, Senate Democrats tried to keep President George W. Bush from moving the federal courts in a more conservative direction. Although the Senate approved 208 of Bush's federal court nominees during his first term, Democrats used the threat of a filibuster—the use of unlimited debate to stop a vote from taking place, a means of protecting the minority's rights that has been part of the Senate's rules for more than 200 years—to block 10 appeals court nominations.

When Bush resubmitted 7 of the 10 nominations in 2005, the Republican Senate leadership announced its intention to keep Democrats from using the filibuster. The leadership's argument, called the "nuclear option" because it was likely to blow up what little comity remained between the Senate's Democrats and Republicans, was that the filibuster could be ruled out of order by the Senate's presiding officer. Upholding that ruling would take only 51 votes; shutting off a filibuster, in contrast, would require 60 votes, beyond the reach of the 55-member Senate Republicans.

The furious Senate Democrats warned that they would shut down Senate business indefinitely in response. Hundreds of interest groups spent millions of dollars on TV and Internet ads and e-mails. The Alliance for Justice, representing 185 liberal groups, claimed that the Republicans were attempting a power grab by breaking Senate rules. Conservative groups came together in the Committee for Justice and Progress for America, charging that Democrats wanted to keep people of faith out of the judiciary and characterizing the Democrats as obstructionists. As the voting on these nominations approached, threats and charges on both sides reached fever pitch.

The night before this remarkable game of chicken was to unfold on the Senate floor, a group of seven Democrats and seven Republicans finally concluded long-standing negotiations with a compromise. Democrats would allow votes to be taken on three of Bush's nominees but would block two others. The "Gang of 14" further agreed to filibuster future judicial nominees only under "extraordinary circumstances."

One of the remarkable aspects of this compromise is that the two parties' Senate leaders had no role in negotiating it; the influence of the more extreme interest groups associated with each party kept the party leaders from backing down. But with the Senate so closely divided by party, these 14 senators had their party leaders over a barrel. The question, however, was whether the compromise would hold when the stakes got even higher. Political Scientist Ross Baker commented, "I think they did what the Senate very often does. They kicked the can down the road. They basically postponed a crisis and set up the predicate for another one in the future on the Supreme Court nomination."

Sources: Charles Babington and Shailagh Murray, "A Last-Minute Deal on Judicial Nominees," *Washington Post,* May 24, 2005, p. A1; and Dan Balz, "Breakthrough Pact Unlikely to End Battle," *Washington Post,* May 24, 2005, p. A1.

required for judgeships in many European nations limits the impact of party organizations and partisan elections, those who become judges will still have political preferences, many of which will have been shaped by their partisanship.

THE PARTY WITHIN THE EXECUTIVE AND THE JUDGE

When we talk about party influence on executives and judges, then, the best explanation for this influence is that executives and judges are people who hold political beliefs, and those beliefs are often related to the individual's party affiliation. Democrats tend to hold different beliefs about government and the economy than Republicans do, and Democratic judges and bureaucrats, similarly, hold different views from Republican judges and bureaucrats. These party differences are reinforced by partisan elements in the process by which presidents and governors, top executive officials, and most judges are chosen. However, we rarely see much evidence of direct influence by the party organization on bureaucrats and courts. The parties don't have the means to enforce party discipline in the executive or judicial branches.

Reformers have tried to wring partisan considerations out of the selection process; one example is the use of the merit system to appoint officials. There is good reason to try. When judgeships are elected, prospective judges can receive campaign money from private interests, just as other candidates can. In 2004, for example, two candidates competing for an Illinois judgeship raised more than $5 million in contributions, and a group in West Virginia financed by business interests spent more than $2.5 million to defeat a sitting State Supreme Court justice. About a third of the contributions to judicial races nationwide came from interest groups, particularly business interests and plaintiffs' lawyers, many of whom try cases before these judges.[37] When citizens suspect that partisan forces are active, as some inevitably believed about the case that opened this chapter, public confidence in courts and administrative agencies can be undermined. However, there is no way to eliminate individuals' beliefs and values, including their partisanship, from their selection as administrators or judges or from their behavior in administrative agencies and in court.

Chapter 15

The Semi-Responsible Parties

The American political parties are an intriguing puzzle. On the one hand, in earlier chapters, we've seen evidence of renewed party activity at all levels, from increased party voting in Congress to greater national and state party success in raising money and recruiting candidates. Even when party organizations are nowhere to be seen, large numbers of voters rely on party labels when choosing among a series of unfamiliar names on the ballot, and judges' and bureaucrats' decisions often reflect their partisan backgrounds.

On the other hand, although parties are ever present in American politics, they have less power over the functioning of government than do parties in many European countries. In the United States, even when a party has won a majority in government, it still can't guarantee that its promises to the nation—the pledges that it has made in its platform—will be carried out. Unified Republican control of Congress and the White House in the early 2000s brought the tax cuts promised by the Republican platform but not the limits on the growth of government spending.

Parties are among the most effective tools available to citizens for controlling their government. If the American parties are not strong enough to hold elected officials accountable, then doesn't that put American democracy at risk?[1] Some observers believe that it does. Bolstered by an early report from leading academic experts on political parties,[2] they argue that the answer is to create a system of more "responsible" parties. The governing party in this system would translate a coherent political philosophy into government action and would then be held responsible for the results. That, they argue, would enhance democracy.

Others see a more limited problem with party politics. For decades, the American parties have been criticized for being too much alike in their platforms, too centrist, and not clear and specific enough on big issues. Conservative Republican activists in 1964 pleaded for a platform that would be "a choice, not an echo" of the Democrats. In his third-party candidacy in 1968, George Wallace scoffed that there was "not a dime's worth of difference" between the major parties. Ralph Nader campaigned for president in 2004 on the charge that both parties were tied to the demands of moneyed special interests, just as Ross Perot had claimed in the 1990s and John McCain in 2000.

These two sets of critics—the scholars who favor party government and the ideologically oriented activists—have different perspectives, but at heart they make the same point. They both want the parties to offer clearer and more detailed stands on issues and for the winning party to put its promises to work in public policy. To some extent, their complaints have been answered. Both parties have become more distinctive in their stands on important policy questions in the past two decades. The Democratic Party is more uniformly liberal now, after many southern conservatives switched into the Republican Party, and the Republicans have followed a more clearly conservative path. Have they become more like "responsible" parties, and does that make them better able to serve the needs of a democracy?

THE CASE FOR RESPONSIBLE PARTY GOVERNMENT

The idea of *party government*, or *responsible parties*, offers a vision of a democracy very different from the traditional American commitment to limited government and the equally traditional American hostility to powerful political parties. Champions of party government believe that we need a strong and decisive government to solve social and economic problems. Our political institutions, they feel, may have been well suited to the limited governing of the early years of American history but do not serve us well today, when we need more vigorous government action against challenges ranging from hurricanes to terrorism.

However, this strong government must be held accountable to the public. The current system doesn't permit that, they charge. Individuals rarely have the time or the information to play an active political role or even to find out what their elected representatives are doing, so they depend on parties to present them with clear alternatives and to hold elected officials accountable for their actions. When parties are unable to do that, voters drift from one meaningless decision to another.[3] In a system of candidate-centered politics and divided party control of government, there can be no genuine public control. The result, they argue, is that government serves the well-financed minorities—corporations, labor unions, single-issue groups—rather than the people.

How Would Party Government (Responsible Parties) Work?

The best way to deal with this problem, party government advocates say, is to restructure the political parties. The parties would then take the lead in organizing and energizing the government and would, in the process, reinvigorate the other institutions of popular democracy. The process of party government would work like this:

- Each party would draw up a clear and specific statement of the principles and programs it favors. It would pledge to carry out those programs if the party wins.

- The parties would nominate candidates loyal to the party program and willing to enact it into public policy if elected.

- Each party would run a campaign that clarifies the policy differences between the two parties, so voters would grasp these differences and vote on that basis.

- Once elected, the party would hold its officeholders responsible for carrying out the party program. Voters could then determine whether they approved of the results and decide whether to keep or throw out the governing party at the next election.

In this system of responsible parties, then, the party's main focus would be on the policies it has pledged to put into effect. Winning elections would not be an end in itself. Nominations and elections would become no more—and no less—than a means to achieve certain public policy goals. For this to happen, all the elected branches of government would have to be controlled by the same party at a particular time. The party would bind the divided institutions of government into a working whole, as happens in parliamentary democracies.

What qualifies the party to play this crucial role? In the words of a prominent party scholar, it is because

> the parties have claims on the loyalties of the American people superior to the claims of any other forms of political organization. . . . The parties are the special form of political organization adapted to the mobilization of majorities. How else can the majority get organized? If democracy means anything at all it means that the majority has the right to organize for the purpose of taking over the government.[4]

So parties would hold a privileged position in politics compared with interest groups, their major rivals as intermediaries between citizens and government.[5]

Those who argue for party government do not always agree on the purposes they feel a strong federal government should serve. Many conservatives, once suspicious of a powerful central government, grew to like it better when conservative Presidents Reagan and Bush used their power to urge Congress to eliminate liberal programs. Similarly, liberals who were frustrated by the separation of powers developed greater enthusiasm for the principle when Congress proved capable of checking some of Reagan's and Bush's initiatives. It is much easier to like party government, apparently, when your party is in charge. In any case, party government advocates feel that a central government pulled together by strong parties would give the public a bigger voice in politics.

THE CASE AGAINST PARTY GOVERNMENT

The proponents of party government are persuasive, but most American political scientists and political leaders remain unconvinced. Their concerns about party government take two forms. One is the argument that party government would not produce desirable results. The other is that it simply would not work in the American context.[6]

It Would Increase Conflict

First, these skeptics fear that the nature of party government—its dedication to providing clear alternatives on major issues—would stimulate more intense and conflict-filled politics. Legislators, they say, would be bound to a fixed party position and would no longer be free to represent their own constituents and to negotiate mutually acceptable solutions. Compromise would become more rare. That would weaken the deliberative character of American legislatures.

Critics of party government also fear that a system that makes parties the main avenue of political representation could undercut or destroy the rich variety of interest groups and other nonparty organizations. Without these other means of representing the nation's diversity, the two major parties might be seriously overloaded. Minor parties would be likely to pop up, which would further fragment the American system. In short, critics fear that politics and legislatures would be dominated by a number of doctrinaire, unyielding political parties unable to resolve problems.

It Wouldn't Work in American Politics

The second major argument against responsible parties is that the idea could not take root in the United States because it is not compatible with American political culture. The biggest problem here is the design of the American government. The principles of separation of powers and federalism were intended to prevent tyranny by dividing constitutional authority among the various levels and branches of government. The separation of powers, for example, allows voters to give control of the executive branch to one party and the legislative branch to the other. Elections for Congress take place on a different schedule from presidential elections, so congressional candidates can try to insulate themselves, although they don't always succeed, from presidential coattails. Federalism permits different parties to dominate in different states. Any change in these basic principles, such as a move to a parliamentary system, which would give the party a powerful reason to remain united in the legislature, would require major revision of the Constitution.

In recent years, American voters have made enthusiastic use of the separation of powers. Until 1950, the president's party controlled both houses of Congress most of the time. However, since then, *divided government* has prevailed: A president or governor faces at least one house of the legislature controlled by the other party. As you can see in Table 15.1, there have been only six years since 1980 when control of the federal government *wasn't* shared by the two parties. Voters have produced divided party control in most state governments as well since the early 1980s.[7]

Divided government makes responsible party government impossible. By giving control of different branches of government to opposing parties, it requires agreement between the parties for successful policy making. The alternative is gridlock, as New Yorkers have so often seen in their state legislature, in which Republicans have controlled the state Senate and Democrats have dominated the state Assembly for decades. Negotiation and bargaining are necessary in any democratic system. When both Democrats and Republicans have their fingerprints on every major piece of legislation, voters find it difficult to figure out which party is responsible for bad policies. Without that ability, voters can't throw out the guilty party and replace it with the opposition—the most effective tool for controlling government.

To party government advocates, divided government helps to explain why the federal government has failed to respond effectively on a number of major concerns from health care to campaign finance. The critics disagree. They contend that unified party government doesn't necessarily produce more significant legislative action, that the federal government has a lot of practice in coping with shared party power,[8] and even that American voters prefer it that way.[9] However, it is clear that divided government is a big problem for those who would like to see responsible parties.

TABLE 15.1   Party Control of Government at the National Level, 1951–2006

| Year | Party in control of the | | | Divided Government |
	President	House	Senate	
1951–1952	D	D	D	
1953–1954	R	R	R	
1955–1956	R	D	D	x
1957–1958	R	D	D	x
1959–1960	R	D	D	x
1961–1962	D	D	D	
1963–1964	D	D	D	
1965–1966	D	D	D	
1967–1968	D	D	D	
1969–1970	R	D	D	x
1971–1972	R	D	D	x
1973–1974	R	D	D	x
1975–1976	R	D	D	x
1977–1978	D	D	D	
1979–1980	D	D	D	
1981–1982	R	D	R	x
1983–1984	R	D	R	x
1985–1986	R	D	R	x
1987–1988	R	D	D	x
1989–1990	R	D	D	x
1991–1992	R	D	D	x
1993–1994	D	D	D	
1995–1996	D	R	R	x
1997–1998	D	R	R	x
1999–2000	D	R	R	x
2001–2002	R	R	D*	x
2003–2004	R	R	R	
2005–2006	R	R	R	

*The Senate was Republican-controlled for the first five months of 2001 until Senator James Jeffords left the Republican Party and the Democrats gained majority control.

Note: D, Democratic control; R, Republican control; x, president, House, and Senate controlled by different parties.

Source: Updated from Harold W. Stanley and Richard G. Niemi, *Vital Statistics on American Politics 1999–2000* (Washington, DC: CQ Press, 2000), pp. 34–38.

The Gingrich Experiment: A Temporarily Responsible Party

Americans did get at least a whiff of party responsibility starting in the mid-1990s. In a move spearheaded by House Republican minority leader Newt Gingrich, the great majority of Republicans running for House seats in 1994 signed a statement they called a "Contract with America." In it, they pledged that if the voters would give the Republicans a House majority, they would guarantee a vote on each of ten pieces of legislation, all embodying conservative principles, within the first one hundred days of the next Congress. The statement concluded, in words that would gladden the hearts of party government advocates: "If we break this contract, throw us out. We mean it."

The Republicans did win a majority of House seats in 1994. They delivered on their promise; once in office, the new Republican leadership used its iron control of the House agenda to vote on each of those bills before the self-imposed deadline. The House Republicans were more unified on these bills than they had been in decades. That, however, is when party government stalled. The Senate Republican majority had not committed itself to the Contract with America and did not feel bound to consider these bills promptly or to pass them when they came up. The House Republicans' efforts were further stymied by divided government; a Democratic president had the power to veto any legislation that made it through both houses.

What can we learn from this experiment? As we have seen, the separation of powers is a mighty roadblock in the path of party government. Even the commitment of a legislative party to a set of clear and consistent principles is not enough to produce responsible party government, as long as the president and the other house of Congress are not willing to go along. There is reason to doubt, as well, that most voters appreciated the experiment; although Republicans kept their House majority in the next elections in 1996, so did the Senate Republicans who had not signed the Contract with America, and the Democratic president was reelected as well.

Since 2002, divided government has given way to Republican control of the White House and both houses of Congress. Yet other obstacles remain to achieving party government. Because party candidates are chosen by voters in primary elections, parties lack the power to insist that their nominees stay loyal to the party program. Even legislators who often buck their party's leaders or its platform are able to keep their jobs as long as their constituents keep voting for them. Critics of the responsible parties model have also argued that:

- American voters are not issue oriented enough to be willing to see politics only through ideological lenses.

- The diversity of interests in American society is too great to be contained within just two platforms.

- The parties themselves are too decentralized to be able to take a single, national position on an issue and then enforce it on all their officeholders.

- Americans distrust parties too much, as seen by their frequent efforts to reduce party influence in politics, to be willing to accept increased party power.

The idea of a responsible governing party, in other words, seems to its critics to ask too much of the voters, the parties, and the institutions of American government.

PARTY COHESION AND IDEOLOGY

Even if genuine party government is unlikely in the United States, it might still be possible to nudge the parties in the direction of greater accountability. The challenge would be to unite the party organization with party voters and the party in government behind a clear and consistent party program—in short, to make each party more cohesive. Perhaps the only feasible way for a party to grow into a more cohesive unit in modern American politics is if its various parts were to agree voluntarily on a party ideology or at least on a set of shared goals. Because their shared commitment to that program would be voluntary, it would not violate the separation of powers or require a basic change in the form of the federal government. What is the chance that more ideological parties could develop in American politics?

Are the American Parties Ideological?

An *ideological party* is one with clear and consistent principles on a wide range of questions, from the purpose of government to the essence of human nature. Good examples include European Socialist parties, the old-style Communist parties, and the Muslim fundamentalist parties that have arisen in Middle Eastern nations. The principles of an ideological party offer straight answers to questions such as these: What should the power relationships in the society look like? How should the society be governed and what values should the government try to achieve? What are the appropriate means to achieve these values?

Throughout their histories, however, the American parties have tended to be more pragmatic than ideological, focusing on concrete problems rather than on the purity of their principles. Ever since their founding, each party has been a blend of its own original tradition (the egalitarian tradition of the Democrats and the Republican tradition of order and industrial capitalism) with those of other groups that associated with it because of personal ties, geographic nearness, or simple expectations of political gain.[10]

Why have the major American parties been relatively free of ideology? Most important, there are only two of them to divide up a tremendous array of interests in American politics. In a system with several parties, a party can cater to one particular ideological niche in the voting public and still hope to survive. In a diverse two-party system, with many different interests and people to represent, such specialized appeals can be made only by minor parties—or by a major party intent on self-destruction.

Do They at Least Offer Clear Choices?

Even though the two parties are not as ideological as are many European parties, they have come to differ clearly in their stands on specific policies, and that could increase voters' ability to hold them responsible. We can see these differences in the platforms they adopt every four years at their national conventions (see box on pages 294–295), in their candidates' speeches, and in the policies they pursue when they win. It would have been hard during either the 2000 or 2004 presidential campaigns, for example, to mistake the tax-cutting proposals of Republican George W. Bush for the spending on social programs favored by his Democratic opponents. "Republicans mostly believe that the role of government is to foster greater individual economic achievement, even if it leads to more economic inequality," one perceptive analyst writes. "The Democratic philosophy is that the government should provide a safety net, even if it leads to economic inefficiency."[11] These differences, most notably the Democratic commitment to federal social programs and the Republican desire to limit them, have been central principles of the two parties since the New Deal.

Each major party has become more unified in its stands during the past few decades as well as more different from the other party. A major contributor was the issue of civil rights. As questions of racial justice emerged as an important focus of national policy, white southerners deserted the Democratic Party in increasing numbers and took with them their more conservative views on a variety of other issues. This lowered the biggest barrier to unity within the Democratic Party on several issues.[12] As Chapter 13 shows, the Democratic congressional party votes more cohesively now than it has in decades. The Republicans have also become more united on conservative principles. State parties tend to divide along issue lines as well, with Democratic parties more liberal, especially when there is real party competition in the state.[13]

A major step in this direction occurred with the election of Ronald Reagan in the 1980s. Reagan, a candidate strongly identified with the conservative wing of the Republican Party, demonstrated the appeal of a simple vision based on one major idea: less government. The clarity of his message appealed even to voters who were not persuaded by its content. His assault on the role of government as it had developed since the New Deal gave a more ideological tone to American politics than had been seen in decades. Since then, more issue-oriented leaders have been selected in both parties.[14] In the same sense, political ideas, or purposive values, have become more prominent in bringing people into party activism.

As a result, a change in party control can now make a noticeable difference in public policy. When Vermont Senator James Jeffords left the Republican Party in mid-2001 and caused the Republicans to lose their one-vote Senate majority, the agenda of the Senate changed quickly. A patients' rights bill, for example, which was regarded as dead under Republican control, went to the head of the legislative line after the Democrats took over, and several environmental measures also took on new life.

But Internal Divisions Remain

These clear differences on major issues, however, do not add up to the kinds of sharply articulated, all-encompassing political philosophies that are found in genuinely ideological parties. Consider, for instance, the interesting relationship between each party's stand on economic policy and its position on issues such as abortion and pornography. Democrats have long stood for an activist federal government with respect to social welfare and economic fairness but a largely hands-off policy with regard to abortion. Republicans generally want to loosen the federal government's grip on the economy and environmental regulation, but argue for government activism in prohibiting abortion.[15] Nimble advocates could probably construct a rationale as to why these sets of positions are actually consistent. But in reality, these stands coexist within each party's platform because the major parties, as they always have, adjust their policy positions to attract groups of potential supporters—in this case, when Democrats reached out to pro-choice women and young people and when Republicans found common cause with conservative Christians.

In addition, because the major American parties are pragmatic and vote-seeking above all, neither party has stayed entirely true to the principles it has articulated. The Republican platform, for example, has long committed the party to the goal of smaller government. Yet since gaining control of Congress in 1994 and the presidency in 2000, the Republican Party in Congress has promoted a number of big-government programs, from a huge ($400–$700 billion) expansion of Medicare entitlements to a major boost in pork barrel spending. The aim is to keep attracting the votes of constituents who are more concerned about economic benefits than about abstract principles. A conservative group

PARTY DIFFERENCES ON MAJOR ISSUES: THE 2004 PARTY PLATFORMS

These selections from the 2004 platforms show some of the most important differences between the Democratic and Republican Parties:

Abortion

Democrats: "We stand proudly for a woman's right to choose, consistent with *Roe v. Wade,* and regardless of her ability to pay."

Republicans: "The unborn child has a fundamental individual right to life which cannot be infringed. . . . We oppose using public revenues for abortion and will not fund organizations which advocate it."

Education

Democrats: "Instead of pushing private school vouchers that funnel scarce dollars away from the public schools, we will support public school choice. . . ."

Republicans: "The Republican Party supports the efforts of parents who choose faith-based and other nonpublic school options for their children."

Environment

Democrats: "In President George Bush's government, where polluters actually write environmental laws and oil company profits matter more than hard science and cold facts, protecting the environment doesn't matter at all. . . . We will . . . end Republican giveaways to special interests that exploit public land without regard for environmental consequences."

Republicans: "Environmental stewardship has been best advanced where property is privately held."

Gay Marriage

Democrats: "We support full inclusion of gay and lesbian families in the life of our nation and seek equal responsibilities, benefits, and protections for these families. . . . We repudiate President Bush's divisive effort to politicize the Constitution by pursuing a 'Federal Marriage Amendment.'"

Republicans: "Legal recognition and the accompanying benefits accorded couples should be preserved for that unique and special union of one man and one woman which has historically been called marriage. . . . Attempts to redefine marriage in a single state or city could have serious consequences throughout the country, and anything less than a Constitutional amendment . . . is vulnerable to being overturned by activist judges."

Health Care

Democrats: "We oppose privatizing Medicare."

Republicans: "Market-based health care has given America the most advanced medical system in the world."

Iraq

Democrats: "This Administration badly exaggerated its case, particularly with respect to weapons of mass destruction and the connection between Saddam's government and al Qaeda. . . . Ignoring the advice of military leaders, this Administration did not send sufficient forces into Iraq to accomplish the mission."

PARTY DIFFERENCES ON MAJOR ISSUES: THE 2004 PARTY PLATFORMS *(continued)*

Republicans: "Today, because America and our coalition helped to end the violent regime of Saddam Hussein, and because we are helping to raise a peaceful democracy in its place, 25 million Iraqis are free and the American people are safer."

Labor Unions

Democrats: "We will ensure that the right to organize a union exists in the real world, not just on paper. . . . That means reforming our labor laws to protect the rights of workers (including public employees) to bargain contracts and organize on a level playing field without interference."

Republicans: "[We believe that] no one should be kept out of a job for which they are qualified simply because they choose to remain independent of labor unions. We therefore support the right of states to enact Right to Work laws."

Race

Democrats: "We support affirmative action to redress discrimination and to achieve the diversity from which all Americans benefit."

Republicans: "Because we are opposed to discrimination, we reject preferences, quotas, and set-asides based on skin color, ethnicity, or gender."

Social Security

Democrats: "We oppose privatizing Social Security or raising the retirement age."

Republicans: "Each of today's workers should be free to direct a portion of their payroll taxes to personal investments for their retirement."

Stem Cell Research

Democrats: "We will reverse [President Bush's] wrongheaded policy. Stem cell therapy offers hope to more than 100 million Americans who have serious illnesses. . . . We will pursue this research under the strictest ethical guidelines."

Republicans: "We strongly support the President's policy that prevents taxpayer dollars from being used to encourage the future destruction of human embryos. . . . We do not end some lives for the medical benefit of others."

Taxes

Democrats: "We will roll back the Bush tax cuts for those making more than $200,000."

Republicans: "The fundamental premise of tax relief is that everyone who pays income taxes should see their income taxes reduced. . . . The taxation system should not be used to redistribute wealth or fund ever-increasing entitlements and social programs."

You can find the full text of the platforms at http://www.democrats.org/pdfs/2004platform.pdf (for the Democrats) and http://www.gop.com/media/2004platform.pdf (for the Republicans) tracking the 30 Republicans first elected to the House in the Republican sweep of 1994 who were still serving in the House in 2004 found that in their first term, most had sponsored bills that would have had a net effect of cutting federal spending, whereas in 2003–2004, all but two sponsored legislation that would have had a net effect of increasing spending.[16]

Finally, as cohesive as the congressional parties have become, they both deal with some internal dissent. A small group of Republican moderates has challenged party leaders' efforts to unite Republican House and Senate members in support of the president's program. Moderate Republicans have organized the Tuesday Group in Congress and the Republican Main Street Partnership, which includes some Republican governors as well,[17] while more than 100 of the most conservative members of Congress have formed the Republican Study Committee to hold their congressional party to what they regard as true conservative principles.[18]

The Democrats have at least as long a history of internal conflict. After the 2004 election, as in 2000, many liberal Democrats claimed that the best way to win back the presidency was to draw sharp ideological contrasts with the Republicans and energize the party's liberal base. Moderate Democrats responded that there weren't enough liberals among likely voters to bring a Democratic victory; rather, the party should stress issues such as security that appeal to swing voters.[19] These recriminations reflected years of dispute between party liberals and centrist "New Democrats" who are less favorable toward big government and more pro-business.[20] The conflicts occur in state parties as well, such as in Idaho, where rural, mainly Mormon Democrats split from urban liberals on abortion, and Democrats from the logging and mining areas vote differently from urban Democrats on environmental issues.[21]

What about party voters? Is it true, as some ideologues charge, that most Americans are committed to ideological principles and want the Democrats and Republicans to provide more clearly defined ideological choices? Or are party voters bored with, or even alienated by, the programmatic concerns of many party activists?

IDEOLOGY AND THE AMERICAN VOTER

Media reports of election results frequently use the terms "liberal" and "conservative" to describe voters' choices. It has been common, for example, to attribute the Republican wins since 1980 and the emergence of several moderate Democratic leaders to a more conservative mood among American voters. The question is more complicated for political scientists, who have long debated the nature and structure of citizens' political attitudes.

How Ideological Is the American Public?

Careful study of American political attitudes since the 1950s raises serious doubt that most voters can be described as "ideological," or even as very consistent on issues. An ideological voter, like an ideological party, would not just hold clear attitudes toward a variety of individual issues but would connect those attitudes into a coherent structure. However, since the early days of opinion research, analysts have found that many individuals with conservative attitudes on, say, taxes may express moderate or liberal attitudes on other issues, such as foreign policy or the environment.[22] It has been one of the staples of American survey research that large numbers of respondents say they want both a smaller government with lower taxes *and* a government that provides more services in areas such as defense, health care, environment, and education. These are understandable goals, but not a likely foundation for consistent thinking.[23]

Most of us, researchers find, hold in our minds a mix of conflicting thoughts about politics and particular issues. We do not necessarily hold a set of fixed and unyielding stands, such as an unqualified "yes" on all forms of affirmative action and a firm "no" to tax breaks for business. Rather, we might feel that affirmative action can help those who need it *and* that it can give an unfair advantage. We can be pulled toward one of these views under some conditions and toward another view under other conditions. Thus, most people react to issues with a degree of ambivalence[24]—a sharp contrast with the more stable, predictable response of an ideologue. Thus, in CNN's 2004 exit poll, almost half of the voters chose to sidestep both ideological poles and define themselves as "moderates." [25]

Even in the case of Ronald Reagan, who campaigned for president in 1980 as a principled conservative, voters' judgments turned more on their *retrospective evaluations* of presidential performance—their feelings as to whether the most recent presidency had turned out well—than on Reagan's issue positions. In fact, many voters supported Reagan in spite of his conservative policy positions, rather than because of them; in both 1980 and 1984, most voters preferred the policy stands of Reagan's opponent.[26] Because many voters' choices tend to be results oriented, focusing on concrete problems and pragmatic efforts to solve them, parties and candidates try to stitch together winning coalitions by appealing to a range of qualities—the candidates' personal characteristics, group interests, single issues, and feelings toward the party in power—but rarely by using ideological appeals.

Yet there is a growing number of people who may be more attracted to these appeals. Compared with 1972, the proportion of people in the University of Michigan's National Election Studies (NES) calling themselves conservative or extremely conservative, and liberal or extremely liberal, rose from 19 percent to 39 percent in 2002.[27] These voters, who tend to be more interested and engaged in politics, have sorted themselves out more accurately by party in recent years.[28] The CNN exit poll, for instance, showed that voters who described themselves as liberal or conservative were very likely to pick the "correct" candidate (liberals selecting Kerry, conservatives choosing Bush). And according to NES data, during the last three decades an increasing proportion of Democrats has called themselves liberals and a substantially greater proportion of Republicans now consider themselves conservatives (see Figure 15.1). Differences between the two parties' activists were even greater.[29]

Why have at least some Americans become more polarized, especially since the early 1990s, and more likely to identify with the "right" party from a policy perspective? Because party leaders and platforms are more polarized now, and because both parties have been increasingly concerned with mobilizing their base in campaigns,[30] Americans are more likely to see a difference between the two parties on big issues (see Figure 15.2) and to divide by party in their attitudes toward candidates and issues.[31] That may improve many voters' ability to approximate the demands of the responsible parties model.[32] Even presidential coattails or voters' perceptions of the behavior of the majority party in Congress could prompt a party to behave in a more accountable manner.[33]

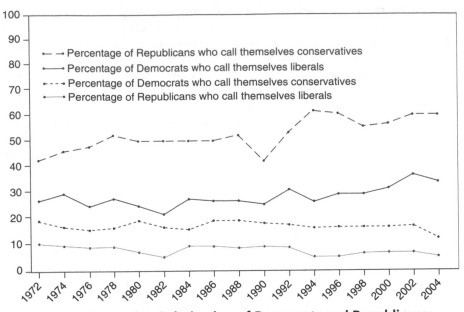

FIGURE 15.1   Increasing Polarization of Democrats and Republicans: 1972–2004

Note: Lines are the percentages of Democrats and Republicans (including strong and weak partisans and "leaners") who classify themselves as liberal (1–3 on a 1–7 liberal to conservative scale) or conservative (5–7) in each year listed.

Source: National Election Study data from the University of Michigan, http://www.umich.edu/~nes/nesguide/2ndtable/t3_1_1.htm and 3_1_3.htm (accessed October 5, 2005).

Note, however, that a large number of Americans has managed to sit out this polarization so far. Paul Allen Beck refers to "two electorates—one partisan and about evenly divided, the other estranged from party politics."[34] Is the polarized portion of the electorate big enough to sustain a movement toward more responsible parties?

Differences Among Voters, Activists, and Candidates

Party activists take more extreme positions on many issues than do party voters. Studies of delegates to the two national parties' nominating conventions have consistently found Democratic activists on the liberal end of the liberal-conservative continuum and Republican activists on the conservative end, with both parties' voters closer to the center. You can find a dramatic illustration of these patterns in Table 10.2, on page 190. The table shows that a full 96 percent of delegates to the 2004 Republican National Convention felt that the United States did the right thing in taking military action against Iraq, for example, compared with only 7 percent of the Democratic convention delegates. The parties' voters were in between; 21 percent of Democratic voters and 78 percent of the Republicans supported military action.

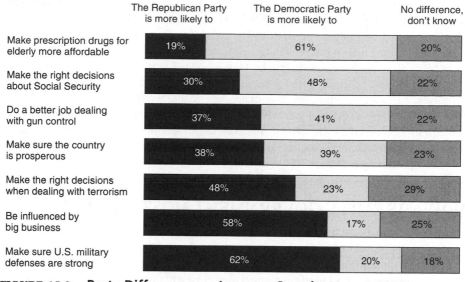

	The Republican Party is more likely to	The Democratic Party is more likely to	No difference, don't know
Make prescription drugs for elderly more affordable	19%	61%	20%
Make the right decisions about Social Security	30%	48%	22%
Do a better job dealing with gun control	37%	41%	22%
Make sure the country is prosperous	38%	39%	23%
Make the right decisions when dealing with terrorism	48%	23%	29%
Be influenced by big business	58%	17%	25%
Make sure U.S. military defenses are strong	62%	20%	18%

FIGURE 15.2   Party Differences on Issues as Seen by Voters, 2002

*Source: New York Times/*CBS Poll conducted October 27–31, 2002, at http://www.nytimes.com/pages/politics/index.html, "Poll Watch, Previous Surveys, Perceptions of the Parties" (accessed November 6, 2003).

A similar pattern appears on other major issues. Only 7 percent of the Republican activists agreed that government should do more to solve national problems, compared with 79 percent of Democratic activists. Again, the parties' voters were in the middle, and in this case, each party's activists were more distant from their own party's voters than the two parties' voters were from one another.[35] In other studies as well, researchers find that the more actively involved in campaigns and politics a partisan is, the more likely he or she is to be liberal or conservative rather than moderate.

A party's candidates and officeholders often find themselves caught in between: closer to the left or right than the party's voters but not as extreme as its activists. That can put candidates in a difficult position. If they try to muffle their conservative or liberal views, they risk alienating their party's activists. But if they express those views candidly, more moderate voters may choose not to support them in the next election.[36] It is no wonder that many candidates prefer to remain ambiguous when asked about issues in their campaigns, at least when they speak to general audiences.

These differences between more ideological activists and more flexible candidates can aggravate the tensions among the party organization, the party in government, and the party's voters. The ideologues in both parties complain periodically about the moderation of at least some parts of the party in government. Liberal Democrats often objected to the more centrist policies of Democratic President Clinton, and although George W. Bush has calmed the fears of many social conservatives about his core values, others remain watchful.

The dilemma of ideology, then, is not whether the American parties can become genuinely ideological parties. That is not likely. The problem is whether the increasing ideological commitment of their activists and of many of their officeholders can be sustained without alienating their more pragmatic supporters. The parties already face a deep well of public suspicion. Much of the public feels alienated from the parties' attachment to organized interests, their affinity for negative campaigns, and their failure to keep their promises.[37] It is entirely possible that many Americans, whose tolerance for politics is low, will find these sharpened party differences to be more of a turnoff than an incentive to learn more.[38] As one writer puts it, voters in the middle may become more convinced that "politics no longer speaks to them, that it has become a dialogue of the deaf, a rant of uncompromising extremes."[39]

WHEN IS PARTY GOVERNMENT MOST LIKELY?

Responsible parties are hard to achieve. Even the British Parliament, so often cited as a model by proponents of party government, has not always had the cohesion and the binding party discipline that a "pure" responsible party government would require.[40] Under what conditions have the American parties come closest to the ideal of responsible parties?

When There Is Strong Presidential Leadership

At times, a strong president—Ronald Reagan and George W. Bush in his first term are good examples—has been able to push Congress to enact important parts of the platform on which he ran for office. That is especially likely, of course, when the president's party controls both houses of Congress. Strong party-oriented presidents can also draw voters' attention to party differences. But the result is likely to be "presidential government" rather than party government; voters are likely to respond to the president's performance rather than that of the party as a whole.

In Times of Crisis

At critical times in American history, the parties have divided in ways that were, if not truly ideological, at least determinedly policy oriented. In the 1936 presidential election, for example, the Democrats and the Republicans offered dramatically different solutions to a nation devastated by the Great Depression. The hardships of that economic collapse probably focused voter attention to an unusual degree on the possible remedies that government could provide. Combined with a campaign centered on the pros and cons of the Roosevelt program for social and economic change, this may well have produced something close to a mandate in the election for both the president and Congress. When strong presidential leadership is combined with crisis conditions, then a degree of responsible party government might be achieved, at least for relatively short periods.

When the Parties' Supporting Coalitions Realign

At times when the parties' supporting coalitions of social groups have undergone real change—often called "realignments"—American politics seems to have most closely approached the requirements for party government. At these times, which often result in the creation of a new party system, the parties have tended to divide more clearly on a single, riveting set of issues, and party leaders, activists, and voters seem to reach their highest levels of agreement with one another and their greatest differences with the other party (see Chapter 7). New party systems typically produce a unified federal government with the same party controlling both houses of Congress, the presidency, and a judiciary that, through the president's appointment power, comes to reflect the new majority. On only five occasions in American history has one party enjoyed control of Congress and the presidency continuously for more than a decade, and each time, this control was first established during a realignment of the parties' coalitions.

Unified party control does not guarantee that the branches of the government will cooperate with one another. However, cooperation is certainly more likely when a president is dealing with a majority of his own party in Congress and especially if its members feel that they owe their election to their party label. Moreover, party cohesion in Congress is especially high at the beginning of a new party system. So it is not surprising that major bursts of comprehensive policy change have followed the realignments of the parties' coalitions after the Civil War and during the 1930s,[41] though there have been periods of major policy innovation during periods of divided party control or shorter periods of unified party control as well.

Even at these times, the American version of party government has been a pale imitation of its European counterparts. The realignment of the 1930s, for example, produced a majority Democratic Party by linking a liberal northern wing, attracted to the party because it represented the hopes of disadvantaged groups and championed the developing welfare state, and a conservative southern wing that often opposed both of these goals. The president at the time, Franklin D. Roosevelt, had a congressional majority large enough to achieve many of his policy goals, but he faced opposition within his own party throughout his long career in the White House.

In short, even when they are most unified around a single political agenda during a major shift in the parties' supporting coalitions, the American parties have typically contained differing interests and goals.

PARTY GOVERNMENT AND POPULAR CONTROL

To many analysts, the idea of party government, or responsible parties, has continuing appeal. When parties stand for clear principles and voters are offered clear choices in elections, it is easier for citizens to hold government responsible for the policies it produces. That may make for a stronger and more vibrant democracy.

The major American parties are not ideological parties like many in Europe. But the congressional parties and, to some extent, the parties in the electorate have become more cohesive in the past two decades than they have been in a very long time. At the federal level and in many states, there is a great deal of conflict between the parties over basic principles of public policy. The national party committees have never been stronger or more engaged than they are today in helping state and local parties and financing campaigns.

Yet, if the parties are to become more accountable, more like responsible parties in a system of party government, clear differences on issues and greater organizational strength are not enough. There must be some set of basic principles that can connect different issues into a single logical structure for each party, some means by which voters and leaders are able to distill the large number of policy issues into one major dimension or a few so that voters can easily understand and predict the party's stands.

That much structure and coherence will be harder and perhaps impossible to achieve. Too many powerful forces stand in the way. Even if party organizations gain immense new resources, they still won't be able to choose their own candidates; prospective office-holders will still have to attract voter support in primary elections. So candidates will still need to run their own campaigns and raise most of their own campaign money. Election ads will still encourage voters to respond to candidates as individuals, not as parts of a party ticket. All of these forces give candidates greater independence from their parties than the increase in party resources can counteract. And no amount of party money can buy an exception to the rules of federalism and the separation of powers.

It is not likely, then, that the American parties and voters can meet the demands of the responsible parties model. The party organizations have not grown into the central role that the reformers so valued—that of drawing up a party program and enforcing it on candidates and officeholders. Many would find that to be cause for celebration. Others would remind us that, in a system of government as fragmented as that of the United States, semiresponsible parties make it even harder to accomplish one of the basic tasks of a democracy: holding public officials accountable for their actions.

Chapter 16

The Place
of Parties in
American Politics

Three decades ago, the American parties appeared to be in decline. Because their troubles seemed to reflect long-term changes in American society, it was easy to assume that the decline was permanent. By the time their decay had become the central theme of books and articles about the parties, however, there were clear signs of resurgence. The parties have grown into different types of organizations than they once were, but in this changed form, they continue to be a vital part of the American political landscape.

To conclude this look at the American parties, this chapter will sum up these changes in relation to a simple but important truth: Political parties are powerfully shaped by the world around them. Parties affect presidents, legislatures, citizens, election rules, interest groups, and campaign finance, but they are also influenced by these forces. The changes in party power and functions over time can be better understood by looking at the relationships between parties and their environment.

PARTIES AND THEIR ENVIRONMENT

Political parties influence their environment in a variety of ways. They promote public policies in response to citizens' beliefs, demands, and fears. They recruit individuals into active roles in politics and government. Through their communications and performance, parties affect public attitudes about the Democrats and the Republicans and about politics more generally. Party organizations and the parties in government structure their own environment even more directly as well: They make the rules governing how the parties' candidates will be nominated and financed and who will have the opportunity to choose them.

In turn, their environment helps to shape the parties' nature, activities, and effectiveness. Three types of environmental factors have been especially important in influencing the American parties as well as those in other western democracies: the nature of the electorate, the nation's basic governmental institutions and rules, and the forces that mold the broader society (Table 16.1).[1]

TABLE 16.1   How Their Environment Influences the American Parties

Types of Influences	Examples
1. Nature of the electorate	Expansion of the right to vote, citizens' political interest and knowledge, social characteristics of the electorate (distributions of age, race, income, education)
2. Political institutions and rules	
(a) Institutions	Federalism, separation of powers, nature of the presidency, single-member districts
(b) Electoral processes	Direct primary, nonpartisan elections
(c) Laws and regulations	Laws governing campaign finance, structure of party organization, patronage
3. Social forces	
(a) National events and conditions	State of the economy, war, other national problems
(b) Other political intermediaries	Types of other organized interests, nature and importance of television and other media, independent consultants
(c) Political culture	Attitudes toward parties and politics

The Nature of the Electorate

The nature and concerns of the voting population are vital influences on a party system. The societal "fault lines" that divide the electorate into opposing groups—race is one of the best and most persistent examples in American politics—help to define the parties' issue agendas. So do the social characteristics that make some groups more likely to vote than others.

The right to vote has expanded enormously in the United States. From an extremely limited suffrage—the small proportion of white male adults who owned property—it now includes the overwhelming majority of citizens over the age of 18. Political information has expanded as well. Mass media and computers have made information about politics much more accessible, and more citizens have the advantage of higher education, which helps them find and understand the information. Voters have gained unprecedented opportunities to take part in political decisions through primary elections, referenda, recall elections, and Internet access to public officials throughout the nation. Yet people's interest in politics and feelings of political effectiveness and trust have not increased. So at the same time that these opportunities for participation expanded, voter turnout dropped and has remained lower than in most other industrialized democracies.

Turnout did not decline to the same degree among all groups in the population, however. There was a steeper decline among lower income Americans than among those with greater wealth.[2] And as we saw in Chapter 8, the turnout rate of college-age Americans, though it rose slightly between 2000 and 2004, remains more than a third lower than the turnout rate of adults over 65. It should come as no surprise, then, that Social Security and Medicare are much more frequent campaign issues than are college loans. The social forces that help to determine who votes and who doesn't are powerful influences on which groups' concerns will dominate the political system.

Political Institutions and Rules

The second cluster of environmental influences on the parties includes the nation's basic framework of political institutions: whether the government is federal or unitary, whether it is parliamentary or has separated powers, and how its positions of power are structured. Then there are the laws that regulate the parties and their activities, ranging from state laws telling the parties when to hold their meetings to federal laws regulating campaign spending. We have discussed, for example, the effects of the separation of powers, the direct primary, and the use of plurality elections in single-member districts on the development and cohesion of the parties.

The American parties are regulated more heavily than are parties in other nations. The direct primary limits their role in the selection of candidates to a degree unknown in most other democracies, and American state laws defining the party organizations have no parallel in the democratic world. The effect of this regulation—and in most cases its aim—is to restrict the development of the party organizations. An unintended effect is to boost the power of the party in government relative to that of the party organization. With the important exceptions of the direct primary and the secret ballot, however, these political rules have probably changed less dramatically over time than has the nature of the electorate.

Societal Forces

A third set of environmental influences refers to events and trends in the larger society that affect politics at a particular time. The horrors of the September 11 attacks, the relocation of U.S. industries to Mexico and China, and the changes in women's roles and family structures have had powerful effects on the nation's agenda. Thus, they have become part of the parties' agenda as well and affect the parties' platforms, campaign appeals, and supporting coalitions.

Other societal forces include the number and character of organized interests in the nation, the types and behavior of the media, and other means of representing interests. If individuals find alternative ways to pursue their political goals that seem more effective than the parties, they will use them. If the "hot line" of a local newspaper is better able to track down a reader's Social Security check that has gotten lost in the bureaucracy or if an interest group is more vocal in opposing abortion or gay marriage, then why should the individual try to achieve her political aims through a party? The nature of the parties at any given time, then, depends in part on the available alternatives to parties and the competition among them.

All these elements of their environment have contributed to the unique character of the American parties. Thus, as we summarize the dramatic changes that have occurred in the parties' structure, supporting coalitions, and strength during the past four decades, we will pay special attention to the effects of their environment and especially to changes in the electorate.

PARTY DECLINE IN THE 1960s AND 1970s

A basic feature of the American parties is that the three party sectors are bound together only loosely. The party organization has not been able to involve large numbers of party identifiers in its structure and activities, nor has it been able to direct the campaigns or the policy making of the party in government. The party decline that was becoming apparent in the 1960s affected the three sectors very differently.

The Parties in the Electorate

During a time of upheaval in many of aspects of American life, voters' loyalty to the parties weakened noticeably in the late 1960s and 1970s. More people began to think of themselves as independents rather than as strong party identifiers. Those who remained attached to a party no longer relied on that identification in elections as much as they once did. The parties, then, found themselves with smaller numbers of less loyal identifiers.

One result was a surge in ticket splitting. By 1968, almost half of the respondents in national surveys said they had voted for more than one party's candidates in state or local elections, and by 1974 that figure topped out at 61 percent. At the aggregate level, the number of congressional districts selecting a presidential candidate of one party and a congressional candidate of the other party exceeded 30 percent for the first time in history in 1964 and had reached 44 percent early in the next decade.[3]

As education levels increased, some voters became more responsive to the increasingly issue-oriented candidacies of the time. The campaigns of Barry Goldwater in 1964, Eugene McCarthy and George Wallace in 1968, and George McGovern in 1972 spurred many people's awareness of political issues and events. As television came to be used more widely in campaigns, others were drawn to candidates' personalities and media images. The handsome faces and ready smiles that television screens convey attracted some of the support that party symbols once commanded.

Voters became more inclined than they had in the 1950s, then, to respond to candidates as individuals rather than as members of a party. Independent candidates for president—McCarthy in 1976 and John Anderson in 1980—and for governor enjoyed some success. Because candidates and issues change far more frequently than parties, the result was a less stable and predictable pattern of voting.

Party Organizations

The last of the great party machines were fading in the 1960s and 1970s. The famous Daley machine in Chicago was ripped apart in a series of tumultuous struggles after Richard J. Daley's death in 1976. Party organizations could no longer depend on the patronage and preferments that once were so vital in recruiting party activists. Instead, more people were being drawn into party activism because of their commitment to particular issues. These were better educated people, and they demanded greater participation in the party's decisions. Some of these new activists felt that compromise was a dirty word; to them, standing for a set of principles was more important than winning an election. If their party did not satisfy their ideological goals, they stood ready to leave it for other groups—candidates' campaigns and single-issue organizations—that were more narrowly targeted to meet their needs.

Other aspects of the party organization were under stress as well. As the direct primary came to dominate presidential nominations, party organizations gave up their control over nominations to whoever voted in the primary. By the time a primary season had ended, the party's presidential nominee had been determined, so its presidential nominating convention no longer had much of an independent role. As grassroots activists came to expect a bigger say within the party organization, its own internal decision making was no longer under the party leaders' control. This was particularly true of the Democrats, who in 1972 and 1976 nominated presidential candidates who were well outside the mainstream of their own party.

In addition to their declining influence over nominations, by the 1960s and 1970s the party organizations had lost their central role in campaigns more generally. Candidates now built their own campaign organizations, raised their own campaign money, and made their own decisions on how to spend it. The campaign assets that they once received from their local party organizations—information about public opinion, strategic advice, fund-raising, willing helpers—could now be obtained directly from pollsters, the media, issue-oriented activists, or campaign consulting firms that were, in effect, "rent-a-party" agencies. The campaign finance reforms gave candidates an incentive to try to raise nonparty money at a time when the technologies for doing so were becoming more effective and widely available.

In fact, in comparison with independent consultants, the campaign skills that local party organizations could offer their candidates were fairly primitive. The national parties began to develop expertise in newer campaign technologies during the 1970s and to share their resources with state and local parties, but consultants and the other nonparty providers of campaign services had already established a beachhead. Even in the face of new vigor in the national committees, the party organizations in the 1970s remained much more decentralized than did life and politics in the United States. Voters were looking more and more to national political leaders and symbols, but the party organizations still tended to be collections of state and local activists.

The Party in Government

In the 1960s and early 1970s, elected officials came to depend more than ever on direct appeals to voters. Officeholders had been freed from reliance on the party organization by the direct primary, their direct access to the media, and the money they could raise and the volunteers they could attract independent of the party's efforts. Because of split-ticket voting, candidates didn't even need to rely on party identification. Through personal style, personal appeals, and personal funds, they developed a "personal vote" independent of party.[4]

It became harder than ever before to unseat an incumbent, especially in Congress. The cycle perpetuated itself; because there was not as much chance of beating an elected official, serious challengers did not appear as frequently. When they did, party organizations were not vigorous enough to provide challengers with the campaign resources they so desperately needed. Holding public office became more of a profession—a lifetime career—even at the state and local level, where political professionals had formerly been rare.

As incumbents became more secure electorally, even though many did not feel that way, the congressional parties gained greater freedom from the party organizations. Even the legislative party leaders found it harder to marshal their members on behalf of the legislative party's bills or the programs of the party's president. Add this to the diversity within the Democratic Party in Congress, divided between southern conservatives and northern moderates and liberals. Democrats in Congress were reluctant to grant much power to their legislative party leaders; neither the southern nor the northern Democrats could trust that leaders selected from the other group would act to serve the needs of all the members of the congressional party. Senate and House Republicans were a varied group as well. So party-line voting in Congress fell to an all-time low in the late 1960s and early 1970s. However, it was a perverse kind of freedom. Protected from the demands of party leaders, legislators were thus more exposed to other pressures, mainly from large numbers of organized interests.

With the legislative parties less cohesive and strong, presidents and governors began to exercise greater leadership. The parties, then, could be viewed as executive-centered coalitions during the late 1960s and 1970s. Presidents did not depend on their party organizations for much; in fact, with the help of federal campaign money after 1974, presidential candidates were able to run their campaigns free of obligation to the party organization at any level. By that time, however, divided government had become the norm. That undercut executives' power by permitting the opposition party to block their leadership.

Shifting Power Centers Within the Parties

These changes produced a major shift of power within the parties. From the decentralized party organization, power had flowed to the individual members of the party in government, especially the executives. The changes also accentuated a shift in influence from the parties to rival political intermediaries, especially organized interests and the mass media.[5]

At the core of these changes was the increasing isolation of the party organization, not only within the parties but also in American politics more generally. Party organizations and their leaders became even more vulnerable to suspicions that they were run by bosses plotting in smoke-filled rooms. Visions of "boss rule" were as much alive at party conventions in the 1960s and 1970s as they were in the early 1900s, even though, ironically, the resources that the party organizations had in the early 1900s, which could have justified the charge of boss rule at that time, were largely eroded by the 1960s.

The result was a peculiar kind of political party. A party organization is the only sector of the party whose interests go beyond the winning of individual elections. It is the party organization that sustains the party when its candidates lose their races. It is the organization that links the party's officeholders and office seekers; it can call them to collective action of the type that parties were created to achieve. Without it, party candidates are individual entrepreneurs seeking individual goals in a political system that requires collective decisions. The decline of the party organizations was clearly a major force in the decline of the parties more generally.

PARTY RENEWAL

This marked decline was not the end of the story, however. The American parties responded to these challenges, just as they have adapted to changing circumstances at other times in the past. The steady decay of the parties was stopped and reversed, but some of the changes that took place in the 1960s and 1970s have left their imprint even now. In some ways, the parties have had to adjust to a new role in American politics.

Change in the Parties' Electoral Coalitions

The slow, steady change in the two parties' supporting coalitions, discussed especially in Chapter 7, has led to regularly recurring speculation that a party realignment has taken place—that the two parties' supporting coalitions have changed in significant enough ways to alter the nature of the party system. The symptoms that normally precede a major coalitional change began to be present in the mid-1960s: lower voter turnout, more ticket splitting, greater support for third-party or independent candidates, less predictable elections, and divided government.

When Republicans won both the presidency and the Senate in 1980 and gained control of the House in 1994—the first time since 1954 that there was a Republican majority in both Houses of Congress—some concluded that the long-awaited realignment had finally occurred. They pointed out that the party coalitions had clearly changed from those of the New Deal period. Black Americans are now steadfastly Democratic, white southerners have moved into the GOP in large numbers, and religious conservatives, southern and nonsouthern, are now a distinctive force within the Republican Party. Other demographic categories such as marital status and sexual orientation have taken on a partisan tinge, as unmarried people (especially women) and gay people have come to identify preponderantly as Democrats. The most striking feature of this new alignment has been the decline of Democratic strength in the South (see Figure 16.1). As a result, Republicans have come closer to parity with the Democrats in both party identification and election results than had been the case since the 1930s.

There is good evidence, then, that we are in a different party system in the early 2000s from that of the New Deal. But this sixth party system has emerged differently from the New Deal party system. In contrast with the tumultuous changes that followed the Depression of the 1930s, the more recent changes in party coalitions and party structure have developed over a period of four decades and continue to evolve. Election results have been mercurial. Republican House candidates went from great success in 1994 to panic in 1998 and back to success in 2002. The proportion of the public calling themselves independents remains high. New parties and independent candidacies have aroused public interest. Polls do not reveal any great public enthusiasm for the major parties or, for that matter, many other aspects of American politics. Even a full-fledged realignment of the parties' coalitions, in a world of primaries, would not give back the party organizations' power to nominate their candidates. Lasting change in the parties' coalitions could not guarantee an end to the more candidate-centered electoral world that has resulted.

Thus, the events of the 1960s and 1970s resulted in a continuing challenge to American party loyalties. Large numbers of voters now rely on sources other than the parties, such as the media and single-issue groups, for their political information. In earlier times, these sources may have helped to reinforce partisan views and loyalties; now, they may not.[6] Even with this formidable competition, however, parties remain important landmarks on most people's political map. Levels of party identification rebounded in the 1990s, and partisanship is at least as strong an influence on people's voting now as it was before the 1960s.[7] Split-ticket voting, especially as measured by the number of districts voting for a presidential candidate of one party and a congressional candidate of the other, hit a 50-year low in 2002.[8]

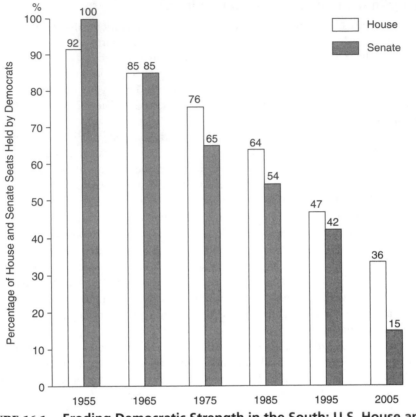

FIGURE 16.1   Eroding Democratic Strength in the South: U.S. House and Senate Seats, 1955–2005

Note: Data points are the percentage of U.S. senators and House members from the 13 southern states who are Democrats.

Source: Data for 1955–1995 from *Congressional Quarterly Weekly Report*, November 12, 1994: 3231. Data for 2005 from *CQ Weekly*, November 6, 2004, pp. 2664–2666, and December 11, 2004, p. 2931

The Rise of More Cohesive Parties in Government

Well before the current revival of partisanship among voters—and thus a possible cause of it—the parties in government had begun a revival of their own. By the mid-1970s, the long decline in party unity in Congress had stopped and the organizational seeds had been sown for greater party strength. By the 1980s, with stronger and more assertive leadership, the congressional parties had become more cohesive than they had been in a century. Their cohesion was enhanced by the coalitional changes within the party electorates. The slow, steady movement from the Democratic "solid South" to a largely Republican South left both congressional parties more homogeneous. This homogeneity made it easier for each party to offer distinctive alternatives on major issues. In a number of states, as well, legislative parties were becoming more unified and taking clearer positions on issues.

Parties also took on greater importance in the executive branch. The Reagan administration came into office in 1981 as the most ideologically committed and the most partisan in decades. Reagan's leadership placed conservative principles at the top of the GOP's agenda and solidified the hold of his brand of conservatives on the party. The Democrats became more unified in response. By the mid-1990s, there was intense partisan warfare in Washington between a programmatically committed Republican majority in Congress and an activist Clinton White House. The battles continued in 2004 between a conservative Republican president and large Democratic minorities in the Senate and House.

The New "Service Parties"

The party organizations have revived in even more dramatic fashion. Facing an environment of candidate-centered campaigns, both parties retooled their national organizations to provide services to the party's candidates. They have used their increased funding and professional staffs to assist state and local parties, recruit candidates for office, offer them more resources, and thus step up their role in campaigns, at least in comparison with the 1960s and 1970s.

The new service party, however, differs a great deal from the grassroots organizations of earlier years. Because its main role is to support candidates, it is not very visible to voters, nor is it assured of making a major impact on campaigns. In the big-spending world of campaign finance, the party organizations do not bring enough money to the table to be able to dominate political campaigning or at times even to be heard very clearly. The service party is one of many forces, including campaign consultants and interest groups, trying to win the attention of candidates, influence elected officials, and mobilize citizens.

The party organizations, in short, are more vigorous now than they have been in years. There is a greater balance of power between the national and state and local parties now than ever existed before. The party organizations have adapted to new conditions by taking on a new form: that of the service party. However, as service parties, the party organizations are no longer as distinctive as they used to be in the sense of providing campaign resources that no other group could deliver.

THE FUTURE OF PARTY POLITICS IN AMERICA

These trends are vital to us because political parties are vital to us. Parties have the potential to do a great deal of good for a democracy. They can enable political leaders to work together in achieving a set of shared interests over time. They can provide cues that permit voters to make decisions on candidates and issues with relatively little effort. Parties can bring voters to the polls, which helps to legitimize a democracy. Perhaps most important, parties organize majorities, which are necessary for governing. Interest groups can effectively represent intense minorities, but there are not many alternatives to the parties for organizing lasting and predictable majorities.

A Changing Intermediary Role

Elections require voters to make large numbers of choices, often on the basis of little information. Parties serve as an efficient guide. The value of the party label in elections is probably greatest when a mass electorate has just begun to develop and has serious need for information. As the electorate matures, its needs change. One explanation for American voters' decreased reliance on party loyalties in the 1960s and 1970s was that voters had become better educated and better informed than was the case 60 or 80 years earlier, so they might have been better able to sift through a broader range of political messages without the need for party labels as a guide.[9]

It is interesting, then, that although education levels have continued to increase since the 1960s, party identification has reasserted itself as an influence on many voters' choices. Why should partisanship help citizens who have so many other sources of information about candidates and issues? Perhaps *because* they are exposed to so much information. Without this simple guide, the blizzard of political communication could serve as more of a deterrent than a tool. At the same time, the fact that the two major parties have drawn farther apart from one another on important issues lends even more meaning to the party labels for politically engaged citizens. Added to the heightened party competition in the early 2000s and the resulting intensity of campaign advertising, changes in the political environment can make an individual's partisanship even more significant to him or her.

Granted, the parties' traditional dominance in politics has been eroded by competition from organized interests and the media. A century ago, someone concerned about environmental quality would probably have had to pursue his or her goals through a political party; not many groups focused specifically on resource conservation or pollution control. Now, however, along with the growing reach of government into most aspects of private life, a huge array of organized interests has developed that permit individuals to establish a "designer link" with the political system. If someone prefers to see politics entirely from the perspective of environmental rights or property rights, several groups exist to make that possible. There is no need to compromise or to support a coalition of other groups' needs and a range of candidates, as a party loyalty would encourage.

In this fractured world of political interests, parties become even more important as a means of broadening individuals' perspectives and improving their ability to hold elected officials accountable. The parties have long struggled with hostile environmental forces, from a system of separated powers that is inhospitable to strong parties to a political culture that regards parties with suspicion. However, as we have seen throughout this book, the parties are adaptable. They are not the intermediaries they were in 1900 or 1950, but for large numbers of Americans and for the process by which policies are made, the major parties remain the most important intermediaries.

The Need for Strong Parties

The problem is that although we need parties, we don't like them. We don't even like to admit that they influence us. Most of us claim that issues and candidates' personal qualities have the biggest impact on our votes. Yet it's clear that partisanship is closely related to our attitudes toward issues and candidates and is the source of much of their influence.[10]

Democracy is unworkable without parties.[11] The United States has probably come closer to testing that principle than any other democracy; much of American local politics has been, at least officially, nonpartisan for some time. But it seems clear that when parties are reduced to playing a smaller role in politics, the quality of democracy is weakened.

Consider the role strong parties can play in Congress and state legislatures. As a representative body, Congress is structured to permit legislators to give their constituents what they want: short-term, tangible benefits such as disaster relief, expanded Medicare benefits, and jobs on pork-barrel projects. Legislators facing reelection seek the Holy Grail of constituent service: a project such as a new dam or highway that provides tangible benefits to their own constituents but whose costs are paid by taxpayers all over the country. Both the individual voter and the individual legislator are motivated to pay close attention to the benefits they can get for their district, but who is motivated to pay attention to the collective cost? Very few voters support the idea of raising their own taxes in order to pay for benefits to others—and often even to pay for benefits to themselves.

Strong legislative parties do have an incentive to take responsibility for the collective costs.[12] Some legislative party members can gain personal career advantages by becoming leaders of their congressional party. When the party's members in Congress are elected from similar districts and hold similar views, they can afford to trust these legislative party leaders with greater power to structure the choices they will make. Members realize that although their own reelection needs are primary, they also need coordination within the legislature in order to pass bills and to help with the endless tasks of legislative life. And most members come to Congress to accomplish something beyond just obtaining the prestige and the pay of the office, and they realize that to do so, they need powerful allies.

By using the carrots and sticks discussed in Chapter 13, legislative party leaders can lead their party colleagues to make truly national policy, not just "Christmas tree" legislation that consists of a pork-barrel ornament for each congressional district. By holding their legislators to this party program, they can create a favorable "brand name" for their party in elections, which voters can come to recognize and associate with their own district's candidate. In the absence of strong parties, it is difficult to imagine where this collective responsibility might come from. Without strong parties, individual members of Congress and state legislatures have every reason to behave in ways that conflict with their collective interest and that of their constituents.[13]

In a society dominated by other intermediaries, most people would not be as well represented. Among the many links between citizens and government, only the parties have the incentive to create majorities in order to win a wide range of elections over a long period. That, in turn, gives the parties, to a greater extent than interest groups, political action committees, or even elected officials, a reason to pay attention to those citizens who are not activists or big campaign contributors. As political scientist Walter Dean Burnham has written, parties are the only devices that can "generate countervailing collective power on behalf of the many individually powerless against the relatively few who are individually—or organizationally—powerful.[14]

It is the parties that mobilize sheer numbers against the organized minorities who hold other political resources. The parties do so in the one political arena where sheer numbers count most heavily: elections. Because of that, parties traditionally have been the means by which newly enfranchised but otherwise powerless groups gained a foothold in American life. The old-style urban machines, for example, provided the instrument with which recent immigrants won control of their cities from the more established Anglo-Saxon Protestant elites.

In other periods of American history as well, the party has been the form of political organization most available to citizens who lack the resources to influence public decisions using other means. In a less party-driven politics, in which bargaining takes place among many more types of political organizations, the well-organized minorities with critical resources—money, insider knowledge, and technological expertise—would probably have even greater advantages than they do now. As we have seen from research on nonpartisan elections, for instance, the elimination of the party symbol and of the party as an organizer has probably helped wealthier and higher status groups of both the right and left to dominate these elections, and has made it more difficult for citizens to hold their representatives accountable.[15] That may be one reason why participation has declined more sharply during the past few decades among lower status and less educated Americans; they may feel less represented by a politics in which the parties are no longer dominant.[16]

Finally, weakened parties would rob the political system of an effective means for creating governing coalitions. Without at least moderately strong parties, it becomes harder to mobilize majorities that can come together in support of policies. Individual candidates, freed from lasting party loyalties, would have to recreate majorities for every new legislative proposal. The result could be political immobility in which legislatures splinter into conflicting and intransigent groups. This can further undermine public confidence in democratic politics.

Laws and policies would continue to be made, but they would be made by shifting coalitions composed of interest groups, campaign contributors, bureaucrats, and elected officials acting as free agents. These coalitions would be less permanent and less identifiable to the public, and therefore much harder to hold accountable, than the parties have been and can be. In a diverse nation, the challenge is whether any of the alternatives could pull together the pieces of a fragmented politics and separated political institutions as effectively as the parties have done.

How to Make the Parties Stronger

Because parties bring so much value to American democracy, some analysts have considered ways to expand the parties' role in political life. The most potent solutions—abolishing the separation of powers, the direct primary, and the antiparty sentiment engrained into the political culture—are not on the table, of course. But there are a variety of less dramatic ways in which the parties might be strengthened.

Larry J. Sabato and Bruce Larson report that most respondents in their recent survey would like the parties to be more active in helping people deal with government. They propose, among other ideas, that the party organizations could create "mobile units" to help citizens in areas where the U.S. (and perhaps the state) representative is from the other party. That would allow the party organization, not just the members of the party in government, to perform constituent service. They note that this idea was especially attractive to respondents who described their commitment to party as having declined in the past five years and who said they were not registered to vote—those, in short, more likely to be alienated from politics.[17]

The parties could help to build long-term loyalty among their activists by providing volunteers with such attractive nonpolitical benefits as low-cost health and life insurance, as many interest groups do now.[18] This would make the American parties into organizations more like European-style mass membership parties. Another way for the parties to renew their connection with citizens is to air campaign ads that promote the party as a whole, rather than just individual candidates. To this point, the bulk of both parties' money goes to fund ads that do not even mention the party itself. In particular, such advertising could strengthen the meaning of party by stressing the link between the party's stands and individuals' daily lives.

The parties will likely benefit as well from the current movement by some cash-starved states to forgo their presidential primary elections and permit the parties to hold caucuses instead. The experience of taking part in a party caucus has brought many polit-ically interested citizens and candidate activists into more active work for their party, which in turn allows the party organization to expand its canvassing and other forms of direct contact with voters.

CONCLUSION: THE PARTIES' PROSPECTS

The American parties have never lacked problems to solve. The electorate has become more and more varied. Traditional group ties have broken down. New groups, from antiabortion to animal liberation, are tilling the ground that the major parties once owned. The great majority of voters still identify with a political party, but they also respond to candidates and issues, stylistic changes, and national trends. The result is a more diverse, complicated politics that no single set of loyalties or political organiza-tions can easily contain.

The parties can't meet every political need. They can't represent the individual agenda of each citizen while trying to build a majority coalition. They can't be pure in their issue stands while still making the compromises necessary to build coalitions and govern. They find it hard to offer policy alternatives in campaigns without engaging in the partisan conflict that many Americans find so distasteful. It is as difficult to mesh the needs and agendas of their candidates and officeholders as it is to satisfy every voter; it can be an impossible task for the parties to unite their elected officials and office seek-ers on a single agenda while giving candidates the independence to choose their own appeals and meet their own districts' needs. The parties can't provide party accountabil-ity to an electorate that wants to choose candidates individually.

We will continue to challenge the parties with these conflicting expectations. The American parties will continue to have to adapt to them while facing attack from a rich assortment of critics. The parties' distinctive character has sustained them longer than any other tool of democratic politics. For the sake of representation, effective policy mak-ing, and accountability in governance, even the most independent-minded citizens have a stake in sustaining vigorous party politics in the United States.

Party Politics on the Internet

The web pages of the two major parties and a variety of minor parties can provide a fascinating glimpse into the world of each party's politics and can serve as the basis for some interesting assignments. Here are the main sites of the Democrats, the Republicans, and 22 American minor parties for you to explore. Later in this section, you'll find a listing of other sites on party politics and a number of sample assignments using these sites.

http://www.democrats.org

This is the official website of the Democratic National Committee (DNC). It contains party news, a blog, critical reports about President Bush and other Republicans, strategic plans, and lists of special events. There are links to state and local Democratic Parties and the party's most recent national platform as well as information for various Democratic constituency groups (women, young people, and others). Visitors can find out how to receive e-mail updates from the DNC, contribute, and register to vote.

http://www.rnc.org

The Republican National Committee's official website provides party statements about current events and issues, biographies of President George W. Bush and other Republican leaders, and information about the party's history. Profiles of candidates are posted here at election time, and the site includes a blog, a calendar of coming events, and a listing of allied groups and constituencies. Links enable the visitor to contact state Republican organizations, donate money, contact elected officials, and register to vote.

http://www.americafirstparty.org

Members of the America First Party broke away from the Reform Party in 2002 to support its 2000 presidential candidate, Pat Buchanan. A socially conservative party aligned with the Christian Right, the America Firsters have experienced a number of internal divisions in their short history. Information is posted about the state party organizations in 12 states and about a party e-mail list. The party has an extensive platform.

http://www.americanreform.org

The American Reform Party split off from the main body of the Reform Party in 1997 in opposition to its founder, Ross Perot. The site contains a history of the organization, position papers, a party platform, profiles of party candidates, and links to state groups. You can get information on how to contribute online and join the party.

http://www.americanheritageparty.org

An explicitly Christian party, the American Heritage Party promotes the Bible as a blue-print for political action and opposes abortion, group-based civil rights, gun control, income and property taxes, and government welfare programs. Its website emphasizes its statement of principles and states its aim to establish voter clubs at the local level, in addition to its existing party organization in the state of Washington.

http://www.cpusa.org

This is the home page of the Communist Party USA. Posted here are position papers stating the party's stands against joblessness, racism, and poverty and a list of party-related journals. There are e-mail addresses for joining the national party, contacting state parties and local clubs, and donating money, listings of party events, and links to a variety of groups with similar aims.

http://www.constitutionparty.com

Formerly the U.S. Taxpayers Party, the Constitution Party favors limited government and opposes abortion, gun control, immigration, taxes, and gay rights. The site offers press releases, a list of party events, its platform, and a place to order campaign materials. There are audio clips, links to state party organizations in almost every state, and online opportunities to volunteer for the party and make contributions.

http://www.dsausa.org/dsa.html

The Democratic Socialists of America's site includes a statement of the party's principles and links to information about socialism in the United States and in other nations. There are reports about the activities of its approximately 25 local parties and an invitation for members to form other local parties, receive e-mail updates, and join Young Democratic Socialists.

http://www.greens.org/na.html

The Green Parties of North America post their platform, which emphasizes environmental issues, peace, and social justice, on this website. The site includes a series of party publications, e-mail services, listings of its election results since 1985, and, at election time, its current candidates. There are links to state Green Parties and to Campus Greens.

http://www.usiap.org

The Independent American Party wants smaller government and an emphasis on Christian values, patriotism, and property rights. It is pro-life and favors a strong military and the free enterprise system. It began as a Utah party in 1998 but currently has contacts in about half of the states. The site contains the national platform, membership information, coming events, and a discussion of party history.

http://www.logcabin.org

Formed in the late 1970s to oppose a California initiative that would have barred gays from teaching in the state's public schools, the Log Cabin Republicans is an organization of gay and lesbian Republicans that aims to influence Republican stands on issues of concern to gays. It now has chapters in 25 states and is headquartered in Washington, DC. Its website includes legislative information, material about party conventions and advocacy campaigns, and a newsletter. Candidate endorsements are listed at election time. Links exist to various local chapters.

http://www.lp.org

The Libertarian Party believes in almost complete freedom from government and taxes. Its home page provides an extensive list of party principles. There is a link to a quiz, "Are You a Libertarian?" You'll also find a list of state chapters. Interested visitors can sign up for the party's e-mail announcement list, register to vote, and contribute online. It describes itself as the third largest party in the United States.

http://www.uspeacegovernment.org

U.S. Peace Government (formerly the Natural Law Party) proposes establishing a group of 8,000 peace-creating experts who use Transcendental Meditation and other new-age practices to eliminate deep-seated political, ethnic, and religious tensions. The site includes the platform, news and events, information about issues such as genetic engineering, and a link to the Student Natural Law Party Club. You'll find links to representatives in the states, recommended readings, and an opportunity to join the group's e-mail list.

http://www.newparty.org

The New Party is a progressive grassroots party concerned mainly with local elections in a variety of cities. It promotes "fusion," the listing of candidates on multiple party lines. The website features materials about the party's principles, including nondiscrimination, affordable housing, a living wage, campaign finance reform, and limits on corporate power, plus an opportunity to join its e-mail list.

http://www.peaceandfreedom.org

Formed in the 1960s to oppose American involvement in the Vietnam War, the Peace and Freedom Party lost but recently regained ballot status in California. It describes itself as a feminist and socialist party dedicated to environmental protection, workers' rights, racial equality, disarmament, and democratic control of industry. The site includes the party's platform, a place to register to vote, and to contribute to the party.

http://www.prohibition.org

Founded in 1870 to oppose the manufacture and sale of alcoholic beverages, the Prohibition Party has taken on a new life as a pro-life, anti-gay, pro-prayer party. There is a link to the party's 2004 national platform, its monthly publication "The National Statesman," and items including historical campaign buttons for sale.

http://www.reformparty.org

This is the site of one branch of the Reform Party, founded in 1996 by Ross Perot. Perot has left the party, and it has split again since then, but it remains committed to campaign finance reform, restrictions on lobbying, term limits for elected officials, and a balanced budget. The party's main principles are posted here, along with a statement of party history and current party news. Visitors to the site can register to vote, contribute online, and join the party's e-mail lists. There are links to 14 state Reform Parties.

http://www.sp-usa.org

The century-old Socialist Party USA stands for principles of democratic socialism, including full employment and an internally democratic party organization. It is an anticommunist socialist group, unlike several other socialist parties. Its website lists a variety of socialist publications and introduces its current candidates. Visitors can find information about joining, locating state parties, current events, and participating in the party's e-mail list.

http://www.socialequality.com

One of the newer socialist parties, the Socialist Equality Party fielded a presidential and a few congressional candidates in 2004. It favors American withdrawal from Iraq, workers' rights, and regulation of big business. The site offers links to stories on the World Socialist website and an opportunity to donate to the party.

http://www.slp.org

The Socialist Labor Party bills itself as the original Socialist Party in the United States, founded in the late 1800s. It no longer runs candidates for president but does take part in a few local races. Its website discusses its principles, including a classless society and collective ownership of industries and social services; contains links to a newsletter and other socialist writings, and provides e-mail links to several local chapters.

http://www.themilitant.com

The Socialist Workers Party broke away from the Communist Party decades ago and now espouses a pro-Castro and workers' rights viewpoint. It runs local candidates in some areas as well as a candidate for president. Its website is a newsletter presenting party views on current issues.

http://www.veteransparty.us

Formed mainly to advocate for veterans' benefits, the Veterans Party of America also stands for term limits, an end to illegal immigration, less foreign aid, and careful oversight of the Department of Veterans' Affairs. It was founded in 2003 and fielded a small number of candidates in 2004 and a few in 2006. It has an official party song: Lee Greenwood's "God Bless the USA."

http://www.wethepeople-wtp.org

The We the People Party views itself as a coalition of independents first organized to take part in the 2004 presidential race. Its primary concern is campaign finance reform, and it hopes to establish party organizations in all 50 states. The website contains newsletters, a statement of principles, a free membership application, and a page encouraging visitors to express their concerns, as well as links to websites dealing with campaign finance. The creation of two founders, it is located in New Hampshire.

http://www.workers.org

The Workers World Party has a 45-year history in the United States since it split off from the Socialist Workers Party. It is an anti-capitalist organization with a pro-Cuba, pro-China approach to communist politics. Its website contains news of issues that the organization finds interesting, events, and a party e-mail list.

Here are some other Internet websites on political parties, elections, and voting.

CAMPAIGN FINANCE

http://www.commoncause.org

Common Cause monitors a variety of political issues as a means of holding government accountable. You can access a long list of research reports, get campaign finance information, and learn about other reforms including those involving media coverage. The group has an internship program.

http://www.fec.gov

This is the Federal Election Commission's website. In addition to information about the Commission itself, it provides access to current and past campaign finance data in federal (presidential, House, and Senate) races.

http://www.opensecrets.org

The Center for Responsive Politics, a nonpartisan research group, distributes information on money in politics. Its databases include presidential and congressional races, political action committees, 527s, soft money, lobbyists, and news links of various kinds.

POLITICS AND POLITICAL ISSUES

http://www.govote.com

This site has a lot of information on elections, issues, and other political news. You can take part in surveys, compare your views with those of a variety of public officials, and track the voting record of your senator or House member on a range of issues.

http://www.heritage.org

The Heritage Foundation is a conservative think tank; its website provides current political news and detailed analyses of policy issues from a conservative perspective.

http://www.mojones.com

Mother Jones, a liberal publication that appears on the web as well as in hard copy, covers American politics and issues and also contains a lot of international news.

http://www.nga.org

You can find information about every state governor at the site of the National Governors' Association, as well as NGA positions on issues of interest to the states. Job opportunities are also listed here. The home page of the Council of State Governments (http://www.statesnews.org) has more information on state policy issues.

http://www.rollcall.com

Roll Call is a newspaper that covers Congress and Capitol Hill. Its website contains news about current legislative action, political campaigns, and "insider" information about Congress.

http://www.vote-smart.org

Project VoteSmart offers a wealth of information on federal and state candidates, including biographical data, interest group ratings, voting records, and candidates' responses to questions about their issue priorities. It contains data on campaign finance, tracks legislation in Congress, and tells website visitors how to register to vote. The group maintains an internship program in Montana.

POLLING

http://www.people-press.org

The Pew Research Center for the People and the Press conducts polls about politics, policy, and public attitudes toward the media. Its website contains a lot of polling data and analysis by Pew and other groups.

http://www.pollingreport.com

This site carries recent survey data from several polling organizations (Fox News, Gallup, CNN, and others) on a variety of political topics, including candidate ratings and public opinion about political issues.

http://www.tarrance.com/battleground.html

The Battleground Poll is a collaboration between Democratic pollster Celinda Lake and Republican strategist Ed Goeas. The website offers public opinion polling data and strategic analyses from both parties' perspectives.

http://www.umich.edu/~nes/

The National Election Studies, based at the University of Michigan, have been conducted since 1952 to provide information on public opinion, political participation, and voting behavior. Students can view and download survey data from current and earlier studies and look at research reports.

MEDIA SITES

http://www.cnn.com/POLITICS

Here are links to current and recent news stories from CNN and *Time* magazine.

http://www.cagle.com/politicalcartoons

You'll find dozens of current political cartoons on this website from the United States and other nations.

http://www.washingtonpost.com

Major national newspapers such as the *Washington Post* can be read on the Internet. The *Post* is notable for the excellence of its political coverage, as are the *New York Times* (http://www.nytimes.com) and the *Los Angeles Times* (http://www.latimes.com).

SAMPLE ASSIGNMENTS USING THESE WEBSITES

- Pick two political issues that interest you. Use the Democratic and Republican Parties' websites to determine where they stand on these issues. How clear are their stands and how much difference do you find between them? Do they offer you a real choice?

- Compare the positions of the two major parties with those of two minor parties. How easy is it to find out where the minor parties stand on the issues that interest you? How different are their stands from those of the Democrats and Republicans? What would be the advantages and disadvantages for American politics if these alternatives were more widely publicized?

- What can you learn from these websites about the parties' organizations? At what levels of government do the major parties have organizations? Where do the minor parties have chapters or branches, other than at the national level?

- What kinds of activities do the Democrats and Republicans sponsor? To what extent do minor parties offer similar activities to their sympathizers?

- Does a party's website show evidence that the party offers material rewards for activists or solidary or purposive rewards (see Chapter 5)? Which type of rewards seems to be most common? Do you find more emphasis on purposive rewards in the major parties' websites or in those of the minor parties? What about solidary rewards?

- Which do the Democrats' and Republicans' home pages stress most: their candidates' experience and personal qualities or the party's issue stands?

- Do the two major parties seem to be targeting particular groups in the population, such as women, Latinos, or others? Which ones? Do the Democrats and Republicans target the same groups or different groups?

- Are the statements on these websites predominantly positive—that is, presenting the party's own beliefs—or predominantly negative, in the sense of criticizing other parties' or groups' actions and views? Do you find the major parties' statements to be more positive (or negative) than those of the minor parties? The liberal parties' statements to be more positive (or negative) than those of the conservative parties?

- In comparison with the major parties, why is the universe of minor parties so splintered? There are, for example, seven socialist parties listed here. How do they differ from one another, and how substantial are their differences? What about the differences among the several conservative minor parties? Do you find anything in these websites that helps to explain this proliferation?

- Are there any major issue positions or views of the world that you do *not* find represented by any party, major or minor? What are they, and why do you think no party espouses them?

- Using the National Election Studies website, familiarize yourself with the results of survey questions on citizens' feelings about the parties. When you read a survey question, predict what you expect the responses to be. Compare your prediction with the actual data. Have the responses changed over time?

- Use this National Election Studies website to create cross-tabulations: How do Democratic and Republican identifiers compare in their views on various issues? Are there big differences among strong identifiers, weak identifiers, and independent leaners? Which group expresses the greatest interest in politics? Would you have expected this finding?

- Using the Opensecrets website, check out the information on campaign contributions by various interest groups and corporations (see Chapter 12). Which types of groups would you expect to give the most campaign money? Compare your prediction with the actual data.

- Using the Federal Election Commission website, click on "Campaign Finance Reports and Data" on the left of the home page. Then click on "Search the Disclosure Database," and finally on "Candidate and PAC/Party Summaries." Find out how much the various candidates for federal office in your state have raised for their next campaign. How much have the incumbents received compared with the challengers and the candidates for open seats? How much have the Democrats raised compared with the Republicans? Have third-party candidates raised any money?

- What interest groups would you expect to give Democrats in Congress high ratings? Republicans? Go to the VoteSmart website and test your guesses against their findings.

- Using the *Washington Post*'s website (or that of any other major newspaper or broadcast media outlet), read articles, columns, and editorials about political issues. Are the major parties mentioned? If so, what aspects of the parties' activities are emphasized? Are political candidates mentioned more frequently than parties are or the reverse? Do you find any mention of minor parties?

Appendix

TABLE A.1 Party Identification: 1952–2004

	1952	1956	1960	1964	1968	1972	1976	1980	1984	1988	1992	1996	2000	2004
Strong Democrats	22%	21%	20%	27%	20%	15%	15%	18%	17%	17%	18%	18%	19%	17%
Weak Democrats	25	23	25	25	25	26	25	23	20	18	18	19	15	16
Independents, closer to Democrats	10	6	6	9	10	11	12	11	11	12	14	14	15	17
Independents	6	9	10	8	11	13	15	13	11	11	12	9	12	10
Independents, closer to Republicans	7	8	7	6	9	10	10	10	12	13	12	12	13	12
Weak Republicans	14	14	14	14	15	13	14	14	15	14	14	15	12	12
Strong Republicans	14	15	16	11	10	10	9	9	12	14	11	12	12	16
Others	3	4	2	1	1	1	1	2	2	2	1	1	1	0
	101%	100%	100%	101%	101%	99%	101%	100%	100%	101%	100%	100%	99%	100%
Cases	1,793	1,762	1,928	1,571	1,556	2,707	2,864	1,614	2,236	2,033	2,478	1,714	1,785	1,197

Note: Based on surveys of the national electorate conducted immediately before each presidential election in recent years as part of the American National Election Studies program at the University of Michigan. Due to rounding, percentages do not always add up to 100 percent.

Source: American National Election Studies, Center for Political Studies, University of Michigan; data made available by the Inter-University Consortium for Political and Social Research..

TABLE A.2   Percent of Party Identifiers Voting for Their Party's Presidential Candidates: 1952–2004

	1952	1956	1960	1964	1968	1972	1976	1980	1984	1988	1992	1996	2000	2004
Strong Democrats	84%	85%	90%	95%	85%	73%	91%	86%	87%	93%	93%	96%	97%	97%
Weak Democrats	62	62	72	82	58	48	74	60	67	70	69	82	89	83
Independents, closer to Democrats	60	68	88	90	52	60	72	45	79	88	71	76	72	84
Independents	—	—	—	—	—	—	—	—	—	—	—	—	—	—
Independents, closer to Republicans	93	94	87	75	82	86	83	76	92	84	62	68	79	83
Weak Republicans	94	93	87	56	82	90	77	86	93	83	60	70	85	89
Strong Republicans	98	100	98	90	96	97	96	92	96	98	87	94	97	98

Note: The table entries are the percentages of each category of partisans who reported a vote for their party's candidate for president. To find the percentage voting for the opposing party's candidate or some other candidate, subtract the entry from 100 percent. Individuals who did not vote for president are excluded from the table.

Source: American National Election Studies, Center for Political Studies, University of Michigan; data made available by the Inter-University Consortium for Political and Social Research.

TABLE A.3   Percent of Party Identifiers Voting for Their Party's Congressional Candidates: 1952–2004

	1952	1956	1960	1964	1968	1972	1976	1980	1984	1988	1992	1996	2000	2004
Strong Democrats	89%	94%	93%	94%	88%	91%	89%	85%	89%	88%	86%	88%	87%	91%
Weak Democrats	77	86	86	84	73	80	78	69	70	82	82	71	73	86
Independents, closer to Democrats	64	83	84	79	63	80	76	70	78	87	74	69	70	80
Independents	—	—	—	—	—	—	—	—	—	—	—	—	—	—
Independents, closer to Republicans	81	83	74	72	81	73	65	68	61	64	65	79	67	68
Weak Republicans	90	88	84	64	78	75	66	74	66	70	63	79	79	81
Strong Republicans	95	95	90	92	91	85	83	77	85	77	82	97	86	88

Note: The table entries are the percentages of each category of partisans who reported a vote for their party's candidate for Congress. To find the percentage voting for the opposing party's candidate or some other candidate, subtract the entry from 100 percent. Individuals who did not vote or did not vote for Congress are excluded from the table.

Source: American National Election Studies, Center for Political Studies, University of Michigan; data made available by the Inter-University Consortium for Political and Social Research.

Endnotes

PART ONE

1. This is the title of Harold Lasswell's pioneering book, *Politics: Who Gets What, When, How* (New York: McGraw-Hill, 1936).
2. E. E. Schattschneider, *Party Government* (New York: Rinehart, 1942), p. 1.
3. See Herbert Kitschelt, Zdenka Mansfeldova, Radoslaw Markowski, and Gabor Toka, *Post-Communist Party Systems* (New York: Cambridge University Press, 1999), and Timothy J. Colton, *Transitional Citizens* (Cambridge: Harvard University Press, 2000).
4. Austin Ranney, *Curing the Mischiefs of Faction* (Berkeley: University of California Press, 1975).

CHAPTER 1

1. These definitions come from Edmund Burke, "Thoughts on the Cause of the Present Discontents" (1770) in *The Works of Edmund Burke* (Boston: Little, Brown, 1839), vol. I, pp. 425–426; Anthony Downs, *An Economic Theory of Democracy* (New York: Harper & Row, 1957), p. 24; William Nisbet Chambers, "Party Development and the American Mainstream," in Chambers and Walter Dean Burnham, eds., *The American Party Systems* (New York: Oxford University Press, 1967), p. 5; John H. Aldrich, *Why Parties?* (Chicago: University of Chicago Press, 1995), pp. 283–284; and V. O. Key, Jr. *Politics, Parties, and Pressure Groups* (New York: Crowell, 1958), pp. 180–182.
2. V. O. Key, Jr., used this "tripartite" conception to organize his classic text, *Politics, Parties, and Pressure Groups.* Key attributed the concept of party-in-the-electorate to Ralph M. Goldman, *Party Chairmen and Party Factions, 1789–1900* (Ph.D. diss., University of Chicago, 1951).
3. See Denise L. Baer and David A. Bositis, *Elite Cadres and Party Coalitions* (Westport, CT: Greenwood Press, 1988), pp. 21–50.
4. See Joseph A. Schlesinger, "The Primary Goals of Political Parties," *American Political Science Review* 69 (1975): 840–849.
5. This image is Joseph A. Schlesinger's in "The New American Political Party," *American Political Science Review* 79 (1985): 1152–1169.
6. State legislative elections in Nebraska are nonpartisan, although the candidates' partisan ties are obvious to many voters, and statewide officials (such as the governor and attorney general) are elected on a partisan ballot.
7. See William N. Chambers, *Political Parties in a New Nation* (New York: Oxford University Press, 1963); A. James Reichley, *The Life of the Parties* (Lanham, MD: Rowman & Littlefield, 2000); and John H. Aldrich, *Why Parties?*
8. Quoted in David Von Drehle, "Origin of the Species," *Washington Post,* July 25, 2004, p. W12.
9. See John H. Aldrich and Ruth W. Grant, "The Antifederalists, the First Congress, and the First Parties," *Journal of Politics* 55 (1993): 295–326; and John F. Hoadley, *Origins of American Political Parties 1789–1803* (Lexington: University of Kentucky Press, 1986).
10. Chilton Williamson, *American Suffrage: From Property to Democracy* (Princeton: Princeton University Press, 1960).
11. Neal R. Peirce and Lawrence D. Longley, *The People's President* (New Haven: Yale University Press, 1981).
12. See Aldrich, *Why Parties?* Chapter 4, and Reichley, *The Life of the Parties*, Chapter 5.
13. See Reichley, *The Life of the Parties*, Chapters. 6–11.
14. See Moisei Ostrogorski, *Democracy and the Organization of Political Parties, Volume II: The United States* (Garden City, NY: Anchor Books, 1964, originally published in 1902).
15. On party reform, see Austin Ranney, *Curing the Mischiefs of Faction* (Berkeley: University of California Press, 1975); and Richard Hofstadter, *The Age of Reform* (New York: Vintage Books, 1955).
16. See Leon Epstein, *Political Parties in the American Mold* (Madison: University of Wisconsin Press, 1986), pp. 155–199.

17. See The NES Guide to Public Opinion and Electoral Behavior, located on the Internet at *http://www.umich.edu/~nes/nesguide/toptable/tab2b_2.htm.*

CHAPTER 2

1. Arend Lijphart, *Electoral Systems and Party Systems* (New York: Oxford University Press, 1994).
2. See John F. Bibby and L. Sandy Maisel, *Two Parties—Or More?*, 2nd ed. (Boulder, CO: Westview, 2003), p. 46.
3. Charles S. Bullock III, "It's a Sonny Day in Georgia," in Larry J. Sabato, ed., *Midterm Madness* (Lanham, MD: Rowman & Littlefield, 2003), p. 177.
4. Interparty competition refers to competition between the parties, as opposed to competition within a particular party (termed "intra-party"). The index was first presented in Austin Ranney, "Parties in State Politics," in Herbert Jacob and Kenneth Vines, eds., *Politics in the American States* (Boston: Little, Brown, 1965), p. 65. For an alternative index based on state legislative races, see Thomas M. Holbrook and Emily Van Dunk, "Electoral Competition in the American States," *American Political Science Review* 87 (1993): 955–962.
5. See Malcolm E. Jewell and Sarah M. Morehouse, *Political Parties and Elections in American States* (Washington, DC: CQ Press, 2001), Chapter 2, and John F. Bibby and Thomas M. Holbrook, "Parties and Elections," in Virginia Gray and Russell L. Hanson, eds., *Politics in the American States,* 8th ed. (Washington, DC: CQ Press, 2003), Chapter 3.
6. In 65 of the 100 races where the winner got 75 percent or more of the vote, he or she had no major-party competitor.
7. See Peverill Squire, "Uncontested Seats in State Legislative Elections," *Legislative Studies Quarterly* 25 (2000): 131–146, and recent issues of *Ballot Access News.*
8. Data from *CQ Weekly* postelection figures. On the influence of incumbency on elections, see Gary C. Jacobson, *The Politics of Congressional Elections,* 6th ed. (New York: Longman, 2004), Chapter 3; Stephen Ansolabehere, James M. Snyder, Jr., and Charles Stewart III, "Old Voters, New Voters, and the Personal Vote," *American Journal of Political Science* 44 (2000): 17–34; and Scott W. Desposato and John R. Petrocik, "The Variable Incumbency Advantage," *American Journal of Political Science* 47 (2003): 18–32.
9. John M. Carey, Richard G. Niemi, and Lynda W. Powell, "Incumbency and the Probability of Reelection in State Legislative Elections," *Journal of Politics* 62 (2000): 671–700.
10. Stephen Ansolabehere and James M. Snyder Jr., "The Incumbency Advantage in U.S. Elections," *Election Law Journal* 1 (2002): 315–338.
11. John R. Alford and David W. Brady, "Personal and Partisan Advantage in U.S. Congressional Elections, 1846–1990," in Lawrence C. Dodd and Bruce I. Oppenheimer, eds., *Congress Reconsidered,* 5th Ed. (Washington, DC: CQ Press, 1993), p. 147.
12. Gary C. Jacobson, "The Congress: The Structural Basis of Republican Success," in Michael Nelson, ed., *The Elections of 2004* (Washington, DC: CQ Press, 2005), pp. 166–167.
13. Bruce I. Oppenheimer, "Deep Red and Blue Congressional Districts," in Dodd and Oppenheimer, eds., *Congress Reconsidered,* 8th ed. (Washington, DC: CQ Press, 2005), pp. 135–157. See also Alan I. Abramowitz, Brad Alexander, and Matthew Gunning, "Incumbency, Redistricting, and the Decline of Competition in U.S. House Elections," *Journal of Politics* 68 (2006), forthcoming.
14. Bill Bishop, "The Schism in U.S. Politics Begins at Home," *Austin American-Statesman,* April 4, 2004, p. 1.
15. Rob Richie, executive director of FairVote, quoted in David S. Broder, "No Vote Necessary," *Washington Post,* November 11, 2004, p. A37.
16. Maurice Duverger, *Political Parties* (New York: Wiley, 1954). See also Octavio Amorim Neto and Gary W. Cox, "Electoral Institutions, Cleavage Structures, and the Number of Parties," *American Journal of Political Science* 41 (1997):149–174.
17. This used to be a frequent occurrence in the United States. In 1955, 58 percent of all state legislative districts were multimember; this number had declined to 10 percent by the 1980s. See Richard Niemi, Simon Jackman, and Laura Winsky, "Candidates and Competitiveness in Multimember Districts," *Legislative Studies Quarterly* 16 (1991): 91–109.
18. Other minorities are affected as well; James D. King, in "Single-Member Districts and the Representation of Women in American State Legislatures," *State Politics and Policy Quarterly* 2 (2002): 161–175 found that a change from multimember to single-member districts decreases the representation of women in state legislatures.

19. See A. James Reichley, *The Life of the Parties* (Lanham, MD: Rowman & Littlefield, 2002), p. 4.

20. Leon Epstein, *Political Parties in the American Mold* (Madison: University of Wisconsin Press, 1986), pp. 129–132.

21. V. O. Key, Jr., *Politics, Parties, and Pressure Groups*, 5th ed. (New York: Crowell, 1964), pp. 229ff.

22. See Louis Hartz, *The Liberal Tradition in America* (New York: Harcourt, Brace and World, 1955). However, this "consensus" is full of mixed feelings; see Stanley Feldman and John Zaller, "The Political Culture of Ambivalence," *American Journal of Political Science* 36 (1992): 268–307.

23. Marjorie Randon Hershey, "Third Parties: The Power of Electoral Laws and Institutions," in Matthew J. Streb, ed., *Law and Election Politics: The Rules of the Game* (Boulder, CO: Lynne Rienner, 2005), pp. 23–42.

24. Brian F. Schaffner, Matthew J. Streb, and Gerald C. Wright, "Teams without Uniforms: The Nonpartisan Ballot in State and Local Elections," *Political Research Quarterly* 54 (2001): 7–30.

25. Gerald C. Wright and Brian F. Schaffner, "The Influence of Party: Evidence from the State Legislatures," *American Political Science Review* 96 (2002): 367–379.

26. J. David Gillespie, *Politics at the Periphery* (Columbia: University of South Carolina Press, 1993).

27. Holly A. Heyser, "Minnesota Governor: The End of the Ventura Interlude," in Sabato, *Midterm Madness*, pp. 233–245.

28. Among the best books on American third parties are Steven J. Rosenstone, Roy L. Behr, and Edward H. Lazarus, *Third Parties in America*, 2nd ed. (Princeton: Princeton University Press, 1996); Paul S. Herrnson and John C. Green, *Multiparty Politics in America*, 2nd ed. (Lanham, MD: Rowman & Littlefield, 2002); and John F. Bibby and L. Sandy Maisel, *Two Parties—Or More?;* 2nd ed. (Boulder, CO: Westview, 2003). Lisa J. Disch makes an argument in favor of third parties in *The Tyranny of the Two-Party System* (New York: Columbia University Press, 2003).

29. Joseph M. Hazlett II, *The Libertarian Party* (Jefferson, NC: McFarland and Company, 1992). Third parties' websites are listed in "Party Politics on the Internet," at the end of this book.

30. As evidence, almost all third-party presidential candidates since 1900 have received less support on Election Day than they did in preelection polls; see Rosenstone, Behr, and Lazarus, *Third Parties in America*, p. 41.

31. Rosenstone, Behr, and Lazarus, *Third Parties in America*, p. 162.

32. See Paul R. Abramson, John H. Aldrich, and David W. Rohde, *Change and Continuity in the 1992 Elections* (Washington, DC: CQ Press, 1994).

33. See Lee Epstein and Charles D. Hadley, "On the Treatment of Political Parties in the U.S. Supreme Court, 1900–1986," *Journal of Politics* 52 (1990): 413–432, Richard Winger's *Ballot Access News* at http://www.ballot-access.org and issues of the *Election Law Journal.*

34. See Howard A. Scarrow, *Parties, Elections, and Representation in the State of New York* (New York: New York University Press, 1983).

35. Orit Kedar, "When Moderate Voters Prefer Extreme Parties," *American Political Science Review* 99 (2005): 185–199.

36. James E. Campbell, "The 2002 Midterm Election," *PS* 36 (2003): 203–207.

PART TWO

1. See Alan Ware, ed., *Political Parties: Electoral Change and Structural Response* (New York: Basil Blackwell, 1987).

CHAPTER 3

1. Andrew M. Appleton and Daniel S. Ward, *State Party Profiles* (Washington, DC: CQ Press, 1997), Appendix.

2. A public utility is a government-regulated provider of services, such as a gas or a water company. Leon Epstein, *Political Parties in the American Mold* (Madison: University of Wisconsin Press, 1986), pp. 155–199.

3. The cases are *Tashjian v. Republican Party of Connecticut,* 479 U.S. 208 (1986); and *Eu v. San Francisco County Democratic Central Committee et al.,* 489 U.S. 214 (1989). See David K. Ryden, "'The Good, the Bad, and the Ugly': The Judicial Shaping of Party Activities," in John C. Green and Daniel M. Shea, *The State of the Parties,* 3rd ed. (Lanham, MD: Rowman & Littlefield, 1999), pp. 50–65.

4. V. O. Key, Jr., *Politics, Parties and Pressure Groups* (New York: Crowell, 1964), p. 316.

5. Samuel J. Eldersveld, *Political Parties: A Behavioral Analysis* (Chicago: Rand McNally, 1964).

6. The organization of American political parties differs from what Robert Michels calls the "iron law of oligarchy"—that organizations are inevitably controlled from the top. See Robert Michels, *Political Parties* (Glencoe, IL: Free Press, 1949).

7. M. Craig Brown and Charles N. Halaby, "Machine Politics in America, 1870–1945," *Journal of Interdisciplinary History* 17 (1987): 587–612.

8. See David Mayhew, *Placing Parties in American Politics* (Princeton: Princeton University Press, 1986), pp. 19–21.

9. See Kenneth Finegold, *Experts and Politicians: Reform Challenges to Machine Politics in New York, Cleveland, and Chicago* (Princeton, NJ: Princeton University Press, 1995).

10. Steven P. Erie, *Rainbow's End: Irish-Americans and the Dilemmas of Urban Machine Politics, 1840–1985* (Berkeley: University of California Press, 1988); but see John F. Bibby, "Party Organizations 1946–1996," in Byron E. Shafer, *Partisan Approaches to Postwar American Politics* (New York: Chatham House, 1998), pp. 142–185.

11. Anne Freedman, *Patronage: An American Tradition* (Chicago: Nelson-Hall, 1994), Chapter 5.

12. Kenneth R. Mladenka, "The Urban Bureaucracy and the Chicago Political Machine," *American Political Science Review* 74 (1980): 991–998.

13. Michael Johnston, "Patrons and Clients, Jobs and Machines," *American Political Science Review* 73 (1979): 385–398.

14. James L. Gibson, Cornelius P. Cotter, John F. Bibby, and Robert J. Huckshorn, "Whither the Local Parties?" *American Journal of Political Science* 29 (1985): 139–160.

15. Cornelius P. Cotter, James L. Gibson, John F. Bibby, and Robert J. Huckshorn, *Party Organization in American Politics* (New York: Praeger, 1984), pp. 49–53

16. See Cotter et al., *Party Organization in American Politics*, p. 54, for 1964–1980. On 1984: James L. Gibson, John P. Frendreis, and Laura L. Vertz, "Party Dynamics in the 1980s," *American Journal of Political Science* 33 (1989): 67–90. On 1988: Charles E. Smith, Jr., "Changes in Party Organizational Strength and Activity 1979–1988," unpublished manuscript, Ohio State University, 1989. See also Samuel J. Eldersveld, "The Party Activist in Detroit and Los Angeles," in William J. Crotty, ed., *Political Parties in Local Areas* (Knoxville: University of Tennessee Press, 1986), pp. 89–119.

17. John Frendreis and Alan R. Gitelson, "Local Parties in the 1990s," in John C. Green and Daniel M. Shea, *The State of the Parties,* 3rd ed., pp. 135–153.

18. Carol S. Weissert, "Michigan," in Appleton and Ward, *State Party Profiles*, pp. 153–160.

19. L. Sandy Maisel, "American Political Parties: Still Central to a Functioning Democracy?" in Jeffrey E. Cohen, Richard Fleisher, and Paul Kantor, eds., *American Political Parties: Decline or Resurgence?* (Washington, DC: CQ Press, 2001), pp. 112–114.

20. Gary F. Moncrief, Peverill Squire, and Malcolm E. Jewell, *Who Runs for the Legislature?* (Upper Saddle River, NJ: Prentice Hall, 2001).

21. John J. Coleman, "The Resurgence of Party Organization? A Dissent from the New Orthodoxy," in Daniel M. Shea and John C. Green, eds., *The State of the Parties* (Lanham, MD: Rowman & Littlefield, 1994), pp. 282–298.

22. A. James Reichley, *The Life of the Parties* (Lanham, MD: Rowman & Littlefield, 2000), pp. 129–130.

23. Malcolm E. Jewell and Sarah M. Morehouse, *Political Parties and Elections in American States*, 4th ed. (Washington, DC: CQ Press, 2001), p. 4.

24. Jewell and Morehouse, *Political Parties and Elections,* p. 1.

25. See James L. Gibson, Cornelius P. Cotter, John F. Bibby, and Robert J. Huckshorn, "Assessing Party Organizational Strength," *American Journal of Political Science* 27 (1983): 193–222.

26. John H. Aldrich, "Southern Parties in State and Nation," *Journal of Politics* 62 (2000), p. 655.

27. Jewell and Morehouse, *Political Parties and Elections*, p. 52; Aldrich, "Southern Parties," 655–659.

28. Jewell and Morehouse, *Political Parties and Elections*, p. 211.

29. Anthony Gierzynski, *Legislative Party Campaign Committees in the American States* (Lexington: University Press of Kentucky, 1992).

30. Robert E. Hogan, "Candidate Perceptions of Political Party Campaign Activity in State Legislative Elections," *State Politics and Policy Quarterly* 2 (2002): 66–85.

31. Raymond J. La Raja, "State Parties and Soft Money," in John C. Green and Rick Farmer, eds., *The State of the Parties,* 4th ed. (Lanham, MD: Rowman & Littlefield, 2003), pp. 132–150.

32. Anthony Corrado, "Political Party Finance under BCRA: An Initial Assessment," Brookings Institution paper, 2004, on the Internet at http://www.brookings.edu/views/papers/corrado20040311_paper.pdf (accessed May 31, 2005).

33. Sarah M. Morehouse and Malcolm E. Jewell, "State Parties: Independent Partners in the Money Relationship," in Green and Farmer, *The State of the Parties,* p. 151. The budget estimates come from Robert J. Huckshorn and John F. Bibby, "State Parties in an Era of Political Change," in Joel L. Fleishman, ed., *The Future*

of American Political Parties (Englewood Cliffs, NJ: Prentice-Hall, 1982), pp. 70–100; Gibson, Cotter, Bibby, and Huckshorn, "Assessing Party Organizational Strength," and Aldrich, "Southern Parties," p. 656.

34. Derek Willis, "State Parties Adjust to McCain-Feingold," Center for Public Integrity press release, Washington, DC, August 26, 2004.

35. Agustin Armendariz and Aron Pilhofer, "McCain-Feingold Changes State Party Spending," Center for Public Integrity press release, Washington, DC, May 26, 2005.

36. See Aldrich, "Southern Parties," pp. 656–657.

37. Aldrich, "Southern Parties," Table 7, pp. 656–657.

38. See Mildred Schwartz, *The Party Network* (Madison: University of Wisconsin Press, 1990) and Jonathan Bernstein and Casey B. K. Dominguez, "Candidates and Candidacies in the Expanded Party," *PS* 36 (2003): 165–169.

39. John H. Kessel, "Ray Bliss and the Development of the Ohio Republican Party During the 1950s," in John C. Green, ed., *Politics, Professionalism, and Power* (Lanham, MD: University Press of America, 1994), pp. 48–61.

40. See Jewell and Morehouse, *Political Parties and Elections,* p. 36. See also Edward G. Carmines and James A. Stimson, *Issue Evolution* (Princeton: Princeton University Press, 1989); and Joseph A. Aistrup, *The Southern Strategy Revisited* (Lexington: University Press of Kentucky, 1996).

41. Charles Prysby, "North Carolina," and Anne E. Kelley, "Florida," in Appleton and Ward, *State Party Profiles,* pp. 234–243 and 62–64.

42. See the articles in John A. Clark and Charles Prysby, eds., "Grassroots Party Activists in Southern Politics, 1991–2001," *American Review of Politics* 24 (Spring and Summer, 2001), pp. 1–223.

43. Walter Dean Burnham, *Critical Elections and the Mainsprings of American Politics* (New York: Norton, 1970), p. 72.

44. Alan Ware, *The Breakdown of the Democratic Party Organization 1940–80* (Oxford, England: Oxford University Press, 1985).

CHAPTER 4

1. Cornelius P. Cotter and Bernard C. Hennessy, *Politics without Power: The National Party Committees* (New York: Atherton, 1964). See also Ralph M. Goldman, *The National Party Chairmen and Committees* (Armonk, NY: M. E. Sharpe, 1990).

2. See Philip A. Klinkner, *The Losing Parties: Out-Party National Committees, 1956–1993* (New Haven: Yale University Press, 1994).

3. James W. Ceaser, "Political Parties—Declining, Stabilizing, or Resurging," in Anthony King, ed., *The New American Political System* (Washington, DC: American Enterprise Institute, 1990), p. 115. See also Sidney M. Milkis, *The President and the Parties* (New York: Oxford University Press, 1993).

4. Jo Freeman, *A Room at a Time* (Lanham, MD: Rowman & Littlefield, 2000).

5. Dan Balz, "GOP Governors Want a Seat at the Table," *Washington Post,* November 22, 2004, p. A2.

6. John C. Green, ed., *Politics, Professionalism, and Power: Modern Party Organization and the Legacy of Ray C. Bliss* (Lanham, MD: University Press of America, 1994).

7. See Austin Ranney, *Curing the Mischiefs of Faction* (Berkeley: University of California Press, 1975); William J. Crotty, *Decisions for the Democrats* (Baltimore: Johns Hopkins University Press, 1978); and Byron E. Shafer, *The Quiet Revolution* (New York: Russell Sage Foundation, 1983).

8. John F. Bibby, "Party Renewal in the Republican National Party," in Gerald M. Pomper, ed., *Party Renewal in America* (New York: Praeger, 1981), pp. 102–115.

9. See Paul S. Herrnson, "The Revitalization of National Party Organizations," in L. Sandy Maisel, ed., *The Parties Respond,* 2nd ed. (Boulder, CO: Westview, 1994), pp. 45–68.

10. See Don Van Natta, Jr. and John M. Broder, "The Few, the Rich, the Rewarded Donate the Bulk of G.O.P. Gifts," *New York Times,* August 2, 2000, p. A1; and Ceci Connolly, "In Final Funding Drive, Parties Eye 'Hard' Cash," *Washington Post,* September 21, 2000, p. A16.

11. Federal Election Commission at: http://www.fec.gov/press/20030320party/20030103party.html (accessed June 11, 2003). Unless otherwise noted, the remaining data in this chapter come from the Federal Election Commission.

12. Paul S. Herrnson, *Congressional Elections,* 4th Ed. (Washington, DC: CQ Press, 2004), pp. 92–93.

13. Mike Allen, "Hard Cash Is Main Course for GOP Fundraiser," *Washington Post,* June 14, 2005, p. A1.

14. F. Christopher Arterton calls them "service vendor" parties, and Paul Herrnson refers to them as "intermediary" parties. See Arterton's "Political Money and Party Strength," in Joel Fleishman, ed., *The Future of*

American Political Parties (Englewood Cliffs, NJ: Prentice Hall, 1982), pp. 101–139; and Paul S. Herrnson, *Party Campaigning in the 1980s* (Cambridge, MA: Harvard University Press, 1988), p. 47.

15. Paul Farhi, "Parties Are Waging Battle of the Databases," *Washington Post,* July 20, 2004, p. A1.

16. See David B. Magleby and J. Quin Monson, eds., *The Last Hurrah?* (Provo, UT: Center for the Study of Elections and Democracy, 2003).

17. Mike Allen, "Bush Goes for 'Icing' in Louisiana," *Washington Post,* December 4, 2002, p. A1.

18. Daniel A. Smith, "Strings Attached: Outside Money in Colorado's Seventh Congressional District," in Magleby and Monson, eds., *The Last Hurrah?,* p. 194.

19. Robin Toner, "Where Candidates May Fear to Tread, National Parties Stampede In," *New York Times,* September 30, 2002, p. A18.

20. Howard Fineman, "How Bush Did It," *Newsweek,* November 18, 2002, pp. 32, 34.

21. Richard L. Berke, "G.O.P. Mobilizes to Help Hopefuls in Primary Races," *New York Times,* March 3, 2002, p. 26.

22. Timothy P. Nokken, "Ideological Congruence Versus Electoral Success," *American Politics Research* 31 (2003): 3–26.

23. Mike Glover, "Iowa Senate: Harkin's Best Yet," in Larry J. Sabato, ed., *Midterm Madness* (Lanham, MD: Rowman & Littlefield, 2003), pp. 78–79.

24. Leon D. Epstein, *Political Parties in the American Mold* (Madison: University of Wisconsin Press, 1986), p. 200.

25. John J. Coleman, "The Resurgence of Party Organization? A Dissent from the New Orthodoxy," in Daniel M. Shea and John C. Green, eds., *The State of the Parties* (Lanham, MD: Rowman & Littlefield, 1994), pp. 311–328.

CHAPTER 5

1. Peter B. Clark and James Q. Wilson, "Incentive Systems: A Theory of Organizations," *Administrative Science Quarterly* 6 (1961): 129–166; and James Q. Wilson, *Political Organizations* (New York: Basic Books, 1973), Chapter 6.

2. See A. James Reichley, *The Life of the Parties* (Lanham, MD: Rowman & Littlefield, 2000), pp. 72, 118, 128–130, 174–176; and Martin Shefter, *Political Parties and the State* (Princeton, NJ: Princeton University Press, 1994).

3. The 1976 case is *Elrod v. Burns,* 427 U.S. 347; the 1980 case is *Branti v. Finkel,* 445 U.S. 507; and the 1990 case is *Rutan v. Republican Party of Illinois,* 111 L. Ed. 2d 52.

4. On the case for patronage, see the dissenting opinions to the Supreme Court's *Elrod, Branti,* and *Rutan* decisions. The case against patronage is well put in Anne Freedman, *Patronage: An American Tradition* (Chicago: Nelson-Hall, 1994), Chapter 5.

5. Cornelius P. Cotter, James L. Gibson, John F. Bibby, and Robert J. Huckshorn, *Party Organizations in American Politics* (New York: Praeger, 1984), p. 42; and Robert J. Huckshorn, *Party Leadership in the States* (Amherst: University of Massachusetts Press, 1976), p. 37.

6. See William Crotty, ed., *Political Parties in Local Areas* (Knoxville: University of Tennessee Press, 1986); and Sidney Verba, Kay Lehman Schlozman, and Henry E. Brady, *Voice and Equality* (Cambridge, MA: Harvard University Press, 1995), pp. 112–121.

7. John C. Green, John S. Jackson, and Nancy L. Clayton, "Issue Networks and Party Elites in 1996," in John C. Green and Daniel M. Shea, eds., *The State of the Parties,* 3rd ed. (Lanham, MD: Rowman & Littlefield, 1999).

8. Samuel J. Eldersveld, "The Party Activist in Detroit and Los Angeles: A Longitudinal View, 1956–1980," in Crotty, *Political Parties in Local Areas,* Chapter 4.

9. John A. Clark, John M. Bruce, John H. Kessel, and William Jacoby, "I'd Rather Switch than Fight," *American Journal of Political Science* 35 (1991): 577–597; Mary Grisez Kweit, "Ideological Congruence of Party Switchers and Nonswitchers: The Case of Party Activists," *American Journal of Political Science* 30 (1986): 184–196; and Dorothy Davidson Nesbit, "Changing Partisanship among Southern Party Activists," *Journal of Politics* 50 (1988): 322–334.

10. Verba, Schlozman, and Brady, *Voice and Equality,* p. 121.

11. See M. Margaret Conway, *Political Participation in the United States,* 2nd ed. (Washington, DC: CQ Press, 1991), p. 61.

12. See Clark and Wilson, "Incentive Systems" and Wilson, *The Amateur Democrat.* Note that the term *professional* as used here does not necessarily refer to someone who is paid for party work.

13. Walter J. Stone and Alan I. Abramowitz, "Winning May Not Be Everything But It's More Than We Thought," *American Political Science Review* 77 (1983): 945–956.

14. Michael A. Maggiotto and Ronald E. Weber, "The Impact of Organizational Incentives on County Party Chairpersons," *American Politics Quarterly* 14 (1986): 201–218.

15. Robert D. Putnam, *Bowling Alone: The Collapse and Revival of American Community* (New York: Simon & Schuster, 2000).

16. Verba, Schlozman, and Brady, *Voice and Equality*, Chapter 3.

17. American National Election Studies data, found at http://www.umich.edu/~nes/nesguide/toptable/tab6b_2.htm and _3.htm.

18. See Paul Allen Beck and M. Kent Jennings, "Updating Political Periods and Political Participation," *American Political Science Review* 78 (1984): 198–201; and Steven E. Finkel and Gregory Trevor, "Reassessing Ideological Bias in Campaign Participation," *Political Behavior* 8 (1986): 374–390.

19. See Verba, Schlozman, and Brady, *Voice and Equality*, pp. 15–16 and Chapters 9–14.

20. Henry E. Brady, Kay Lehman Schlozman, and Sidney Verba, "Prospecting for Participants," *American Political Science Review* 93 (1999): 153–168.

21. Verba, Schlozman, and Brady, *Voice and Equality*, pp. 135 and 139–144.

22. See, for example, Patrick R. Cotter, Samuel H. Fisher III, and Patrick Fuller, "Alabama: Maturing Party Competition," *American Review of Politics* 24 (2003): 26.

23. See Verba, Schlozman, and Brady, *Voice and Equality*, p. 190, Chapters 7 and 12, for campaign activists; Kyle L. Saunders and Alan I. Abramowitz, "Ideological Realignment and Active Partisans in the American Electorate," *American Politics Research* 32 (2004): 285–309, for party activists more generally; Ronald B. Rapoport, Alan I. Abramowitz, and John McGlennon, *The Life of the Parties* (Lexington: University of Kentucky Press, 1986), Chapter 3, for state convention delegates; and Chapter 10 of this book for national convention delegates and on protest activity, American Political Science Association Task Force Report, "American Democracy in an Age of Rising Inequality," *Perspectives on Politics* 2 (2004): 655

24. See Michael Margolis and Raymond E. Owen, "From Organization to Personalism," *Polity* 18 (1985): 313–328.

25. Malcolm E. Jewell and Sarah M. Morehouse, *Political Parties and Elections in American States*, 4th ed. (Washington, DC: CQ Press, 2001), p. 86.

26. Verba, Schlozman, and Brady, *Voice and Equality*, pp. 84–91.

27. Verba, Schlozman, and Brady, *Voice and Equality*, pp. 220–225.

28. Alan Abramowitz and Kyle Saunders, "Ideological Realignment in the U.S. Electorate," *Journal of Politics* (1998): 634.

29. See, for example, Cotter, Fisher, and Fuller, "Alabama: Maturing Party Competition," pp. 27–29; and Charles Prysby and John A. Clark, "Conclusion: Changes in Southern Political Party Organizations and Activists," *American Review of Politics* 24 (2003): 214–215.

PART THREE

1. See Angus Campbell, Philip E. Converse, Warren E. Miller, and Donald E. Stokes, *The American Voter* (New York: Wiley, 1960), Chapter 6.

2. Steven E. Finkel and Howard A. Scarrow, "Party Identification and Party Enrollment: The Difference and the Consequence," *Journal of Politics* 47 (1985): 620–642.

CHAPTER 6

1. Party identification is developing in newer democracies such as Russia and the Ukraine as well, even in the face of overwhelmingly negative attitudes toward political parties more generally. See Arthur H. Miller and Thomas F. Klobucar, "The Development of Party Identification in Post-Soviet Societies," *American Journal of Political Science* 44 (2000): 667–685; and Ted Brader and Joshua A. Tucker, "The Emergence of Mass Partisanship in Russia, 1993–1996," *American Journal of Political Science* 45 (2001): 69–83.

2. For a summary of these approaches, with an argument for party identification as social identity, see Donald Green, Bradley Palmquist, and Eric Schickler, *Partisan Hearts and Minds* (New Haven: Yale University Press, 2002), Chapter 5.

3. John R. Petrocik, "An Analysis of the Intransitivities in the Index of Party Identification," *Political Methodology* 1 (1974): 31–47; and Herbert F. Weisberg, "A Multidimensional Conceptualization of Party Identification," *Political Behavior* 2 (1980): 33–60. See also Green, Palmquist, and Schickler, *Partisan Hearts and Minds,* Chapter 2.

4. Paul Allen Beck and M. Kent Jennings, "Family Traditions, Political Periods, and the Development of Partisan Orientations," *Journal of Politics* 53 (1991): 742–763.
5. Paul Allen Beck, Russell J. Dalton, Steven Greene, and Robert Huckfeldt, "The Social Calculus of Voting," *American Political Science Review* 96 (2002): 57–73.
6. Richard G. Niemi and M. Kent Jennings, "Issues and Inheritance in the Formation of Party Identification," *American Journal of Political Science* 35 (1991): 970–988.
7. Green, Palmquist, and Schickler, *Partisan Hearts and Minds,* pp. 7–8.
8. See William Clagett, "Partisan Acquisition vs. Partisan Intensity," *American Journal of Political Science* 25 (1981): 193–214.
9. James E. Campbell, "Sources of the New Deal Realignment," *Western Political Quarterly* 38 (1985): 357–376; and Warren E. Miller, "Generational Changes and Party Identification," *Political Behavior* 14 (1992): 333–352.
10. The seminal report of these studies is Angus Campbell, Philip E. Converse, Warren E. Miller, and Donald E. Stokes, *The American Voter* (New York: Wiley, 1960). Note that Figure 6.1 combines strong and weak identifiers of each party with those independents who say they "lean" toward that party. The data in the Appendix (Table A.1) show the full range of categories of party ID.
11. See Paul Allen Beck, "The Dealignment Era in America," in Russell J. Dalton, Scott C. Flanagan, and Paul Allen Beck, eds., *Electoral Change in Advanced Industrial Democracies* (Princeton, NJ: Princeton University Press, 1984), pp. 244–246.
12. Philip E. Converse and Gregory B. Markus, "Plus ça change. . . : The New CPS Election Study Panel," *American Political Science Review* 73 (1979): 32–49. See also Donald Philip Green and Bradley Palmquist, "How Stable Is Party Identification?" *Political Behavior* 16 (1994): 437–466; and Paul Goren, "Party Identification and Core Political Values," *American Journal of Political Science* 49 (2005): 881–896.
13. Russell Dalton, "The Decline of Party Identification," in Russell J. Dalton and Martin P. Wattenberg, eds., *Parties without Partisans* (Oxford, UK: Oxford University Press, 2000), pp. 19–36. On split-ticket voting, see Barry C. Burden and David C. Kimball, *Why Americans Split Their Tickets* (Ann Arbor: University of Michigan Press, 2002).
14. Martin P. Wattenberg, *The Decline of American Political Parties, 1952–1994* (Cambridge, MA: Harvard University Press, 1996), p. ix.
15. See James H. Kuklinski, Paul J. Quirk, Jennifer Jerit, and Robert F. Rich, "The Political Environment and Citizen Competence," *American Journal of Political Science* 45 (2001): 410–424; and Paul M. Sniderman, "Taking Sides: A Fixed Choice Theory of Political Reasoning," in Arthur Lupia, Mathew D. McCubbins, and Samuel L. Popkin, eds., *Elements of Reason* (New York: Cambridge University Press, 2000).
16. David G. Lawrence, "On the Resurgence of Party Identification in the 1990s," in Jeffrey E. Cohen, Richard Fleisher, and Paul Kantor, eds., *American Political Parties: Decline or Resurgence?* (Washington, DC: CQ Press, 2001), pp. 30–54.
17. James W. Ceaser and Andrew E. Busch, *Red Over Blue* (Lanham, MD: Rowman & Littlefield, 2005), p. 136.
18. The classic here is Bernard R. Berelson, Paul F. Lazarsfeld, and William N. McPhee, *Voting* (Chicago: University of Chicago Press, 1954), pp. 215–233.
19. The poll data are from Green, Palmquist, and Schickler, *Partisan Hearts and Minds,* pages 127 and 49, respectively. They see these poll results, however, as evidence that the two groups of partisans are using different standards of evaluation rather than as an indicator of perceptual bias.
20. See Wendy M. Rahn, "The Role of Partisan Stereotypes in Information Processing about Political Candidates," *American Journal of Political Science* 37 (1993): 472–496; and Michael W. Wagner, "Think of It This Way," Ph.D. dissertation, Indiana University, 2006
21. See, for example, Larry M. Bartels, "Partisanship and Voting Behavior, 1952–1996," *American Journal of Political Science* 44 (2000): 35–50.
22. Paul Allen Beck, Lawrence Baum, Aage R. Clausen, and Charles E. Smith, Jr., "Patterns and Sources of Ticket Splitting in Subpresidential Voting," *American Political Science Review* 86 (1992): 916–928.
23. See Barry C. Burden and David C. Kimball, "A New Approach to the Study of Ticket-Splitting," *American Political Science Review* 92 (1998): 533–544; and Malcolm E. Jewell and Sarah M. Morehouse, *Political Parties and Elections in American States* (Washington, DC: CQ Press, 2001), p. 277.
24. Beck, Baum, Clausen, and Smith, "Patterns and Sources of Ticket Splitting"; and Burden and Kimball, "A New Approach."
25. Scott Basinger and Howard Lavine, "Ambivalence, Information, and Electoral Choice," *American Political Science Review* 99 (2005): 169–184.

26. See Morris P. Fiorina, *Retrospective Voting in American National Elections* (New Haven: Yale University Press, 1981); and Michael B. MacKuen, Robert S. Erikson, and James A. Stimson, "Macropartisanship," *American Political Science Review* 83 (1989): 1125–1142.

27. Paul R. Abramson, John H. Aldrich, and David W. Rohde, *Change and Continuity in the 2000 and 2002 Elections* (Washington, DC: CQ Press, 2003), Chapter 6.

28. See Bartels, "Partisanship and Voting Behavior"; and Abramson, Aldrich, and Rohde, *Change and Continuity,* Chapter 8.

29. Overall turnout in 2004 among citizens of voting age was estimated at 60 percent. Reported turnout levels in the 2004 American National Election Studies survey are considerably higher for reasons specified in Chapter 8.

30. Abramson, Aldrich, and Rohde, *Change and Continuity,* pp. 178–189.

31. Sidney Verba and Norman H. Nie, *Participation in America* (Chicago: University of Chicago Press, 1987), Chapter 12.

32. See Bruce E. Keith, David B. Magleby, Candice J. Nelson, Elizabeth Orr, Mark Westlye, and Raymond E. Wolfinger, *The Myth of the Independent Voter* (Berkeley: University of California Press, 1992).

33. V. O. Key, Jr. (with Milton C. Cummings), *The Responsible Electorate* (Cambridge, MA: Harvard University Press, 1966).

34. See Paul R. Abramson, John H. Aldrich, and David W. Rohde, *Change and Continuity in the 1992 Elections* (Washington, DC: CQ Press, 1995), p. 245.

35. Data from the 1992 and 1996 American National Election Studies were made available by the Inter-University Consortium for Political and Social Research.

36. See Martin P. Wattenberg, *The Rise of Candidate-Centered Politics* (Cambridge, MA: Harvard University Press, 1991).

CHAPTER 7

1. See, for example, Edward G. Carmines and James A. Stimson, *Issue Evolution* (Princeton: Princeton University Press, 1989) and Paul M. Sniderman and Thomas Piazza, *The Scar of Race* (Cambridge: Harvard University Press, 1995).

2. See, for example, Jerome M. Clubb, William H. Flanigan, and Nancy H. Zingale, *Partisan Realignment* (Beverly Hills, CA: Sage, 1980, Chapter 3.

3. See John H. Aldrich, *Why Parties?* (Chicago: University of Chicago Press, 1995).

4. See V. O. Key, Jr., "A Theory of Critical Elections," *Journal of Politics* 17 (1955): 3–18; Walter Dean Burnham, *Critical Elections and the Mainsprings of American Politics* (New York: Norton, 1970); and James L. Sundquist, *Dynamics of the Party System* (Washington, DC: Brookings Institution, 1973).

5. These events typically unfold over a period of time, but for convenience, the beginning of each party system is located in the year in which the new majority party coalition first took office.

6. Michael Holt, *The Rise and Fall of the American Whig Party* (New York: Oxford University Press, 2003). See also Richard P. McCormick, *The Second American Party System* (Chapel Hill: University of North Carolina Press, 1966), Chapter 7.

7. The third party system actually contained two distinct periods. From the end of the Civil War in 1865 through 1876, Democratic voting strength in the South was held in check by the occupying Union army and various Reconstruction policies and laws. So to reflect the true party balance during this time, it is helpful to differentiate between 1861–1876 and the 1877–1896 period.

8. A. James Reichley, *The Life of the Parties* (Lanham, MD: Rowman & Littlefield, 2000), p. 104.

9. Jeff Manza and Clem Brooks, *Social Cleavages and Political Change* (Oxford: Oxford University Press, 1999).

10. James Madison, *The Federalist No. 10,* November 22, 1787.

11. See Paul R. Abramson, John H. Aldrich, and David W. Rohde, *Change and Continuity in the 2000 and 2002 Elections* (Washington, DC: CQ Press, 2003), pp. 113–115.

12. Jeffrey M. Stonecash, *Class and Party in American Politics* (Boulder, CO: Westview Press, 2000), pp. 13 and 139, and Chapter 4.

13. See Russell J. Dalton, Scott C. Flanagan, and Paul Allen Beck, eds., *Electoral Change in Advanced Industrial Democracies* (Princeton, NJ: Princeton University Press, 1984).

14. Henry E. Brady, "Trust the People: Political Party Coalitions and the 2000 Election," in Jack N. Rakove, *The Unfinished Election of 2000* (New York: Basic Books, 2001), p. 55.

15. Steven M. Cohen and Charles S. Liebman, "American Jewish Liberalism," *Public Opinion Quarterly* 61 (1997): 405–430. See also L. Sandy Maisel and Ira N. Forman, eds., *Jews in American Politics* (Lanham, MD: Rowman & Littlefield, 2003).

16. Robin Toner, "Voters Are Very Settled, Intense and Partisan, and It's Only July," *New York Times*, July 25, 2004, p. 1.

17. See David C. Leege and Lyman A. Kellstedt, eds., *Rediscovering the Religious Factor in American Politics* (Armonk, NY: M. E. Sharpe, 1993); and Russell Muirhead, Nancy L. Rosenblum, Daniel Schlozman, and Francis X. Shen, "Religion in the 2004 Presidential Election," in Larry J. Sabato, ed., *Divided States of America* (New York: Longman, 2006), pp. 221–242.

18. "Stay or Go?" *Washington Post*, December 17, 2002, p. A8.

19. CNN exit poll data at http://www.cnn.com/ELECTION/2004/pages/results/states/US/P/00/epolls.0.html (accessed June 29, 2005).

20. On black political behavior, see Katherine Tate, *From Protest to Politics* (Cambridge, MA: Harvard University Press, 1994). On racial differences in issue attitudes, see Donald R. Kinder and Nicholas Winter, "Exploring the Racial Divide," *American Journal of Political Science* 45 (2001): 439–453.

21. Dan Balz, "Incumbent Reaches Beyond His Base," *Washington Post*, January 8, 2004, p. A1.

22. "Most Hispanics Say They're Democrats," *Washington Post*, October 4, 2002, p. A8.

23. Brian Faler, "Women Returning to Democratic Party, Poll Finds," *Washington Post*, May 10, 2005, p. A9.

24. Janet M. Box-Steffensmeier, Suzanna De Boef, and Tse-Min Lin, "The Dynamics of the Partisan Gender Gap," *American Political Science Review* 98 (2004): 515–528; and Karen M. Kaufman and John R. Petrocik, "The Changing Politics of American Men," *American Journal of Political Science* 43 (1999): 864–887.

25. Kira Sanbonmatsu, *Democrats, Republicans, and the Politics of Women's Place* (Ann Arbor: University of Michigan Press, 2002), Chapter 3; see also Christina Wolbrecht, *The Politics of Women's Rights* (Princeton: Princeton University Press, 2000); and Brian Schaffner, "Priming Gender," *American Journal of Political Science* 49 (2005): 803–817.

26. Calculated from *CQ Weekly*'s "Special Report: Election 2002: New Senators, New Representatives," November 9, 2002, pp. 2948–2970.

27. Located at http://www.pollingreport.com/2004.htm#Exit (accessed June 26, 2005).

28. David O. Sears, Richard R. Lau, Tom R. Tyler, and Harris M. Allen, Jr., "Self-Interest vs. Symbolic Politics in Policy Attitudes and Presidential Voting," *American Political Science Review* 74 (1980): 670–684; and Abramson, Aldrich, and Rohde, *Change and Continuity*, pp. 156–160.

29. CNN exit poll data, as cited in note 19.

30. Greg D. Adams, "Abortion: Evidence of an Issue Evolution," *American Journal of Political Science* 41 (1997): 718–737.

31. Quoted in Thomas B. Edsall, "Political Party Is No Longer Dictated By Class Status," *Washington Post*, November 9, 2000, p. A37.

32. See Geoffrey C. Layman, *The Great Divide* (New York: Columbia University Press, 2001).

33. Nicholas A. Valentino and David O. Sears, "Old Times There Are Not Forgotten," *American Journal of Political Science* 49 (2005): 673.

34. Merle Black, "The Transformation of the Southern Democratic Party," *Journal of Politics* 66 (2004): 1001–1017.

35. Valentino and Sears, "Old Times There Are Not Forgotten," p. 676.

36. Martin P. Wattenberg, *The Decline of American Political Parties 1952–96* (Cambridge, MA: Harvard University Press, 1998).

37. Donald Green, Bradley Palmquist, and Eric Schickler, *Partisan Hearts and Minds* (New Haven: Yale University Press, 2002), pp. 141 and 158.

38. Helmut Norpoth, "Under Way and Here to Stay: Party Realignment in the 1980s?" *Public Opinion Quarterly* 51 (1987): 376–391; and Warren E. Miller, "Party Identification, Realignment, and Party Voting," *American Political Science Review* 85 (1991): 557–570.

39. Harold W. Stanley and Richard G. Niemi, "The Demise of the New Deal Coalition," in Herbert Weisberg, ed., *Democracy's Feast* (Chatham, NJ: Chatham House, 1994), pp. 220–240.

40. Ronald Brownstein, "GOP Has Lock on South, and Democrats Can't Find Key," *Los Angeles Times*, December 15, 2004, p. A1.

41. See Earl Black and Merle Black, *The Rise of Southern Republicans* (Cambridge, MA: Harvard University Press, 2002); Michael F. Meffert, Helmut Norpoth, and Anirudh V. S. Ruhil, "Realignment and Macropartisanship," *American Political Science Review* 95 (2001): 953–962; and Paul Frymer, "The 1994 Electoral Aftershock," in Philip A. Klinkner, ed., *Midterm: The Elections of 1994 in Context* (Boulder: Westview, 1996), pp. 99–113.

42. Alan Cooperman and Thomas B. Edsall, "Evangelicals Say They Led Charge for the GOP," *Washington Post*, November 8, 2004, p. A1.

43. David R. Mayhew, *Electoral Realignments* (New Haven: Yale University Press, 2002); see also Carmines and Stimson, *Issue Evolution*; Byron E. Shafer, ed., *The End of Realignment?* (Madison: University of Wisconsin Press, 1991); and Peter F. Nardulli, "The Concept of a Critical Realignment, Electoral Behavior, and Political Change," *American Political Science Review* 89 (1995): 10–22.

44. See Paul Allen Beck, "A Tale of Two Electorates," in John C. Green and Rick Farmer, eds., *The State of the Parties*, 4th ed. (Lanham, MD: Rowman & Littlefield, 2003), pp. 38–53.

CHAPTER 8

1. Because of the difficulties in estimating American turnout, most "official" turnout figures *underestimate* it. The percentages here and in Figure 8.1 follow the method of Walter Dean Burnham, which carefully corrects for this underestimation. Their denominator is an effort to estimate the *eligible* population: the voting-age population minus the number of noncitizens living in the United States. The numerator of the turnout fraction is the number of voters who cast a vote for president or for the office with the highest vote in midterm elections. Estimated turnout would be slightly higher if we had a reliable way to include blank or spoiled ballots, write-in votes for the office with the highest vote total, and voters who did not vote for that office, and to exclude from the denominator citizens who are not eligible to vote in various states because they are inmates of prisons or mental hospitals. See Walter Dean Burnham, "The Turnout Problem," in A. James Reichley, ed., *Elections American Style* (Washington, DC: Brookings, 1987), pp. 97–133.

2. Robin Toner, "Voters Are Very Settled, Intense and Partisan, and It's Only July," *New York Times*, July 25, 2004, p. 1.

3. See Benjamin Barber, *Strong Democracy* (Berkeley: University of California Press, 1994).

4. Walter Dean Burnham, "The Changing Shape of the American Political Universe," *American Political Science Review* 59 (1965): 7–28.

5. Stephen J. Wayne, *The Road to the White House 2004* (Belmont, CA: Wadsworth, 2004), p. 71.

6. "Suffrage" means the right to vote. See Chilton Williamson, *American Suffrage* (Princeton, NJ: Princeton University Press, 1960).

7. The Supreme Court case overturning the poll tax was *Harper v. Virginia State Board of Elections,* 383 U.S. 663 (1966).

8. *Oregon v. Mitchell,* 400 U.S. 112 (1970).

9. Raymond E. Wolfinger and Jonathan Hoffman, "Registering and Voting with Motor Voter," *PS: Political Science and Politics* 34 (2001): 85–92; and Michael D. Martinez and David Hill, "Did Motor Voter Work?" *American Politics Quarterly* 27 (1999): 296–315.

10. Paul Kleppner, *Continuity and Change in Electoral Politics, 1893–1928* (Westport, CT: Greenwood, 1987), pp. 165–166.

11. Peverill Squire, Raymond E. Wolfinger, and David P. Glass, "Residential Mobility and Voter Turnout," *American Political Science Review* 81 (1987): 45–65.

12. Walter Dean Burnham, "Theory and Voting Research," *American Political Science Review* 68 (1974): 1002–1023; and Frances Fox Piven and Richard A. Cloward, *Why Americans Still Don't Vote* (Boston: Beacon Press, 2000).

13. See Robert L. Dudley and Alan R. Gitelson, *American Elections: The Rules Matter* (New York: Longman, 2002), pp. 7–15.

14. Ruy A. Teixiera, *The Disappearing American Voter* (Washington, DC: Brookings, 1992), Chapter 4; and Glenn E. Mitchell and Christopher Wlezien, "The Impact of Legal Constraints on Voter Registration, Turnout, and the Composition of the American Electorate," *Political Behavior* 17 (1995): 179–202.

15. The white primary was finally overturned by the Supreme Court in *Smith v. Allwright,* 321 U.S. 649 (1944).

16. See V. O. Key, Jr., *Southern Politics in State and Nation* (New York: Knopf, 1949).

17. Chandler Davidson and Bernard Grofman, eds., *Quiet Revolution in the South* (Princeton, NJ: Princeton University Press, 1994).

18. Thomas B. Edsall, "Parties Play Voting Rights Role Reversal," *Washington Post,* February 25, 2001, p. A1. See also Kevin A. Hill, "Does the Creation of Majority Black Districts Aid Republicans?" *Journal of Politics* 57 (1995): 384–401, and David Lublin and D. Stephen Voss, "Racial Redistricting and Realignment in Southern State Legislatures," *American Journal of Political Science* 44 (2000): 792–810.

19. The cases are *Miller v. Johnson* 515 U.S. 900 (1995) and *Easley v. Cromartie* 532 U.S. 234 (2001), respectively. On majority-minority districts, see David T. Canon, *Race, Redistricting, and Representation* (Chicago: University of Chicago Press, 1999); David Lublin, "Racial Redistricting and African-American Representation," *American Political Science Review* 93 (1999): 183–186; and Katherine Tate, "Black Opinion on the

Legitimacy of Racial Redistricting and Minority-Majority Districts," *American Political Science Review* 97 (2003): 45–56.

20. Robert E. Pierre and Peter Slevin, "Fla. Vote Rife With Disparities, Study Says," *Washington Post*, June 5, 2001, p. A1. See also Michael Tomz and Robert P. Van Houweling, "How Does Voting Equipment Affect the Racial Gap in Voided Ballots?," *American Journal of Political Science* 47 (2003): 46–60.

21. See Jeff Manza and Christopher Uggen, "Punishment and Democracy," *Perspectives on Politics* 2 (2004): 491–505.

22. Robert A. Jackson, "The Mobilization of U.S. State Electorates in the 1988 and 1990 Elections," *Journal of Politics* 59 (1997): 520–537.

23. Thomas E. Cronin, *Direct Democracy* (Cambridge, MA: Harvard University Press, 1989).

24. Steven J. Rosenstone and John Mark Hansen, *Mobilization, Participation, and Democracy in America* (New York: Longman, 2003), pp. 178–188.

25. Barry C. Burden, "An Alternative Account of the 2004 Presidential Election," *The Forum* 2 (2004) on the Internet at http://www.bepress.com/cgi/viewcontent.cgi?article=1057&context=forum.

26. The role of party competition in this turnout decline has been debated by Burnham, "The Changing Shape of the American Political Universe," and Jerrold G. Rusk, "The American Electoral Universe," *American Political Science Review* 68 (1974): 1028–1049.

27. Mark N. Franklin, "Electoral Participation," in Lawrence LeDuc, Richard Niemi, and Pippa Norris, eds., *Comparing Democracies* (London: Sage, 1996).

28. See Alan S. Gerber and Donald P. Green, "The Effects of Canvassing, Direct Mail, and Telephone Contact on Voter Turnout," *American Political Science Review* 94 (2000): 653–663; and Alan S. Gerber and Donald P. Green, "Correction to Gerber & Green (2000)," *American Political Science Review* 99 (2005): 301–313.

29. Thomas Patterson, press release from the Vanishing Voter Project, John F. Kennedy School of Government, Harvard University, November 11, 2004.

30. On the mobilization of black voters, see Lawrence Bobo and Franklin D. Gilliam, Jr., "Race, Sociopolitical Participation, and Black Empowerment," *American Political Science Review* 84 (1990): 377–393; and Richard Timpone, "Mass Mobilization or Governmental Intervention," *Journal of Politics* 57 (1995): 425–442.

31. Gerald M. Pomper, "The Presidential Election," in Michael Nelson, ed., *The Elections of 2004* (Washington, DC: CQ Press, 2005), pp. 46–47.

32. Alan S. Gerber, Donald P. Green, and Ron Chachar, "Voting May Be Habit-Forming," *American Journal of Political Science* 47 (2003): 540–550; and Eric Plutzer, "Becoming a Habitual Voter," *American Political Science Review* 96 (2002): 41–56.

33. See John H. Aldrich, "Rational Choice and Turnout," *American Journal of Political Science* 37 (1993): 246–278.

34. Paul R. Abramson, John H. Aldrich, and David W. Rohde, *Change and Continuity in the 2000 and 2002 Elections* (Washington, DC: CQ Press, 2003), pp. 82–85; and Robert A. Jackson, "Clarifying the Relationship between Education and Turnout," *American Politics Quarterly* 23 (1995): 279–299.

35. Raymond E. Wolfinger and Steven J. Rosenstone, *Who Votes?* (New Haven, CT: Yale University Press, 1980), pp. 35–36.

36. See Sidney Verba, Norman H. Nie, and Jae-On Kim, *Participation and Political Equality* (Cambridge: Cambridge University Press, 1978).

37. See Thomas E. Patterson, "Young Voters and the 2004 Election," John F. Kennedy School of Government, Harvard University, 2005; and Daniel M. Shea and John C. Green, *The Fountain of Youth* (Allegheny College: Center for Political Participation, 2004).

38. Amy Goldstein and Richard Morin, "Young Voters' Disengagement Skews Politics," *Washington Post,* October 20, 2002, p. A8.

39. Bobo and Gilliam, "Race, Sociopolitical Participation, and Black Empowerment."

40. Laura Stoker and M. Kent Jennings, "Life-Cycle Transitions and Political Participation: The Case of Marriage," *American Political Science Review* 89 (1995): 421–436; and Nancy Burns, Kay Lehman Schlozman, and Sidney Verba, "The Public Consequences of Private Inequality," *American Political Science Review* 91 (1997): 373–389.

41. See Rosenstone and Hansen, *Mobilization, Participation, and Democracy in America*, pp. 141–156.

42. See Mark N. Franklin and Wolfgang P. Hirczy de Mino, "Separated Powers, Divided Government, and Turnout in U.S. Presidential Elections," *American Journal of Political Science* 42 (1998): 316–326.

43. Diana C. Mutz, "The Consequences of Cross-Cutting Networks for Political Participation," *American Journal of Political Science* 46 (2002): 838–855.

44. Harold D. Clarke, David Sanders, Marianne C. Stewart, and Paul F. Whiteley, "Britain (Not) at the Polls, 2001," *PS: Political Science and Politics* (2003): 59–64.

45. Richard A. Brody, "The Puzzle of Participation in America," in Anthony King, ed., *The New American Political System* (Washington, DC: American Enterprise Institute, 1978), pp. 287–324.

46. Lyn Ragsdale and Jerrold G. Rusk, "Who Are Nonvoters?," *American Journal of Political Science* 37 (1993): 721–746.

47. Abramson, Aldrich, and Rohde, *Change and Continuity*, pp. 86–91.

48. Claudine Gay, "The Effect of Black Congressional Representation on Political Participation," *American Political Science Review* 95 (2001): 589–602.

49. Paul S. Martin, "Voting's Rewards," *American Journal of Political Science* 47 (2003): 110–127; and Steven Balla, Eric Lawrence, Forrest Maltzman, and Lee Sigelman, "Partisanship, Blame Avoidance, and the Distribution of Legislative Pork," *American Journal of Political Science* 46 (2002): 515–525.

50. Sidney Verba, Kay Lehman Schlozman, and Henry E. Brady, *Voice and Equality* (Cambridge, MA: Harvard University Press, 1995), p. 511.

51. James DeNardo, "Turnout and the Vote: The Joke's on the Democrats," *American Political Science Review* 74 (1980): 406–420. See also Jack Citrin, Eric Schickler, and John Sides, "What If Everyone Voted?;" *American Journal of Political Science* 47 (2003): 75–90.

PART FOUR

1. See Murray Edelman, *Constructing the Political Spectacle* (Chicago: University of Chicago Press, 1988).

CHAPTER 9

1. See Alan Ware, *The American Direct Primary* (Cambridge: Cambridge University Press, 2002). On the spread of the primary to other democracies, see James A. McCann, "The Emerging International Trend toward Open Presidential Primaries," in William G. Mayer, ed., *The Making of the Presidential Candidates 2004* (Lanham, MD: Rowman & Littlefield, 2004), pp. 265–293.

2. Stephen J. Wayne, *The Road to the White House 2004* (Belmont, CA: Wadsworth, 2004), pp. 6–13.

3. See Charles E. Merriam and Louise Overacker, *Primary Elections* (Chicago: University of Chicago Press, 1928).

4. Robert M. La Follette, *La Follette's Autobiography* (Madison, WI: R. M. La Follette, 1913), pp. 197–198.

5. Some states allow third parties to nominate their candidates through conventions.

6. *The Book of the States 2003 Ed.* (Lexington, KY: The Council of State Governments, 2003), pp. 295–296; Malcolm E. Jewell and Sarah M. Morehouse, *Political Parties and Elections in American States*, 4th ed. (Washington, DC: CQ Press, 2001), Chapter 4; and the Federal Election Commission *Record, Party Guide Supplement* 31 (May 2005).

7. See Craig L. Carr and Gary L. Scott, "The Logic of State Primary Classification Schemes," *American Politics Quarterly* 12 (1984): 465–476; and Steven E. Finkel and Howard A. Scarrow, "Party Identification and Party Enrollment: The Difference and the Consequence," *Journal of Politics* 47 (1985): 620–652.

8. The numbers of states in each category are updated from John F. Bibby and Thomas M. Holbrook, "Parties and Elections," in Virginia Gray and Russell L. Hanson, eds., *Politics in the American States*, 8th ed. (Washington, DC: CQ Press, 2003), Chapter 3. Note that experts disagree on these definitions and on the dividing line between an "open" and a "closed" primary.

9. A 1986 Supreme Court decision (*Tashjian v. Republican Party of Connecticut,* 106 S. Ct. 783 and 1257) upheld the Connecticut party's efforts to establish an open primary by overriding the state's closed primary law. This decision affirmed the authority of the party, rather than the state, to control its own nomination process. However, most state parties would prefer a closed primary to an open one.

10. The case was *California Democratic Party v. Jones*, 530 U.S. 567(2000). On blanket primaries, see Bruce E. Cain and Elisabeth R. Gerber, eds., *Voting at the Political Fault Line: California's Experiment with the Blanket Primary* (Berkeley: University of California Press, 2002).

11. Lynn Vavreck, "The Reasoning Voter Meets the Strategic Candidate," *American Politics Research* 29 (2001): 507–529. See also Philip Paolino and Daron R. Shaw, "Lifting the Hood on the Straight-Talk Express," *American Politics Research* 29 (2001): 483–506.

12. Gary D. Wekkin, "Why Crossover Voters Are Not 'Mischievous' Voters," *American Politics Quarterly* 19 (1991): 229–247.

13. The monthly newsletter *Ballot Access News* reports current efforts to change the rules governing ballot access, especially for third parties and independents. It can be found on the Internet (http://www.ballot-access.org).

14. See Harold Stanley, "The Runoff: The Case for Retention," *PS: Political Science and Politics* 18 (1985): 231–236; and Charles S. Bullock, III, and Loch K. Johnson, *Runoff Elections in the United States* (Knoxville: University of Tennessee Press, 1991).

15. See V. O. Key, Jr., *American State Politics: An Introduction* (New York: Knopf, 1956), p. 195.

16. About a third of all state legislative races have been uncontested in recent years. See L. Sandy Maisel, Linda L. Fowler, Ruth S. Jones, and Walter J. Stone, "Nomination Politics: The Roles of Institutional, Contextual, and Personal Variables," in L. Sandy Maisel, ed., *The Parties Respond* (Boulder, CO: Westview, 1994), pp. 148–152.

17. See John G. Geer and Mark E. Shere, "Party Competition and the Prisoner's Dilemma: An Argument for the Direct Primary," *Journal of Politics* 54 (1992): 741–761.

18. See, for example, Jewell and Morehouse, *Political Parties and Elections in American States*, p. 123.

19. Theodore H. White, *The Making of the President 1960* (New York: Atheneum, 1961), p. 78.

20. See Walter J. Stone, "The Carryover Effect in Presidential Elections," *American Political Science Review* 80 (1986): 271–280.

21. Studies differ in their conclusions about the impact of divisive primaries, in part depending on the way they define "divisive." See, for example, James I. Lengle, Diana Owen, and Molly W. Sonner, "Divisive Nominating Mechanisms and Democratic Party Electoral Prospects," *Journal of Politics* 57 (1995): 370–383; Lonna Rae Atkeson, "Divisive Primaries and General Election Outcomes," *American Journal of Political Science* 42 (1998): 256–271; and Robert E. Hogan, "The Effects of Primary Divisiveness on General Election Outcomes in State Legislative Elections," *American Politics Research* 31 (2003): 27–47.

22. See Paige L. Schneider, "Factionalism in the Southern Republican Party," *American Review of Politics* 19 (1998): 129–148.

23. Matt Bai, "Fight Club," *New York Times Magazine,* August 10, 2003, pp. 24–27.

24. Quoted in David S. Broder and Juliet Eilperin, "Of Primary Importance," *Washington Post,* April 20, 2002, p. A1.

25. Gary F. Moncrief, Peverill Squire, and Malcolm E. Jewell, *Who Runs for the Legislature?* (Upper Saddle River, NJ: Prentice Hall, 2001), p. 39.

26. Sarah McCally Morehouse, *The Governor as Party Leader* (Ann Arbor: University of Michigan Press, 1998), pp. 22–23.

27. Jewell and Morehouse, *Political Parties and Elections in American States*, pp. 109–110.

28. See Maisel, Fowler, Jones, and Stone, "Nomination Politics," pp. 155–156.

29. See Jewell and Morehouse, *Political Parties and Elections in American States*, pp. 118–120 and Jay Goodliffe and David B. Magleby, "Campaign Finance in U.S. House Primary and General Elections," in Peter F. Galderisi, Marni Ezra, and Michael Lyons, eds., *Congressional Primaries and the Politics of Representation* (Lanham, MD: Rowman & Littlefield, 2001), pp. 62–76.

30. Malcolm E. Jewell, "Northern State Gubernatorial Primary Elections: Explaining Voting Turnout," *American Politics Quarterly* 12 (1984): 101–116.

31. Patrick J. Kenney, "Explaining Primary Turnout: The Senatorial Case," *Legislative Studies Quarterly* 11 (1986): 65–74; and John G. Geer, "Assessing the Representativeness of Electorates in Presidential Primaries," *American Journal of Political Science* 32 (1988): 929–945.

32. Jewell and Morehouse, *Political Parties and Elections in American States*, pp. 124–125.

33. Karen M. Kaufmann, James G. Gimpel, and Adam H. Hoffman, "A Promise Fulfilled? Open Primaries and Representation," *Journal of Politics* 65 (2003): 457–476.

CHAPTER 10

1. See John S. Jackson III and William J. Crotty, *The Politics of Presidential Selection,* 2nd ed. (New York: Longman, 2001), Chapters 3 and 4.

2. See James W. Ceaser, *Presidential Selection* (Princeton, NJ: Princeton University Press, 1979); and Larry M. Bartels, *Presidential Primaries and the Dynamics of Public Choice* (Princeton, NJ: Princeton University Press, 1988), pp. 17–21.

3. Michael G. Hagen and William G. Mayer, "The Modern Politics of Presidential Selection," in William G. Mayer, ed., *In Pursuit of the White House 2000* (New York: Chatham House, 2000), pp. 1–55.

4. Byron E. Shafer, *Bifurcated Politics* (Cambridge, MA: Harvard University Press, 1988), pp. 181–184.

5. See Gary D. Wekkin, *Democrats versus Democrats* (Columbia: University of Missouri Press, 1983).

6. William G. Mayer and Andrew E. Busch, *The Front-Loading Problem in Presidential Nominations* (Washington, DC: Brookings Institution Press, 2004).

7. Marjorie Randon Hershey, "Shedding Light on the Invisible Primary," in Larry J. Sabato, ed., *Get in the Booth! The Presidential Election of 2004* (New York: Longman, 2004), pp. 27–47.

8. Howard Kurtz, "Funny, the Calendar Doesn't Say 2004," *Washington Post,* February 10, 2003, p. C1.

9. Hershey, "Shedding Light on the Invisible Primary," pp. 42–43.

10. See John H. Aldrich, *Before the Convention* (Chicago: University of Chicago Press, 1980); and Paul-Henri Gurian and Audrey A. Haynes, "Campaign Strategy in Presidential Primaries," *American Journal of Political Science* 37 (1993): 335–341.

11. See Andrew E. Busch and William G. Mayer, "The Front-Loading Problem," in William G. Mayer, ed., *The Making of the Presidential Candidates 2004* (Lanham, MD: Rowman & Littlefield, 2004), pp. 1–43.

12. Richard Herrera, "Are 'Superdelegates' Super?" *Political Behavior* 16 (1994): 79–92.

13. See Patrick J. Kenney and Tom W. Rice, "Voter Turnout in Presidential Primaries: A Cross-Sectional Examination," *Political Behavior* 7 (1985): 101–112; and Barbara Norrander and Gregg W. Smith, "Type of Contest, Candidate Strategy, and Turnout in Presidential Primaries," *American Politics Quarterly* 13 (1985): 28–50.

14. Sen. Carl Levin of Michigan, quoted in Dan Balz, "First-in-Nation Status of Iowa, N.H. May Be Up for Grabs," *Washington Post,* March 12, 2005, p. A4.

15. Bartels, *Presidential Primaries and the Dynamics of Public Choice*, pp. 140–148.

16. Will Lester, "Poll: Some Voters Not Familiar With Dems," Associated Press, January 17, 2004, on the Internet at http://www.washingtonpost.com/wp-dyn/articles/A25923-2004Jan17.html (accessed January 17, 2004).

17. See Scott Keeter and Cliff Zukin, *Uninformed Choice* (New York: Praeger, 1983); and John G. Geer, *Nominating Presidents* (New York: Greenwood Press, 1989).

18. Samuel L. Popkin, *The Reasoning Voter* (Chicago: University of Chicago Press, 1991), Chapters 6–8.

19. Bartels, *Presidential Primaries and the Dynamics of Public Choice*, Chapter 4.

20. Paul R. Abramson, John H. Aldrich, Phil Paolino, and David W. Rohde, "'Sophisticated' Voting in the 1988 Presidential Primaries," *American Political Science Review* 86 (1992): 55–69.

21. See Walter J. Stone, Ronald B. Rapoport, and Alan I. Abramowitz, "Candidate Support in Presidential Nomination Campaigns: The Case of Iowa in 1984," *Journal of Politics* 54 (1992): 1074–1097.

22. Hagen and Mayer, "The Modern Politics of Presidential Selection," pp. 17–21.

23. L. Sandy Maisel, "The Platform-Writing Process: Candidate-Centered Platforms in 1992," *Political Science Quarterly* 108 (1993–1994): 671–699.

24. Gerald M. Pomper, "Party Responsibility and the Future of American Democracy," in Jeffrey E. Cohen, Richard Fleisher, and Paul Kantor, eds., *American Political Parties: Decline or Resurgence?* (Washington, DC: CQ Press, 2001), pp. 170–172.

25. See Lee Sigelman and Paul J. Wahlbeck, "The 'Veepstakes': Strategic Choice in Presidential Running Mate Selection," *American Political Science Review* 91 (1997): 855–864.

26. These data and those cited in the rest of the chapter come from the *New York Times*/CBS News Polls of Democratic and Republican National Convention delegates. The Democratic survey was done during June 16–July 17, 2004, with 1,085 delegates participating, and the Republican survey was held on August 3–23 with 1,200 delegates responding.

27. Herbert McClosky, Paul Hoffman, and Rosemary O'Hara, "Issue Conflict and Consensus among Party Leaders and Followers," *American Political Science Review* 54 (1960): 406–427.

28. See Jeane Kirkpatrick, *The New Presidential Elite* (New York: Russell Sage Foundation, 1976).

29. See John S. Jackson III, Barbara L. Brown, and David Bositis, "Herbert McClosky and Friends Revisited," *American Politics Quarterly* 10 (1982): 158–180; and Warren E. Miller and M. Kent Jennings, *Parties in Transition* (New York: Russell Sage Foundation, 1986), Chapters 7–9.

30. See John W. Soule and Wilma E. McGrath, "A Comparative Study of Presidential Nomination Conventions: The Democrats 1968 and 1972," *American Journal of Political Science* 19 (1975): 501–517.

31. Denise L. Baer and David A. Bositis, *Elite Cadres and Party Coalitions* (New York: Greenwood Press, 1988), Chapter 7.

32. Shafer, *Bifurcated Politics*, Chapter 8.

33. Thomas E. Patterson, "Young Voters and the 2004 Election," John F. Kennedy School of Government, Harvard University, 2005.

34. See Emmett H. Buell, Jr., "The Changing Face of the New Hampshire Primary," in William G. Mayer, ed., *In Pursuit of the White House 2000* (New York: Chatham House, 2000), pp. 87–144.

35. Nelson W. Polsby, *The Consequences of Party Reform* (Oxford: Oxford University Press, 1983).

CHAPTER 11

1. Jerrold G. Rusk, "The Effect of the Australian Ballot Reform on Split Ticket Voting: 1876–1908," *American Political Science Review* 64 (1970): 1220–1238.

2. Joanne M. Miller and Jon A. Krosnick, "The Impact of Candidate Name Order on Election Outcomes," *Public Opinion Quarterly* 62 (1998): 291–330; and Jonathan GS Koppell and Jennifer A. Steen, "The Effects of Ballot Position on Election Outcomes," *Journal of Politics* 66 (2004): 267–281.

3. Walter Dean Burnham, "The Changing Shape of the American Political Universe," *American Political Science Review* 59 (1965): 7–28. See also Stephen M. Nichols and Gregory A. Strizek, "Electronic Voting Machines and Ballot Roll-off," *American Politics Quarterly* 23 (1995): 300–318.

4. Guy Gugliotta, "Study Finds Millions of Votes Lost," *Washington Post,* July 17, 2001, p. A1; and Justin Buchler, Matthew Jarvis, and John E. McNulty, "Punch Card Technology and the Racial Gap in Residual Votes," *Perspectives on Politics* 2 (2004): 517–524.

5. Robin Toner, "For Those Behind the Scenes, It's Old News That Elections Are Not an Exact Science," *New York Times,* November 17, 2000, p. A23.

6. Abby Goodnough, "Lost Record of Vote in '02 Florida Race Raises '04 Concern," *New York Times,* July 28, 2004, p. 1.

7. The landmark Supreme Court cases are *Baker v. Carr,* 369 U.S. 186 (1962); *Reynolds v. Sims,* 377 U.S. 533 (1964); and *Wesberry v. Sanders,* 376 U.S. 1 (1964).

8. Gregory L. Giroux, "Democrats Regenerating for Long Haul to a Majority," *CQ Weekly,* June 7, 2003, pp. 1364–1367.

9. See Gary W. Cox and Jonathan N. Katz," The Reapportionment Revolution and Bias in U.S. Congressional Elections," *American Journal of Political Science* 43 (1999): 812–841; Richard G. Niemi and Alan I. Abramowitz, "Partisan Redistricting and the 1992 Congressional Elections," *Journal of Politics* 56 (1994): 811–817; Andrew Gelman and Gary King, "Enhancing Democracy through Legislative Redistricting," *American Political Science Review* 88 (1994): 541–559; and John D. Cranor, Gary L. Crawley, and Raymond H. Scheele, "The Anatomy of a Gerrymander," *American Journal of Political Science* 33 (1989): 222–239.

10. See Paul S. Herrnson, *Congressional Elections,* 4th ed. (Washington, DC: CQ Press, 2004); Marjorie Randon Hershey, *Running for Office* (Chatham, NJ: Chatham House, 1984); and on presidential campaigns, Stephen J. Wayne, *The Road to the White House 2004* (Belmont, CA: Wadsworth, 2004).

11. Herrnson, *Congressional Elections*; and Gary C. Jacobson, *The Politics of Congressional Elections,* 6th ed. (New York: Longman, 2004).

12. Edward I. Sidlow, *Challenging the Incumbent* (Washington, DC: CQ Press, 2003).

13. See, for example, David A. Dulio, *For Better or Worse: How Political Consultants Are Changing Elections in the United States* (Albany, NY: SUNY Press, 2004).

14. James A. Thurber and Candice J. Nelson, eds., *Campaign Warriors* (Washington, DC: Brookings, 2000).

15. Paul Farhi, "Toledo Tube War: 14,273 Ads and Counting," *Washington Post,* October 11, 2004, p. A1.

16. Darrell M. West, *Air Wars,* 4th ed. (Washington, DC: CQ Press, 2005); and Paul Farhi, "Campaigns Buying More Ads but Targeting Fewer States," *Washington Post,* September 25, 2004, p. A1.

17. See Doris A. Graber, *Mass Media and American Politics,* 7th ed. (Washington, DC: CQ Press, 2005), Chapter 4.

18. Dave Barry, "Scandal Sheep," *The Boston Globe Magazine,* March 15, 1998, pp. 12–13.

19. See Matthew Robert Kerbel, "The Media: The Challenge and the Promise of Internet Politics," in Michael Nelson, ed., *The Elections of 2004* (Washington, DC: CQ Press, 2005), pp. 88–107; and Bruce Bimberg and Richard Davis, *Campaigning Online* (New York: Oxford University Press, 2003).

20. Michael Cornfield, "Going Broadband, Getting Netwise," in Larry J. Sabato, ed., *Divided States of America* (New York: Longman, 2006), p. 219.

21. John Bart and James Meader, "South Dakota Senate Race 2002," in David B. Magleby and J. Quin Monson, eds., *The Last Hurrah?* (Provo, UT: Center for the Study of Elections and Democracy, Brigham Young University, 2003).

22. Richard J. Semiatin, *Campaigns in the 21st Century* (Boston: McGraw Hill, 2005), p. 178.

23. Elizabeth Theiss-Smith and Richard Braunstein, "The Nationalization of Local Politics in South Dakota," in David B. Magleby, J. Quin Monson, and Kelly D. Patterson, eds., *Dancing without Partners* (Brigham Young University: Center for the Study of Elections and Democracy, 2005), p. 240.

24. American National Election Study, University of Michigan, 2004, and CNN 2004 exit poll.

25. See Magleby and Monson, *The Last Hurrah?*, Chapters 1 and 12.

26. Gerald M. Pomper, "The Presidential Election," in Michael Nelson, ed., *The Elections of 2004* (Washington, DC: CQ Press, 2005), p. 57.

27. See Richard R. Lau and Gerald M. Pomper, "Effectiveness of Negative Campaigning in U.S. Senate Elections," *American Journal of Political Science* 46 (2002): 47–66; Stephen Ansolabehere and Shanto Iyengar, *Going Negative* (New York: Free Press, 1995); and, for a different view, Steven E. Finkel and John G. Geer, "A Spot Check: Casting Doubt on the Demobilizing Effect of Attack Advertising," *American Journal of Political Science* 42 (1998): 573–595.

28. Paul Farhi, "Campaigns Buying More Ads but Targeting Fewer States."

29. Paul R. Abramson, John H. Aldrich, and David W. Rohde, *Change and Continuity in the 2000 and 2002 Elections* (Washington, DC: CQ Press, 2003), pp. 261–262; Dan Balz, "Exuberant RNC Seeks More Voters," *Washington Post*, February 1, 2003, p. A5.

30. Quoted in Thomas B. Edsall and James V. Grimaldi, "On Nov. 2, GOP Got More Bang For Its Billion," *Washington Post*, December 30, 2004, p. A1.

31. Stephen T. Mockabee, Michael Margolis, Stephen Brooks, Rick Farmer, and John C. Green, "The Battle for Ohio," in Magleby, Monson, Patterson, *Dancing without Partners*, pp. 145, 151–152.

32. Pomper, "The Presidential Election," pp. 57 and 61.

33. Alan Abramowitz, "Terrorism, Gay Marriage, and Incumbency," *The Forum* 2 (2004), on the Internet at http://www.bepress.com/forum; Andrew Gelman and Gary King, "Why Are American Presidential Election Polls So Variable When Votes Are So Predictable?" *British Journal of Political Science* 23 (1993): 409–451; and Thomas M. Holbrook, "Campaigns, National Conditions, and U.S. Presidential Elections," *American Journal of Political Science* 38 (1994): 973–998.

34. See Robert Huckfeldt and John Sprague, "Political Parties and Electoral Mobilization," *American Political Science Review* 86 (1992): 70–86; Peter W. Wielhouwer, "The Mobilization of Campaign Activists by the Party Canvass," *American Politics Quarterly* 27 (1999): 177–200; and Steven J. Rosenstone and John Mark Hansen, *Mobilization, Participation, and Democracy in America* (New York: Longman, 2003), Chapter 6.

35. Donald P. Green and Alan S. Gerber, *Get Out the Vote!* (Washington, DC: Brookings Institution Press, 2004); and John C. Blydenburgh, "A Controlled Experiment to Measure the Effects of Personal Contact Campaigning," *Midwest Journal of Political Science* 15 (1971): 365–381.

36. John P. Frendreis, James L. Gibson, and Laura L. Vertz, "The Electoral Relevance of Local Party Organizations," *American Political Science Review* 84 (1990): 225–235.

37. Harold W. Stanley and Richard G. Niemi, *Vital Statistics on American Politics 1999–2000* (Washington, DC: CQ Press, 2000), Table 4.5, p. 173.

38. Kathleen Hall Jamieson and Paul Waldman, *The Press Effect* (New York: Oxford University Press, 2003), p. 67.

39. Daron R. Shaw, "The Effect of TV Ads and Candidate Appearances on Statewide Presidential Votes, 1988–96," *American Political Science Review* 93 (1999): 345–61; and Carroll J. Glynn, Susan Herbst, Garrett J. O'Keefe, and Robert Y. Shapiro, *Public Opinion* (Boulder, CO: Westview, 1999), pp. 436–441.

40. Thomas M. Holbrook, *Do Campaigns Matter?* (Thousand Oaks, CA: Sage, 1996); Daron R. Shaw, "A Study of Presidential Campaign Effects from 1952–1992," *Journal of Politics* 61 (1999): 387–422; and Adam Simon, *The Winning Message* (Cambridge: Cambridge University Press, 2002).

41. See Paul Freedman, Michael Franz, and Kenneth Goldstein, "Campaign Advertising and Democratic Citizenship," *American Journal of Political Science* 48 (2004): 723–741.

42. D. Sunshine Hillygus and Simon Jackman, "Voter Decision Making in Election 2000," *American Journal of Political Science* 47 (2003): 583–596.

43. Russell J. Dalton, Paul A. Beck, and Robert Huckfeldt, "Partisan Cues and the Media: Information Flows in the 1992 Presidential Election," *American Political Science Review* 92 (1998): 111–126.

44. See Robert Huckfeldt and John Sprague, "Networks in Context: The Social Flow of Political Information," *American Political Science Review* 81 (1987): 1197–1216; and Paul Allen Beck, "Voters' Intermediation Environments in the 1988 Presidential Contest," *Public Opinion Quarterly* 55 (1991): 371–394.

45. The classics are Paul Lazarsfeld, Bernard Berelson, and Hazel Gaudet, *The People's Choice* (New York: Columbia University Press, 1948); and Bernard Berelson, Paul Lazarsfeld, and William McPhee, *Voting* (Chicago: University of Chicago Press, 1954).

46. Donald Shaw and Maxwell E. McCombs, *The Emergence of American Political Issues* (St. Paul, MN: West, 1977). On priming, see Joanne M. Miller and Jon A. Krosnick, "News Media Impact on the Ingredients of Presidential Evaluations," *American Journal of Political Science* 44 (2000): 295–309; and Shanto Iyengar and Donald Kinder, *News That Matters* (Chicago: University of Chicago Press, 1987).

47. See Marjorie Randon Hershey, "The Campaign and the Media," in Gerald M. Pomper, ed., *The Election of 2000* (New York: Chatham House, 2001), pp. 46–72.

48. Iyengar and Kinder, *News That Matters;* see also Jamieson and Waldman, *The Press Effect.*

49. Shanto Iyengar and John R. Petrocik, " 'Basic Rule' Voting: Impact of Campaigns on Party- and Approval-Based Voting," in James A. Thurber, Candice J. Nelson, and David A. Dulio, eds., *Crowded Airwaves* (Washington, DC: Brookings, 2000), p. 142.

50. John J. Coleman, "Party Images and Candidate-Centered Campaigns in 1996," in John C. Green and Daniel M. Shea, eds., *The State of the Parties,* 3rd ed. (Lanham, MD: Rowman & Littlefield, 1999), pp. 337–354.

51. See John Kenneth White and Daniel M. Shea, *New Party Politics,* 2nd ed. (Belmont, CA: Wadsworth, 2004), p. 98.

52. David B. Magleby, ed., *The Other Campaign* (Lanham, MD: Rowman & Littlefield, 2003). On the impact of party money, see Thomas M. Holbrook and Scott D. McClurg, "The Mobilization of Core Supporters," *American Journal of Political Science* 49 (2005): 689–703.

53. Quoted in David B. Magleby and Eric A. Smith, "Party Soft Money in the 2000 Congressional Elections," in Magleby, ed., *The Other Campaign,* p. 44.

54. See Paul S. Herrnson and Diana Dwyre, "Party Issue Advocacy in Congressional Election Campaigns," in Green and Shea, *The State of the Parties,* pp. 86–104.

CHAPTER 12

1. Unless otherwise noted, all figures cited in this chapter come from Federal Election Commission reports. For excellent analysis of campaign finance in 2004, see Michael J. Malbin, ed., *The Election after Reform* (Lanham, MD: Rowman & Littlefield, 2006); and David B. Magleby, Kelly Patterson, and Anthony Corrado, eds., *Financing the 2004 Election* (Washington, DC: Brookings Institution Press, 2006).

2. George Thayer, *Who Shakes the Money Tree?* (New York: Simon & Schuster, 1973), p. 25.

3. FEC data in "Congressional Candidates Spend $1.16 Billion During 2003–2004," press release issued June 9, 2005.

4. Gary C. Jacobson, "The First Congressional Elections after BCRA," in Michael J. Malbin, ed., *The Election after Reform* (Lanham, MD: Rowman & Littlefield, 2006), Chapter 9.

5. Michael Cooper, "At $92.60 a Vote, Bloomberg Shatters An Election Record," *New York Times,* December 4, 2001, p. A1.

6. Kaitlin Gurney, "N.J. Finds 'Clean Elections' Tempting," *Philadelphia Inquirer,* March 19, 2004, p. 1.

7. Neil A. Lewis, "Gifts in State Judicial Races Are Up Sharply," *New York Times,* February 14, 2002, p. A27.

8. See John J. Coleman and Paul F. Manna, "Congressional Campaign Spending and the Quality of Democracy," *Journal of Politics* 62 (2000): 757–789.

9. Gary C. Jacobson, *The Politics of Congressional Elections,* 6th ed. (New York: Longman, 2004), p. 44.

10. See these articles in the *American Journal of Political Science:* Donald Philip Green and Jonathan S. Krasno, "Salvation for the Spendthrift Incumbent," 32 (1988): 884–907; Gary C. Jacobson, "The Effects of Campaign Spending in House Elections," 34 (1990): 334–362; and Donald Philip Green and Jonathan S. Krasno, "Rebuttal to Jacobson's 'New Evidence for Old Arguments,'" 34 (1990): 363–372.

11. On state elections, see Michael J. Malbin and Thomas L. Gais, *The Day after Reform* (Albany, NY: Rockefeller Institute, 1998).

12. Peter Francia, John C. Green, Paul S. Herrnson, Lynda W. Powell, and Clyde Wilcox, *The Financiers of Congressional Elections* (New York: Columbia University Press, 2003).

13. Michael Cornfield, "Going Broadband, Getting Netwise," in Larry J. Sabato, ed., *Divided States of America* (New York: Longman, 2006), pp. 212–213.

14. Larry J. Sabato and Bruce A. Larson, *The Party's Just Begun,* 2nd ed. (New York: Longman, 2002), pp. 84–88.

15. Frank J. Sorauf, *Inside Campaign Finance* (New Haven, CT: Yale University Press, 1992), Chapter 4.

16. Gregory Wawro, "A Panel Probit Analysis of Campaign Contributions and Roll-Call Votes," *American Journal of Political Science* 45 (2001): 563–579.

17. See Richard L. Hall and Frank W. Wayman, "Buying Time," *American Political Science Review* 84 (1990): 797–820.

18. John R. Wright, "PACs, Contributions, and Roll Calls," *American Political Science Review* 79 (1985): 400–414.

19. Diana Dwyre and Robin Kolodny, "The Parties' Congressional Campaign Committees in 2004," in Malbin, ed., *The Election after Reform,* Chapter 3.

20. 424 U.S. 1 (1976). See Thomas E. Mann, "Linking Knowledge and Action: Political Science and Campaign Finance Reform," *Perspectives on Politics* 1 (2003): 69–83.

21. Anthony Corrado and Heitor Gouvea, "Financing Presidential Nominations under the BCRA," in William G. Mayer, *The Making of the Presidential Candidates 2004* (Lanham, MD: Rowman & Littlefield, 2004), p. 47

22. The cases are *Colorado Republican Federal Campaign Committee v. Federal Election Commission*, 116 S. Ct. 2309 (1996), known as "Colorado I," and *McConnell v. Federal Election Commission*, 124 S. Ct. 619 (2003).

23. From the record in *McConnell v. Federal Election Commission*, quoted in Adam Cohen, "Buying a High-Priced Upgrade on the Political Back-Scratching Circuit," *New York Times*, September 15, 2003, p. A22.

24. See Anthony Corrado, Sarah Barclay, and Heitor Gouvea, "The Parties Take the Lead," in John C. Green and Rick Farmer, eds., *The State of the Parties*, 4th ed. (Lanham, MD: Rowman & Littlefield, 2003), pp. 97–114; and Diana Dwyre and Victoria A. Farrar-Myers, *Legislative Labyrinth* (Washington, DC: CQ Press, 2001).

25. John Kenneth White and Daniel M. Shea, *New Party Politics* (Belmont, CA: Wadsworth, 2004), p. 258.

26. Thomas B. Edsall, "After Late Start, Republican Groups Jump Into the Lead," *Washington Post*, October 17, 2004, p. A15.

27. Thomas B. Edsall, "In Boost for Democrats, FEC Rejects Proposed Limits on Small Donors," *Washington Post*, May 14, 2004, p. A9.

28. Daniel A. Smith, "Strings Attached: Outside Money in Colorado's Seventh Congressional District," in David B. Magleby and J. Quin Monson, eds., *The Last Hurrah?* (Provo, UT: Center for the Study of Elections and Democracy, Brigham Young University, 2003).

29. Paul S. Herrnson, "The Congressional Elections," in Gerald M. Pomper, ed., *The Election of 2000* (New York: Chatham House, 2001), p. 170.

30. Steve Weissman and Ruth Hassan, "BCRA and the 527 Groups," in Malbin, ed., *The Election after Reform*, Chapter 5.

31. Michael Toner, "The Impact of the New Campaign Finance Law on the 2004 Presidential Election," in Sabato, ed., *Divided States of America*, pp. 193–194.

32. Weissman and Hassan, "BCRA and the 527 groups."

33. Thomas B. Edsall and James V. Grimaldi, "New Routes for Money to Sway Voters," *Washington Post*, September 27, 2004, p. A1.

34. Karen Foerstel and Peter Wallsten, "Campaign Overhaul Mired in Money and Loopholes," *CQ Weekly*, May 13, 2000, p. 1084.

35. Michael J. Malbin, "Political Parties Under the Post-*McConnell* Bipartisan Campaign Reform Act," *Election Law Journal* 3 (2004): 183.

36. Foerstal and Wallsten, "Campaign Overhaul."

37. Mike Allen, "GOP Takes in $33 Million at Fundraiser," *Washington Post*, May 15, 2002, p. A1.

38. Raymond J. La Raja, "State Parties and Soft Money," in Green and Farmer, *The State of the Parties*, 4th ed., pp. 132–150.

39. Jonathan Krasno and Kenneth Goldstein, "The Facts About Television Advertising and the McCain-Feingold Bill," *PS Political Science & Politics* 35 (2002): 210.

40. Richard Morin and Claudia Deane, "Exit Polls in Doubt for Nov. Elections," *Washington Post on the Web*, http://www.washingtonpost.com/wp-dyn/articles/A26071-2002Aug16.html (accessed August 16, 2002).

41. Raymond J. LaRaja, "State and Local Political Parties," in Malbin, *The Election after Reform*, Chapter 4.

42. Michael M. Franz, Joel Rivlin, and Kenneth Goldstein, "Much More of the Same," in Malbin, *The Election after Reform*, Chapter 7.

43. In fact, after the 2000 election, one-third of Bush's biggest contributors, 57 people, were given appointments to high-level government jobs, including agency positions or advisory committees. See Marian Currinder, "Campaign Finance: Funding the Presidential and Congressional Elections," in Michael Nelson, ed., *The Elections of 2004* (Washington, DC: CQ Press, 2005), p. 121.

44. David S. Broder, "A Win for Campaign Reform," *Washington Post*, February 3, 2005, p. A27.

45. Joseph E. Sandler and Neil P. Reiff, "State and Local Parties Must Tread Carefully Through the Campaign Finance Minefield," *Campaigns & Elections* 25 (2004), pp. 50–51; and LaRaja, "State and Local Political Parties."

46. Malbin, "Political Parties Under the Post-*McConnell* Bipartisan Campaign Reform Act," p. 184.

47. Data from National Conference of State Legislatures at http://www.ncsl.org/programs/legman/about/ContribLimits.htm (accessed May 25, 2005).

48. See Harold W. Stanley and Richard G. Niemi, *Vital Statistics on American Politics, 1999–2000* (Washington, DC: CQ Press, 2000), Tables 2.2 and 2.3, pp. 84–87.
49. See Malbin and Gais, *The Day after Reform,* Chapter 4.

PART FIVE

1. David Firestone and Richard W. Stevenson, "G.O.P. Leader Brushes Off Pressure by Bush on Taxes," *New York Times,* June 11, 2003, p. 1.
2. See the report of the Committee on Responsible Parties of the American Political Science Association, *Toward a More Responsible Two-Party System* (New York: Rinehart, 1950).
3. Associated Press, "AP: GOP Changed Spending of Billions," *New York Times on the Web,* August 5, 2002.

CHAPTER 13

1. Edmund L. Andrews, "Pleas and Promises by G.O.P. as Cafta Wins by 2 Votes," *New York Times,* July 29, 2005, p. 1.
2. Jim VandeHei and Juliet Eilperin, "GOP Leaders Tighten Hold In the House," *Washington Post,* January 13, 2003, p. A1.
3. Keith Krehbiel, "Where's the Party?" *British Journal of Political Science* 23 (1993): 225–266.
4. Gary W. Cox and Keith T. Poole, "On Measuring Partisanship in Roll-Call Voting," *American Journal of Political Science* 46 (2002): 477–489; and Gerald C. Wright and Brian F. Schaffner, "The Influence of Party," *American Political Science Review* 96 (2002): 367–379. See also Jeffery A. Jenkins, "Examining the Bonding Effects of Party," *American Journal of Political Science* 43 (1999): 1144–1165.
5. D. Roderick Kiewiet and Mathew D. McCubbins, *The Logic of Delegation* (Chicago: University of Chicago Press, 1991).
6. Even Cannon faced limits, however; see Eric D. Lawrence, Forrest Maltzman, and Paul J. Wahlbeck, "The Politics of Speaker Cannon's Committee Assignments," *American Journal of Political Science* 45 (2001): 551–562.
7. Joseph Cooper, "From Congressional to Presidential Preeminence," in Lawrence C. Dodd and Bruce I. Oppenheimer, eds., *Congress Reconsidered,* 8th ed. (Washington, DC.: CQ Press, 2005), Chapter 16.
8. Gary W. Cox and Mathew W. McCubbins, *Legislative Leviathan* (Berkeley and Los Angeles: University of California Press, 1993), pp. 279–282.
9. Barbara Sinclair, "Evolution or Revolution? Policy-oriented Congressional Parties in the 1990s," in L. Sandy Maisel, ed., *The Parties Respond,* 3rd ed. (Boulder, CO: Westview, 1998).
10. David W. Rohde, *Parties and Leaders in the Postreform House* (Chicago: University of Chicago Press, 1991). See also Barbara Sinclair, *Legislators, Leaders, and Lawmaking* (Baltimore: Johns Hopkins University Press, 1995). Rohde and John H. Aldrich term this "conditional party government."
11. See, for example, Vincent G. Moscardelli, Moshe Haspel, and Richard S. Wike, "Party Building through Campaign Finance Reform," *Journal of Politics* 60 (1998): 691–704.
12. Barbara Sinclair, *Unorthodox Lawmaking,* 2nd ed. (Washington, DC: CQ Press, 2000), pp. 103–106.
13. See Lawrence C. Evans and Walter J. Oleszek, *Congress Under Fire* (Boston: Houghton Mifflin, 1997); and Lawrence C. Dodd and Bruce I. Oppenheimer, "A Decade of Republican Control," in Dodd and Oppenheimer, eds., *Congress Reconsidered,* 8th ed. (Washington, DC: CQ Press, 2005), Chapter 2.
14. Jim Jordan, quoted in Jeffrey H. Birnbaum and Dana Milbank, "Indictment Ends the DeLay Era on Capitol Hill," *Washington Post,* September 29, 2005, p. A7.
15. Mike Allen, "GOP Leaders Tighten Their Grip on House," *Washington Post,* January 9. 2005, p. A5.
16. Barbara Sinclair, "The New World of U.S. Senators," in Dodd and Oppenheimer, eds., *Congress Reconsidered,* 8th ed., pp. 1–22.
17. Steven S. Smith and Gerald Gamm, "The Dynamics of Party Government in Congress," in Dodd and Oppenheimer, eds., *Congress Reconsidered,* 8th ed., pp. 181–205.
18. Bruce I. Oppenheimer, "Delayed Republican Revolution?" *Extensions* (publication of the Carl Albert Congressional Research and Studies Center), Spring 2005, pp. 10–15.
19. The exceptions are some southern states and Nebraska, which is nominally nonpartisan. See Malcolm E. Jewell and Sarah M. Morehouse, *Political Parties and Elections in American States,* 4th ed. (Washington, DC: CQ Press, 2001), Chapter 8.
20. Jewell and Morehouse, *Political Parties and Elections,* pp. 234–235.
21. Jewell and Morehouse, *Political Parties and Elections,* pp. 236–238.

22. See Keith E. Hamm and Robert Harmel, "Legislative Party Development and the Speaker System: The Case of the Texas House," *Journal of Politics* 55 (1993): 1140–1151; and Malcolm E. Jewell and Marcia Lynn Whicker, *Legislative Leadership in the American States* (Ann Arbor, MI: University of Michigan Press, 1994).

23. See Barbara Sinclair, "Majority Party Leadership Strategies for Coping with the New U.S. House," *Legislative Studies Quarterly* 6 (1981): 391–414; and Steven Smith, *Call to Order* (Washington, DC: Brookings Institution, 1989).

24. Thomas Stratmann, "Congressional Voting over Legislative Careers," *American Political Science Review* 94 (2000): 665–676.

25. See Paul S. Herrnson, *Congressional Elections: Campaigning at Home and in Washington,* 4th ed. (Washington, DC: CQ Press, 2004), and Kathryn Pearson, "Congressional Party Discipline: Carrots on the Campaign Trail?" Paper delivered at the 2002 Annual Meeting of the Midwest Political Science Association.

26. Juliet Eilperin, "House GOP Practices Art of One-Vote Victories," *Washington Post,* October 14, 2003, p. A1.

27. See Keith T. Poole and Howard Rosenthal, *Congress: A Political-Economic History of Roll Call Voting* (New York: Oxford University Press, 1997).

28. Julius Turner, *Party and Constituency: Pressures on Congress,* rev. ed., Edward V. Schneier, ed. (Baltimore: The Johns Hopkins University Press, 1970), pp. 16–17.

29. Gregory L. Giroux, "GOP's Effectiveness Shows in Party Unity Votes," *CQ Weekly,* April 19, 2003, p. 923.

30. Jason M. Roberts and Steven S. Smith, "Procedural Contexts, Party Strategy, and Conditional Party Voting in the U.S. House of Representatives, 1971–2000," *American Journal of Political Science* 47 (2003): 305–317.

31. Barbara Sinclair, "The New World of U.S. Senators," p. 4.

32. See Nelson W. Polsby, "The Institutionalization of the United States House of Representatives," *American Political Science Review* 62 (1968): 144–168, and Walter Dean Burnham, *Critical Elections and the Mainsprings of American Politics* (New York: Norton, 1970), pp. 91–134.

33. See Dodd and Oppenheimer, "A House Divided," pp. 38.

34. Jewell and Morehouse, *Political Parties and Elections*, p. 251.

35. Rohde, *Parties and Leaders in the Postreform House,* Chapter 3. See also M. V. Hood III, Quentin Kidd, and Irwin L. Morris, "Of Byrd[s] and Bumpers: Using Democratic Senators to Analyze Political Change in the South, 1960–1995," *American Journal of Political Science* 43 (1999): 465–487.

36. Stanley P. Berard, *Southern Democrats in the U.S. House of Representatives* (Norman: University of Oklahoma Press, 2001).

37. Jason M. Roberts and Steven S. Smith, "Procedural Contexts."

38. Gary C. Jacobson, "Congress: Elections and Stalemate," in Michael Nelson, ed., *The Elections of 2000* (Washington, DC: CQ Press, 2001), pp. 204–205.

39. Barry Burden, "Candidate Positioning in U. S. Congressional Elections," *British Journal of Political Science* 34 (2004): 211–227. See also Bruce I. Oppenheimer, "Deep Red and Blue Congressional Districts," in Dodd and Oppenheimer, *Congress Reconsidered,* 8th ed., pp. 135–157.

40. See Mark A. Peterson, *Legislating Together* (Cambridge, MA: Harvard University Press, 1990); and Cary R. Covington, J. Mark Wrighton, and Rhonda Kinney, "A 'Presidency-Augmented' Model of Presidential Success on House Roll Call Votes," *American Journal of Political Science* 39 (November 1995): 1001–1024.

41. Gary C. Jacobson, *The Politics of Congressional Elections,* 6th ed. (New York: Longman, 2004), p. 243.

42. Cox and Poole, "On Measuring Partisanship."

43. See James M. Snyder, Jr., and Tim Groseclose, "Estimating Party Influence in Congressional Roll-Call Voting," *American Journal of Political Science* 44 (2000): 187–205.

44. See Barbara Sinclair, "Party Realignment and the Transformation of the Political Agenda: The House of Representatives, 1925–1938," *American Political Science Review* 71 (1977): 940–953.

45. David Nather and Adriel Bettelheim, "Moderates and Mavericks Hold Key to 107th Congress," *CQ Weekly,* January 6, 2001, p. 49.

46. Gerald C. Wright, Tracy Osborn, and Jonathan Winburn, "Parties and Representation in the American Legislatures." Paper presented at the 2004 Annual Meeting of the Midwest Political Science Association, April 15–18.

47. Jewell and Morehouse, *Political Parties and Elections,* p. 244.

48. David Denemark, "Partisan Pork Barrel in Parliamentary Systems: Australian Constituency-Level Grants," *Journal of Politics* 62 (2000): 896–915.

49. See Jewell and Morehouse, *Political Parties and Elections*, pp. 212–215; Anthony Gierzynski, *Legislative Party Campaign Committees in the American States* (Lexington: University of Kentucky Press, 1992); and

Daniel M. Shea, *Transforming Democracy: Legislative Campaign Committees and Political Parties* (Albany: State University of New York Press, 1995).

50. Cox and McCubbins, *Legislative Leviathan*; see also Kiewiet and McCubbins, *The Logic of Delegation*.

51. See Austin Ranney, "Candidate Selection and Party Cohesion in Britain and the U.S.," in William J. Crotty, ed., *Approaches to the Study of Party Organization* (Boston: Allyn and Bacon, 1968), pp. 139–168; Gary Cox, *The Efficient Secret* (New York: Cambridge University Press, 1987); and Leon D. Epstein, "A Comparative Study of Canadian Parties," *American Political Science Review* 58 (1964): 46–59.

52. See Richard Fleisher and Jon R. Bond, "Polarized Politics: Does It Matter?" in Bond and Fleisher, eds., *Polarized Politics* (Washington, DC: CQ Press, 2000), pp. 195–200.

CHAPTER 14

1. See David Von Drehle, Peter Slevin, Dan Balz, and James V. Grimaldi, "Anxious Moments in the Final Stretch," *Washington Post*, February 3, 2001, p. A1.

2. See Clive Bean and Anthony Mughan, "Leadership Effects in Parliamentary Elections in Australia and Britain," *American Political Science Review* 83 (1989): 1165–1180.

3. Quoted in Adam Clymer, "Not So Fast: Suddenly Bush's Smooth Ride Turns Bumpy," *New York Times*, April 1, 2001, sec. 4, p. 1.

4. Thune lost this very close contest but went on to win the state's other Senate seat in 2004.

5. Quoted in Edwin Chen and Janet Hook, "Bush Team Plays Role Fit for a Kingmaker," *Los Angeles Times*, April 25, 2001, p. A13.

6. Quoted in Jim VandeHei and Dan Balz, "In GOP Win, a Lesson in Money, Muscle, Planning," *Washington Post*, November 10, 2002, p. A1.

7. See John A. Ferejohn and Randall L. Calvert, "Presidential Coattails in Historical Perspective," *American Journal of Political Science* 28 (1984): 127–146; Richard Born, "Reassessing the Decline of Presidential Coattails," *Journal of Politics* 46 (1984): 60–79; and James E. Campbell, "Predicting Seat Gains from Presidential Coattails," *American Journal of Political Science* 30 (1986): 164–183.

8. See Bruce Cain, John Ferejohn, and Morris Fiorina, *The Personal Vote* (Cambridge, MA: Harvard University Press, 1987).

9. Paul R. Abramson, John H. Aldrich, and David W. Rohde, *Change and Continuity in the 2000 and 2002 Elections* (Washington, DC.: CQ Press, 2003), pp. 249–250.

10. Gary C. Jacobson, *The Politics of Congressional Elections*, 6th ed. (New York: Longman, 2004), pp. 162–163.

11. See James E. Campbell, "Presidential Coattails and Midterm Losses in State Legislative Elections," *American Political Science Review* 80 (1986): 45–63.

12. See, for example, Robin F. Marra and Charles W. Ostrom, Jr., "Explaining Seat Change in the U.S. House of Representatives, 1950–86," *American Journal of Political Science* 33 (1989): 541–569.

13. Quoted in Michael Nelson, "The Setting: George W. Bush, Majority President," in Nelson, ed., *The Elections of 2004* (Washington, DC.: CQ Press, 2005), p. 17.

14. The classic statement is Angus Campbell, "Surge and Decline: A Study of Electoral Change," in Campbell, Philip E. Converse, Warren E. Miller, and Donald E. Stokes, eds., *Elections and the Political Order* (New York: Wiley, 1966), pp. 40–62.

15. Samuel Kernell, "Presidential Popularity and Negative Voting," *American Political Science Review* 71 (1977): 44–66. See also Richard Born, "Surge and Decline, Negative Voting, and the Midterm Loss Phenomenon," *American Journal of Political Science* 34 (1990): 615–645.

16. Walter R. Mebane and Jasjeet S. Sekhon, "Coordination and Policy Moderation at Midterm," *American Political Science Review* 96 (2002): 141–157.

17. Abramson, Aldrich, and Rohde, *Change and Continuity*, pp. 249–250.

18. For one convincing explanation, see Gary C. Jacobson and Samuel Kernell, *Strategy and Choice in Congressional Elections*, 2nd ed. (New Haven: Yale University Press, 1983).

19. Alan Rosenthal, *Governors and Legislatures* (Washington, DC: CQ Press, 1990).

20. Victoria Allred, "Versatility With the Veto," *CQ Weekly*, January 20, 2001, pp. 175–177.

21. Hugh Heclo, "Issue Networks and the Executive Establishment," in Anthony King, ed., *The New American Political System* (Washington, DC: American Enterprise Institute, 1979), pp. 87–124.

22. Hugh Heclo, *A Government of Strangers* (Washington, DC: Brookings Institution, 1977).

23. See, for example, B. Dan Wood, "Principals, Bureaucrats, and Responsiveness in Clean Air Enforcements," *American Political Science Review* 82 (1988): 213–234.

24. See Terry M. Moe, "The Politicized Presidency," in John E. Chubb and Paul E. Peterson, eds., *The New Direction in American Politics* (Washington, DC: Brookings Institution, 1985), pp. 235–271.

25. Joel Aberbach and Bert A. Rockman, "Clashing Beliefs Within the Executive Branch," *American Political Science Review* 70 (1976): 456–468.

26. Joel D. Aberbach and Bert A. Rockman, "The Political Views of U.S. Senior Federal Executives, 1970–1992," *Journal of Politics* 57 (1995): 838–852.

27. Dana Milbank, "Bush Seeks to Rule The Bureaucracy," *Washington Post,* November 22, 2004, p. A4.

28. Robert A. Carp and Ronald Stidham, *Judicial Process in America* (Washington, DC: CQ Press, 2001), p. 292.

29. Stuart S. Nagel, "Political Party Affiliations and Judges' Decisions," *American Political Science Review* 55 (1961): 843–850. See also Jeffrey A. Segal and Harold J. Spaeth, *The Supreme Court and the Attitudinal Model* (Cambridge: Cambridge University Press, 1993).

30. Juliet Eilperin, "Environmental Group Cites Partisanship in the Judiciary," *Washington Post,* October 9, 2004, p. A2.

31. See Randall D. Lloyd, "Separating Partisanship from Party in Judicial Research," *American Political Science Review* 89 (1995): 413–420.

32. Sheldon Goldman, "The Bush Imprint on the Judiciary," *Judicature* 74 (1991), 294–306.

33. Sheldon Goldman, Elliot Slotnick, Gerard Gryski, and Gary Zuk, "Clinton's Judges," *Judicature* 84 (2001): 244, 249.

34. Daniel J. Parks, "Senate Judicial Nominations Spat Again Frustrates Appropriators," *CQ Weekly,* October 20, 2001, pp. 2470–71. See also Sarah A. Binder and Forrest Maltzman, "Senatorial Delay in Confirming Federal Judges, 1947–1998," *American Journal of Political Science* 46 (2002): 190–199.

35. *The Book of the States 2005* (Lexington, KY: Council of State Governments, 2005), pp. 318–321.

36. See Henry R. Glick and Craig F. Emmert, "Selection Systems and Judicial Characteristics," *Judicature* 70 (1987), 228–235; and Melinda Gann Hall, "State Supreme Courts in American Democracy," *American Political Science Review* 95 (2001): 315–330.

37. Adam Liptak, "Judicial Races in Several States Become Partisan Battlegrounds," *New York Times,* October 24, 2004, p. 1.

CHAPTER 15

1. See E. E. Schattschneider, *Party Government* (New York: Rinehart, 1942), pp. 131–132.

2. Committee on Political Parties of the American Political Science Association, *Toward a More Responsible Two-Party System* (New York: Rinehart, 1950).

3. See Austin Ranney, *The Doctrine of Responsible Party Government* (Urbana: University of Illinois Press, 1964), Chapters 1 and 2.

4. Schattschneider, *Party Government*, p. 208.

5. E. E. Schattschneider, *The Semi-Sovereign People* (New York: Holt, Rinehart, and Winston, 1960).

6. See Evron Kirkpatrick, "Toward a More Responsible Two-Party System," *American Political Science Review* 65 (1971): 965–990; and John Kenneth White and Jerome M. Mileur, eds., *Challenges to Party Government* (Carbondale: Southern Illinois University Press, 1992).

7. See Malcolm E. Jewell and Sarah M. Morehouse, *Political Parties and Elections in American States,* 4th ed. (Washington, DC: CQ Press, 2001), p. 222; and Morris Fiorina, *Divided Government* (New York: MacMillan, 1992), Chapter 3.

8. See John J. Coleman, "Unified Government, Divided Government, and Party Responsiveness," *American Political Science Review* 93 (1999): 821–835; George C. Edwards III, Andrew Barrett, and Jeffrey Peake, "The Legislative Impact of Divided Government," *American Journal of Political Science* 41 (1997): 545–563; and David R. Mayhew, *Divided We Govern,* 2nd ed. (New Haven, CT: Yale University Press, 2005).

9. See Richard Born, "Split-Ticket Voters, Divided Government, and Fiorina's Policy-Balancing Model," *Legislative Studies Quarterly* 19 (1994): 95–115.

10. See A. James Reichley, *The Life of the Parties* (Lanham, MD: Rowman & Littlefield, 2000), Chapter 6.

11. David E. Rosenbaum, "Bush to Return to 'Ownership Society' Theme in Push for Social Security Changes," *New York Times,* January 16, 2005, p. 20.

12. Edward G. Carmines and James A. Stimson, *Issue Evolution* (Princeton, NJ: Princeton University Press, 1989); see also Geoffrey C. Layman and Thomas M. Carsey, "Party Polarization and 'Conflict Extension' in the American Electorate," *American Journal of Political Science* 46 (2002): 786–802.

13. Charles Barrilleaux, Thomas Holbrook, and Laura Langer, "Electoral Competition, Legislative Balance, and American State Welfare Policy," *American Journal of Political Science* 46 (2002): 415–427.

14. Jason M. Roberts and Steven S. Smith, "Procedural Contexts, Party Strategy, and Conditional Party Voting in the U.S. House of Representatives, 1971–2000," *American Journal of Political Science* 47 (2003): 305–317.

15. See "The Main GOP Factions," *CQ Weekly,* September 4, 2004, p. 2027.

16. Sheryl Gay Stolberg, "The Revolution That Wasn't," *New York Times,* February 13, 2005, section 4, p. 1. Data are from the National Taxpayers Union.

17. See Robin Kolodny, "Moderate Party Factions in the U.S. House of Representatives," in John C. Green and Daniel M. Shea, *The State of the Parties,* 3rd ed. (Lanham, MD: Rowman & Littlefield, 1999), pp. 271–285.

18. Christopher Lee, "Putting a New Face on Conservatism," *Washington Post,* March 22, 2005, p. A15.

19. Thomas B. Edsall, "Report Warns Democrats Not to Tilt Too Far Left," *Washington Post,* October 7, 2005, p. A7.

20. Nicol C. Rae, "Party Factionalism, 1946–1996," in Byron E. Shafer, *Partisan Approaches to Postwar American Politics* (New York: Chatham House, 1998), pp. 41–74. See also John S. Jackson, Nathan S. Bigelow, and John C. Green, "The State of Party Elites: National Convention Delegates, 1992–2000," in Green and Rick Farmer, eds., *The State of the Parties,* 4th ed. (Lanham, MD: Rowman & Littlefield, 2003), pp. 54–78.

21. Stephanie L. Witt, "Idaho," in Andrew M. Appleton and Daniel S. Ward, *State Party Profiles* (Washington, DC: CQ Press, 1997), pp. 82–88.

22. The seminal study is Philip E. Converse, "The Nature of Belief Systems in Mass Publics," in David Apter, ed., *Ideology and Discontent* (New York: Free Press, 1964), pp. 206–261. Also see Russell J. Dalton, *Citizen Politics,* 3rd ed. (New York: Chatham House, 2002), Chapter 2.

23. Kathleen A. Frankovic and Monika L. McDermott, "Public Opinion in the 2000 Election: The Ambivalent Electorate," in Gerald M. Pomper, ed., *The Election of 2000* (New York: Chatham House, 2001), pp. 76–78 and 88–89.

24. John Zaller and Stanley Feldman, "A Simple Theory of the Survey Response," *American Journal of Political Science* 36 (1992): 579–616.

25. CNN exit poll on the Internet at: http://www.cnn.com/ELECTION/2004/pages/results/states/US/P/00/epolls.0.html

26. Paul R. Abramson, John H. Aldrich, and David W. Rohde, *Change and Continuity in the 1984 Elections* (Washington, DC: CQ Press, 1986), Chapter 6.

27. Data from http://www.umich.edu/~nes/nesguide/toptable/tab3_1.htm.

28. Morris P. Fiorina with Samuel J. Abrams and Jeremy C. Pope, *Culture War?* (New York: Pearson Longman, 2005).

29. Alan Abramowitz and Kyle Saunders, "Why Can't We All Just Get Along?" *The Forum* 3 (2005), http://www.bepress.com/forum (accessed July 22, 2005).

30. Jacob S. Hacker and Paul Pierson, "Abandoning the Middle," *Perspectives on Politics* 3 (2005): 33–53.

31. Marc J. Hetherington, "Resurgent Mass Partisanship: The Role of Elite Polarization," *American Political Science Review* 95 (2001): 619–631.

32. Gerald M. Pomper and Marc D. Weiner, "Toward a More Responsible Two-Party Voter," in John C. Green and Paul S. Herrnson, eds., *Responsible Partisanship?* (Lawrence: University Press of Kansas, 2002), pp. 181–200.

33. David R. Jones and Monika L. McDermott, "The Responsible Party Government Model in House and Senate Elections," *American Journal of Political Science* 48 (2004): 1–12.

34. Paul Allen Beck, "A Tale of Two Electorates," in John C. Green and Rick Farmer, eds., *The State of the Parties,* 4th ed. (Lanham, MD: Rowman & Littlefield, 2003), pp. 38–53.

35. See William Crotty, John S. Jackson III, and Melissa Kary Miller, "Political Activists Over Time," in Birol A. Yesilada, ed., *Comparative Political Parties and Party Elites* (Ann Arbor: University of Michigan Press, 1999), pp. 259–286.

36. See Brandice Canes-Wrone, David W. Brady, and John F. Cogan, "Out of Step, Out of Office," *American Political Science Review* 96 (2002): 127–140.

37. John R. Hibbing and Elizabeth Theiss-Morse, "Process Preferences and American Politics," *American Political Science Review* 95 (2001): 145–153.

38. David C. King, "The Polarization of American Political Parties and Mistrust of Government," in Joseph S. Nye, Philip Zelikow, and David C. King, eds., *Why People Don't Trust Government* (Cambridge, MA: Harvard University Press, 1997), pp. 155–178.

39. David Von Drehle, "Political Split Is Pervasive," *Washington Post,* April 25, 2004, p. A1.

40. Leon D. Epstein, "What Happened to the British Party Model?" *American Political Science Review* 74 (1980): 9–22.

41. Jerome M. Clubb, William H. Flanigan, and Nancy H. Zingale, *Partisan Realignment* (Beverly Hills, CA: Sage, 1980), pp. 155–188.

CHAPTER 16

1. See Robert Harmel and Kenneth Janda, *Parties and Their Environments* (New York: Longman, 1982).
2. See Ruy A. Teixeira, *The Disappearing American Voter* (Washington, DC: Brookings Institution, 1992), Chapter 3
3. These figures are taken from Harold W. Stanley and Richard G. Niemi, *Vital Statistics on American Politics 1999–2000* (Washington, DC: CQ Press, 2000), pp. 44 and 133.
4. Bruce E. Cain, John Ferejohn, and Morris P. Fiorina, *The Personal Vote* (Cambridge, MA: Harvard University Press, 1987).
5. Jeffrey E. Cohen and Paul Kantor, "Decline and Resurgence in the American Party System," in Jeffrey E. Cohen, Richard Fleisher, and Paul Kantor, eds., *American Political Parties: Decline or Resurgence?* (Washington, DC: CQ Press, 2001), pp. 255–257.
6. See Robert Huckfeldt and Paul Allen Beck, "Contexts, Intermediaries, and Political Activity," in Lawrence C. Dodd and Calvin Jillson, eds., *The Dynamics of American Politics* (Boulder, CO: Westview Press, 1994), Chapter 11. On the other hand, organized interests have become more polarized by party since the Reagan years; see Jack L. Walker, Jr., *Mobilizing Interest Groups in America* (Ann Arbor: University of Michigan Press, 1991), Chapter 8, and media coverage frequently refers to party; see Marjorie Randon Hershey, "If 'The Party's in Decline,' Then What's That Filling the News Columns?" in Nelson W. Polsby and Raymond E. Wolfinger, *On Parties* (Berkeley: Institute of Governmental Studies, 1999), pp. 257–278.
7. Larry M. Bartels, "Partisanship and Voting Behavior, 1952–1996," *American Journal of Political Science* 44 (2000): 35–50.
8. Gary C. Jacobson, *The Politics of Congressional Elections,* 6th ed. (New York: Longman, 2004), p. 158.
9. See Ronald Inglehart, *Culture Shift* (Princeton, NJ: Princeton University Press, 1990), Chapters 10 and 11.
10. Larry J. Sabato and Bruce Larson, *The Party's Just Begun* (New York: Longman, 2002), pp. 2–4.
11. John H. Aldrich, *Why Parties?* (Chicago: University of Chicago Press, 1995), p. 3.
12. David R. Mayhew, *Congress: The Electoral Connection* (New Haven: Yale University Press, 1974), especially pp. 141–149. See also Gary C. Jacobson, *The Politics of Congressional Elections,* pp. 226–230.
13. See Marjorie Randon Hershey, "Political Parties as Mechanisms of Social Choice," in Richard S. Katz and William Crotty, eds., *Handbook of Party Politics* (London: Sage, 2005), pp. 75–88.
14. Walter Dean Burnham, *Critical Elections and the Mainsprings of American Politics* (New York: Norton, 1970), p. 133.
15. See Brian F. Schaffner, Matthew J. Streb, and Gerald C. Wright, "Teams without Uniforms: The Nonpartisan Ballot in State and Local Elections," *Political Research Quarterly* 54 (2001): 7–30, and Gerald C. Wright and Brian F. Schaffner, "The Influence of Party: Evidence from the State Legislatures," *American Political Science Review* 96 (2002): 367–379.
16. See Steven J. Rosenstone and John Mark Hansen, *Mobilization, Participation, and Democracy in America* (New York: Macmillan, 1993), Chapter 8.
17. Sabato and Larson, *The Party's Just Begun,* pp. 156–157.
18. Sabato and Larson, *The Party's Just Begun,* pp. 159–160.

Index

Page numbers followed by *italicized* letters *f* and *t* indicate figures and tables, respectively